FINANCIAL SOURCEBOOK FOR SOUTHEAST ASIA AND HONG KONG

FINANCIAL SOURCEBOOK FOR SOUTHEAST ASIA AND HONG KONG

TAN CHWEE HUAT
Faculty of Business Administration
National University of Singapore

SINGAPORE UNIVERSITY PRESS
NATIONAL UNIVERSITY OF SINGAPORE

World Scientific
Singapore • New Jersey • London • Hong Kong

© 2000 Singapore University Press
Yusof Ishak House
National University of Singapore
31 Lower Kent Ridge Road
Singapore 119078

and

World Scientific Publishing Co. Pte. Ltd.
PO Box 128, Farrer Road, Singapore 912805
USA office : Suite 1B, 1060 Main Street, River Edge, NJ 07661
UK office : 57 Shelton Street, Covent Garden, London WC2H 9HE

ISBN 9971-69-231-7 (Case)

Typeset by: Scientifik Graphics (Singapore) Pte Ltd
Printed by: Humanities Press

CONTENTS

PREFACE

The Asian financial crisis has attracted much attention to this part of the world, especially Southeast Asia where the crisis first emerged. While there are signs of economic recovery in the affected countries, financial events in Southeast Asia remain the focus of international attention.

Part I of this book highlights the basic features of the financial systems of Southeast Asian countries. For easy reference, it summarises the various types of institution and market in each country.

Although Hong Kong is not strictly located in Southeast Asia, it is included in this book for two reasons. It is an important financial centre in Asia. Financial events in Hong Kong have important implication for other regional centres especially Kuala Lumpur and Singapore.

Part II highlights the financial reforms that have been implemented in several Southeast Asian countries and Hong Kong. These reforms are closely studied by international institutions as their success remains the key to a financially stable Southeast Asia.

Part III is a convenient directory of the various financial institutions in Southeast Asia and Hong Kong. The number of world-class institutions present in each city reflects the status and sophistication of that market.

Part IV is a list of abbreviations and Part V is a lexicon or dictionary of financial terms arranged from A to Z. Many of these terms are specific to Southeast Asia. They are not found in most standard dictionaries on banking and finance.

January 2000

PART I

FINANCIAL SYSTEMS IN SOUTHEAST ASIA AND HONG KONG

Brunei
Cambodia
Indonesia
Laos
Malaysia
Myanmar
Philippines
Singapore
Thailand
Vietnam
Hong Kong

BRUNEI DARUSSALAM

The financial system in Brunei Darussalam comprises the following: Currency Board, banks, finance companies and insurance companies.

Currency Board

There is no central bank in Brunei. The main functions of a central bank are carried out by the Department of Financial Services (Treasury), the Currency Board and the Brunei Investment Agency. They are under the jurisdiction of the Ministry of Finance.

The Brunei Currency Board was set up in 1967. It issues the Brunei currency and controls its circulation. It also licenses and monitors all the banks and finance companies. There is no foreign exchange control in Brunei.

The Brunei dollar is the only legal tender. However, under the interchangeability at par agreement between Brunei Darussalam and Singapore, the Singapore dollar is also accepted in Brunei. Brunei depends on oil revenue. As there is no need to raise funds, there are no government securities.

Commercial Banks

In Brunei, there are seven banks providing the whole range of banking services. Except for the locally-incorporated Islamic Bank of Brunei Berhad, the others are foreign banks.

Local Bank

Islamic Bank of Brunei Berhad
(formerly International Bank of Brunei Berhad and Island Development Bank Berhad)

Foreign Banks

1. Citibank (USA)
2. Hongkong & Shanghai Banking Corp (Hong Kong)
3. Malayan Banking Berhad (Malaysia)
4. Overseas Union Bank (Singapore)
5. Standard Chartered Bank (UK)
6. United Malayan Banking Corp (Malaysia)

Finance Companies

There are several finance companies providing hire purchase financing, mortgage loans and financing for small businesses. Finance companies are governed by the Finance Companies Act which is administered by the Ministry of Finance.

Finance Companies

1. Credit Corporation Berhad (Brunei)
2. IRB Finance Berhad (Brunei)
3. Mortgage and Finance Berhad (Brunei)

Insurance Companies

There are several locally incorporated as well as international insurance companies in Brunei. There are no special regulation on insurance business except for motor vehicle insurance. To carry out motor vehicle insurance, a company must have a licence, pay a deposit to the government and provide a bank guarantee.

Insurance companies are supervised by the Economic Development Board.

Economic Development Board

The Economic Development Board was set up in 1976 to assist in industrial growth under the Five Year National Development Plan.

The EDB is also in charge of tourism and is responsible for licensing travel agents. It also administers the law concerning third party motor vehicle insurance.

References

KPMG (1991). *Banking and Finance in ASEAN*. KPMG Peat Marwick, Singapore.

KPMG (1993). *Investing in Brunei.* KPMG Peat Marwick, Brunei Darussalam.

CAMBODIA

The financial system in Cambodia comprises the National Bank of Cambodia (NBC) (central bank), state-owned commercial banks and about 20 commercial banks. Some of these are branches of foreign banks while others are joint venture banks with Cambodian partners.

National Bank of Cambodia

The National Bank of Cambodia (formerly known as the Bank of the People of Cambodia) is the central bank of Cambodia. It is authorised to issue licences to the various types of financial institutions.

It is supervised by the Council of Ministers and has the status of a ministry. It is managed by a 5-member board of directors and is chaired by the Governor who has the status of a minister. The vice chairman is also the Vice Governor. The other three members act as advisers and are attached to various departments.

The major departments are: the cabinet, organisation, planning and operations, accounting, auditing, research, management of reserves, issuing of currency, foreign exchange and banking.

Authority of NBC

The NBC has the power to approve, supervise and regulate all financial institutions in Cambodia. It fixes foreign exchange rates and interest rates for the purpose of the purchase and discounting of commercial papers. It has the power to intervene in the financial markets to stabilise the national currency.

As a Central Bank

As Cambodia's central bank, the NBC regulates foreign exchange and local currency reserves. It is the sole authority to issue and print the national currency. It receives deposits from all financial institutions which are required to deposit 5% to 15% of their capital with the central bank. All financial institutions are required to submit weekly reports on the following:

— the amount of loans made during the week
— the amount of money held in cash and in kind
— all re-discount transactions
— the balance sheet.

The NBC regulates the supply of money to financial institutions to support economic development and to control inflation. It purchases and re-discounts promissory notes and commercial papers. It purchases from and sells foreign currencies to other banks in Cambodia.

When the NBC was established in 1979, the Minister of Finance also served as the Governor of the national bank until 1982 when the two functions were separated. The Minister dealt with matters related to national finance and the Governor concentrated on the supervision of banks in the country. In 1980, a new Cambodian currency, the riel, was issued.

Banking Laws

The first piece of legislation was the Decree on the Change of the Structure, Organisation, Function and Law of the National Bank of Cambodia.

Two laws were promulgated in 1992:

— Decree on the Changing Organisation and Function of the National Bank of Cambodia;
— Decree on the Management of Commercial Banks.

After the enactment, the former branches of the National Bank became autonomous commercial, agricultural or development banks while the National Bank became the central bank.

Foreign Joint Venture Banks

Under the Foreign Investment Law (FIL), foreign banks are allowed to form joint venture banks with local partners. For example, in 1991, the Cambodia Commercial Bank was set up as the first joint venture bank between the National Bank of Cambodia and the Siam Commercial Bank. In 1992, the Cambodia Finance Bank was set up as a joint venture between the National Bank of Cambodia and a Thai-Cambodia group. Approval has also been given for foreign banks to set up branches in Cambodia.

Licensing of Banks

Bank licensing is done in two stages. The NBC first issues a temporary licence called a "Letter of Agreement in Principle" which is valid for 12 months. During this period, the bank must comply with the requirements set by the NBC. An official licence is granted after all the requirements are fulfilled.

Some of the legal provisions governing banks include the following:

— Minimum capital of 10 billion Riel (US$4 million)
— Deposit the full amount of the capital with NBC before the licence is issued
— During their operations, banks must maintain reserve accounts with NBC at 5% of their registered capital, and 5% of their total deposits
— Lending by the bank should not exceed 20% of its capital.

Foreign Exchange Control

In 1991, the Law on the Management of Exchange, Precious Metal and Stones ("Foreign Exchange Law") and the Decree on the Practice of Law on Management of Exchange, Precious Metal and Stones were introduced in Cambodia.

They authorise the Ministry of Finance and the National Bank of Cambodia to deal with all matters related to foreign exchange, precious metals and precious stones. For example, all transfer of foreign capital into and out of Cambodia must be approved by the National Bank of Cambodia.

Only authorised banks can deal in foreign exchange transactions. They may sell foreign currencies to customers to pay for imports of goods and services, to repay foreign debts and to repatriate capital and transfer profits from foreign investment. They sell and buy foreign currencies at a rate within the limits set by the National Bank of Cambodia.

Resident and Non-resident Accounts

Residents may open foreign exchange accounts for the following reasons:

— to deposit proceeds from export of goods and services
— to deposit transfers from abroad which do not result from export of goods or services
— to deposit transfers from other foreign currency accounts in Cambodia
— to deposit foreign currency notes.

Non-residents may open foreign exchange accounts and convertible Riel accounts for the following reasons:
Foreign exchange account:

— to deposit transfers from abroad
— to deposit transfers from foreign currency accounts of residents or non-residents
— to deposit foreign currency notes.

Convertible Riel account:

— to deposit Riel proceeds from the sale of foreign currencies
— to deposit transfers from other convertible Riel accounts of non-residents.

Insurance Companies

Insurance business is controlled by the Ministry of Economy and Finance. The only insurance company is the state-owned Cambodian National Insurance Company (CAMINCO) which provides mainly marine cargo insurance cover. There is only one insurance broking firm, Indochine Insurance Union. It provides a wide range of insurance covers.

References

Brahm, L. J. (1992). *Banking and Finance in Indochina,* Woodhead-Faulkner, Hemel Hempstead, Hartfordshire.
Singapore Trade Development Board (1996). *Market Research Report: Cambodia,* Trade Development Board and Coopers & Lybrand, Singapore.

INDONESIA

The Indonesian financial system comprises two main groups: banking and non-banking institutions.

Banking Institutions

The banking institutions include commercial banks, foreign exchange banks, development banks, savings banks, cooperative banks and rural banks.

Non-banking Institutions

The non-banking institutions are the finance companies, leasing companies, insurance companies, pawnshops and others.

BANK INDONESIA (CENTRAL BANK)

Bank Indonesia was set up in 1953 as a result of nationalising De Javasche Bank, a Dutch bank which was assigned by the Dutch colonial government to serve as the Dutch East Indies circulation bank.

As the central bank, Bank Indonesia regulates the banking system and foreign exchange. It supervises financial institutions (except insurance companies) and assesses their performance. BI regulates the liquidity position of banks by adjusting the minimum liquidity ratio and the minimum reserve requirements that the banks must maintain.

BI issues the Indonesian rupiah and maintains its stability. It acts as the banker of the government and advises on monetary policies. The governor of Bank Indonesia has the status of a cabinet minister. The vision of BI is reflected in its strategic plan known as RENSTRA which comprises a range of targets to be realised within every five years.

Commercial Banks

Before 1998, commercial banks included 7 state banks and more than 200 private banks. The state banks were:

— Bank Bumi Daya (BBD)
— Bank Dagang Negara (BDN)
— Bank Ekspor Impor Indonesia (EXIM)
— Bank Negara Indonesia (BNI)
— Bank Pembangunan Indonesia (Bapindo)
— Bank Rakyat Indonesia (BRI)
— Bank Tebungan Negara (BTN)

In 1998, as part of the restructuring, EXIM, Bapindo, BBD, BDN and the corporate business of BRI were merged into one bank.

Most of the private banks were owned by family or business groups. The major ones were:

— Bank Central Asia (Salim Group)
— Bank Danamon (Admadjaja family)
— Bank Internasional Indonesia (Sinar Mas Group)
— Lippobank (Lippo Group)

During the 1998 financial crisis, numerous private banks had financial difficulties and were taken over by the government.

Foreign Exchange Banks

Foreign Exchange banks are commercial banks which are authorised by Bank Indonesia to deal in foreign exchange. Most of them are foreign banks and joint venture banks.

Development Banks

Development banks deal in medium and long term financing and the issue of bonds and securities subject to the approval of Bank Indonesia. There is one state development bank (Development Bank of

Indonesia) with 26 offices and one private development bank with 5 offices, and 27 regional development banks with 326 offices. Regional development banks are wholly or partly owned by provincial governments.

Savings Banks

Savings banks collect savings and time deposits. There is one state savings bank and two private savings banks.

Cooperative Banks

Cooperative banks are banks incorporated in the legal form of cooperatives.

Rural Banks

Rural banks are located in the villages. They collect demand, time and savings deposits from local residents and give short term loans to retailers and farmers. There are several thousand rural banks.

A rural savings bank or rural credit bank may be upgraded to a commercial bank if it meets the minimum capital requirement set by the Bank Indonesia.

Stock Exchanges

The Jakarta Stock Exchange (JSX) was established in 1977. It is supervised by Capital Market Supervisory Board (BAPEPAM). As a result of the capital market reforms, in 1989 the Surabaya Stock Exchange (SSX) was set up as a private stock exchange in Indonesia's second largest city. In 1990, Bursa Paralel Indonesia (BPI) was set up for the listing of medium size enterprises as its listing requirements were less stringent than those on JSX and SSX.

In 1992, JSX was privatised. In 1995, BPI merged with the SSX.

CAPITAL MARKET

Capital market activities are supervised by the Capital Market Supervisory Agency (BAPEPAM). In 1996, the Capital Market Law came into effect.

Development of Capital Market — Major Highlights

The Early Period

1912 The first stock exchange was set up in Jakarta by some Dutch broker companies.

1925 Stock exchanges were established in Surabaya and Semarang. During the Second World War, the stock exchanges ceased operations.

The 1950s

1952 The stock exchange was reopened for the trading of Indonesian government bonds.

1958 The exchange ceased operations due to the unstable economic conditions.

The 1970s, 1980s and 1990s

1976 The Capital Market Executive Agency (BAPEPAM) and PT Dana Reksa were established.

1977 The capital market was reopened.

1987 Several deregulation packages were introduced to develop the capital market.

1989 Surabaya Stock Exchange and the Parallel Stock Exchange were established.

1992 Jakarta Stock Exchange was privatised.

1993 The following institutions were set up:
- Indonesian Securities Clearing and Depository (KDEI)
- The Indonesian Credit Rating Agency (PEFINDO)

1995 Surabaya Stock Exchange and Parallel Stock Exchange were merged.
Jakarta Stock Exchange introduced the Jakarta Automated Trading System (JATS).

1996 The Capital Market Law 1995 took effect on 1 January.

Capital Market Supervisory Agency (BAPEPAM)

The basic role of BAPEPAM is to supervise, regulate and monitor capital market activities and to protect the interests of investors. It ensures that market activities are efficient.

Capital Market Law 1995 — Highlights

The Capital Market Law came into effect on 1 January 1996. Important features included the following:

— Extending the authority of BAPEPAM. As the supervisor of the capital market, it grants and cancels licences to persons or institutions engaged in capital market activities. As the regulator, BAPEPAM creates rules within the context of the Capital Market Law. As the enforcement agency, it conducts investigation if a person or an institution violates the Law.
— Establishment of stock exchanges, a clearing guarantee institution and a central depository as self-regulatory organizations.
— Introduction of open-end investment funds and contractual type investment funds.
— Registration of capital market supporting institutions and professionals. These included trustees, accountants, legal consultants, appraisers and notaries.
— Registration of issuers and public companies.
— Strict sanction on violators of capital market regulations.

Jakarta Stock Exchange

Early History

The first stock exchange in Indonesia was set up in 1912 by the Dutch colonial government in Batavia (Jakarta). Exchanges were later set up in Surabaya and Semarang. All trading ceased in 1942 during the Japanese Occupation. In 1952, the Jakarta exchange was reopened to trade in stocks and bonds issued before the war by Dutch companies. After the nationalisation program was launched in 1956, all trading was suspended.

Recent History

On 10 August 1977, the Jakarta exchange was opened under the management of the Capital Market Executive Agency (*Badan Pelaksana Pasar Modal* BAPEPAM). During the first ten years, growth was slow. The exchange attracted only 24 companies to be listed. It was only in 1988 that the exchange became active after banking and capital market reforms were introduced under PAKTO 1988 (Paket Oktober 1988, or Reform Packet October 1988).

In early 1990s, steps were taken to privatise the stock exchanges. In 1990, Bursa Efek Surabaya (Surabaya Stock Exchange SSX) was set up in 1990 and Bursa Efek Jakarta (Jakarta Stock Exchange JSX) was set up in 1991, followed by the over-the-counter market Bursa Paralel Indonesia.

On 13 July 1992, JSX was privatised when its management was transferred from BAPEPAM to the Jarkata Stock Exchange Inc. BAPEPAM changed its function from Captial Market Executive Agency to Capital Market Supervisory Agency.

The members of JSX are broker-dealers with licences from BAPEPAM and are shareholders of the Jakarta Stock Exchange Limited Company.

Listing Requirements

Shares

- Shares are issued by limited liability company
- Registration statement is declared effective by BAPEPAM
- Financial statement has been audited by an accountant registered with BAPEPAM
- A minimum of 1 million shares are to be listed
- The company is owned by at least 200 shareholders
- The company may list all paid-up shares as long as the listing does not violate the rule regarding maximum ownership by foreign investors
- The company has been established and operated for 3 years
- The company has net operating profit for the last 2 years
- The company has total assets of Rp 20 billion
- The company has authorised capital of Rp7.5 billion and paid-up capital of Rp2 billion
- Board of directors and commissioners have a good reputation

Bonds

- Bonds are issued by a legal entity
- Registration statement is declared effective by BAPEPAM
- Financial statement has been audited by an accountant registered with BAPEPAM

— Total value of bonds must be at least Rp 25 billion
— The period between the effective date of the registration statement and the listing should not exceed 6 months with a minimum remaining maturity for bonds of 4 years
— The company has been established and operated for 3 years
— The company has operating profit for the last 2 years
— Board of directors and commissioners have a good reputation

Surabaya Stock Exchange

Surabaya Stock Exchange (SSX) was set up in 1989. It was the first private stock exchange in Indonesia. In 1995 Bursa Paralel Indonesia merged with Surabaya Stock Exchange to form Surabaya Stock Exchange Limited Company. Its basic role is to organise and provide facilities for buying and selling securities. Its members are broker-dealers with licences from BAPEPAM and are shareholders of the Surabaya Stock Exchange Limited Company.

Indonesian Clearing and Settlement Corporation (KPEI)

The basic role of KPEI is to provide clearing service and guarantee efficient securities settlement in an exchange. Its major shareholders are Jakarta Stock Exchange Ltd (90%) and Surabaya Stock Exchange Ltd (10%).

Indonesian Securities Custodian and Depository (KDEI)

The basic function of KDEI is to provide central custodian service and settle securities transaction. Its shareholders are: Bank Rakyat Indonesia, Bank Exim, Bank Tabungan Negara, Bapindo, Bank BNI, Bank Bumi Daya, Bank Dagang Negara (13.33% each), Jakarta Stock Exchange Ltd (5%) and Surabaya Stock Exchange Ltd (1.67%).

Indonesian Credit Rating Agency (PT PERFINO)

PERFINDO was established in 1994. Its basic role is to rate bonds and other debt instruments. It provides information to investors about the ability of companies to pay their loans and interest.

Privatisation of SOEs

In the early 1990s, several big state-owned enterprises (SOEs) were privatised and listed on the JSX and SSX. They included cement maker Semen Gresik, telecommunication services company Indosat, tin-mining company Tambang Timah, and telecommunication company Telkom. The largest listing in the history of JSX was Telkom with a value of Rp 25 trillion or 16% of the market capitalisation.

References

Binhadi (1994), "Financial deregulation and bank supervision: the case of Indonesia", in Faruqi, Shakil (ed.) *Financial Sector Reforms, Economic Growth and Stability: Experiences in Selected Asian and Latin American Countries,* World Bank, Washington, D.C., 81–102.

Cole, D.C. and Slade, B.F. (1995), "Money markets in Indonesia", in Cole D.C., Scott, H.S. and Wellons, P.A. (eds.) *Asian Money Markets,* Oxford University Press, New York, 95–158.

Cole, D.C. and Slade, B.F. (1996), *Building a Modern Financial System: the Indonesian Experience,* Cambridge University Press, New York.

Nasution, Anwar (1999), "The financial crisis in Indonesia", in Masuyama, S., Vanderbrink, D. and Chia, S.Y. (eds.) *East Asia's Financial Systems: Evolution and Crisis,* Nomura Research Institute, Tokyo and Institute of Southeast Asian Studies, Singapore, 74–108.

LAOS

The financial system in Laos comprises the following:

— the Central Bank (Bank of Lao PDR)
— state-owned commercial banks
— state-owned agricultural development bank
— state-private joint venture bank
— branches of foreign banks
— private joint venture bank between Lao and foreign interest
— general insurance company

Bank of Lao PDR

The main function of the Bank of Lao PDR (BOL, the central bank) is to maintain monetary control and to promote the development of financial markets. The main objective of monetary control is to reduce inflationary rate while recognising the need for continued credit growth to finance the development needs of the country. The objective is achieved through high interest rate structure (to absorb excess liquidity and encourage savings) and using monetary policy instruments such as reserve requirement ratio, credit and discount window, and the issue of treasury bills.

Issue of Treasury Bills

The first treasury bills were issued in 1994.

Reserve with BOL

A non-state bank must deposit USD 5 million with the BOL as start-up capital once its licence is approved. The bank may draw down on this deposit after operations have begun, provided it maintains a deposit of 10% of the capital with BOL at all times. All banks are required to provide information to the BOL on a regular basis.

Commercial Banks

Commercial banks collect deposits from and grant loans to individuals, business firms, joint ventures and other organisations. The Bank of Lao PDR used to have branches in all the provinces. As BOL now plays the role of a central bank, some of these branches have become regional commercial banks serving the northern, central and southern regions of the country. For example, the bank at Luang Prabang serves eight northern provinces, Pak Thai Bank in Savannakhet serves three central provinces and Lao Mai Bank in Pakse serves the southern provinces.

BRIEF HISTORICAL DEVELOPMENT

For several decades, the banking sector in Laos remained an undeveloped sector in the economy. During the pre-liberation period (before the creation of the Lao People's Democratic Republic), there were two separate and independent financial sectors: that of the Lao Patriotic Front and the Vientiane government. During the post-liberation period (1975–88), there was only one nationalised and centralised banking system. There were no other banking entity except the State Bank. It acted as a government treasury, issued money and transferred funds from the central budget to provincial and district budgets in line with plans approved by the National Assembly, and extended loans to state enterprises.

Banking Reforms in 1988 and 1990

In March 1988, the Council of Ministers passed Decree No. 11 on the Reform of the Lao Banking System. The objective was to move away from state planning and control. As a result, the various branches of the State Bank became autonomous commercial banks. These were:

— Bank Sethathilath
— Bank Nakhoneluang
— Foreign Commercial Bank of Lao PDR
(Banque pour le Commerce Exterrior Lao)

The State Bank was renamed the Bank of Lao PDR (BOL) to function as the central bank. It has been enpowered to license, supervise and regulate financial services. It also keeps the national reserves. The Foreign Commercial Bank acts as the nation's main foreign exchange bank.

In 1989, a state-private joint venture bank was set up. After Bangkok Bank opened a branch in Vientiane in 1993, several other foreign banks were also allowed to open branches.

Banking Regulation

By 1993, most guidelines on interest rates were removed except for a minimum savings rate and a maximum loan rate. Since 1985, residents have been allowed to hold foreign currency accounts.

Foreign Exchange Control

Before the introduction of banking reform in Lao PDR, the Foreign Commercial Bank of Lao PDR (Banque pour le Commerce Exterrior Lao) had a monopoly over foreign exchange transactions. After the reforms, commercial banks are allowed to deal in foreign exchange. In the market, the Lao kip, Thai baht and the US dollars are circulated widely.

Foreign travellers and investors are required to declare their foreign currencies upon arrival. They may then export those that they have brought in.

In 1991, Decree No. 53 governing the Management of Foreign Exchange and Precious Metals was passed. Foreign exchange control was implemented. Under the Foreign Exchange Decree, all foreign exchange transactions must be carried out through institutions authorised by the Bank of the Lao PDR. These institutions include commercial banks and foreign exchange dealers. They are required to submit periodic reports to the BOL.

In 1994, the Law on the Promotion and Management of Foreign Investment was passed. It has replaced the Foreign Investment Law of 1988.

Insurance Company

In 1991, an Insurance Code was adopted. In 1992, a new company Assurances Generales du Lao (AGL) was formed as a joint venture between the Lao Government and Assurances Generales de France. It was granted a monopoly by the government on the condition that it provided a full range of insurance services including fire insurance for factories.

References

Brahm, L. J. (1992). *Banking and Finance in Indochina,* Woodhead-Faulker, Hemel Hempstead, Hertfordshire, UK.

Brahm, L. J. and Macpherson, N. T. (1991). *Investment in the Lao People's Democratic Republic,* Hong Kong: Longman.

Khamsay Souphanouvong (1995), "Developments in the banking and finance industry — how can foreign investors capitalise on the opportunities in the emerging markets: the case of People's Democratic Republic of Laos", Paper presented at the Conference on Banking & Finance in Indochina and Myanmar, 30–31 March 1995, Bangkok, Thailand.

Sunshine, Russell (1995) *Managing Foreign Investment: Lessons From Laos,* Honolulu, Hawaii, East-West Centre, 1995.

United Nations Industrial Development Organisation (1994), *Lao People's Democratic Republic — Industrial Transition,* Industrial Development Reviews Unit, UNIDO, Vienna, Austria.

Varit Lekprasert (1995), "Banking operations: what you should know about the People's Democratic Republic of Laos", Paper presented at the Conference on Banking & Finance in Indochina and Myanmar, 30–31 March 1995, Bangkok, Thailand.

MALAYSIA

Financial Institutions

Financial institutions in Malaysia comprise two major groups: banking institutions and non-bank institutions.

Banking Institutions

The banking institutions are:

— Bank Negara (Central Bank)
— Islamic Bank
— Commercial banks (domestic & foreign)
— Representative office of foreign banks
— Finance companies
— Merchant banks
— Discount houses

Non-bank Institutions

The non-bank institutions are:

— Leasing companies
— Factoring companies
— Venture capital companies
— Credit token companies

Development Finance Institutions

— Agricultural Bank of Malaysia
— Borneo Development Corporation

— Development Bank of Malaysia
— Industrial Bank of Malaysia
— Malaysian Industrial Development Finance
— Sabah Credit Corporation
— Sabah Development Bank

Saving Institutions

— National Savings Bank
— Urban Credit Cooperatives
— Rural Credit Cooperatives
— Bank Rakyat

Insurance Companies

— General insurance companies
— Life insurance companies
— Composite insurance companies
— Reinsurance companies
— Islamic insurance (Takaful)
— Offshore insurance companies

Provident and Pension Funds

— Employees Provident Fund
— Social Security Organisation
— Pension Trust Fund
— Other statutory and private provident funds

Unit Trusts

— Unit trust companies
— Unit trust funds
— Amanah Saham Bumiputera
— Amanah Saham Nasional

Property Trusts

— Property trust funds

Housing Credit Institutions

— Malaysian Building Society Bhd
— Borneo Housing Mortgage Finance
— Government Housing Loan Division
— Cagamas Berhad

Other Institutions

— Pilgrims Fund Board
— Credit Guarantee Corporation
— Malaysia Export Credit Insurance Bhd

Rating Companies

— Rating Agency Malaysia Bhd
— Malaysia Rating Corporation Bhd

FINANCIAL MARKETS

The financial markets in Malaysia include the following:

Money and Foreign Exchange Markets

The participants in these markets include commercial banks, finance companies, merchant banks, money brokers and foreign exchange brokers.

Malaysian Government Securities

In the Malaysian Government Securities market, there are 13 principal dealers.

Stock Exchanges

There are two stock exchanges. The main exchange is the Kuala Lumpur Stock Exchange (KLSE) which has 60 broking companies. The Bumiputera Stock Exchange has 5 companies.

Options and Futures Exchanges

There were 3 exchanges:

— Kuala Lumpur Commodity Exchange (KLCE)
— Monetary Exchange of Malaysia (MME)
— Kuala Lumpur Options and Financial Futures Exchange (KLOFFE)

In 1998, KLCE and MME merged to become the Commodity and Monetary Exchange of Malaysia (COMMEX Malaysia). In January 1999, the KLSE acquired KLOFFE.

Labuan International Offshore Financial Centre

In 1990, the Malaysian decided to develop Labuan as an international offshore financial centre. Much progress has been made. By 31 December 1997, there were 64 offshore banks, 11 insurance companies, 19 insurance-related companies, 20 trust companies and 5 fund managers.

BANK NEGARA MALAYSIA (CENTRAL BANK OF MALAYSIA)

Bank Negara Malaysia (BNM) was set up in 1959 as the central bank of Malaysia. It supervises and controls all banks and other financial institutions which are governed by the Banking and Financial Institutions Act (BAFIA). It issues the Malaysian currency and enforces exchange controls. It is the financial adviser to the Malaysian government.

Objectives

The objectives of BNM are:

— to issue currency and keep reserves safeguarding the value of the currency
— to act as a banker and financial adviser to the government
— to promote monetary stability and a sound financial structure
— to influence the credit situation to the advantage of the country.

In meeting these objectives, the BNM is guided by the principle that it should act only in the economic interest of the nation and without regard to profit as a primary consideration.

The functions of the Bank are carried out within the context of the broader goals of promoting economic growth, a high level of employment, maintaining price stability and a reasonable balance in the country's international payments position, eradicating poverty and restructuring society.

In particular, the BNM ensures that the availability and cost of money and credit in the economy are consonant with national macroeconomic objectives. In this respect, the BNM acts as the banker for currency issue, keeper of international reserves and safeguarding the value of the ringgit, banker and financial adviser to the government, agency responsible for monetary policy and management of the financial system and banker to the banks.

Laws Enforced by BNM

As the central bank, BNM is vested with legal powers to regulate and supervise the financial system. The laws include:

1. Central Bank of Malaysia Act 1958 (Revised 1994)

The Act states the powers and the duties of the Central Bank in relation to the issuance of currency, maintenance of external reserve, authorised business of the bank, specific powers to deal with ailing institutions, its relationship with the government and financial institutions.

2. Banking and Financial Institutions Act 1989 (BAFIA)

The BAFIA came into effect on 1 October 1989. It regulates institutions carrying on banking, finance company, merchant banking, discount house and money-broking businesses. It also regulates non-bank institutions such as credit and charge card companies, building societies, factoring, leasing companies and development finance institutions.

3. Exchange Control Act 1953

The Act restricts dealings in gold and foreign currencies, payments to and from residents, issuance of securities outside Malaysia, imports and exports and settlements. The Act also empowers the Controller for Foreign Exchange to enforce the provisions of the Act.

4. Islamic Banking Act 1983

The Act regulates Islamic banking business. It states the financial requirements and duties of an Islamic Bank, ownership, control and management of Islamic banks, restrictions on its business, powers of supervision and control over Islamic bank and other general provisions.

5. Insurance Act 1996

The Act deals with the licensing of insurers, insurance brokers adjusters and reinsurers. It also deals with the setting up of subsidiary and offices, establishment of insurance fund, direction and control of defaulting insurers, the control on management of licensee, accounts of licensee, examination and investigation powers of the Central Bank, winding-up, transfer of business of licensee.

The Act also provides for matters relating to policies, insurance guarantee scheme fund, enforcement powers of the Central Bank, offences and other general provisions.

6. Takaful Act 1984

The Act regulates takaful business in Malaysia and for other purposes relating to takaful. "Takaful" means a scheme based on brotherhood, solidarity and mutual assistance which provides for mutual financial aid to the participants.

7. Emergency (Essential Powers) Act, 1979 Essential (Protection of Depositors) Regulations 1986

The Act empowers the Central Bank to investigate the affairs of any person it suspects or has reason to believe is a deposit-taker. It empowers the Bank to freeze the properties of the deposit-taker and other persons associated with the deposit-taker, assume control over the deposit-taker, and to appoint receivers and managers. The Act also enumerates the powers of the managers, provisions on priority of payment and cost.

8. Loan (Local) Ordinance, 1959

This Ordinance authorises the Central Bank to be the agent of the government in raising loans.

9. Treasury Bills (Local) Act 1946 (Revised 1977)

This Act authorises the issue of Treasury Bills in Malaysia and appoints the Central Bank as the agent of the government.

10. Government Investment Act 1983

This Act empowers the Minister to receive investment money and to pay dividend. It appoints the Central Bank as the agent of the government.

KUALA LUMPUR STOCK EXCHANGE

(Source: www.klse.com.my)

History of the KLSE

In 1930, the Singapore Stockbrokers' Association was formed. It was the first formal organisation in the securities business in Malaysia. It was re-registered as the Malayan Stockbrokers' Association in 1937. Public trading of shares in Malaysia only began on 9 May 1960 when the Malayan Stock Exchange was formed.

In 1961, the board system was introduced with two trading rooms, in Singapore and Kuala Lumpur, that were linked by direct telephone lines into a single market with the same stocks and shares listed at a single set of prices on both boards.

After the separation of Singapore from Malaysia in 1965, the common stock exchange continued to function but as the Stock Exchange of Malaysia and Singapore (SEMS). In 1973, currency interchangeability between Malaysia and Singapore was terminated and SEMS was separated into Kuala Lumpur Stock Exchange (KLSE) and Stock Exchange of Singapore (SES). During this period, Malaysian companies continued to be listed on SES and vice-versa. In 1990, Singapore incorporated companies were delisted from the KLSE and vice-versa.

Vision, Goals and Development Plan

KLSE's Vision

The KLSE's vision is to become a world-class stock exchange offering unique investment opportunities in a fast developing capital market within the industrialising Malaysian economy.

KLSE's Goals (by the year 2000)

1. To achieve a sustainable market capitalisation of RM1.25 trillion.
2. To enhance accessibility of the market to as many investors as possible, locally and abroad.
3. To achieve an efficient trading and settlement system capable of handling 1 million trades or four billion shares a day.
4. To have a full fledged Central Depository System, handling all aspects of depository operations.
5. To have an efficient information dissemination system through infrastructure improvements.
6. To have a high level of investors' confidence through the implementation, recommendation, and effective enforcement of laws and regulations.
7. To uphold a high level of professionalism at all levels of the industry.
8. To be the most efficient and cost effective market in the region.
9. To achieve a 100% disaster recovery environment.
10. To have an efficient office automation system and management information system for the entire KLSE group.

Development Plan

In order to achieve world class status, the KLSE has formulated Development Plan containing 56 benchmark areas and 47 strategic action plans spanning over five years.

It has identified the area of infrastructure and information technology to be the main driver for KLSE to face future challenges and opportunities.

Several IT related projects have been included in the Development Plan such as the Brokers' Integrated Operation Study and System that will improve post trade integration between KLSE and its member companies, and webbing KLSE with the outside world through Internet-working.

The Development Plan also emphasises the effectiveness of its rules and regulations through mechanisms such as Code of Ethics for members, Minimum Capital Requirements and Capital Adequacy Requirements.

The Development Plan also stresses the importance of timely and accurate information with respect to market promotional activities and programs, investor education as well as other investor services.

The Development Plan will be updated from time to time according to the needs and requirements for KLSE to become a leading stock exchange.

KLSE Group of Companies

The KLSE is a company limited by guarantee. It is a self-regulatory organisation with its own Memorandum and Articles of Association and a set of rules which govern the conduct of stockbroking companies. It is responsible for the surveillance of the market place, and for the enforcement of its Listing Requirements which spell out the criteria for listing, disclosure requirements and standards to be maintained by public listed companies.

The KLSE has several subsidiary and affiliate companies.

Securities Clearing Automated Network Services Sdn Bhd (SCANS)

SCANS is a clearing house wholly owned by the KLSE. It provides all the information technology related services to the KLSE Group of Companies.

Malaysian Central Depository Sdn Bhd (MCD)

MCD is a subsidiary which operates the Central Depository System (CDS), the KLSE electronic settlement system.

KLSE-Bernama Real-Time Information Services Sdn Bhd (KULBER)

KULBER is a subsidiary of SCANS. It compiles and disseminates real-time share price, financial and economic information to information vendors and subscribers.

Research Institute of Investment Analysts Malaysia (RIIAM)

RIIAM is an affiliate company of KLSE. Its main objectives are to conduct investment research as well as organise courses, seminars and workshops for the public.

KLSE's Computerised Trading System

Since its introduction in 1989, KLSE's computerised trading system has been constantly upgraded until it became a fully automated system in 1992. By 1995, all stockbroking companies were equipped with the KLSE's latest computerised broker front end system known as the WinSCORE system.

SCORE (System on Computerised Order Routing and Execution) is the central computer responsible for the matching of all orders. WinSCORE is the broker front end trading system. It is responsible for credit control management, order and trade routing as well as confirmation.

Stockbroking Companies

Trading in securities is carried out by stockbroking companies which are referred to as member companies of the KLSE. The terms member company and stockbroking company are interchangeable.

Stockbroking companies are either private or public companies. The operation of stockbroking business in the form of partnership or sole proprietorship is not allowed in Malaysia.

A member company is not a member of the KLSE. Members of the KLSE are either natural persons or corporations who are the shareholders of the member companies or stockbroking companies.

Stockbroking companies in Malaysia are governed by several laws and regulations of which the main ones are:

1. Securities Industry Act 1983
2. Securities Commission Act 1993
3. Securities Industry (Central Depository) Act 1991
4. Companies Act 1965
5. Rules and Regulations of the KLSE

KLSE Regulatory Structure

The Securities Industry Act came into force in 1976. It required a stockbroker, being a director and shareholder of a stockbroking company as well as a member of the KLSE to hold a dealer's licence issued by the Registrar of Companies (ROC). An investment adviser was required to hold an investment adviser's licence. The ROC was not only the custodian of the Companies Act 1965 but also the Securities Industry Act.

SIA 1983

The 1976 Act was replaced by the Securities Industry Act 1983 (SIA). The Act gave formal recognition to the Capital Issues Committee (CIC) with the primary functions of advising the MOF on matters relating to the securities industry and approving the listing and quotation of securities on the KLSE.

A stockbroker continued to hold a dealer's licence while his representatives each required a dealer's representative licence issued by the Registrar of Companies.

1986 Amendments

Amendments were made in 1986. The amendments stipulated that only corporations could hold dealer's licences. This enabled corporations, in addition to individuals, to be members of the KLSE and to contribute to the KLSE's fidelity fund. The amendments also enabled parties concerned to announce a proposal for scheme of arrangement, a scheme of reconstruction or take-over scheme to be made prior to submitting the proposal to the CIC.

Securities Industry (Central Depositories) Act

In 1991, under the Securities Industry (Central Depositories) Act (SICDA), a central depository system was set up.

Securities Commission Act

In 1993, under the Securities Commission Act (SCA), the Securities Commission (SC) was set up. Among some of its functions, the SC took over the Capital Issue Committee (CIC) and the Panel on Takeovers and Mergers.

SIA Amendments in 1993

In 1993, amendments were made to the SIA to give recognition to the SC while deleting provisions relating to the CIC and also, established the Licensing Officer (MOF) as the issuer of licences.

SCA, SICDA and SIA Amendments in 1996

The SCA was amended in 1996 to accord three additional specific functions to the SC, namely:

1. to promote self-regulation by professional associations or market bodies in the securities and futures industries;
2. to license and supervise all licensed persons as may be provided for under any securities law;
3. to promote and maintain the integrity of all licensed persons in the securities and futures industries.

Amendments were made to the SICDA to transfer the powers of regulation of the central depository system from the ROC to SC.

Amendments to the SIA were wide ranging. They included:

1. defines securities law to mean the SIA, the SICDA and the SCA;
2. empowers the MOF to exempt any stock market from the requirement to comply with the relevant subsection. In granting such exemption, the MOF may impose any conditions or restrictions as he thinks reasonable and appropriate;
3. specifies the statutory duty of the stock exchange to ensure an orderly and fair market in the securities traded through its facilities, and, to act in the public interest and to ensure that its members, member companies and listed corporations comply with its rules;
4. enables the MOF to close a stock market of the stock exchange where orderly trading on the stock exchange is or is likely to be prevented by emergencies or related disaster or by economic or financial crisis whether in Malaysia or elsewhere;
5. empowers the SC to prohibit trading in particular securities or classes of securities under specified circumstances;
6. empowers the MOF to issue suspension orders against a stock exchange, recognised clearing house or central depository under specified circumstances;

7. introduces a new class of licence for fund managers in which they were formerly licensed as dealers;
8. transfers licensing powers from the Licensing Officer (MOF) to the SC;
9. replaces the fidelity fund of the stock exchange with a compensation fund whereby the scope of the claims which can be made against the compensation fund is broadened and to ensure that investors can be adequately protected not only in cases of defalcation but also in cases of fraudulent misuse of property and in the event of insolvency of Member companies;
10. facilitates regulated short selling on the stock exchange; and
11. empowers the MOF to make regulations with respect to the giving of contract notes by dealers and fund managers who carry on the business of managing a portfolio of securities. This will provide flexibility and also enable the MOF to prescribe appropriate regulations on business conducted by dealers and fund managers in step with market developments.

Main Board Listing Requirement

(Source: www.klse.com.my/klse31.htm)

Pre-Requisites for Admission

— The company must have a minimum paid-up capital of RM50 million, comprising ordinary shares of RM1 each.

— At least 25% of the issued and paid-up capital is in the hands of a minimum number of public shareholders holding not less than 1,000 shares each, as follows:

Nominal value of issued and paid-up capital:	Minimum number of shareholders:
Less than RM100 million	750
RM100 million and above	1,000

— The minimum number of public shareholders shall exclude employees of the company. However, up to 5% of the issued and paid-up capital of the company held by employees is allowed to make up the 25% public shareholding spread.

— The company must issue a prospectus regardless of method of flotation and the advertisement of the full prospectus.

— The company must have either:

1. Profit track record of 3 financial years (*), with an after-tax profit of not less than RM4 million per annum and an aggregate after-tax profit of not less than RM25 million over the said 3 financial years; or
2. Profit track record of 5 financial years, with an after-tax profit of not less than RM2 million per annum and an aggregate after-tax profit of not less than RM25 million over the said 5 financial years.

(*) Notwithstanding the shorter period of profit track record now permitted, the requirements that the applicant company or the core company must have commenced business for a period of at least 5 years remains unchanged.

Second Board Listing Requirements

The Second Board Listing Requirements are essentially the same as those of the Main Board. Second Board companies are subject to the same Corporate Disclosure Policy.

Some major differences of the Second Board Listing Requirements from those of the Main Board:

— Paid up capital of at least RM10 million but less than RM50 million, comprising ordinary shares of RM1 each.
— Profit track record of 3 financial years, with an after-tax profit of not less than RM1 million per annum, and should have achieved an average after-tax profit of not less than RM2 million per annum.
— At least 25% but not more than 50% of the issued and paid-up capital is in the hands of a minimum number of 500 public shareholders holding not less than 1,000 shares each.

The minimum number of public shareholders shall exclude employees of the company. However, up to 5% of the issued and paid-up capital of the company held by employees is allowed to make up the 25% public shareholding spread.

— Only a summary of the prospectus needs to be advertised.

Corporate Disclosure Policy

Corporate disclosure policy, which all listed companies must observe, forms part of the continuing listing requirements. These include:

— Policy on immediate public disclosure of material information
— Policy on thorough public dissemination
— Policy on clarification or confirmation of rumours and reports
— Policy on response to unusual market action
— Policy on unwarranted promotional disclosure
— Policy on insider trading

Moratorium or Profit Guarantee

The major shareholders of Main Board companies involved in construction, services or specialised activities can either choose to place their shares under moratorium or to be governed by a minimum profit guarantee requirement.

Moratorium

Under moratorium, major shareholders are prohibited from selling, transferring or assigning their shareholdings for one year from date of admission of company to the Main Board. Thereafter, the major shareholders are allowed to sell, transfer or assign only up to a maximum of 20% of their shareholdings per annum.

Profit Guarantee

For the profit guarantee requirement, the major shareholders are required to provide a profit guarantee of 90% of the forecast profit as stated in the prospectus and also 90% of the annual maintainable earnings for the following two financial years.

All Second Board applicant companies for direct listing are required to provide a profit guarantee in the form of bank guarantee instead of being given the option of either profit guarantee or moratorium on disposal of shares.

Procedures for Initial Listing

1. Company submits application to Securities Commission
2. Company submits Memorandum and Articles of Association to the Exchange for approval

3. Company files Initial Listing Application and supporting papers with the Exchange
4. Securities Commission approves listing
5. Exchange approves listing
6. Company files final copy of prospectus with Registrar of Companies and the Exchange
7. Companies advertises and issues prospectus to public and offer period opens
8. Company announces basis for allotment
9. Notice of Allotment is despatched to successful applicants. Company issues shares pursuant to the allotment
10. Shares admitted to the Official List
11. Shares traded on the Exchange 3 market days after the Exchange has received confirmation that Notice of Allotment has been despatched to successful applicants.

NEW MALAYSIAN CODE ON TAKE-OVERS AND MERGERS

(Source: Securities Commission press release on 2 January 1999)

On 1 January 1999, the new Malaysian Code On Take-overs and Mergers came into effect to replace the 1987 Code.

The new Code ensures that minority shareholders are given a fair opportunity to consider the merits and demerits of an offer and to enable them to decide whether they should retain or dispose of their shares.

The new Code also requires offer documents, board of directors circulars and independent advice circulars to include all relevant information required by shareholders and their professional advisers to make informed assessments of the merits and risks of accepting or rejecting a take-over offer.

New Provisions

The new Code includes provisions imposing criminal liability on the relevant parties to a take-over offer for providing false or misleading information to the SC and shareholders.

Provisions relating to "creeping" take-overs have been amended to allow an acquirer who holds between 33% and 50% of the voting shares in a company to acquire 2% within a period of 6 months instead of 12 months and hence, effectively reduce the time taken to "creep" into control of the company.

Previously, such persons were not allowed to acquire more than 2% of the voting shares in the company in any 12-month period. The purpose of a creeping provision is to restrict the time frame whereby a person can obtain statutory control of a company. The amendment is made in order to be more consistent with international practices such as those of Hong Kong, Singapore and Australia.

SC as Sole Authority

The SC is the sole authority to grant exemptions from provisions of the new Code. It has to ensure that take-overs and mergers take place in an efficient, competitive and informed market. It has to ensure that:

— the shareholders and directors of an offeree and the market for the shares that are the subject of the take-over offer are aware of the identity of the acquirer and offeror, have reasonable time in which to consider a take-over offer, and are supplied with sufficient information necessary to enable them to assess the merits of any take-over offer;
— all shareholders of an offeree have equal opportunity to participate in benefits accruing from the take-over offer, including in the premium payable for control;
— shareholders, in particular, minority shareholders, are treated fairly and equally; and
— directors of the offeree and acquirer act in good faith and that minority shareholders are not disadvantaged by the treatment and conduct of the directors of the offeree or the acquirer.

Practice Notes

The Practice Notes to the new Code govern the treatment of specific situations or elaborate on the interpretation of certain sections of the Code. The Practice Notes also list the circumstances or transactions which the SC would consider granting exemptions to.

Amending Listing Requirements for Mergers and Takeovers

(Source: KLSE press release on 4 January 1999)

In line with the introduction of the new Code, the SC has also approved amendments to the Listing Requirements submitted by the

KLSE. These requirements are part of the regulatory framework governing take-overs and mergers. The amendments will enhance disclosure by public listed companies on matters relating to mergers and take-overs. The amendments are made to Part 5 of the Main Board Listing Requirements and Part 6 of the Second Board Listing Requirements relating to take-overs.

The amendments seek to achieve the following:

— clarify and strengthen existing provisions in relation to the relevant obligations of the offeror and the offeree;
— extend compliance with the provisions of the Securities Commission Act 1993 relating to take-over and mergers and the code, to the listed companies' directors, officers and advisers and any other person to whom the code purports to apply;
— prescribe the standard of disclosure for take-overs by stipulating the type of information within the knowledge of specified persons that require disclosure;
— enhance the content of disclosure in announcements and documents sent to shareholders by the prescription of additional disclosure requirements consonant with the new code;
— enhance the timeliness of announcements in relation to take-overs by requiring an immediate announcement to be made in the following circumstances:
  (a) in the event of unusual market activity where discussions are on-going;
  (b) where the offeror has sent a written notice of a take-over offer in relation to securities or voting shares pursuant to the new code;
  (c) in the event of dealings in the voting shares of the offeror and offeree company by specified persons during the offer period.

NEW CAPITAL ADEQUACY REQUIREMENTS FOR STOCKBROKERS

(Source: Press statement dated 2 January 1999)

The Securities Commission (SC) approved on 31 December 1998 the Capital Adequacy Requirements for stockbroking companies, which will refine the prudential benchmark for maintaining better market integrity at the level of the exchange and clearing house.

The new requirements have replaced the old Minimum Liquid Fund rules when they were implemented through the KLSE's business rules in 1999. These have enabled both KLSE and its stockbroking companies to identify more clearly the capital available to cover the risks of running a securities business from the actual level of risk faced by the business at any given point in time.

STANDARD REMISIERS AGREEMENT

(Source: KLSE website press release dated 9 February 1999)

The KLSE, in consultation with the Securities Commission, has approved a standard remisiers agreement which took effect from 9 February 1999.

The standard agreement applies to all stockbroking companies and their remisiers. Contracting parties — stockbroking companies and remisiers — who have no current remisiers' agreement have to comply with the standard agreement beginning 9 February 1999. Contracting parties who had a remisiers' agreement in place were given a 6 months grace period from 9 February 1999 to comply with the new agreement.

The standard remisiers agreement covers the following areas:

- Duties and obligations of remisiers
- Remisiers' security deposit
- Remisiers' commission
- Remisiers' transfers
- Rights of the stockbroking company
- Duties of the stockbroking company

KLSE ACQUIRED KLOFFE

(Source: KLSE website press release dated 4 January 1999)

In January 1999, KLSE acquired KLOFFE Capital Sdn Bhd (KLOFFE Capital), the holding company of KLOFFE Berhad, the operator of the Kuala Lumpur Options & Financial Futures Exchange (KLOFFE). KLSE signed the sale and purchase agreement to acquire KLOFFE Capital in July 1998 to acquire KLOFFE Capital for RM35 million cash. The vendors of KLOFFE Capital were Renong Bhd, Rashid Hussain Bhd, The New Straits Times Press (Malaysia) Bhd and HLG Capital Bhd. Subsequently, the vendors and KLSE agreed to revise the purchase price to RM27 million.

References

Bank Negara Malaysia (1989), *Central Banking in an Era of Change: Landmark Speeches, 1959–88*, Bank Negara Malaysia, Kuala Lumpur.

Bank Negara Malaysia (1994), *Money and Banking in Malaysia*, 4th ed. Economic Department, Bank Negara Malaysia, Kuala Lumpur.

Lin, See Yan and Chung, Tin Fah (1995), "Money markets in Malaysia", in Cole, D.C., Scott, H.S. and Wellons, P.A. (eds.) *Asian Money Markets*, Oxford University Press, New York, 209–272.

Ong, Hong Cheong (1999), "Evolution of the Malaysian financial system", in Masuyama, S., Vanderbrink, D. and Chia, S.Y. (eds.) *East Asia's Financial Systems: Evolution and Crisis*, Nomura Research Institute, Tokyo and Institute of Southeast Asian Studies, Singapore, 144–65.

Sieh-Lee, Mei Ling *et al.* (1995), *The Finance Company Industry of Malaysia: Current Status and Future Directions*, University of Malaya Press, Kuala Lumpur.

MYANMAR

The financial system in Myanmar includes the Central Bank of Myanmar, specialised state-owned banks, a state-owned finance company and a state-owned insurance company. It also includes domestic private banks, representative offices of foreign banks.

Central Bank of Myanmar

The Central Bank of Myanmar was set up under the Central Bank of Myanmar Law enacted in 1990 which replaced the old Bank Law of 1975. The main objective of the bank is to preserve the internal and external value of the kyat. It promotes efficient payment mechanisms, and a sound financial system to foster monetary, credit and financial conditions conducive for economic development.

The Central Bank advises the government on economic matters, issues currency, formulates and implements monetary policies, and manages the international reserves of the country. It implements exchange rate policy and controls foreign exchange transactions. It licenses, inspects, supervises and regulates financial institutions.

The Central Bank sets reserve requirements, maximum discount rates, maximum and minimum interest rates on loans and deposits, asset and liability ratios and minimum cash margins.

State-owned Specialised Banks

The state-owned specialised banks are:

— Myanma Agricultural and Rural Development Bank (MARDB)
— Myanma Economic Bank (MEB)
— Myanma Foreign Trade Bank (MFTB)
— Myanma Investment and Commercial Bank (MICB)

In addition, there is a Government Employees Bank, a state-owned finance company and an insurance company.

Myanma Agricultural and Rural Development Bank (MARDB)

The MARDB was first set up in 1953 as the State Agricultural Bank (SAB). In 1976, the name was changed to Myanma Agricultural Bank. The MARDB was set up under the Myanma Agricultural and Rural Bank Law enacted in 1990 to take over the functions of the Myanma Agricultural Bank.

The MARDB supports the development of agricultural livestock and rural socio-economic enterprises. It has a nation-wide network of 14 regional offices, about 170 branches and 50 agency offices. It provides short and long term credit to farmers for crop production, livestock, fish and dairy farming. In 1993, it introduced the Rural Savings Scheme to encourage savings among farmers and to develop a rural banking system.

Myanma Economic Bank (MEB)

The MEB was set up in 1976 to provide commercial and industrial banking services. It has a nation-wide network of about 300 branches. It is the agent of the Central Bank of Myanmar for the operation of currency chests throughout the country. Foreign Exchange Certificates issued by the Central Bank are handled by the MEB. The bank also maintains the accounts of government departments and state-owned enterprises. Its former Small Loans Department is now a separate state-owned finance company.

Myanma Foreign Trade Bank (MFTB)

The MFTB focuses on foreign trade and foreign currency transactions. It issues guarantees and letters of credit and deals in traveller cheques. Its major customers are the state-owned enterprises and foreign companies which transmit their capital in foreign currencies. It has a network of about 120 correspondent banks in 60 countries.

Myanma Investment and Commercial Bank (MICB)

The MICB was formerly part of the Myanma Economic Bank. It became a separate bank under the Financial Institutions of Myanmar

Law 1990. It provides a wide range of investment, development and commercial banking services to both local and foreign enterprises.

Government Employees Bank (GEB)

The Government Employees Bank was set up in 1996 to provide loans to government employees and pensioners.

State-owned Finance Company

Myanma Small Loans Enterprise

Myanma Small Loans Enterprise was formerly the Small Loans Department in the Myanma Economic Bank. It was set up as a finance company to provide small loans. It has a network of about 200 branches throughout Myanmar.

State-owned Insurance Company

Myanmar Insurance Institution

In 1993, the Myanmar Insurance Law was enacted to replace the Insurance Business Law of 1975 to provide a wider coverage of insurance business. The Myanmar Insurance Institution is the sole insurance institution in Myanmar. It underwrites a wide range of insurance policies. It has a network of about 35 branches throughout Myanmar.

BRIEF HISTORY

The financial history of Myanmar dates back to 1861 when Burma (old name for Myanmar) was under British rule. At that time, Myanmar was considered as part of India by the British Administration until separation in 1937. The first bank to be set up was the Presidency Bank of Bengal (India) which opened two branches in 1865 and 1866. The Chartered Bank of India, Australia and China (now Standard Chartered Bank) also opened branches in Yangon, Moulmein and Akyab.

In 1913, post offices began to collect saving deposits. Before the Second World War, there were 400 post office savings bank branches. The 22 commercial banks were mostly foreign-owned.

After the independence of Myanmar in 1948, the Union Bank of Burma was set up in 1952 as the Central Bank. The State Agricultural Bank was set up in 1952 and State Commercial Bank in 1953. By that time, there were 14 foreign banks and 10 national banks (Ng, 1995).

After the Revolutionary Council came into power in 1962, all banks were nationalised. In 1967, the People's Bank of the Union of Burma was set up by merging all the nationalised banks. It performed the functions of a central bank as well as those of a commercial, industrial and agricultural bank. It had a special division dealing with insurance. In 1972, the name was changed to Union of Burma Bank.

In 1975, the Union Bank Law came into effect and the banking system was comprised of four banks:

— Union Bank of Burma: the central bank
— Myanma Economic Bank: commercial bank
— Myanma Foreign Trade Bank: foreign trade bank
— Myanma Agricultural Bank: agricultural bank.

Market-Oriented

In 1988, the State Law and Restoration Council (SLORC) took over power and introduced a market-oriented economic system.

In 1993, the Central Bank issued 3-year and 5-year treasury bonds on behalf of the government.

In November 1994, the Ministry of Planning and Economic Development and Daiwa Securities of Japan signed a memorandum of understanding whereby Daiwa would help Myanmar to develop its capital market by setting up a stock market and to privatise its state-owned economic enterprises.

Allowing Private Banks

In 1992, the Central Bank of Myanmar granted licence to 15 private domestic banks. Representative offices of foreign banks were also allowed to operate in Myanmar. With effect from 1994, some domestic private banks were allowed to conduct foreign exchange transactions. Another three were allowed to issue credit cards.

Foregin Exchange Certificates

In 1993, the Central Bank issued Foreign Exchange Certificates in denominations of 1 unit, 5 units and 10 units which were equivalent of US$1, US$5 and US$10. This was meant for the convenience of tourists and foreign currency account holders.

Exchange Control

Exchange control is administered by the Central Bank of Myanmar in accordance with instructions from the Ministry of Finance and Revenue. With effect from April 1993, non-residents may bring in foreign currency of up to US$2,000 without the need to declare to the Customs Department on arrival.

Laws Related to Financial Institutions

The main laws and regulations related to financial institutions are:

— Financial Institution of Myanmar Law 1990.
— Rules Relating to Financial Insitution of Myanmar Law 1991.
— Myanmar Insurance Law 1993.

Requirements for Commercial Banks

Commercial banks must have a minimum paid up capital of 15 million kyat. They are allowed to operate normal banking activities. They may grant short term loans of not exceeding one year. Banks with an additional capital of 15 million kyat may be granted a foreign exchange licence.

Banks with capital of more than 60 million kyat are permitted to collect time deposits of over one year and to grant loans with matching tenure.

Reserves Requirement

A bank is required to set aside 25% of its net profit as reserves until this amount reaches 100% of its capital. The capital adequacy ratio is 10% against risk weighted assets. The lending limit to a single customer is 20% of capital and reserves.

Statutory Reserves

Banks are required to maintain the following statutory reserves: 5% on time and saving deposits and 10% on demand deposits. Of these statutory reserves, 75% should be kept as reserves with the Central Bank. The cash ratio is 25% and the liquidity ratio is 20%.

Central Bank Guidelines

The interest rates on deposit and loan are guided by the Central Bank rate. Deposit rate should not be less than 3% below Central Bank rate. The rate on advances should not be more than 6% above Central Bank rate.

Foreign Investment

The Foreign Investment Law was enacted in 1988 to encourage foreign investments. It provides incentives for the inflow of direct foreign investment. The important features of this Law include non-nationalisation, tax holiday of up to three years and 100% foreign ownership. The law also guarantees the repatriation in foreign currency the rightful entitlement of the foreign investor. Foreign investors may incorporate enterprise on a 100% ownership basis. For a joint venture with local partners, the foregin investor must contribute at least 35% of the equity capital.

MONETARY POLICY

1948–63 Period

During the 1948–63 period, the Central Bank used the reserves requirements of commercial banks as an instrument of monetary policy. For example, the reserve requirements of commercial banks were raised for the first time in August 1957 and again in July 1961 to moderate the expansion of bank credit.

1963–88 Period

During the 1963–88 period, in the centrally-planned economy, cash plan and credit plan were used for monetary control. Implementation of control was based on the annual credit plan which determined the amount of total credit available and its sectoral allocation. Interest rates played only a limited role in regulating and allocating credit but were important in mobilising savings. The cash plan was prepared to enable the Central Bank to project the permissable level of money supply (Kyaw, 1995).

Since 1990

In 1990, the Central Bank of Myanmar was set up to formulate and implement monetary policies. The aim of the monetary policy is to ensure expansion of the money supply appropriate to support a growing economy at reasonable stable prices. The instruments used include reserve requirements, liquidity ratio, interest rates and the issue of Treasury bonds (Kyaw, 1995).

Reserve Requirements

Financial institutions are required to maintain reserves with the Central Bank of Myanmar (CBM). The reserves shall not exceed 35% of the total liabilities of the bank. If there is serious inflationary pressure, the CBM may increase the requirement beyond the 35% limit. The CBM shall pay interest on the reserves exceeding the 35% limit.

The CBM shall impose a levy not exceeding 1/5 of 1% per day on the shortfall of required reserves.

Liquidity Ratio

Financial institutions are required to maintain a liquidity ratio of 20%. The CBM imposes a levy of not more than 1/5 of 1% per day on the shortfall of liquid assets.

Interest Rate

The CBM has the authority to determine its rates for discount, rediscount and rate of interest on advances. For example, the CMB bank rate was raised from 11% to 12.5% with effect from 1 January 1995.

Treasury Bonds

The CBM is authorised to buy and sell, discount and rediscount securities, treasury bills and other financial instruments. For example, since 1993, it has issued 3-year and 5-year treasury bonds on behalf of the government.

Financial Institutions of Myanmar Law

Under the old Bank Law of 1975, only state-owned banks were allowed to operate in Myanmar. In 1990, the Financial Institutions of Myanmar Law was enacted to allow the setting up of financial institutions, whether state-owned, privately owned, or jointly owned by the State and the private sector subject to the approval from the Central Bank of Myanmar.

Private Banks

There are about 20 domestic private banks which have been granted banking licences by the Central Bank. Examples are Myanmar Citizens Bank, Cooperative Bank, Myawaddy Bank and Yangon City Bank. Some have been licensed to deal in foreign exchange.

Functions of Banks

The functions of both state-owned and private banks include borrowing and lending of money; buying, selling and collecting and dealing in bills of exchange, promissory notes, drafts, bills of lading, securities; granting and issuing of letters of credit, traveller cheques, buying and selling of foreign exchange, acting as agents of local government authorities or the Central Bank.

Foreign Bank Representative Offices

There are about 44 foreign bank representative offices in Yangon. As they are not allowed to perform banking services, they perform mainly trade-related business and correspondent banking.

Joint Venture Banks

There are four joint venture banks. These are:

— Mayflower Bank with Siam City from Thailand

— Tun Foundation Bank with Maybank from Malaysia
— Asia Wealth Bank with Thai Farmers Bank from Thailand
— Yoma Bank with Fuji Bank from Japan.

MYANMAR SECURITIES EXCHANGE CENTRE

The Myanmar Securities Exchange Centre is a joint venture between Myanma Economic Bank and Daiwa Research Institute of Japan. In 1997, it began to establish a stock exchange. It issued its first prospectus for the placement of 45% of the shares of the Union of Myanmar Forest Products Joint Venture with Myamar citizens and companies in the over-the-counter (OTC) market (Christie and Smith, 1997).

The major criteria for companies to participate in the OTC market include the following:

— a public company formed under the Companies Act
— paid up capital of at least 50 million kyat
— at least 100 shareholders
— no restriction on the transfer of shares among Myanmar citizens
— financial statements are published regularly
— profitable for at least three years.

References

Christie, A. and Smith, S. (1997), *Foreign Direct Investment in Myanmar*, Sweet & Maxwell Asia, Hong Kong.

Daw Ommar Sein (1995), "Central Bank and the regulation of the Myanmar financial markets", Paper presented at the Myanmar Banking & Finance Conference, 6 September 1995, Singapore.

Foo, T. W., Goh, Y. H., Tan, A. T. and Tham, Y. H. (1996) "Banking and Finance in Myanmar", in Tan, T. M., Low, A. M., Williams, J. J. and Polunin, I. P. (eds) (1996), *Business Opportunities in Myanmar*, Prentice Hall, Singapore, 205–215.

Fore, Millard (1995), "Financing opportunities for Myanmar in the international financial markets", Paper presented at the Myanmar Banking & Finance Conference, 6 September 1995, Singapore.

Kyaw Kyaw (1995), 'The banking and finance industry in perspective — internationalisation of the market and the place for foreign investors", Paper presented at the Myanmar Banking & Finance Conference, 6 September 1995, Singapore.

Lai, Andrew (1995), "Using technological advances to enhance the Myanmar financial banking industry", Paper presented at the Myanmar Banking & Finance Conference, 6 September 1995, Singapore.

Lunbeck, John (1995), "Portfolio investment in Myanmar", Paper presented at the Myanmar Banking & Finance Conference, 6 September 1995, Singapore.

Michel, Jacques (1995), "Potential of credit card business and credit facilities in Myanmar", Paper presented at the Myanmar Banking & Finance Conference, 6 September 1995, Singapore.

Myat Kyaw (1996) "Myanmar's banking and financial system", in Tan, T. M., Low, A. M., Williams, J. J. and Polunin, I. P. (eds) (1996), *Business Opportunities in Myanmar*, Prentice Hall, Singapore, 195–204.

Ng Thiam Watt (1995), "The banking and financial system in Myanmar — prospects and challenges", Paper presented at the Myanmar Banking & Finance Conference, 6 September 1995, Singapore.

Quinn, John (1995), "Establishing the equity market in Myanmar", Paper presented at the Myanmar Banking & Finance Conference, 6 September 1995, Singapore.

Sein Maung (1995), "Banking operations: what you should know — the Union of Myanmar", Paper presented at the Conference on Banking & Finance in Indochina and Myanmar, 30–31 March 1995, Bangkok.

Soe Win (1995), "Developments in the banking and finance industry — how can foreign investors capitalise on the opportunities in these emerging markets? the Union of Myanmar", Paper presented at the Conference on Banking & Finance in Indochina and Myanmar, 30–31 March 1995, Bangkok.

Website: www.myanmar.com/gov/trade/fin.htm

PHILIPPINES

The financial system in the Philippines comprises the following:

Financial Institutions

— Bangko Sentral ng Pilipinas (Central Bank)
— Commercial banks
— Thrift banks
— Rural banks
— Specialised government banks
— Offshore banking units
— Investment houses
— Finance companies

Other Financial Institutions

— Board of Investments
— Philippine Export & Foreign Loan Guarantee Corporation
— Philippine Deposit Insurance Corporation (PDIC)

Bangko Sentral ng Pilipinas

The Bangko Sentral ng Pilipinas (BSP) is the central bank of the Philippines. The BSP was established under the New Central Bank Act of 1993 as part of the restructuring of the old Central Bank of the Philippines (CBP), which dated back to 1949.

The New Central Bank Act has granted the BSP more fiscal and administrative autonomy from other sectors of the government. It no longer undertakes the quasi-fiscal activities and is not engaged in development banking or financing.

The Monetary Board

The highest policy making body of the BSP is the Monetary Board (MB). Its members are appointed by the President of the Republic.

Objectives of the BSP

The BSP formulates and implements policy on money, banking and credit, with the objective of maintaining stable prices conducive to economic growth. It also promotes and preserves monetary stability and the convertibility of the national currency.

Functions of the BSP

The BSP performs the following functions:

— conducting monetary policy
— issuing currency
— lending to other banks and the government
— managing foreign currency reserves
— supervising and regulating financial institutions
— determining exchange rate policy
— acting as banker, financial advisor and official depository of the government
— representing the government in international financial institutions, such as the IMF and the World Bank.

Commercial Banks

In the Philippines, the first commercial bank was set up in 1851 by the Banco Espanol-Filipino de Isabel (now known as the Bank of the Philippine Islands). In 1873, the Chartered Bank of Australia, India and China (now Standard Chartered Bank) also set up a branch. This was followed by the Hongkong and Shanghai Banking Corporation in 1875.

The Philippine National Bank (PNB) was set up in 1916 to take over the note issuing duties of the privately-owned Bank of the Philippine Islands and to be the sole depository of government funds.

Expanded Commercial Banks

Commercial banks in the Philippines perform the whole range of banking activities. In recent years, some of these banks (known as expanded commercial banks EKBs or universal banks) have been authorised to expand their activities to include investment banking activities such as underwriting, securities dealership and equity investment. Commercial banks are governed by the General Banking Act (RA 337).

The minimum capital requirement for a commercial bank is P2.0 billion while that of an expanded commercial bank is P4.5 billion.

Foreign Banks

Subsidiaries and branches of foreign banks are allowed to perform the same functions and subject to the same limitations of a domestic bank of the same category. Foreign banks are governed by the General Banking Act (RA 337) as well as the Act Liberalizing the Entry and Scope of Operations of Foregin Banks in the Philippines (RA 7721).

The bank liberalising law passed in 1994 has allowed the entry of ten foreign banks in 1995. Most foreign banks specialise in niche markets such as international finance and investment banking.

Offshore Banking Unit

The Philippine offshore banking system was established by a Presidential Decree in 1976. An offshore banking unit (OBU) may be a branch, subsidiary or affiliate of a bank which is authorised by the BSP as a separate accounting unit to transact offshore banking business in the Philippines. An OBU may transact in any currency other than the Philippine peso.

Thrift Banks

Thrift banks accept saving and time deposits and invest them in loans and provide a wide range of services especailly to small and medium enterprises. Thrift banks are governed by the Thrift Banks Act of 1995 (RA 7906).

The minimum capital requirement for a thrift bank is P250 million if its head office is within Metro Manila or P40 million if it is outside Metro Manila.

Thrift banks are exempted from all taxes, fees and charges (except corporate income tax and local taxes, fees and charges) for five years from their date of commencement of operations.

Thrift banks include savings and mortgage banks, savings and loan associations, and private development banks.

Savings and Mortgage Banks

Savings and mortgage banks accept savings and time deposits and invest them in loans secured by bonds, real estate mortgages and long term loans for home building.

Savings and Loan Associations

Savings and loan associations accept savings and time deposits from members and grant small personal loans and long term loans for home building.

Private Development Banks

Private development banks accept savings and time deposits. They use the funds to provide medium and long term loans to finance industry and agriculture. They may act as correspondent and collection agents and rediscount papers with any bank.

Rural Banks

Rural banks provide credit to small farmers and merchants. They may only be owned by Filipino citizens. With the permission from the BSP, some are allowed to collect deposits, open current accounts, act as collection agents or act as trustees for farmers' estates. They may also invest in the equities of companies engaged in related businesses. Rural banks are governed under the Rural Banks Act of 1992 (RA 7353).

The minimum capital requirements for rural banks are P20 million if they are located in major cities and municipalities. The capital requirements range from P2 million to P10 million if they are located in smaller cities and municipalities.

Rural banks are exempted from all taxes, fees and charges for five years from their date of commencement of operations.

Specialised Government Banks

These are government banks set up by special laws to provide credit for specific projects to promote economic development. Examples are the Development Bank of the Philippines, the Land Bank of the Philippines and the Philippine Amanah Bank.

Development Bank of the Philippines (DBP)

The Development Bank of the Philippines was set up in 1946 under the name of Rehabilitation Finance Corporation. It provided credit facilities for the rehabilitation and development of agriculture and industry and the reconstruction of war-damaged properties. Its activities have expanded and now allocates government funds to all sectors of the economy.

Land Bank of the Philippines

The Land Bank of the Philippines provides financial support for agragrian reform in the Philippines. Its charter is contained in the Code of Agrarian Reforms. Its main activities include collecting deposits and granting loans to farmers' associations for the production, marketing of crops and commodities.

Al-Amanah Islamic Investment Bank of the Philippines

The Al-Amanah Islamic Investment Bank of the Philippines (AAIIBP) was set up by a Presidential Decree in 1973 to provide banking facilities to the Muslim community in Mindanao.

Investment Houses

Investment houses underwrite the issue of securities by companies. They also provide financial consultancy, portfolio management, and assist in mergers and acquisitions.

Finance Companies

Finance companies provide credit facilities to consumers and business enterprises. They discount commercial papers and factor account receivables. They may be involved in the leasing of equipment, machines and motor vehicles.

Other Financial Institutions

Board of Investments (BOI)

The Board of Investments (BOI) is a government agency in the Department of Trade & Industry. It promotes investments in the Philippines. Its One-stop Action Center offers prospective investors what they need to know about investing in the Philippines. Its annual Investment Priorities Plan indicates the preferred areas needed for economic development. It has representative offices in London, Bonn, San Francisco and Tokyo.

Philippine Export & Foreign Loan Guarantee Corporation (Philguarantee)

Philguarantee is a government agency that provides guarantee cover to Filipino exporters on their loans obtained from domestic and foreign sources. It thus enhances the credit-worthiness of these exporters and enables them to obtain funds.

Philippine Deposit Insurance Corporation (PDIC)

The PDIC insures the deposit liabilities of banks. The maximum amount of the insured deposit of any depositor is P40,000.

FINANCIAL MARKETS

The Money Market

The Philippine money market is where short term financial instruments are transacted. It deals with government securities, commercial papers as well as interbank loans. It enables the banks and large companies to invest their surplus funds on a short term basis to maximise their returns. It helps borrowers with liquidity shortfalls to borrow short term funds.

The Stock Market

There were two stock exchanges in the Philippines: the Manila Stock Exchange and the Makati Stock Exchange. In 1994, they merged to become the Philippine Stock Exchange.

Brokers and Dealers

Stockbrokers are licensed by the Securities and Exchange Commission. They are middlemen who match sellers and buyers to earn a commission. They do not transact on their own accounts. Securities dealers are authorised to buy and sell securities for profit.

References

KPMG (1991), *Banking and Finance in ASEAN*, KPMG, Singapore.

Harrison, M. (1994), *Asia Pacific Securities Markets* (2nd ed), Longman, Hong Kong.

Ng, Jimmy and Yong, Alex (1996), "The Philippine banking system", in Tan, T. M., Low, A. M., Williams, J. J. and Calingo, L. M. (eds.), *Business Opportunities in the Philippines*, Prentice Hall, Singapore, 77–96.

Yap, J.T., Lamberte, M.B., Untalan, T.S. and Zingapan, M.S.V. (1995), "Money markets in the Philippines", in Cole, D.C., Scott, H.S. and Wellons, P.A. (eds.) *Asian Money Markets*, Oxford University Press, New York, 273–348.

Zialcita, E.P. (1994), "Capital account liberalisation: the Philippines experience", in Faruqi, Shakil (ed.) *Financial Sector Reforms, Economic Growth and Stability: Experiences in Selected Asian and Latin American Countries*, World Bank, Washington, D.C., 225–42.

SINGAPORE

The Singapore financial system comprises the Monetary Authority of Singapore (MAS), the Board of Commissioners of Currency (BCCS) and a wide range of financial institutions.

The major types of financial institution are:

— commercial bank
— merchant bank
— finance company
— leasing company
— insurance company
— international money broker
— stock broking company
— futures broking company
— unit trust
— investment adviser
— venture capital company

MONETARY AUTHORITY OF SINGAPORE

As the de facto central bank, the Monetary Authority of Singapore (MAS) promotes stable and non-inflationary growth of the economy as well as fosters a sound and progressive financial services sector. It formulates and implements monetary and exchange rate policies. It regulates financial institutions by administering laws such as: Banking Act, Finance Companies Act, Insurance Act, Securities Industry Act, Futures Trading Act, Development Loan Act and the Local Treasury Bills Act.

The MAS is a banker to the government to whom it provides current account and deposit facilities. It is the official depository of international financial institutions. As financial agent of the government, the MAS manages its external assets and public debt. It issues government securities.

The MAS is a banker to financial institutions and provides banking facilities to commercial banks and finance companies. These institutions maintain cash balances with the MAS to satisfy statutory reserve requirements.

The MAS supervises financial institutions to ensure that they maintain high standards in their operations. The supervision is done through field inspection and examination of reports, accounts and other information submitted by these institutions.

BOARD OF COMMISSIONERS OF CURRENCY OF SINGAPORE

The main functions of the BCCS are to issue and redeem currency notes and coins. The BCCS maintains a Currency Fund into which foreign currencies it recieves in exchange for issue of Singapore currency are paid. This Fund is used for backing currency-in-circulation and for redeeming currency. It also maintains a Currency Fund Income Account for receiving income and profit earned from the foreign investment of Currency Fund reserves.

COMMERCIAL BANKS

Types of Bank Licence

There are three types of bank based on the licence granted by the MAS:

Full Licence Bank

A full licence bank provides the whole range of banking services, both personal and corporate, domestic and foreign. It may apply for an Asian Currency Unit (ACU) licence to operate in the Asian dollar market. In 1999, a new category of full bank licence known as Qualifying Full Bank (QFB) was issued to selected foreign banks. Each QFB may have more branches, off-premises ATMs and shared ATMs.

Restricted Licence Bank

A restricted licence bank provides a wide range of banking services except the following:

— It is not permitted to accept time deposits of less than S$250,000 from non-bank customers.
— It is not allowed to accept savings deposits.
— It is not allowed to have more than one office in Singapore.

Offshore Licence Bank

An offshore bank engages mainly in Asian dollar and foreign exchange transactions and is subject to the following restrictions:

— It is not allowed to have more than one office in Singapore.
— It is not allowed to accept savings deposits.
— It is not allowed to accept Singapore dollar deposits from Singapore residents who are non-bank customers. It can, however, accept Singapore dollar deposits of not less than S$250,000 from non-residents or other banks and financial institutions in Singapore.
— It is permitted to engage in Singapore dollar financing of local industries provided that total loans do not exceed S$100 million at any one time.

The restrictions on deposit-taking by restricted licence and offshore banks and the limit imposed on offshore banks loans to non-bank Singapore residents do not apply to ACUs.

Asian Currency Unit

A bank or a merchant bank may get MAS approval to set up a separate accounting unit called Asian Currency Unit for dealing in non-Singapore dollar transactions.

Features of an ACU

The operations of an ACU are subject to the following terms and conditions:

— It is subject to Singapore law including the Banking Act. However, it is exempted from some provisions of the Act. For example, there is no need to maintain a minimum cash balance with the MAS, or to comply with minimum liquidity requirements.

— It must maintain a separate accounting system.
— It may accept time and demand deposits (including savings and current accounts) and to borrow in foreign currency. Savings accounts are subject to MAS approval.
— It may issue fixed rate and floating rate US$ NCDs subject to MAS approval.
— It may accept foreign currency deposits from and grant foreign currency credit facilities to both residents and non-residents.
— It may invest in foreign currency securities, deal in foreign exchange, open and advise letters of credit, discount bills and issue guarantees.
— It may manage or underwrite new issues of securities denominated in foreign currency.
— Its head office must furnish an undertaking to the MAS that it will maintain a sound liquidity position at all times and that the head office will on demand provide adequate funds for any liquidity shortfall.
— It shall only maintain accounts in the actual names of the account holders.
— It may manage funds denominated in foreign currency.
— It may provide financial advisory services.
— Its total assets and liabilities shall not exceed the limit fixed by the MAS.
— It is supervised by the MAS and shall submit financial statements as required by the MAS.

Banking Legislation, Regulation and Supervision

Banking activities are regulated by the Banking Act, notices and guidelines issued by the MAS. The Banking Act requires banks to maintain a minimum cash balance with the MAS and a minimum amount of liquid assets. Banks are supervised by the MAS and are required to submit periodic reports to the MAS. The reports include: income and expenditure statement, monthly balance sheet data, monthly schedules on loans to directors, staff and related companies.

MERCHANT BANKS

Merchant banks serve mainly institutional clients. Their range of activities include offshore banking, corporate finance, underwriting of share and bond issues, mergers and acquisition, portfolio management, investment and financial advice.

FINANCE COMPANIES

The main activities of finance companies are to collect fixed and savings deposits from the public. The funds are used to provide loans for the purchase of consumer durables, motor vehicles and properties. Some finance companies also provide account receivable financing, factoring, inventory financing and leasing.

LEASING COMPANIES

Leasing companies provide finance to enable users of industrial equipment to benefit from its possession instead of ownership. Under a leasing agreement, the lessor purchases the equipment and permits the lessee to use it in return for periodic rental payments.

In addition to the registered leasing companies, leasing business is also carried out by finance companies, banks and other financial institutions. Non-financial enterprises such as equipment manufacturers may engage in leasing operations as lessors.

INSURANCE COMPANIES

There are three types of insurance companies in Singapore: direct insurers, reinsurers and captive insurers. Direct insurers provide cover for the public. Reinsurers provide cover for insurers by spreading their risks. Captive insurers underwrite in-house insurance for large corporations and their related companies. Some insurers specialise in life insurance while others provide both general and life insurance. General insurance includes motor, fire, workmen's compensation, marine, aviation, and others. Life insurance includes whole life, endowment and term insurance.

INTERNATIONAL MONEY BROKERS

International money brokers are financial middlemen in the money market, matching the needs of buyers and sellers, borrowers and lenders of short term funds. They maintain close contacts with their clients through an international telecommunications network to provide timely information and instant service.

Their main task is to find a suitable price for their clients to make a deal. They are not obliged to disclose the identities of their clients before a deal is closed. They are expected to maintain high standards of professional ethics.

Money brokers in Singapore must comply with the rules stated in the "Guide to Conduct and Market Practices in Foreign Exchange and Currency Deposit Transactions", provided by the Foreign Exchange Market Committee.

STOCK BROKING COMPANIES

The Stock Exchange of Singapore (SES) was set up in 1973. It is a company limited by shares. Each of its member companies owns a share and is entitled to use the trading facilities at the Exchange.

The SES operates a floorless, computerised trading system. Buy and sell orders are automatically matched by a computerised Central Limit Order Book System (CLOB). Settlement is done on a scripless basis where there is no physical delivery of share certificates. Settlement is effected by book entries between scrip accounts maintained by all clients at the Central Depository (CDP).

Stockbroking companies are licensed by the MAS under the Securities Industry Act.

FINANCIAL FUTURES BROKING COMPANIES

By virtue of the Futures Trading Act, financial futures brokers are licensed by the MAS. If they are members of SIMEX, they have to comply with its rules.

In SIMEX, there are three types of corporate membership and one type of individual membership. These are: corporate clearing members, corporate non-clearing members and commercial associate members. Members who trade only for their own account do not need to have a futures trading licence.

UNIT TRUST

A unit trust company is a financial institution set up to pool the financial resources of unit-holders and invest the funds in securities by professional fund managers. It is established by a tripartite arrangement between the fund manager, the trustee and the unit-holders.

In Singapore, a unit trust is constituted by a Trust Deed which sets out the rights, responsibilities and duties of the fund manager, the trustee and the unit-holders. The Trust Deed must be approved by the Registrar of Companies before the units in a fund can be advertised for sale to the public. Before a fund can be set up, the fund manager must issue a prospectus to be approved by the Registrar.

Prices of these units are publicised in the daily newspapers by the fund managers. Investors buy from or sell to the managers at these prices.

INVESTMENT ADVISERS

Investment advisers are licensed by the MAS and are regulated by the Securities Industry Act. They give advice to clients, issue reports on matters relating to securities and manage clients' funds. Most of them are related to financial institutions.

VENTURE CAPITAL COMPANIES

A venture company provides start-up capital to young companies with growth potential. They also fund the expansion of companies with track record but without access to stock markets. A venture company monitors the growth of these investee companies and helps them to get a listing on the stock exchange. The venture company may then realise its profits by selling its shareholding in the investee companies.

FINANCIAL MARKETS IN SINGAPORE

The financial markets in Singapore include the following:

— Asian dollar market
— Asian bond market
— Money market
— Government securities market
— Foreign exchange market
— Corporate securities market

— Stock Exchange of Singapore
— Financial futures market
— Commodities futures market

ASIAN DOLLAR MARKET

The Asian Dollar Market is an international money market for foreign currencies such as US dollar, Deutschemark and Japanese yen. It is the Asian counterpart of the Eurodollar Market.

The market had its beginning when the first Asian Currency Unit (ACU) was started in 1968 by the Singapore branch of the Bank of America. With numerous tax incentives provided by the Singapore government, the growth of the market has been rapid.

Asian Currency Unit

The Asian Currency Unit (ACU) is an operation unit within a financial institution which has been granted such a licence by the MAS to deal in the Asian Dollar Market. Although the unit remains an integral part of the bank, it maintains separate accounting records for its transactions. This is to ensure that the free flow of funds to and from the Asian Dollar Market will not disrupt domestic monetary management.

The ACU is supervised by the MAS and is subject to Singapore banking legislation. However, it is exempted from some provisions of the Banking Act. For instance, it is not required to maintain a minimum cash balance with the MAS, nor does it need to comply with the statutory liquidity requirement.

The ACU is allowed to accept external non-resident deposits without reference to the exchange control authorities. It may deposit with or lend to another ACU, and non-residents. It may lend to residents subject to approval.

The ACU may engage in the opening and advising of letters of credit, the discounting of bills, and the issuing of guarantees in dealings with non-residents. It may engage in investment in foreign currency securities, and foreign exchange transaction with non-residents. No reports on the individual deposits or loans are required.

ASIAN DOLLAR BOND MARKET

Asian Dollar Bonds are international bonds denominated in US dollars, Japanese yen or any other major currency. They are listed on the Stock Exchange of Singapore. The issues are lead managed by Asian financial institutions and placed mostly in Asia.

THE MONEY MARKET

A money market is a financial market dealing in short term instruments such as treasury bills, NCDs, short-dated government securities, bills of exchange, and other commercial papers. In the market, money brokers match institutions in need of short term funds with those with surplus funds which may range from overnight fund to those with 12-month maturity. The participants are commercial banks, government securities dealers and money brokers and the MAS.

THE GOVERNMENT SECURITIES MARKET

The Singapore Government Securities Market was restructured in 1987. All settlements are scripless and are done through electronic book entries at the MAS. The market deals mainly in government bonds and treasury bills. Treasury bills are of 3, 6 and 12-month maturities whereas bonds are of 2 to 5-year maturity. In the Government Securities Market, there are 7 primary dealers. They are market-makers who bid for new issues and make two-way quotes to ensure liquidity in the market. The secondary dealers are financial institutions which deal on their own account or for their clients.

FOREIGN EXCHANGE MARKET

In Singapore, foreign exchange control was lifted in 1978. Financial institutions and individuals are free to deal in all foreign exchange transactions. Major participants in the market include forex dealers of banks, corporate treasurers of MNCs or international trading companies, speculators, money brokers, and central banks.

CORPORATE SECURITIES MARKET

In the corporate securities market, there are two major types of securities: (1) equities, and (2) bonds. A public company raises equity capital by floating its shares in the primary market. These shares are then listed and traded in the secondary market, which is the stock exchange. A company may also float bond issues in the capital market. In Singapore, the volume of corporate bond issues is negligible compared to equity issues. Companies which have raised capital through public subscription of shares have to seek a listing on the Stock Exchange of Singapore.

The Stock Market

The Stock Exchange of Singapore (SES) is a self-regulatory body governed by its own bye-laws and rules. Besides the main board, there is a second board called SESDAQ (Stock Exchange of Singapore Dealing and Automated Quotation System) where listing requirements are less stringent in order to cater for young and growing companies.

There is an over-the-counter (OTC) market called CLOB International which facilitates trading in Malaysian and international stocks. With effect from September 1998, CLOB International ceased to trade in Malaysina shares, after the Malaysian government announced that it would not recognise transactions of Malaysian shares made in CLOB International in Singapre.

Transactions in SES and SESDAQ are settled under a scripless system. Ownership is transferred electronically through the Central Depository (CDP), a SES wholly-owned company which serves as the clearing house for all transactions. Every investor has to maintain a CDP securities account for transaction purposes.

FINANCIAL FUTURES MARKET

Singapore International Monetary Exchange

The Singapore International Monetary Exchange (SIMEX) was formed in 1983 to trade in financial futures.

Mutual Offset with CME

For some of its contracts, SIMEX has a mutual offset system with Chicago Mercantile Exchange (CME). These contracts include the Deutschemark contract and the Eurodollar deposit interest rate contract. Under the mutual offset system, a trader can open a contract in one exchange and close it in the other. There is a computer link-up in the clearing system between SIMEX and CME. The offset eliminates overnight risks, reduces transaction costs and bridges the 13-hour time gap between the two cities.

Trading System

Trading in SIMEX is done by the open outcry system. It is an auction conducted in designated pits on the exchange floor.

When an order is placed through a SIMEX member's office, it is transmitted by telephone from the member's office to its booth on the exchange. The order is time-stamped and taken by a messenger to the appropriate pit for execution. After a deal is transacted, details are passed back to the member firm's booth and time-stamped. The customer is then notified of the transaction.

SINGAPORE COMMODITY EXCHANGE

Formerly known as RAS Commodity Exchange, the Singapore Commodity Exchange (SICOM) trades in futures contracts of rubber and other commodities. They include:

— 1RSS (ribbed smoked sheet grade 1)
— 3RSS (ribbed smoked sheet grade 3)
— TSR 20 (technically specified rubber grade 20)
— RCS index contract.
— Robusta coffee contract

References

Ariff, M., Kapur, B.K. and Tyabji, A. (1995), "Money markets in Singapore", in Cole, D.C., Scott, H.S. and Wellons, P.A. (eds.) *Asian Money Markets*, Oxford University Press, New York, 349–87.

Monetary Authority of Singapore, *Annual Report*, various years.

Monetary Authority of Singapore (1989) *Financial Structure of Singapore*, 3rd ed. Monetary Authority of Singapore.

Monetary Authority of Singapore (1999), "Monetary policy operating procedures in Singapore", in Bank for International Settlements, *Monetary Policy Operating Procedures in Emerging Market Economies*, BIS Policy Papers, No. 5, March 1999, Bank for International Settlements, Basle, Switzerland, 218–29.

Montes, Manuel F. and Tan, Khee Giap (1999), "Developing the financial services industry in Singapore", in Masuyama, S., Vanderbrink, D. and Chia, S.Y. (eds.) *East Asia's Financial Systems: Evolution and Crisis*, Nomura Research Institute, Tokyo and Institute of Southeast Asian Studies, Singapore, 231–59.

Ng, Kah Hwa (1996) (ed.), *Commercial Banking in Singapore*, Addison-Wesley, Singapore.

Tan, Chwee Huat (1999) *Financial Markets and Institutions in Singapore*, 10th ed. Singapore University Press, Singapore.

Tan, Chwee Huat (1997) *Singapore Financial Sourcebook*, Singapore University Press, Singapore.

THAILAND

The financial system in Thailand comprises the following:

Financial Institutions

— Bank of Thailand (Central Bank)
— commercial banks
— finance and securities companies
— credit foncier companies
— leasing companies

Other Financial Institutions

— special government banks
— Industrial Finance Corporation of Thailand
— Small Industries Finance Corporation
— agricultural co-operatives

Bank of Thailand

The Bank of Thailand (BOT) was set up in 1942 as the central bank to replace the former National Banking Bureau. It performs the functions of a typical central bank. It issues currency notes and acts as a banker to the government and other banks. It is the government's agent to deal with international monetary organisations.

It is responsible for maintaining monetary stability and promoting economic development. It supervises the financial institutions and administers exchange control and manages the public debt.

Commercial Banks

There were 16 domestic banks in 1997. During the financial crisis, the Bank of Thailand intervened in the operations of 6 of them. After consolidation and merger, by the end of 1998, there were only 10 local banks. There were about 20 branches of foreign banks. Another 19 have been issued international banking facility licences.

The main activities of commercial banks are to collect deposits and to provide credit. Deposits include demand, time and savings deposits. Credit facilities include overdraft and other short term loans.

Finance and Securities Companies

Finance companies provide short term fund and are involved in hire purchase and securities trade. However, they may not collect deposits from the public. Their source of fund is through the issue of promissory notes.

In 1997, the mismanagement of several companies created a crisis of confidence in the financial sector. In 1998, the government intervened and closed down more than 10 of these companies. The industry was overhauled under the close supervision of the Bank of Thailand.

Credit Foncier Companies

Credit foncier companies provide finance for immovable properties. They give loans secured by immovable properties or buy immovable properties with the sellers' right of redemption. They are also allowed to mobilise medium-term funds.

These institutions were affected by the 1984 recession and several had to close down. The Bank of Thailand had to intervene to restore confidence in the financial community.

Leasing Companies

The first leasing company started in 1978. There are now about 12 leasing companies, some of which are joint ventures with foreign companies. Most leasing companies provide finance for the rental of equipment and immovable properties.

Special Government Banks

The special government banks are non-profit organisations and are supervised by Ministry of Finance. They include:

— Government Savings Bank (GSB),
— Bank of Agriculture and Agricultural Co-operatives (BAAC),
— Government Housing Bank (GHB).

Government Savings Bank

The Government Savings Bank (GSB) was set up in 1947 as a non-profit organisation under the control and guarantee by the government. It mobilises small savings and fixed deposits. It encourages savings through the sale of popular savings certificates with a lottery feature. Its extensive network of branches and mobile units reach out to common people throughout the country. Most of its depositors are students, farmers, small traders, workers and civil servants. It also has a normal banking division and a life insurance business.

The GSB invests most of the funds in government securities. It also grants low interest housing loans to civil servants under a special assistance scheme from the government for that purpose.

Bank for Agriculture and Agricultural Co-operatives

The Bank for Agriculture and Agricultural Co-operatives (BAAC) was set up in 1966 to take over the Bank of Co-operatives which had existed since 1947.

The BAAC provides funds directly to farmers and through agricultural cooperatives. Its funds are derived from deposits, and loans from the Bank of Thailand. Its main shareholder is the Ministry of Finance.

Government Housing Bank

The Government Housing Bank (GHB) is wholly-owned government bank set up in 1953. It operates on a commercial basis without government subsidy and provides low-interest mortgage loans to moderate income families. It works closely with the National Housing Authority which is responsible for the government's large scale public housing program.

The GHB collects deposits from the public through current, savings and time deposit accounts. Its other sources of fund include long term loans from the Bank of Thailand, Government Savings Bank and other institutions. It issues bonds guaranteed by the Ministry of Finance.

Industrial Finance Corporation of Thailand

The Industrial Finance Corporation of Thailand (IFCT) was set up in 1959 to replace the Industrial Bank of Thailand. The Ministry of Finance is one of the shareholders. The others are local and foreign financial institutions, corporations and individuals. The IFCT provides medium and long term loans to industry. It guarantees, underwrites and manages special funds set up by the government. Its main sources of fund include long term credit from the Asian Development Bank, the World Bank, and the Bank of Thailand.

The IFCT has four affiliates:

— Mutual Fund Co. Ltd which mobilises public savings for investment in securities.
— Thai Factory Development Co Ltd which provides factories for sale or lease with long-term financing arrangement.
— Industrial Management Co Ltd which provides technical and management assistance to companies.
— Thai Orient Leasing Co Ltd which provides financing for machinery and equipment.

Small Industries Finance Corporation

The Small Industries Finance Corporation (SIFC) was formed in 1993 to take over the functions of the Small Industries Finance Office (SIFO) which was set up in 1964 as the Loan Office for Small Industries Development within the Ministry of Industry. The SIFC provides low-interest fund to cottage and handicraft industries as well as technical assistance. It receives funds from the government budget and deposits them at the government-owned Krung Thai Bank. The bank provides additional funds with three times the amount of the SIFC account which will provide loans to small industries. The bank administers the loans as well as assumes the credit risks.

Agricultural Co-operatives

There are about 1,600 agricultural co-operatives in Thailand. They are organised by farmers for mutual help and to finance members at low interest rates. Their main source of fund is from the Bank of Agriculture and Agricultural Co-operatives.

THE CAPITAL MARKET

The Stock Exchange of Thailand (SET) (formerly known as the Securities Exchange of Thailand) was set up in 1974. Trading on the SET was computerised in 1991.

Under the 1992 Securities Act, the SET was reorganised as a non-profit organisation to serve as a secondary market for transacting securities. It is self-regulated with powers to enforce accounting standard and rules against unfair trading practices. It is supervised by the Securities and Exchange Commission (SEC) which oversees the development of financial institutions dealing in securities. There are about 400 securities listed on SET. They include stocks, debentures and mutual funds.

In 1997, a futures market was introduced in baht. Three contracts are traded: currency contracts (yen-baht and deutschemark-baht), short term interest rate contracts, and stock index contract.

In the bond market, government bonds have been issued since 1933 to finance government budget deficits. The sole underwriter is the Bank of Thailand. Government enterprise bonds have been issued by the Electricity Generating Authority of Thailand (EGAT) and the National Housing Authority since 1972. These bonds range from 3 to 10 years of maturity. Debentures are issued by public companies registered with the SET. Floating rate notes have also been issued by companies since 1987.

THE MONEY MARKET

The money market in Thailand is basically an interbank market used by banks to adjust their liquidity. The Baht Interbank Offer Rate (BIBOR) is the rate used among the banks to settle their transactions. Other instruments in the money market include treasury bills, commercial bills and certificates of deposit.

In 1979, the government bond repurchase market was initiated by the Bank of Thailand. It has increased the liquidity of government bonds held by banks, finance companies, the BAAC, GHB and GSB.

BRIEF HISTORY OF BANKING

The Early Years

In 1888, the Hongkong & Shanghai Bank was the first bank to set up a branch in Thailand. During the early years, banking in Thailand was dominated by foreign banks. The first local bank was the Siam Commercial Bank which started business in 1906. After the Second World War, more Thai banks were set up to finance the economic expansion.

The 1950s and 1960s

In the 1950s, banking laws and regulations were introduced. Many of these were adopted from the experience of the American and British banks. In the 1960s, the Thai government enacted its first comprehensive banking law. The Commercial Banking Act of 1962 was introduced to support the National Economic Plan of 1961.

The 1970s

In the 1970s, as the Thai economy expanded, the Commercial Banking Act was amended in 1979 to allow banks to play a more active role in the economy. Banks were encouraged to become public companies so that more shareholders could invest in their equity capital. At the same time, more control measures were introduced to protect the interest of investors.

For example, banks were required to maintain specified percentage of cash reserve, liquid asset ratio in relation to their deposits or borrowings. Investment by banks in any non-banking business was restricted to 10% of the firm's equity and the total of such investments could not exceed 20% of the capital of the bank. A bank could not undertake business other than those types specified in the Act of 1979.

The 1980s

In the 1980s, instability in the world economy resulted in a series of financial crises in Thailand. Several finance companies and credit foncier companies were closed. In 1985, the Commercial Bank Act was further amended to help prevent the collapse of more financial institutions. For example, the Bank of Thailand was authorised to be the auditor of banks and to help solve their financial problems. The scope of commercial banking was enlarged to allow banks to act as handling agents for securities. These activities included the delivery of securities, transacting payments and dividends related to the securities. However, banks were not allowed to do broking business. In 1988, the Finance, Securities and Credit Foncier Act was similarly amended to enlarge the scope of these institutions.

The Fund for Rehabilitation and Development of Financial Institutions was set up. All financial institutions were required to become members and contribute to the fund which would be used to help institutions in financial difficulty.

The Early 1990s

As a result of the economic boom in the late 1980s, the Thai government deregulated the financial system to support the rapid growth and to prepare Thai institutions for the intensified competition from abroad after the Uraguay Round of trade negotiations. The Commercial Banking Act of 1992 came into effect in April and further extended the scope of financial institutions. For example, commercial banks were permitted to underwrite debt instruments, act as agents for mutual funds and as share registrars. Finance companies were permitted to deal in foreign exchange. The deregulation was aimed to allow market forces determine interest rate movements. It would also lift foreign exchange controls on current account transactions by allowing free flow of funds in and out of the country.

In 1992, the Bangkok International Banking Facility (BIBF) was introduced. Banks with BIBF licences could set up offshore banking units (OBUs) to facilitate the inflow of foreign capital to finance economic development. Incentives were provided for offshore banking activities. Income was taxed at 10% instead of the normal 30%. Municipal taxes and stamp duty were waived.

In 1994, BIBF units were permitted to issue floating rate certificates of deposit (FRCDs) and floating rate notes (FRNs). More measures were introduced to strengthen competition in offshore banking. Foreign banks were allowed to set up provincial international banking facilities (PIBF) units in the provinces.

SECURITIES AND EXCHANGE COMMISSION

(Source: www.sec.or.th.)

The Securities and Exchange Commission (SEC) was set up in 1992 by virtue of the Securities and Exchange Act B.E. 2535 (1992) or "the SEC Act". It is an independent regulatory authority responsible for the following:

- supervise and develop the Thai capital market,
- enhance financing through the issue and offer of securities such as equities, debt instruments or hybrid instruments,
- protect investors and prevent unfair practices,
- promote securities businesses and capital market.

Securities and Exchange Act

The main features of the SEC Act are:

Issue of Securities

The SEC Act allows companies to issue securities, such as equities, debt instruments or hybrid instruments for sale to the public.

Securities Business

Under the SEC Act, securities business includes securities brokerage, securities dealing, securities underwriting, investment advisory service, mutual fund management and private fund management. These businesses must apply for a licence from the Minister of Finance upon the recommendation of the SEC.

The Securities Exchange

The SEC Act empowers the SEC to supervise securities exchanges which include the Stock Exchange of Thailand (SET) and the Bangkok Stock Dealing Center (BSDC).

Protecting Shareholders

The SEC Act protects the interests of shareholders or holders of any convertible securities of listed companies on the SET or traded in the BSDC or public limited company.

Unfair Trading Practices

The SEC Act states that unfair trading practices (including the dissemination of misleading information) are criminal offences with severe penalties under the Act. The SET and the BSDC are responsible for monitoring unfair trading practices before submitting the cases to the SEC for further legal proceeding.

Members of SEC

The SEC comprises the following:

— Minister of Finance as the chairman,
— Governor of the Bank of Thailand,
— Permanent Secretary of the Ministry of Finance,
— Permanent Secretary of the Ministry of Commerce,
— Secretary General of the Office of the SEC,
— Four to six persons, appointed by the Cabinet upon the recommendation of the Minister of Finance. They must include experts from the following professions: legal, accounting, and finance.

Office of the Securities and Exchange Commission

The Office of the SEC comprises numerous departments such as: Secretary General's office, corporate finance, market intermediaries supervision, investment management supervision, enforcement, legal, market supervision, capital market policy and planning, capital market research and development, information technology, human resource development, internal audit, general administration and security.

Achievements of the SEC

The achievements of the SEC include the following:

Establish Infrastructure for the Capital Market

The infrastructure includes the following:

— a secondary market for debt instruments ("Bond Dealers Club"),

— OTC for trading shares which are not listed on the SET ("Bangkok Stock Dealing Center"),
— guideline to supervise a derivatives market,
— short selling and securities borrowing and lending,
— approval for securities companies to purchase or sell securities under the repurchase agreement (repo),
— the OTC derivatives market,
— credit rating agencies.

Issue of Rules and Regulations

The SEC issues rules and regulations related to the following:

— supervision of the SET and the BSDC,
— private fund and investment advisors,
— financial advisors, property valuers and accountants,
— responsibilities of securities companies,
— employee stock ownership plan,
— accounting standards concerning the issue of debentures,
— business take-overs,
— offer of debentures, short-term warrant and covered warrant,
— management of mutual fund,
— cross border listing,
— listing requirements.

Expanding the Scope of Business

The SEC has expanded the scope of business such as:

— overseas representative offices for securities companies,
— establishing rural equity funds,
— broadening the scope of business of securities companies,
— approving commercial banks to accept buy and sell orders of mutual fund units listing on the SET,
— permitting mutual fund management companies to do business other than securities business,
— permitting financial institutions to apply for license to operate securities dealing business or underwriting business for debt instruments,
— liberalising SET policy to accept new members.

Supervising Securities Businesses and Capital Market

In supervising the securities business and the capital market, the SEC has done the following:

— establishment of compliance units to oversee the operations of securities companies,
— maintenance of net capital rule,
— consolidation of securities companies,
— development of central credit file,
— permission for securities related organizations to participate in the supervision of securities businesses,
— registration of fund manager.

Strengthening International Relations

The SEC has strengthened international relations by:

— becoming a member of International Organization of Securities Commissions,
— exchanging information with foreign capital market supervisory authorities.

References

Kiriwat, Ekamol (1994), "Securities markets regulations and reforms in Thailand", in Faruqi, Shakil (ed.) *Financial Sector Reforms, Economic Growth and Stability: Experiences in Selected Asian and Latin American Countries*, World Bank, Washington, D.C., 139–44.

Vajragupta, Y. and Vichyanond, P. (1999), "Thailand's financial evolution and the 1997 crisis", in Masuyama, S., Vanderbrink, D. and Chia, S.Y. (eds.) *East Asia's Financial Systems: Evolution and Crisis*, Nomura Research Institute, Tokyo and Institute of Southeast Asian Studies, Singapore, 34–73.

VIETNAM

The financial system in Vietnam comprises the following institutions:

— State Bank of Vietnam (Central bank)
— state commercial banks
— shareholding banks
— foreign banks
— joint venture banks
— finance companies
— credit co-operatives

STATE BANK OF VIETNAM (SBV)

As the central bank, the State Bank of Vietnam issues and controls money supply. It is the banker to the banks and to the government. It also manages and controls foreign exchange.

Banker to Banks

As the banker to banks, the SBV grant licences to banks and other financial insitutions. It keeps accounts for and accepts deposits from financial institutions. It provides funds to banks by credit allocations, rediscount facilities and trading of commercial papers. It organises local and national inter-bank and intra-bank clearing. It supervises all financial institutions and imposes reserve requirement and liquidity ratios.

Banker to the Government

As banker to the government, the SBV participates in preparing the State Budget and advises the Council of Ministers on economic and monetary matters. It acts as the agent of the State Treasury in issuing and managing bills and bonds. It is the custodian of foreign exchange reserves and gold owned by the state. It represents the government in dealing with international monetary institutions.

Foreign Exchange Control

In exercising exchange control, SBV aims to maintain international balance of payments, to meet national foreign currency requirements and to stabilise the value of the dong. It participates in foreign exchange transactions in the international market.

Administration of the SBV

The SBV is administered by the Board of Management which comprises the following 10 members:

- a president who is the Governor of the Bank
- a vice president who is the First Deputy Governor
- four members with the rank of Vice Ministers representing ministries such as the Ministry of Finance, Ministry of Commerce and Tourism, Ministry of Planning and Investment
- four members who are economic and monetary specialists.

The SBV Governor is also a member of the Council of Ministers. The Board of Management has autonomous administrative powers in matters such as determining reserve ratio, rediscount rate, the underwriting of treasury bonds and the issue of currency notes.

Organisation of the SBV

The Governor reports to the Board of Management. He is assisted by Deputy Governors. In the Governor's Office is the Legal Department while there is Inspector Controller General who reports to the Board of Management.

FINANCIAL INSTITUTIONS

The financial institutions include public commercial banks, shareholding banks, foreign banks, joint venture banks, finance companies and credit co-operatives.

State Commercial Banks

There are four state-owned commercial banks. Each of these specialises in a field prescribed by the government:

— *Agricultural Bank of Vietnam (ABV)* offers credit and financial services to agriculture, forestry and fisheries. It also supports rural development projects.
— *Bank for Foreign Trade (Vietcombank)* specialises in trade financing and foreign currency transactions. It has a network with 700 banks in more than 80 countries.
— *Industrial and Commercial Bank of Vietnam (ICBV)* operates in industries, domestic trade, services, communications and transport.
— *Vietnam Investment and Development Bank (VIDBank)* deals in investment and development.

Joint Stock Banks

Joint stock banks are joint venture institutions formed among state-owned enterprise and private enterprises. They are governed by the Decree Law on Credit Institutions.

Foreign Banks

These are branches, representative offices or joint ventures of foreign banks operating under Vietnamese laws.

Joint Venture Bank

A joint venture bank is set up jointly by a Vietnamese bank and a foreign bank. It may deal in Vietnamese dong and foreign currencies stipulated in the licence.

Finance Companies

A finance company may be publicly owned or a shareholding finance company. Its main function is to lend money for the purchase and sale of goods and services.

Credit Co-operatives

These are credit institutions whose capital are subscribed by members. They provide credit to their members.

BRIEF HISTORICAL DEVELOPMENT

After the Socialist Republic of Vietnam was founded, all monetary matters were controlled by the Ministry of Finance.

After the Second Party Congress in 1951, the government centralised fiscal management in order to control production development and to balance the state budget.

In 1951, the National Bank of Vietnam was set up to issue notes and to implement monetary policy. The objective was to increase revenue by developing the economy and controlling inflation. In 1960, the National Bank was renamed the State Bank of Vietnam (SBV) and was expanded to play a wider role in the economy.

During the first 5-year Plan (1961–65), in order to support the national industrialisation policy, the SBV raised funds to finance the working capital of public enterprise, and to give loans to agricultural co-operatives for developing infrastructure.

After the liberation of the South in 1975, the SBV revamped the banking system and issued notes to be circulated throughout the country.

In 1977, the Council of Ministers promulgated Ordinance No. 163/CP to re-organise the banking system. In addition to the State Bank, there were specialised banks such as the Industrial Bank, Trade Bank, Agricultural Bank, Foreign Trade Bank and the Socialist Saving Funds. These specialised banks were controlled by the General Director of the State Bank and operated as functional departments of the State Bank.

It was only in 1988 that some of these banks became commercial banks to be supervised by the State Bank. They were legal entities responsible for their own operations. These included:

— Vietnam Bank for Foreign Trade
— Agriculture Development Bank of Vietnam
— Industrial and Commercial bank of Vietnam
— Investment and Construction Bank of Vietnam

The banking reform took place after the hyper inflation period from 1986 to 1988. Inflation rate was brought down from 487% in 1986, to 390% in 1988 and 34% in 1989.

Two-Tier Banking System

In 1990, a two-tier banking was introduced with the promulgation of these laws:

— Law on the State Bank
— Law on Banks, Credit Co-operatives and Finance Companies.

The State Bank now assumes the monetary management functions of a central bank. Other functions on money, credit and banking are assumed by the commercial banks, credit cooperatives and finance companies. Since then, the banking system in Vietnam has been reformed. Foreign banks and joint venture banks are now allowed to operate in Vietnam.

New Banking Law

In December 1997, the National Assembly adopted the Law on Credit Institutions which took effect on 1 October 1998.

Important provisions include the following areas:

— grant and withdrawal of banking licences,
— board of management: such as persons who may be admitted to the board,
— need to have a board of inspection to ensure internal control,
— loan security,
— credit risk, including mandatory liquidity and capital adequacy ratio,
— bankruptcy: the establishment of a Special Control Board to investigate the possibility of saving ailing businesses,
— the establishment of foreign banks in Vietnam.

Commercial Law of Vietnam

The Commercial Law came into effect on 1 January 1998. It governs the formation of contracts, agency bidding, branches, and representative offices, sales promotion, commercial advertising, commercial paper, remedies and commercial disputes.

References

Ang, S. H., Lee, B.L., Tan, T. K. and Tan, T. A. "Reforms in Vietnam's financial and banking system", in Tan, T. M., Low, A. M., Williams, J. J. and Gilbert, A. L. and Luu, T. (eds.) (1997) *Business Opportunities in Vietnam*, Prentice Hall, Singapore, 57–76.

Brady, Mark (1998) "Banking: A matter of principles", *Vietnam Business Journal*, April 1998, 44.

Brahm, L. J. (1995) *Vietnam Banking and Finance*, Butterworths Asia, Singapore.

Nguyen Duc Thao and Pham Dinh Thuong (1994), *Viet Nam — Banking System and Its Payment Modalities*, Statistical Publishing House, Hanoi.

HONG KONG

Hong Kong became a Special Administrative Region (SAR) of China on 1 July 1997. Its Basic Law is based on the concept of "one country, two systems" and guarantees a high degree of autonomy to Hong Kong. It also ensures that Hong Kong's capitalist system will remain for at least fifty years.

Banking System

Hong Kong is the sixth largest international banking centre. Of the top 100 largest banks, 79 have offices in Hong Kong. It has a three-tier banking system comprising licensed banks (LB), restricted licence banks (RLB) and deposit-taking companies (DTC). Under the Banking Ordinance, these institutions are known as authorised institutions (AIs). They may operate as either locally incorporated companies or branches of foreign banks.

As of 1999, there were about 170 LBs, 60 RLBs and 90 DTCs in Hong Kong. Of these 320 institutions, 308 were from over 30 countries. There were about 140 local representative offices (Source: HKMA website as updated on 6 September 1999).

Licensed Banks

Licensed banks (LBs) provide the full range of banking services. Until recently, interest rates paid to depositors on all HK dollar deposits of less than $500,000 and a maturity of less than 15 months were governed by the Interest Rate Rules of the Hong Kong Association of Banks (HKAB) of which all banks must be members. The Interest Rate Rules (IRR), established since 1964 have been liberalised in stages:

— In October 1994, HKAB removed the interest rate cap on HK dollar time deposits fixed for more than one month.
— In January 1995, the interest rate cap on all time deposits fixed for more than seven days were abolished.
— In November 1995, HKAB removed the cap on all time deposits fixed for seven days or with a call or notice period of seven days.

The Interest Rate Rules now only apply to deposits with a maturity of below seven days.

Restricted Licence Banks

Restricted licence banks (RLBs) are mainly involved in merchant banking and capital market activities. They take deposits in amounts of $500,000 and above.

Deposit-taking Companies

Most deposit-taking companies (DTCs) are owned by or related to banks. They specialise in consumer finance, trade finance or securities business. They are allowed to take deposits of $100,000 or above and with maturity of at least three months.

STRUCTURE OF THE NON-BANK FINANCIAL SYSTEM

[Source: HKMA (1997) *Prudential Supervision in Hong Kong*]

The non-bank financial system comprises the following:

— securities business
— commodities trading
— leveraged foreign exchange trading
— insurance market
— money lenders

Securities Business

Under the Securities Ordinance, any person or corporation dealing in securities or giving advice on securities must be registered as securities dealer or investment adviser with the Securities and Futures Commission (SFC).

Any person who deals or advises on behalf of a registered dealer or investment adviser must be registered as a dealing director or investment adviser director, or a dealer representative or investment adviser representative (for all other employees). Registration is not required for persons who trade in securities on their own account through registered dealers.

In 1997, there were about 690 registered dealers (of which 245 were corporations controlled by overseas interests), 1,200 dealing directors, 7,500 dealer representatives, 620 registered investment advisers, 1,040 investor adviser directors and 2,460 adviser representatives.

Commodities Trading

Under the Commodities Trading Ordinance, a person or corporation must be registered as a commodity dealer or commodity trading adviser with the SFC to trade in commodity futures contracts or give advice on commodity trading. The main businesses are securities index futures, securities index options and currency futures.

In 1997, there were about 150 commodities dealers (all were corporations of which 80 were controlled by overseas interests), 330 dealing directors, 300 dealer representatives, 130 commodity trading advisers, 170 adviser directors and 170 adviser representatives.

Leveraged Foreign Exchange Trading

Under the Leveraged Foreign Exchange Trading Ordinance (LFETO) any trader in leveraged foreign exchange must be licensed by the SFC and such a licence will only be granted to a limited company. AIs are exempt from the licensing requirement. Leveraged forex traders act either as principals or brokers for retail clients. In 1997, there were about 20 licensed traders and 1,340 trader representatives.

Insurance Market

Insurance activities include general business, reinsurance, insurance agencies and brokerage. In 1997, there were about 220 authorised insurers, of which 120 were branches of overseas insurers from 27 countries. There were 320 insurance brokers and 31,340 insurance agents.

Money Lenders

Money lenders include all persons and companies in the business of making loans but exclude AIs. Loans include any advance, discount or money paid. In 1997, there were about 1,030 licensed money lenders, most of which were incorporated in Hong Kong.

HONG KONG MONETARY AUTHORITY

(Website: www.info.gov.hk/hkma)

The HKMA was set up in 1993 as a result of merging the Office of the Exchange Fund and the Office of the Commissioner of Banking. It performs central banking functions with the following objectives:

— maintain currency stability, within the framework of the linked exchange system, through management of the Exchange Fund and monetary policy operations,
— promote stability of the banking system through regulation and supervision,
— promote efficiency and integrity of the financial system, particularly payment and settlement arrangements.

Regulatory Framework

Banking in Hong Kong is regulated by the Banking Ordinance. The framework is in line with international standards, especially those recommended by the Basle Committee on Banking Supervision. Authorised institutions must maintain adequate liquidity and capital adequacy ratios, submit returns to the HKMA on financial information, adhere to limits on loans to any one customer or to directors and employees, and to seek approval for the appointment of directors, chief executives and controllers. However, branches of overseas banks are not required to hold capital in Hong Kong and are not subject to capital ratio requirements or to capital-based limits on large exposures.

Supervision by HKMA

The HKMA supervises by on-site examination, off-site review, prudential meeting, co-operation with external auditors and sharing information with other supervisors. It uses the "CAMEL" rating system (Capital, Asset quality, Management, Earnings, and Liquidity) to identify weak institutions which require special supervisory attention.

On-site and Off-site Supervision

On-site examination ranges from an investigation of specific areas to a comprehensive review of an institution's operations. These examinations show how an institution is managed. They are used to assess asset quality and the adequacy of internal control. On-site examination is supplemented by off-site analysis of the financial condition of each institution. The scope ranges from analysis of statistical returns to an annual review of the financial position of the institution. These reviews are followed by a meeting with senior management. Discussions with both internal and external auditors form an important part of supervision. They include the annual audit, adequacy of provisions and compliance with prudential standards and the Banking Ordinance.

Loan Classification System

In 1994, the HKMA introduced a loan classification system and required all AIs to submit quarterly report on their assets according to this new system. Under the system, loans are classified as Pass, Special Mention, Sub-standard, Doubtful or Loss, with the last three categories treated as "classified assets".

The system enables the HKMA to understand the loan quality of individual institutions and of the banking industry as a whole. The system is supplemented by regular reporting on provisions set aside for each category of classified loans and for different sectors in Hong Kong. Such information also enables the HKMA to monitor the adequacy of provisioning by the institutions.

In June 1998, the HKMA issued the "Guideline on Recognition of Interest" to promote uniformity in the interest recognition policies of all AIs. As of September 1998, the ratio of classified loans to total credit exposures was 4.9% for the banking sector.

Capital Adequacy

Since 1989, Hong Kong has followed the BIS capital adequacy rule. As of September 1998, the capital adequacy ratio for locally incorporated institutions was 18.6%, well above the BIS minimum standard of 8%.

Liquidity

In 1994, the HKMA introduced a new approach to supervise the liquidity of AIs. Under this approach, the liquidity is assessed on six factors:

— liquidity ratio,
— maturity mismatch profile,
— ability to borrow in the interbank market,
— intra-group transactions,
— loan to deposit ratio,
— diversity and stability of the deposit base.

The new approach ensures that AIs can meet their obligations and that they have sufficient liquid assets during a liquidity crisis.

Financial Disclosure

The HKMA has encouraged banks to be more transparent in their financial reporting to enable shareholders, depositors and credit agencies to assess their performance. To be in line with disclosure requirements for local banks, branches of overseas incorporated institutions are required to disclose financial information on their local operations. The disclosure framework is contained in the booklet on Best Practice Guide on Financial Disclosure by Authorised Institutions.

Authorisation Criteria

The HKMA is responsible for the authorisation, suspension and revocation of all authorised institutions. Criteria are set out in schedules to the Banking Ordinance.

Institutions licensed after 1978 could operate only in one branch, a condition designed to avoid over-crowding in retail banking. This restriction was relaxed in 1994 when foreign banks were allowed to open one regional office and one back office in separate buildings. These restrictions were further relaxed in September 1999. Foreign banks may maintain offices in three separate buildings.

Overseas Representative Offices

In 1996, HKMA opened its first overseas representative office in New York. A second office started operation on 1 October 1999 in London. It performs the following functions:

— monitor European financial markets
— liaise with the Bank of England and other European regulatory authorities and Exchange Fund managers
— provide convertibility undertaking to overseas offices of licensed banks in Hong Kong with clearing accounts with HKMA

LEGISLATION ON NON-BANK FINANCIAL INSTITUTIONS

[Source: HKMA (1997), *Prudential Supervision in Hong Kong*]

Securities, Commodities and Leveraged Foreign Exchange Trading

Under the following laws, the Securities and Futures Commission (SFC) regulates securities, commodities and leveraged foreign exchange trading:

— Securities and Futures Commission Ordinance
— Securities Ordinance
— Commodities Trading Ordinance
— Leveraged Foreign Exchange Trading Ordinance
— Protection of Investors Ordinance
— Insurance Companies Ordinance
— Money Lenders Ordinance

Securities and Futures Commission Ordinance

Under the Securities and Futures Commission Ordinance, the SFC is responsible for the following:

— oversee the Stock Exchange of Hong Kong, the Hong Kong Futures Exchange and their clearing, settlement and depository systems
— license securities and futures dealers, advisers and forex traders
— vet application by persons wishing to distribute to the public

collective investment schemes, including unit trust, mutual fund, investment-linked insurance and pooled retirement fund
— supervise activities through inspection and other means
— enforce regulatory requirements

Securities Ordinance

The Securities Ordinance sets out the registration requirements in the securities business. It provides regulatory powers on the following:

— restriction on the establishment of stock markets
— keeping of trading records by dealers
— preventing improper trade practices
— keeping of accounts and audit of the books of dealers
— administering the Compensation Fund for losses arising from default of registered dealers
— inspecting and investigating

Commodities Trading Ordinance

The Commodities Ordinance regulates commodity dealers and trading advisers. It is similar to the Securities Ordinance such as the establishment of the commodity exchange, registration, accounts and audits, prevention of improper practices, and the administration of the Compensation Fund.

Leveraged Foreign Exchange Ordinance

This ordinance sets out the licensing requirements for leveraged foreign exchange dealers and provides for the investigation of trading malpractice. It is supplemented by rules governing the conduct of business, maintenance of financial resources, contract notes, accounts and audit, arbitration of disputes and appeal procedures.

Protection of Investors Ordinance

The Protection of Investors Ordinance prohibits the use of fraudulent means to induce investors to buy or sell securities. It also prohibits advertisements or documents which invite the public to invest in collective investment schemes unless they are authorised by the SFC. Examples of such schemes are unit trust, mutual fund, investment-linked insurance, pooled retirement fund, and investment-linked immigration scheme.

Insurance Companies Ordinance

The Insurance Companies Ordinance brings insurance business under the control of the Commissioner of Insurance. It protects the interest of policyholders and promotes stability in the insurance industry. It provides legal backing for the self-regulation of insurance agents and brokers.

Money Lenders Ordinance

Companies which lend money and which are not AIs, must register under the Money Lenders Ordinance. The ordinance protects against excessive interest rates and extortionate stipulations with respect to loans.

CURRENCY BOARD SYSTEM

The primary objective of the HKMA is to maintain exchange rate stability within the framework of the linked exchange rate system through management of the Exchange Fund and monetary operations.

The linked exchange rate system is a currency board system. The monetary base (which comprises banknotes and coins issued, the Aggregate Balance of the clearing accounts of licensed banks maintained with the HKMA and all the Exchange Fund Bills and Notes outstanding) is fully backed by foreign reserves. Any change in the monetary base is fully matched by foreign reserves.

The exchange rate of the Hong Kong dollar has remained remarkably stable and stayed close to the linked exchange rate of HK$7.80 to US$1 since 1983. The important underpinnings of the linked exchange rate system include the strong official reserves of Hong Kong (US$89 billion at end-1998), a sound banking system, fiscal prudence and a flexible economic structure.

Strengthening the Currency Board Arrangement
(Source: www.info.gov/hkma/eng/currency/index.htm dated 5 September 1998)

There is no foreign exchange control in Hong Kong. The government is committed to maintain the linked exchange rate system and adhere to currency board arrangements under that system.

To strengthen the currency board arrangements and make them less susceptible to manipulation by speculators to produce extreme conditions in the interbank market and interest rates, the HKMA on 5 September 1998 announced a package of seven technical measures, which include the following:

1. Providing a clear undertaking to all licensed banks in Hong Kong to convert Hong Kong dollars in their clearing accounts into US dollars at the fixed exchange rate of HK$7.75 to US$1.
   — This explicit Convertibility Undertaking demonstrates the government's commitment to the linked exchange rate system. The HKMA intends to move the rate of the Convertibility Undertaking to 7.80 when market circumstances permit.

2. Removing the bid rate of the Liquidity Adjustment Facility (LAF).
   — As licensed banks have improved their liquidity management through the interbank payment system, there was no longer a need for the LAF deposit facility to facilitate interbank market activities.

3. Replacing LAF by a Discount Window with the Base Rate (formerly known as the LAF Offer Rate) to be determined from time to time by the HKMA.
   — In determining the Base Rate, the HKMA will ensure that interest rates are responsive to capital flows while allowing excessive interest rate volatility to be dampened.

4. Removing the restriction on repeated borrowing to provide overnight Hong Kong dollar liquidity through repo transactions using Exchange Fund Bills and Notes.
   — Allowing free access to day-end liquidity through the use of Exchange Fund paper which is fully backed by foreign currency reserves will make Hong Kong's monetary system less

susceptible to manipulation and dampen excessive interest rate volatility without departing from the discipline of the Currency Board arrangement.

5. New Exchange Fund papers will be issued only when there is an inflow of funds.
   — This will ensure that all new Exchange Fund papers are fully backed by foreign currency reserves.

6. Introducing a schedule of discount rates applicable for different percentage thresholds of holdings of Exchange Fund paper by the licensed banks for the purpose of accessing the Discount Window.
   — This will ensure that the interest rate adjustment mechanism will work when the Hong Kong dollar is under pressure.

7. Retaining the restriction on repeated borrowing in respect of repo transactions involving debt securities other than Exchange Fund paper.
   — No new issue of papers other than Exchange Fund papers will be accepted at the Discount Window. This will prevent significant liquidity to be provided to licensed banks against paper not backed by foreign currency reserves.

EFAC Sub-Committee on Currency Board Operations

The Exchange Fund Advisory Committee has a Sub-committee on Currency Board Operations. Its terms of reference are:

— to ensure Currency Board arrangements operate according to the policies determined by the Financial Secretary in consultation with the Exchange Fund Advisory Committee,
— to report to the Financial Secretary through the Exchange Fund Advisory Committee on the operation of the Currency Board arrangements,
— to recommend to the Financial Secretary through the Exchange Fund Advisory Committee, measures to enhance the effectiveness of the Currency Board arrangements,
— to ensure transparency in the Currency Board arrangements by publicising information on such arrangements,
— to promote better understanding of the Currency Board arrangements.

MORTGAGE CORPORATION
(Source: www.info.gov.hk/hkma/eng/mortgage/index.htm)

The Hong Kong Mortgage Corporation (HKMC), wholly owned by the Government through the Exchange Fund, was incorporated in 1997 to develop Hong Kong's secondary mortgage market.

It is developing its business in two phases. Phase I involves the purchase of mortgage loans for its own portfolio and funding the purchases through issuing unsecured debt securities. In Phase II, the HKMC securitises the mortgages into mortgage-backed securities (MBS) and offers them for sale to investors.

HONG KONG INSTITUTE FOR MONETARY RESEARCH

The Hong Kong Institute for Monetary Research (HKIMR) was set up in August 1999. Its main objective is to conduct research in monetary policy, banking and finance areas that are of strategic importance to Hong Kong and Asia. The directors of the Institute are appointed by the Financial Secretary of Hong Kong SAR. HKIMR is affiliated to the Hong Kong Monetary Authority and is funded by grants from the Exchange Board.

HONG KONG EXCHANGES AND CLEARING LTD

In September 1999, the Hong Kong Exchanges and Clearing Ltd (HKEC) was formed as a result of merging the Stock Exchange of Hong Kong and the Hong Kong Futures Exchange.

References

Chen, Edward K.Y. and Ng, Raymond C.W. (1999), "The financial sector and economic development in Hong Kong: Implications for developing countries", in Masuyama, S., Vanderbrink, D. and Chia, S.Y. (eds.) *East Asia's Financial Systems: Evolution and Crisis*, Nomura Research Institute, Tokyo and Institute of Southeast Asian Studies, Singapore, 200–230.

Ghose, T.K. (1995), *The Banking System of Hong Kong*, 2nd ed. Butterworths, Hong Kong.

Ho, Richard Y.K., Scott, R.H. and Wong, K.A. (eds.) (1991), *Hong Kong Financial System*, Oxford University Press, Hong Kong.

Ho, Richard Y.K., Lui, Y. H. and Cheung, Daniel W.W. (1995), "Money markets in Hong Kong", in Cole, D.C., Scott, H.S. and Wellons, P.A. (eds.) *Asian Money Markets*, Oxford University Press, New York, 39–94.

Hong Kong Institute of Bankers (1998), *Hong Kong Banking System and Practice*, 4th ed. Hong Kong Institute of Bankers, Hong Kong.

Hong Kong Monetary Authority (1997), *Core Principles for Effective Banking Supervision: An Assessment of the Position in Hong Kong*, Hong Kong Monetary Authority, Hong Kong.

Hong Kong Monetary Authority (1997), *Prudential Supervision in Hong Kong*, Hong Kong Monetary Authority, Hong Kong.

Hong Kong Monetary Authority (1998), *Best Practice Guide on Financial Disclosure by Authorised Institutions 1998*, Hong Kong Monetary Authority, Hong Kong.

Hsu, Berry F.C. (1998), *Laws of Banking and Finance in the Hong Kong SAR*, Open University of Hong Kong Press and University of Hong Kong Press, Hong Kong.

Jao, Y.C. (1997), *Hong Kong As An International Financial Centre*, City University of Hong Kong Press, Hong Kong.

Roebuck, D., Srivastava, D.K. and Zafrullah, H.M. (1995), *Banking Law in Hong Kong*, Butterworths Asia, Hong Kong.

Yam, Joseph (1998), *Review of Currency Board Arrangements in Hong Kong*, Hong Kong Monetary Authority, Hong Kong.

Yau, Richard (1998), *Securities Investment Practice in Hong Kong*, Hong Kong Institute of Bankers, Hong Kong.

Websites:

Hong Kong Futures Exchange: www.hkfe.com

Hong Kong Government: www.info.gov.hk

Hong Kong Monetary Authority: www.info.gov.hk/hkma

Hong Kong Securities Futures Commission: www.hksfc.org.hk

Stock Exchange of Hong Kong: www.sehk.com.hk

PART II

FINANCIAL REFORMS IN SELECTED SOUTHEAST ASIAN COUNTRIES AND HONG KONG

Indonesia
Malaysia
Singapore
Thailand
Hong Kong

INDONESIA

During the past decade, the banking sector in Indonesia went through a series of reforms. In the early 1980s, oil prices began to weaken. The government realised that it could no longer depend on oil revenue to finance economic development. In order to mobilise savings, it deregulated the banking sector which had been dominated by state banks controlled by the Bank Indonesia (BI), the central bank.

The first reform was introduced in June 1983. The government lifted several restrictions on the state-owned banks. These included credit ceiling and interest rate control. It also phased out subsidised refinancing facilities provided by BI to the state banks.

With the reduction of direct control, BI had to introduce new ways to exercise indirect and market-oriented monetary management. In 1984, lender of last resort facility was re-introduced with the opening of two discount windows for banks wtih temporary liquidity problems. Discount instruments were introduced. Examples were the *Sertifikat Bank Indonesia* (SBIs or Bank Indonesia Certificates) with different denominations and maturities. These were traded among the banks before redemption by BI upon maturity. In 1985, new money market instruments known as *Surat Berharga Pasar Uang* (SBPUs) were introduced. These were promissory notes issued by banks and could be re-discounted with BI.

Reform Packages

In 1988, two important reform packages were introduced in October and December respectively. The October Package (Paket Oktober, or Pakto 1988) removed restrictions in the banking system and allowed the entry of private domestic banks and foreign banks. The December package (Paket Desember, or Pakdes 1988) provided incentives for the entry of new institutions including foreign joint ventures in securities trading, leasing, factoring, venture capital and consumer financing.

More reform packages were introduced in 1989 and 1990. As a result of these deregulation measures, the number of private banks increased from 88 in 1988 to 166 in 1994. The number of branches rose from 560 to 3,200. The number of foreign banks increased from 11 to 40 during the same period.

The rapid expansion resulted in keen competition for loans and deposits among the banks. Subsequent packages were introduced to improve bank supervision. For example, the February 1991 package included a time schedule for banks to meet the capital adequacy ratio (CAR) of 8% as recommended by the Bank for International Settlements (BIS). Other reform packages in 1991 restricted the growth of foreign debt and offshore liabilities of banks.

Collapse of Some Banks

The liberal lending by some banks resulted in many non-performing loans. The situation was worsened by the recession. Several banks began to have financial difficulties. These included Bank Summa which was a private bank owned by a prominent business group. The case involving the state-owned development bank Bank Pembangunan Indonesia (Bapindo) also affected public confidence in the banking system.

INDONESIAN BANK RESTRUCTURING AUTHORITY

Badan Penyehatan Perbankan Nasional (BPPN)
website: www/indoexchange.com/bppn

IBRA, the Indonesian Bank Restructuring Authority (Badan Penyehatan Perbankan Nasional — BPPN) was established by Presidential Decree No. 27/1998. It is an independent body reporting to the Ministry of Finance. Its main objective is to restore confidence in the banking sector and regulate banks by an internationally-accepted standard.

To overcome the financial crisis which happened during the second half of 1997, IBRA was set up to improve the national banking sector shortly after the issuance of the government's guarantee to depositors in January 1998. The guarantee covers all banks including banks placed under IBRA supervision or management control.

IBRA has four rehabilitation units and a coordination unit for administering the government's guarantee program. An Asset Management Unit was also formed to focus on debt recovery.

To strengthen the banking sector, IBRA has a three-prong strategy:

- to conduct a bank normalisation program: identifying, controlling and resolving the condition of banks which pose the greatest threat to the soundness of the financial system.
- to manage the operation of the government's guarantee.
- to resolve bad debts using a specially-formed Asset Management Unit.

The Bank Normalisation Program

As the entire banking system had been affected by the financial crisis, IBRA focussed on banks which were in poorest condition and which could do the most damage to the system. The criteria for selection were:

Category A Banks

- Liquidity support needed in excess of 500% of total equity and equal to or in excess of 75% of total assets.

The action taken included the immediate freezing of all operations, transfer liabilities to a healthy bank, suspension of shareholders' rights and a replacement of management. IBRA would function in place of the former shareholders with full control over the bank.

Category B Banks

- Liquidity support needed in excess of Rp. 2 trillion and in excess of 500% of total equity.

The action taken included the immediate suspension of shareholders' rights and a replacement of management. IBRA would function in place of the former shareholders. A state-owned bank would provide new management with full control over the bank.

The Government's Guarantee

Under Presidential Decree No. 26/1998 the government provided a guarantee for the liabilities of 212 commercial banks and authorised IBRA to administer the guarantee.

BANK RESTRUCTURING MEASURES

(Source: www.indoexchange.com/updates/19980824a.htm)

On 21 August 1998, the government introduced measures to revitalise the banking industry. The measures included:

(a) recapitalisation,
(b) improvement of banking regulations and laws,
(c) improvement and enforcement of prudential regulations.

Bank Recapitalisation Program

The recapitalisation program was conducted in various stages:

1. All banks were audited by Bank Indonesia (BI) and international auditors. Audits were conducted on six banks under the Indonesian Bank Restructuring Authority (IBRA) and 16 banks under BI supervision. This auditing program was completed by the end of October 1998.
2. Based on the results of the audits, Bank Indonesia (BI) decided by November 1998, which banks had to be recapitalised.
3. Banks which needed recapitalisation were asked to submit a recapitalisation plan, which included the determination of the owner to inject fresh funds or arrange local and/or foreign investors.
4. Banks whose recapitalisation plan was considered feasible, could obtain capital investment from the government with the following requirements:
   a. The owners should initially absorb the losses from loans extended to affiliated parties;
   b. Government capital participation would be available only if the owners were committed to injecting fresh money into the banks;
   c. Government participation was temporary and its title of ownership was represented by IBRA;

d. All bank obligations to BI were transferred to IBRA, which would then convert these obligations into equity or subordinated loans.

Improvement of Rules and Regulations

In 1998, the Banking Act No. 7 of 1992 was amended with the following changes:

1. Bank licensing, previously vested with the finance minister, was transferred to BI;
2. Foreign investors were given opportunities to acquire local bank shares;
3. Commercial banks would only be established by Indonesian citizens and / or Indonesian legal entities or by these parties together with foreign citizens and / or foreign legal entities;
4. Bank secrecy, which previously covered all asset and liability information, was changed to merely cover information related to depositors and their deposits;
5. It provided legal basis for IBRA's operations.

Improvement of Prudential Regulation

1. As part of the refinement of banking regulations, several improvements were made, particularly on:
   (a) extension of the leverage of earning assets quality and required loan loss provisions;
   (b) guidance on problem loan restructuring.

   These improvements were intended to achieve more realistic banking performance and to give flexibility to banks and debtors to survive the crisis.
2. Banks must fulfill the Capital Adequacy Ratio of 4%, 8% and 10% by the end of 1998, 1999 and 2000 respectively, as announced by the government in June 1998.
3. In order to coordinate the departments related to the restructuring program, the Financial Sector Action Committee was formed. Its members comprised the Coordination Minister for Economy, Finance and Industry, the governor of Bank Indonesia, the Minister of Finance, the Minister of Industry and Trade, the IBRA chairman and the chairman of the National Development Planning Board.

4. Stricter legal action would be taken against bank owners and managements who violate regulations.

RESTRUCTURING THE BANKS

Within the framework of banking restructuring, several actions were taken:

Merging Some State Banks

In 1998, Bank Ekspor Impor Indonesia (EXIM), Bank Pembangunan Indonesia (Bapindo), Bank Bumi Daya (BBD), Bank Dagang Negara (BDN) and the corporate business of Bank Rakyat Indonesia (BRI) were merged into one bank.

BRI was retained to only handle small credits and retail banking business, to sustain the development of small enterprises and cooperatives. The performing corporate credits in BRI were transferred to the merged bank.

Non performing loans of BBD, BDN and Bapindo, and non performing corporate loans of BRI were transferred to the Asset Management Unit (AMU) of IBRA.

Suspending Some Banks

In April 1998, seven banks were suspended, namely Bank Surya, Bank Subentra, Bank Kredit, Bank Pelita, Hokindo Bank, Deka Bank and Centris International Bank.

Their assets were transferred to the AMU of IBRA. They included claims to debtors, public funds, fixed assets and bank subsidiaries. These banks were liquidated soon after all the assets were transferred.

Taking Over Some Banks

Some banks were taken over by IBRA. They included Bank Danamon, Bank Modern, Bank Umum Nasional (BUN), Bank Dagang Nasional Indonesia (BDNI), Bank PDFCI, Bank Tiara and Bank Central Asia (BCA). The following actions were taken:

— Suspend the operations of BDNI, BUN, and Bank Modern.
— Hold the ownership of BCA, Bank Danamon, Bank PDFCI and Bank Tiara.

In line with the restructuring program, the government received statements from the owners of BCA, Bank Danamon, BDNI and BUN on their willingness to provide certain amounts of funds and assets. The government required that the total amount provided by owners should cover all the credits extended to their groups or affiliated parties and BI liquidity support.

To protect the interests of depositors and employees, the following actions were taken:

All savers and depositors of BDNI, BUN and Bank Modern were guaranteed by the government. Creditors of BDNI, BUN and Bank Modern were advised to contact IBRA for settlement. All employees of BDNI, BUN and Bank Modern were protected in accordance with labour regulations.

All performing debtors of BDNI, BUN and Bank Modern were contacted by IBRA to maintain their business activities. All non performing debtors were transferred to IBRA for further resolution.

THE 1999 BANKING REFORM

Source: Press Release on 13 March 1999
www.bi.go.id/intl/press/sweeping.html

Government Announced Sweeping Bank Reform

On 13 March 1999, the government announced actions to recapitalise viable private domestic banks, while closing and taking over those that did not meet minimum financial requirements.

The decision was made after months of careful evaluation and planning, conducted with support from the International Monetary Fund (IMF), World Bank, and Asian Development Bank (ADB). The actions dealt with 128 private domestic banks which fell into four main groups.

1. Category A Banks

There were 73 Category A banks. The government decided that these banks met Bank Indonesia's minimum capital adequacy standards, and could compete without any public financial assistance. Recent capital injections into these banks had been approved by the evaluation committees (Bank Indonesia, Ministry of Finance, IBRA). These banks would be reviewed regularly to ensure that they remained in good financial health and continued to observe all rules and regulations, focusing on three main criteria — their business plans, the "fit and proper" test of their owners, and the nature of any capital injections. The first full review was conducted by 21 April 1999, and subsequent ones would be held every six months.

2. Category B Banks (for recapitalisation)

There were 9 banks in Category B. They were eligible for recapitalisation by the government to bring them to the minimum capital requirements. All these banks (out of 48 banks originally in Category B) were chosen by the evaluation committees, based on a thorough assessment of their financial position, quality of management, and future prospects. This evaluation process was conducted according to international best practice, with the assistance of international consulting firms, and in consultation with the IMF, World Bank, and ADB.

Owners of these 9 banks were given until 21 April 1999 to inject at least 20% of the banks' capital requirements and enter into investment contract with the government. The government, in turn, would provide the remaining capital (up to 80%) in the form of bonds.

3. Category B Banks (for take-over by IBRA)

There were 7 banks in this category. They were taken over by the government (IBRA). These were the largest among the Category B banks, with extensive branch networks, and were taken over in the public interest to minimise disruption to the payments system. With 100% government ownership, the former owners would have no role in the operation of these banks and, where considered necessary by IBRA, senior management would be replaced.

Former owners were required to settle excess connected lending, in line with the precedents set on previous occasions when banks were taken over. These banks would be restructured to improve their financial performance, reduce their burden on the budget, and to prepare for privatisation.

[The 7 nationalised banks were: Bank Duta, Bank Nusa Nasional (BNN), Bank Risjad Salim Internasional, Bank Pos Nusantara, Jaya Bank Internasional, Bank Rama and Bank Tamara.]

4. Banks to be Closed

There were 38 banks that were closed. These banks — the 21 remaining Category B and all 17 Category C banks — were insolvent and had no prospect of regaining financial viability. Their owners were required to repay their connected lending.

All depositor accounts were transferred, with immediate effect, to near-by branches of the following 5 banks: BNI, BRI, BDN, BCA and Bank Danamon. The government reassured depositors that all deposits in private domestic banks were guaranteed by the government.

Table: List of Banks Closed and Paring Banks
(Source: www.bi.go.id/intl/press/sweeping.html)

Name of Bank Closed		Number of Branches	Name of Paring Bank
1	Bank Sewu	13	BNI
2	Bank Papan Sejahtera	11	
3	Bank Indonesia Raya	44	
4	Bank Ficorinvest	5	
5	Bank Central Dagang	45	
6	Bank Dharmala	31	
7	Bank Ciputra	14	
8	Bank Sembada Artanugroho	10	
9	Bank Aken	44	BRI
10	Bank Intan	12	
11	Bank Alfa	14	
12	Bank Dewa Rutji	5	
13	Bank Kharisma	12	
14	Bank Umum Servitia	39	
15	Bank Arya Panduarta	11	
16	Bank Sino	5	
17	Bank Danahutama	9	BDN
18	Bank Budi Internasional	4	
19	Bank Orient	6	
20	Bank Sahid Gadhah Perkasa	7	
21	Bank Dana Asia	8	
22	Bank Yakin Makmur	9	
23	Bank Asia Pacific	42	

(cont'd overleaf)

Table: *(continued)*

24	Bank Putra Surya Perkasa	32	BCA
25	Bank Pesona Kriyadana	25	
26	Bank Bepede Indonesia	1	
27	Bank Mashill Utama	33	
28	Bank Dagang Dan Industria	7	
29	Bank Indotrade	2	
30	Bank Bumiraya Utama	5	
31	Bank Baja	10	
32	Bank Tata	19	Danamon
33	Bank Lautan Berlian International	14	
34	Bank Uppindo	3	
35	Bank Metropolitan Raya	11	
36	Bank Hastin Internasional	38	
37	Bank Namura Internusa	6	
38	Bank Bahari	18	

BNI = Bank Negara Indonesia
BRI = Bank Rakyat Indonesia
BDN = Bank Dagang Negara
BCA = Bank Central Asia
Danamon = Bank Danamon

JAKARTA INITIATIVE

(Source: www.indoexchange.com/jakarta.initiative)

In 1998, the Indonesian government established the Jakarta Initiative as a voluntary framework for creditors and debtors to follow.

The basic objective is to speed up debt recovery by facilitating negotiation between creditors and debtors. However, if a debtor is not cooperating within this framework, the public prosecutor under the bankruptcy law may initiate bankruptcy proceedings against the company for reasons of public interest.

The Task Force

The government has formed a Jakarta Initiative Task Force whose mandate is to facilitate negotiations between creditors and debtors. Although the Task Force does not have authority to dictate the terms of a restructuring plan, it plays an important role in the following:

— facilitate out-of-court negotiations,
— provide "one-stop" facilities for regulatory filings needed for corporate restructuring,
— recommend legal, regulatory or administrative changes needed to facilitate corporate restructuring,
— when appropriate to serve the public interest, making referrals to the commercial court to move the restructuring negotiations to a court-supervised process under the suspension of payment clause of the bankruptcy law, or to facilitate court rulings to legalise out-of-court settlements.

Corporate Restructuring Advisory Committee

The Task Force has formed a Corporate Restructuring Advisory Committee (CRAC) comprising representatives from domestic and foreign banks, Indonesian companies and bondholders. IBRA (Indonesian Bank Restructuring Authority) and INDRA (Indonesian Debt Restructuring Agency) are represented in the Committee to coordinate other aspects of government policy.

The CRAC may propose new approaches and actions, review the effectiveness of these actions and make recommendations on how to implement the Jakarta Initiative.

The Principles

In order to facilitate negotiations, the government has announced the following principles:

a. Organisation and Representation

Negotiation may be initiated by the company or its creditors. Creditors should form a representative committee which should select a chairperson, financial advisor and legal advisor who are experienced in debt restructuring. Costs will be borne by the debtor, unless otherwise agreed.

b. Critical Role of Senior Managers

The company and the committee members appoint senior managers with authority to participate in the debt restructuring.

c. Standstill and Interim Financing

The creditors should agree to a standstill for a reasonable period. Debtors and creditors should agree on rules what they can and cannot do during that standstill period.

Creditors should subordinate their claims to any new funds brought in after the standstill commences.

Creditors should consider providing (or subordinating to others who are willing to provide) working capital necessary to finance the company's operations during the negotiation. Permissible use of such interim financing should be agreed between creditor and debtor.

d. Information

Committee members and their advisors should sign confidentiality agreements. The company should then submit up-to-date, detailed financial information to the committee and its advisors.

The information should include current, accurate and complete reporting, consistent with internationally acceptable accounting standards (unless the committee agrees otherwise).

The following is an example of that information:

— the company's group structure and all shareholdings and details of all outstanding borrowings and financial arrangements (including which group companies are obligors or guarantors, which borrowings and arrangements are secured, and the repayment schedule for each borrowing and arrangement),

— a balance sheet as of the standstill date and for each quarter ending during the three-year period leading up to the standstill date and a balance sheet forecast for the following three-to-five years,

— details of all collateral documents, guarantee agreements, and subordination agreements,

— details of all inter-company obligations (including security, guarantee and subordination agreements if applicable),

— an income statement for the 3-year period leading up to the standstill date and an income forecast for the following three-to-five years (all on a quarterly basis),

— a cash flow statement for the 3-year period leading up to the standstill date and a cash flow forecast for the following three-to-five years,

— details of the company's major contracts (including those with creditors, suppliers, customers, management, shareholders, etc.),

— the company's business plan, including its goals and strategies, its position in the marketplace, and its competition, and
— such other information as may be necessary for the committee to evaluate the rescue proposal.

e. Company Restructuring Proposal

The company should propose a restructuring plan to the committee with full disclosure of the information as agreed between the parties.

The proposal should be based on the company's business plan and financial forecasts, the preparation of which should heed creditors' contractual priorities, including collateral positions.

f. Committee's Advisory Report

The company should give full access to the committee's advisors to review the company's business and financial status. The advisors will use this information to prepare an advisory report.

The report should include a review and analysis of the company's business operations and management and future prospects. It should recommend on the viability of the company, its ability to service the debt and its working capital needs.

g. Negotiation of a Restructuring Plan

Using the company's restructuring proposal and the committee's advisory report, the debtor and the committee should enter into negotiation to achieve a corporate and debt restructuring plan. The agreed plan should preserve creditors' contractual positions, including creditors collateral rights and positions under subordination agreements. No party should be forced to make any concession, but commercial considerations should control each party's decision-making process.

h. Pre-Negotiated Bankruptcy Plans

The corporate and debt restructure plan should be presented to all creditors, except those creditors whose rights will not be affected.

i. Non-Discrimination

There shall be no discrimination between domestic and foreign creditors.

Jakarta Initiative and INDRA

INDRA is designed to facilitate foreign exchange payments made by Indonesian companies to their foreign creditors. However, it is only available to creditors and debtors who have already negotiated a debt restructuring agreement. The Jakarta Initiative provides a framework for these negotiations. Unlike INDRA, the Jakarta Initiative applies to both domestic and external creditors.

RULES TO HASTEN BUSINESS RECOVERY

In September 1998, the government introduced 10 rules to hasten business recovery. The rules were:

1. Revaluation of fixed assets (revision of an old rule)

This rule makes it easier for companies to reevaluate their fixed assets, so that the reserves created from the reevaluation can be converted into new paid-in shares. Furthermore, this rule covers matters such as:

(a) In addition to land and groups of buildings, the types of assets that can be reevaluated include categories other than buildings.
(b) The ownership period, that formerly was five years, is not limited.
(c) Reevaluation can be done yearly and companies that made a reevaluation in fiscal year 1988, based on the old rule, can now reevaluate based on the new rule.
(d) In calculating income tax, the asset reevaluation surplus is first charged against losses in the current fiscal year and the balance against tax losses in previous years (vertical and horizontal losses).
(e) In the event that reevaluated assets are transferred as a result of a merger or consolidation, the transfer is exempt from the final tax of 15%.
(f) In the event of a business consolidation, the final (10%) tax on the excess reevaluation after charging off vertical and horizontal losses, if any, can be paid as late as five years after the reevaluation was done.

2. Income tax on forgiven loans

In accordance with current regulations, a forgiven loan is considered to be income that is subject to tax at the general rate (Article 4, paragraph 1, section k of the 1983 Income Tax Law).

The current regulations do not stipulate that the benefit received by the company is calculated after first subtracting losses of the current year and the balance of tax losses of previous years (vertical and horizontal losses).

3. The use of foreign currency in financial reports

As of 21 August 1998, the Indonesian Accountants Association (IAI) has issued Accounting Standard (PSAK) Number 52 with respect to foreign currency reporting that makes it possible for a company to use foreign currency (functional currency) in its financial reports if certain criteria are met.

The criteria are as follows:

(a) *Cash Flow Indicator*. When the cash flow related to the principal activity of a company is denominated in a certain currency.
(b) *Selling Price Indicator*. When the selling price of products of the company in the short run and heavily influenced by movements in a certain exchange rate or when the company's products are primarily marketed for export.
(c) *Cost Indicator*. When the costs of a company are heavily influenced by movements of certain currencies.
(d) In the special case of companies that have already sold shares to the public (issuers and public companies), the government, by means of the Capital Market Supervisory Agency (Bapepam) has already issued the following rules that are related to corporate restructuring.

4. Mergers

Based on current rules, mergers with the use of book value and without the incidence of tax are only allowed for banks, insurance companies, pension funds, financial institutions, and companies that have made initial public offers. With respect to others, the requirements call for mergers to be allowed only if the companies are affiliated.

Because of this, to encourage companies to undertake restructuring by means of merger, there will be issued rules that allow mergers in various lines of business and that permit book value to be used by companies that are not affiliated.

5. Issuance of shares in different series of categories

Based on provisions of the Company Law, there is a possibility for companies to undergo restructuring with an influx of new investment with respect to the issuance of new shares in series or categories that are different and with lower par value to the outstanding shares.

Considering that some companies have gone public and others have not, the rule will be as follows:

(a) For ordinary companies, the value of the shares will first be calculated by an independent appraiser.
(b) For companies with shares listed on an exchange that are quoted below par, there will be a possibility to issue shares in different series or categories, with the stipulation that each class or series will have the same rights with respect to voting, dividends, and liquidation.

6. Capital increases without preemptive rights

This rule makes it possible for companies to increase capital without issuing preemptive rights to current shareholders, as long as certain conditions are met.

The criteria are as follows:

(a) A bank that has received a loan from Bank Indonesia or other governmental institutions of an amount that exceeds 200% of the paid-in capital or other circumstances that would result in a restructuring of the bank by the competent governmental authority.
(b) A non-bank corporation that has negative working capital and liabilities that are greater than 80% of the assets of the company.
(c) A corporation that has failed or that is not able to avoid failing to pay its obligation to a non-affiliated lender, when the lender agrees to receive equity or convertible debt in settlement of the loan.
(d) A corporation that increases its capital by issuing equity type securities in an amount up to 5% of paid-in capital in any three-year period.

7. Repurchase of shares by issuers and public companies

This rules makes it possible for issuers and public companies to repurchase shares in circulation, with the conditions established in Law No. 1 of 1995 on Limited Liability Companies, and other conditions such as:

(a) The repurchase is limited to 10% of paid-in capital.
(b) The repurchase must be paid out of net profit.
(c) Approval of the shareholders' meeting is required.

Rules with respect to disclosure, fairness, and liquidity must be observed. In the event that such shares are resold, the sale can only be done at the same or higher price as the purchase. Companies with shares listed on an exchange may not repurchase shares to a level that could significantly reduce liquidity or result in delisting.

8. Registration and prospectus for a rights issue

The existing rules have been revised to speed up document processing with respect to a rights issue of a public company or issuer.

The revision includes the following:

(a) A simplified process, so that what formerly took 107 days now takes only 42 days.
(b) The requirement for underwriting the unsubscribed portion has been eliminated.
(c) In the interest of protecting investors, the quality of disclosure has been improved.

9. Accounting for foreign currency transactions

This new rule was issued in response to developments in the rupiah foreign exchange market as a result of the current national economic situation, as well as the Financial Accounting Standards Statements (PSAK) Number 10 concerning transactions in foreign currency that at this time is being reviewed by IAI.

In principle, the accounting treatment of exchange differences resulting from foreign currency transactions of issuers and public companies is governed by the terms of PSAK 10, with the following additions:

(a) For companies that are not hedging, the accounting treatment of differences that arise from postings to assets and long-term monetary liabilities can be postponed and recognised as profit or loss in current or future periods, as long as the posting to assets of monetary liabilities is done systematically.

(b) If the company chooses to carry forward exchange differences then the company must disclose the cumulative exchange differences that will be carried forward and the amount that will be charged to the current period.

(c) These provisions are valid for financial reports prepared for periods ending after 1 January 1998.

10. Improvement in the exchange listing rules

Based on conditions that companies face during the economic crisis, the shares of many companies may be delisted because of difficult financial conditions. This will have a negative effect on investors who may be pressured to sell.

In order to anticipate this matter, the Jakarta Stock Exchange will immediately revise delisting criteria and refrain from using these criteria as a check list. It will instead pay attention to corporate governance and compliance with disclosure rules.

POLICY ON ASSESSING THE BANKS

(www.bi.go.id/intl/policies/bankingpolicy.htm)

Banks are assessed by a "CAMEL" qualitative approach which includes the following factors:

— Capital factors,
— Productive Asset quality,
— Management,
— Earning ability,
— Liquidity.

The assessment of the factors has a rating of 0 to 100. There are four categories to reflect the soundness of a bank: (a) sound, (b) fairly sound, (c) fairly poor, and (d) poor.

The Weighting

The weighting of the various factors is as follows:

Factor	Weighting
Capital	25%
Productive Asset Quality	30%
Management Quality	25%
Earning Ability	10%
Liquidity	10%

Capital

Banks must meet the minimum capital adequacy ratio (CAR). The formula for the provisioning of minimum capital is as follows:

Capital x 100% = minimum 8% of RWA

i. Capital consists of core capital and supplementary capital
ii. RWA is Risk Weighted Asset

The stipulations for the fulfillment of CAR:

(a) Until the end of September 1997 = 10%
(b) October 1997 – September 1999 = 10%
(c) October 1999 – September 2001 = 12%
(d) October 2001 onwards = 12%

The computation of CAR is based on the principle that every amount of investment which carries the burden of risk should be provisioned with an amount of capital at a certain percentage of that amount of investment.

Productive Asset Quality (PAQ)

It is compulsory to have Provision for Productive Asset Write-offs (PPAW). The measurement is as follows:

— Standard of measurement: A ratio of 0% or has a reserve, the credit value = 0.

— For every increase of 1%, the credit value is added by 1, up to a maximum of 100.

Productive Asset Quality (PAQ) is assessed by the recoverability of the asset. Recoverability is the repayment of the principal and interest amount of the asset. This is grouped into 4 categories, namely, performing, less performing, doubtful and non-performing.

Management

The capability of the management is measured by a questionnaire. There are 100 questions for a foreign exchange licensed bank and 85 for a non-foreign exchange licensed bank. Each question has a credit value of 0.25 for foreign exchange licensed banks, and 0.294 for non-foreign exchange licensed banks.

Earning Ability

Earning ability is measured by the following:

(a) profit before tax for the last 12 months
(b) average business volume during the same period
  — For 0% or negative the credit value = 0
  — For each increase of 0.015% from 0%, credit value shall be added by 1, up to a maximum of 100.

Liquidity

The following formula is used for liquidity based on loan deposit ratio (LDR)

(a) If the value is <110%, sound standard measurement;
(b) 90%, the credit value = 100
(c) For every increase of 1%, the credit value is reduced by 4. For an LDR of 115%, the credit value will be 0.

The liquidity factor shows whether a bank is able to meet its current liabilities.

Other Factors

There are other factors which may decrease the sound conditions of banks. These include:

— Internal dispute
— Involvement of external parties
— Window dressing
— Bank within a bank
— Suspension from clearing
— Other banking practices which may jeopardize the sound conditions of banks.

Stipulations that affect the assessment

Some stipulations affect the assessment. These include:

— The violation of the Maximum Limit of Loan Extension (MLLE), calculated on the basis of the total cumulative violations of the MLLE to an individual debtor, group debtors and parties related to the bank, against the capital of the bank.
— Small business credit is exempted from being assessed.
— Export credits are exempted from being assessed.

NEW CENTRAL BANK LAW

(Source: website: www.bi.go.id)

On 16 April 1999, a new Central Bank Law was introduced to provide greater independence for Bank Indonesia (BI). A law covering foreign exchange movement and exchange rate system was also passed. This allows BI to monitor capital flows and to implement the exchange rate system adopted by the government.

Under the new Central Bank Law, a new institutional framework was introduced. Features of the framework include:

— the specification of price stability as the overriding objective for monetary policy and a primary focus for Bank Indonesia's activities
— a clear mandate and accountability for BI to pursue and conduct monetary policy at its own discretion in attaining its price stability objective

— BI will be required to submit regular reports on the country's state of economic affairs, as well as to provide forecast of the monetary aggregates, inflation, and other economic variables.

These features reflect more transparency in monetary policies and greater accountability of the central bank.

NEW BANKING REGULATIONS

(Source: Bank Indonesia press release 14 May 1999)
(www.bi.go.id/Intl/press/press32-22.html)

In May 1999, in order to create a strong banking system which can stimulate economic recovery, Bank Indonesia issued new banking regulations to implement Law No. 10 of 1998. The regulations cover the following:

— capital
— ownership
— management
— rural banks
— foreign bank branches
— Syariah banks
— merger, consolidation and acquisition
— liquidation of banks.

Capital

The minimum paid up capital to set up various types of bank is as follows:

— new commercial bank: Rp 3 trillion
— new rural bank
  # Jabotabek area: Rp 2 billion
  # provincial capital: Rp 1 billion
  # other areas: Rp 500 million

Funding for the paid up capital has to meet these requirements:

— does not originate from a loan
— does not originate from illegal activities
— for Syariah banks, does not originate from sources forbidden by Syariah principles

Ownership

- ownership can be through direct investment or purchase of shares on the stock exchange
- foreign investors can own up to 99% of bank shares
- foreign ownership of rural banks is not allowed

Management

Bank management consists of board of commissioners and board of directors. The composition is as follows:

- commercial bank: at least three directors and two commissioners
- banks with foreign ownership can have foreigners as directors and commissioners, provided that there is at least one Indonesian director and one Indonesian commissioner
- rural banks: at least two directors and one commissioner

Other prerequisites for management are:

- not on the list of bad bankers drawn up by Bank Indonesia
- high integrity and good character
- ability to manage a bank
- directors should have at least 5 years of banking experience
- for a rural bank, at least half of the directors should have two years of funding experience
- commissioners should have knowledge or experience in banking
- no family relationship between most commissioners and directors
- director should not hold executive position in another bank, company or institution
- board members should not own, either individually or as a group, more than 25% of paid up capital in another company
- potential management has to be examined and interviewed by Bank Indonesia.

Rural Banks

Under the new regulations, rural banks may be set up in big cities. They can extend services to other cash activities including payment point, mobile cash, floating cash and cash services.

Foreign Banks

Foreign banks planning to open branches in Indonesia should:

— be among the 200 largest banks in the world
— have at least "A" rating by Moody's and Standard and Poor's
— have capital of Rp 3 trillion in rupiah and foreign currency.

Syariah Banks

A bank based on Syariah principle may be set up by:

— establishing a new bank
— converting from a conventional bank
— opening a Syariah branch by a conventional bank

A Syariah bank must have a Syariah supervisory board to ensure that the product and services are in line with the Syariah principle on the *fatwa* of the National Syariah Board.

A conventional bank with Syariah branches must have a Syariah Business Unit at its head office. This unit will supervise all activities of Syariah branches and manage funds from these branches. The head of this unit should have experience in Syariah banking and be at least one position below the board of directors.

Merger, Consolidation and Acquisition

Merger, consolidation and acquisition can take place upon:

— the initiative of a bank owner
— request from Bank Indonesia

At the time of the merger, consolidation or acquisition, the total assets of the combined bank should not exceed 20% of the total assets of all the banks in Indonesia.

The merger, consolidation or acquisition should take into account:

— the interests of banks, creditors, minority shareholders and bank employees
— the interests of the community and healthy competition in the banking business

In granting a permit for the merger, consolidation or acquisition, Bank Indonesia assesses whether the result:

— will strengthen the bank performance and the national banking system
— does not create a concentration of economic power in one person or group monopoly which is not beneficial for the community
— does not harm the bank's customers.

Liquidation

A bank's licence will be revoked if:

— a bank has difficulties which are detrimental to its survival and where measures taken are not sufficient to overcome the problems
— based on Bank Indonesia's assessment, the bank's condition can harm the banking system
— there is a request from the bank owners or shareholders.

After the banking licence has been revoked, settlements are made by a liquidation team to be formed by a shareholders' meeting within 60 days. If such a meeting cannot be held, Bank Indonesia will form the liquidation team.

The liquidation team may consist of three to seven persons who may be outside parties or a combination of management and outside parties. After the team has been formed, directors and commissioners are forbidden from taking legal action related to the assets and obligations of the bank.

For the interest of the property of the liquidating bank, the team can request a court cancellation of the bank's legal actions that have incurred losses to the bank's property, where those actions were undertaken within the year before the revocation of the bank's licence.

The bank's liabilities are to be paid in the following order:

— employee salaries, court expenses, auction expenses and tax
— bank customers (depositors and account holders)
— other parties with claims on the bank.

If liquidation is made at the request of the bank owners, Bank Indonesia will revoke the bank's licence after all obligations have been settled.

References

Binhadi (1994), "Financial deregulation and bank supervision: the case of Indonesia", in Faruqi, Shakil (ed.) *Financial Sector Reforms, Economic Growth and Stability: Experiences in Selected Asian and Latin American Countries,* World Bank, Washington, D.C., 81–102.

Chant, J. and Pangestu, M. (1994), "An assessment of financial reform in Indonesia, 1983–90", in Caprio, G., Atiyas, I. and Hanson, J.A. (eds.) *Financial Reform: Theory and Experience,* Cambridge University Press, New York, 223–75.

Cole, D.C. and Slade, B.F. (1995), "Money markets in Indonesia", in Cole, D.C., Scott, H.S. and Wellons, P.A. (eds.) *Asian Money Markets,* Oxford University Press, New York, 95–158.

Cole, D.C. and Slade, B.F. (1996), *Building a Modern Financial System: the Indonesian Experience,* Cambridge University Press, New York.

Nasution, Anwar (1999), "The financial crisis in Indonesia", in Masuyama, S., Vanderbrink, D. and Chia, S.Y. (eds.) *East Asia's Financial Systems: Evolution and Crisis,* Nomura Research Institute, Tokyo and Institute of Southeast Asian Studies, Singapore, 74–108.

MALAYSIA

Introduction

In Malaysia, financial reforms began with the setting up of the National Economic Action Council in January 1998 to advise the government on the economy. The National Economic Recovery Plan was formulated and implemented.

Pengurusan Danaharta Nasional Berhad (or Danaharta) is a wholly-owned government company set up in June 1998 as the national asset management company to deal with non-performing loans (NPLs).

Danamodal is a limited liability company wholly-owned by Bank Negara Malaysia. It serves as an interim funding institution for banks that cannot raise capital directly.

In September 1998, the government imposed exchange controls to insulate its economy from external risks. In February 1999, these controls were partially relaxed with the imposition of a levy on portfolio capital repatriation. The levy was aimed at encouraging existing portfolio investors to take a longer term view on their investments in the country and discourage destabilising short-term flows. The new policy would allow portfolio investors to repatriate their capital and profits as well as encourage new capital inflow into the country.

NATIONAL ECONOMIC ACTION COUNCIL

(Website: www.topspot.com/neac)

The National Economic Action Council (NEAC) or Majlis Tindakan Ekonomi Negara (MTEN) was set up by the Malaysia government in January 1998 as a consultant to the Cabinet to deal with economic problems.

Objectives of the NEAC

The NEAC assists in formulating and implementing strategies to:

- — ensure that the country does not enter into an economic recession as a result of the decline in the value of the ringgit and the fall in the share market,
- — restore investor confidence, particularly that of foreign investors with regard to the economy,
- — make the national economy competitive globally by implementing decisions of the NEAC with regard to enhancing international competitiveness,
- — strengthen the economic base to achieve a developed nation status through rapid and sustainable economic growth.

Structure of NEAC

The NEAC is assisted by an Executive Committee (Exco) which is supported by a working committee on aspects that are critical to restoring the economy. Its Executive Director is responsible for the implementation of decisions.

Terms of Reference of NEAC

The terms of reference are:

- — identify economic issues based on observation by members of the NEAC or on the analysis by the Working Committee of the NEAC,
- — guide the Secretariat or Working Committee in studying all issues identified,
- — propose strategies to address these issues,
- — prepare action plans for the proposals submitted,
- — discuss proposals and make decisions in accordance with the provisions of the law,
- — monitor the implementation of the decisions,
- — submit to the Cabinet all important decisions for its information and endorsement.

Members of the NEAC

The NEAC is chaired by the Prime Minister. Its members include economic ministers and representatives from various fields in the private sector and selected organisations.

Exco to the NEAC

To ensure that current economic problems can be resolved and decisions of the NEAC implemented effectively, an Exco to the NEAC has been established.

The Exco includes:

— Prime Minister
— Executive Director
— Two members to be appointed by the Prime Minister
— Two members in attendance (Minister of Finance and Bank Negara Malaysia Governor)

Decisions of the Exco are submitted to the NEAC for endorsement. However, matters which are sensitive and constitute official and commercial secrets are submitted directly to the Cabinet for endorsement.

Executive Director

The terms of reference of the Executive Director are:

— responsible to the Chairman or Deputy Chairman based on what is deemed fit by the Chairman of the NEAC,
— coordinate activities of the relevant authorities in reviving the national economy,
— formulate and implement strategies to attain the objectives of the NEAC,
— chair the Working Committee on aspects critical to reviving investor confidence and strengthening the national economy,
— prepare and submit reports to the Chairman or Deputy Chairman.

Working Committee

To implement and assist the Exco, a Working Committee has been formed to study the following issues:

1. direct foreign investment
2. banking & finance
3. capital market
4. currency

5. current account deficit
6. development of key economic sectors
7. social issues caused by the current economic crisis

The Working Committee is chaired by the Executive Director of the NEAC. The Secretariat for this Committee is in the Economic Planning Unit at the Prime Minister's Department.

NATIONAL ECONOMIC RECOVERY PLAN

For national economic recovery, Malaysia focuses on six major objectives. It has also outlined key areas for action to achieve these objectives. The six objectives of the Recovery Plan are to:

1. stabilise the ringgit
2. restore market confidence
3. maintain financial market stability
4. strengthen economic fundamentals
5. continue the equity and socio-economic agenda
6. restore adversely affected sectors

Key Areas for Action

The key areas for action to achieve the above objectives are:

Objective 1: Stabilise the Ringgit

— appropriate choice of exchange rate regime
— reduce over-dependence on the US dollar
— increase external reserves
— adopt a balanced interest rate policy

Objective 2: Restore Market Confidence

— improve transparency and regulatory environment
— establish rules for assisting industries and companies in trouble
— increase consistency of policies
— adopt liberal and market-based policies
— improve public relations
— improve the dissemination of economic information

Objective 3: Maintain FInancial Market Stability

— preserve the integrity of the banking system
— establish agencies along the lines of FDIC or RTC
— recapitalise the banking sector
— monitor credit expansion
— improve the capital market
— develop the PDS (public debt securities) market
— industrial development financial institutions
— insurance and reinsurance

Objective 4: Strengthen Economic Fundamentals

— increase the quality of investments
— improve the balance of payments
— maintain a balanced public sector financial position
— maintain an appropriate monetary policy
— maintain price stability
— increase labour competitiveness

Objective 5: Continue the Equity and Socio-Economic Agenda

— ameliorate the hardship from poverty
— address the issues on Bumiputera equity ownership
— expand employment opportunities
— expand tertiary education
— address the problem of graduate unemployment
— control the influx of foreign workers
— gear up state corporations to face the crisis
— revamp cooperatives and cooperative banks
— protect the environment for sustainable development

Objective 6: Revitalise Affected Sectors

— primary commodities and resource-based industries
— mining and petroleum
— manufacturing
— information technology and the multimedia super corridor
— motor industry
— construction

— property
— infrastructure
— transportation
— freight forwarding
— tourism

DANAHARTA

(Website: www.danaharta.com.my)

Pengurusan Danaharta Nasional Berhad is a wholly-owned government company set up in June 1998 by the Malaysian government as the national asset management company to deal with NPLs.

Organisation Structure

Danaharta specialises in NPLs. Its main objectives are:

— to buy NPLs from banks
— to manage these assets
— to maximise their values
— to dispose of these assets.

Danaharta removes NPLs from the banking system so that banks can concentrate on normal banking business. When buying NPLs from the banks, Danaharta pays with government bonds and cash at a mutually agreed price.

As Danaharta has a special mission, new laws have been introduced to enable it to buy, manage and sell NPLs. Examples of these laws are:

— Pengurusan Danaharta Nasional Berhad Act 1998 (Danaharta Act), which came into effect on 1 September 1998;
— National Land Code (Amendment) Act 1998 which came into effect on 11 September 1998.

Status of Borrowers

After Danaharta has bought an NPL from a bank, it works closely with the borrower. Their activities may include the following steps to rejuvenate the business.

— restructure the loan and reschedule repayments
— inject additional fund into the business
— convert some of the loans into equity
— take over the management of the borrower (through the appointment of Special Administrators)

Interest Rate

In deciding on the interest rate for the credit facilities, Danaharta refers to the base lending rate of Malayan Banking Berhad.

Benefits to the Banking System

The banking system will be revitalised. By getting rid of their NPLs, the banks can concentrate on normal banking activities to help the economy to recover. Without the help from a asset management company such as Danaharta, some weaker banks may have gone bankrupt. The loss of confidence in the banking system will have serious effects on the economy.

Benefit to the Borrowers

Companies whose NPLs have been bought by Danaharta receive advice to strengthen their business.

Payment

Danaharta will issue government guaranteed bonds and cash to the banks to pay for NPLs. These bonds are tradeable and are issued with an initial tenor of five years and a roll-over option for another five years. These are zero coupon bonds with yields approximating Malaysian Government securities with similar tenor.

The Danaharta Act

The Pengurusan Danaharta Nasional Berhad Act 1998 provides the legal framework for Danaharta. The Act authorises Danaharta to buy, manage, finance and dispose of assets and liabilities.

Under the Act, Danaharta has a board of nine directors appointed by the Minister of Finance. Most of them are from the private sector.

As the shareholder, the government has two representatives on the board. Danaharta's management is led by a managing director who is a non-voting member of the board.

The Act has provisions to protect Danaharta's independence and integrity. These include the requirement to disclose conflicts of interests and obligations of secrecy. Danaharta's powers and how it will operate are regulated by its Memorandum and Articles of Association.

Danaharta's Special Powers

The Act confers on Danaharta two special powers:

— to buy assets through statutory vesting, i.e. with certainty of title,
— to appoint special administrators to manage distressed companies.

Statutory Vesting

Before Danaharta buys an asset, it must agree on the terms and conditions of the acquisition (including price) with the selling bank. The Danaharta Act allows Danaharta and the selling bank to effect the purchase by statutory vesting. After buying the asset, Danaharta will issue a vesting certificate which will be used for the purpose of registration.

Upon presentation of the vesting certificate at the Land Registry or Land Office, the Registrar of Land or Land Administrator will record Danaharta's interest as the new chargee in place of the selling bank. The effect of statutory vesting is to allow Danaharta to take the same interest and enjoy the same priority as the selling bank.

For example, if the selling bank has a first charge over land as security for the NPL, Danaharta will also have a first charge over the land.

Special Administrator

If the borrower is a company, Danaharta may appoint a Special Administrator if the borrower is unable to pay its debts or fulfil its obligations.

Before a Special Administrator can be appointed, Danaharta must seek the approval of an Oversight Committee formed for this purpose.

The Special Administrator will take over the management of the corporate borrower. In order to preserve those assets until the Special Administrator is able to finish its job, a 12-month moratorium automatically takes effect. During that time, no one may take action against the corporate borrower.

The Special Administrator will prepare a proposal which is given to an Independent Advisor approved by the Oversight Committee. The Independent Advisor's role is to review the proposal taking into consideration the interests of all creditors and shareholders. The proposal with the Independent Advisor's report are then given to Danaharta for approval.

If the proposal is approved, the Special Administrator will call for a meeting of secured creditors to vote on the proposal. Once approved by these creditors, relevant regulatory approvals (such as from the Securities Commission) will be obtained.

Oversight Committee

The Oversight Committee comprises three representatives, one each from the Ministry of Finance, the Securities Commission and Bank Negara Malaysia. It performs the following tasks:

— approve the appointment of Special Administrators and Independent Advisors,
— approve the extension of moratorium periods,
— approve the termination of the services of Special Administrators.

Board of Directors

The activities of Danaharta are supervised by a Board of Directors through its executive and non-executive committees.

DANAHARTA BOND ISSUE PROGRAM

Under its Bond Issue Program, Danaharta will issue RM15 billion government guaranteed zero coupon redeemable bonds. They will be in four series with maturing on 31 December 2003, 31 March 2004, 30 June 2004 and 30 September 2004.

These bonds will be issued progressively, the timing and size of which will be in line with Danaharta's acquisition process which is expected to be completed by the end of 1999.

Pricing

The bonds are priced at RM 71.301 for every RM100 in face value. The yield on the bonds is 6.654%, being the latest indicative yield to maturity of Malaysian Government Securities (MGS) of similar tenor as published by Bank Negara Malaysia (BNM) on 15 January 1999. The yield to maturity of the subsequent issues will be adjusted according to the published yield at the time of issue.

Roll-over Option

Danaharta has the option of refinancing any of the bonds upon maturity for an additional period of one year, three years or five years. These refinanced bonds will bear a coupon equivalent to the then-latest indicative yield of MGS of similar tenor as published by BNM. The coupon would be payable semi-annually in arrears.

Characteristics of the Bonds

The bonds are tradeable in the secondary market. They are designated as Class-1 assets under the new liquidity framework and are eligible for rediscounting with BNM as lender of last resort. Since these bonds are guaranteed by the government, they carry zero risk weight for capital adequacy purposes.

Example of Such Issue

A total of RM2.6014 billion bonds were issued under the first series of the Program which will mature on 31 December 2003. The bonds are issued to banks as consideration for non-performing loans (NPLs) purchased by Danaharta.

On 29 January 1999, Danaharta issued RM 1.1054 billion nominal value bonds under its Bond Issue Program. These bonds will mature on 31 March 2004. They form the first tranche issued under the second series of its Bond Issue Program.

Appointing Special Administrators

For example, on 12 February 1999, Danaharta appointed Special Administrators to manage the assets of six stockbroking companies.

They were: Alor Star Securities, WK Securities, Labuan Securities, Taiping Securities, MBF Northern Securities and Halim Securities.

In order to preserve the assets of these stockbroking companies until the administrators are able to complete their task, a 12-month moratorium took effect from the date of the appointment. During the 12-month period, no creditor may take action against the stockbroking companies.

Advantage of Selling NPLs to Danaharta

By selling their NPLs to Danaharta, banks are able to fetch a fair price and get rid of the NPLs which represent a drain on their resources. This reduces their NPL ratio which is often used as an indicator of the quality of their assets.

They are also able to amortise any resulting shortfall, which is the difference between the fair value of the loan and the principal outstanding, over a period of five years.

If the banks decide not to sell to Danaharta. They are required by Bank Negara Malaysia to write down the value of the NPLs immediately and either restructure these loans at their own expense or refer them to the Corporate Debt Restructuring Committee (CDRC).

Size of Loan

To be cost effective, Danaharta does not acquire loans that are less than RM5 million.

Danaharta versus CDRC

Danaharta's main objective is to remove the NPL problems faced by the banks. CDRC, on the other hand, has the objective of restructuring problem loans of borrowers. Through restructuring of these loans, it is hoped that the loans can be avoided from turning into NPLs, or if they are already non-performing, can be restructured so that they become performing again. Both agencies play an important role in tackling the growing NPL problems.

In general, in the event of NPL problems, financial institutions turn to Danaharta whereas borrowers turn to CDRC.

DANAMODAL NASIONAL BERHAD
(Website: www.bnm.gov.my/danamodal)

Danamodal is a limited liability company wholly-owned by Bank Negara Malaysia (BNM). It has an initial capital of RM1 billion. BNM will invite participation from other institutional investors, both domestic and foreign.

Danamodal serves as an interim funding institution for banks that cannot raise capital directly. It encourages mergers to create well capitalised banks which can compete in the global market.

Objectives of Danamodal

The objectives of the Danamodal are to:

(a) raise funds to recapitalise and strengthen the banking industry,
(b) restore investor confidence and encourage the mobilisation of domestic capital as well as inflows of foreign capital.

The creation of Danamodal is part of the overall financial sector restructuring which aims to:

(a) promote the development of a safe, sound and efficient domestic banking system,
(b) minimize the use of public funds over the long-term,
(c) initiate market oriented reform, and
(d) ensure burden sharing between shareholders and management.

The setting up of Danamodal ensures that the recapitalisation process is commercially-driven and that investment decisions are made according to market-based principles.

Life Span of Danamodal

Danamodal has a life span of about five years. It is expected to complete its task of recapitalisation within the first two years. By then, it will own a portfolio of bank investments which it will then sell over the next three years.

Danamodal will dispose of its stakes by:

— initial public offers,

— strategic sales of its holdings,
— selling directly in the market.

Danamodal will provide capital to banks which have difficulty meeting minimum capital requirements but only after their capital needs, business strategies and rehabilitation plans have been carefully evaluated.

Management of Danamodal

Danamodal is governed by a board of directors which ensures that its activities are independent, consistent with government policies, and properly coordinated with Bank Negara. The daily operations will be headed by a CEO with full-time staff. Danamodal's employees will not be involved in the daily operations of banks where it has acquired shareholding. However, they may sit on the boards of banks where Danamodal has substantial stakes.

Funding of Danamodal

The total funding is about RM16 billion. This allows for a higher peak NPL level than is currently expected and a minimum risk weighted capital adequacy requirement of 9%.

In assisting banks in their restructuring, Danamodal encourages them to raise equity independently. This may include the granting of a guarantee by Danamodal to improve pricing and broaden distribution. Danamodal itself may support such bank capital raisings. Danamodal works closely with Bank Negara to encourage banks to merge.

Danamodal and Danaharta

In recapitalising the banks, the NPLs of these banks will be separated and sold to Danaharta. The sale proceeds will inject some liquidity into the banks and improve their asset quality.

After NPL sales to Danaharta, Danamodal will encourage banks to raise more capital on their own (equity, hybrid or subordinated debt). Danamodal will then recapitalise the banks and facilitate mergers.

With Bank Negara, Danamodal will assess the long-term viability of these banks. They are required to submit rehabilitation plans to

Danamodal and BNM. These plans will be evaluated by Danamodal to determine the bank's fundamental strength before it injects capital.

FOREIGN EXCHANGE CONTROL

In September 1998, Malaysia implemented a series of exchange controls to insulate its economy from external risks. From 1 September 1998, the Malaysian ringgit ceased to be legal tender outside Malaysia and would not be convertible. Within Malaysia, the ringgit would remain convertible for most banking transactions. All offshore ringgit funds had to be repatriated to Malaysia within one month, or else would become worthless.

According to Bank Negara, the objective was to have a stable exchange rate and a domestic economy insulated from adverse global developments. Once these objectives were achieved, the measures would be removed.

Under the new regime, Malaysians and foreigners could still remit funds abroad. All funds for purchases or remittances must be converted first at local commercial banks, which were authorised depository institutions. These transactions would be more tightly monitored: all sums remitted above RM10,000 or equivalent currency had to be recorded by banks. The previous limit was RM100,000 (Toh and Tharmaratnam, 1998).

Bank Negara's statement

Source: Bank Negara (as reported in *Business Times*, 2 September 1998)

These changes, however, would not affect the business operations of traders and investors or the normal conduct of economic activity and would continue to guarantee:

- general convertibility of current account transactions,
- free flows of direct foreign investment and repatriation of interest, profits and dividends and capital,
- result in minimal inconvenience to the general public.

The changes were directed at containing speculation on the ringgit and at minimising the impact of short-term capital inflows on the domestic economy.

The main changes in the exchange control rules were:

External or non-resident accounts

Approval was required for transfer of funds between external accounts. Transfers to residents' accounts were permitted only until 30 September 1998. Thereafter, approval was required. Withdrawal of ringgit from external accounts required approval except for the purchase of ringgit assets.

Authorised depository institutions

All purchases and sales of ringgit financial assets could only be transacted through authorised depository institutions.

Trade settlement

All settlement of exports and imports must be made in foreign currency.

Currency held by travellers

From 1 October 1998, travellers were allowed to import or export ringgit currency of not more than RM1,000 per person. There were no limits on the import of foreign currencies by resident and non-resident travellers. The export of foreign currencies by resident travellers was permitted, up to a maximum of RM10,000 equivalent. The export of foreign currencies by non-resident travellers was permitted, up to the amount of foreign exchange brought into Malaysia.

STEPS TO REGAIN MONETARY INDEPENDENCE

Dealings in gold and foreign currency

— No change except for external account holders

External Accounts

— Transfer of any amounts between external accounts would require prior approval
— Transfers to resident accounts in Malaysia banks are permitted until 30 September 1998, thereafter require approval

Sources of funding the external account are limited to:

(1) proceeds from sale of ringgi instruments, securities registered in Malaysia or other assets in Malaysia
(2) salaries, wages, commissions, interest, dividend
(3) sale of foreign currency — use of funds in the account is limited to buying ringgit assets in Malaysia.

General payments

Residents were freely allowed to make payments to non-residents for any purpose up to RM10,000 in ringgit or its equivalent in foreign currency (reduction in amount) except for payment for imports of goods and services.

Residents were freely allowed to make payments to non-residents in foreign currency only for amounts exceeding RM10,000 equivalent. However, investments abroad in any form and payments under a guarantee for non-trade purpose required approval.

Export of goods

Prescribed manner of payment for exports is in foreign currency only, other than currencies of Israel, Serbia and Montenegro.

Credit facilities to non-residents

Domestic credit facilities to non-resident correspondent banks and non-resident stockbroking companies were no longer allowed.

Investments abroad

Residents with no domestic borrowing were allowed to make payment to non-residents for purposes of investing abroad, up to an amount of RM10,000 or its equivalent in foreign currency per transaction.

All residents required approval to make payments to non-residents for purposes of investing abroad, for an amount excedding RM10,000 equivalant in foreign currency.

Foreign currency credit facilities and ringgit credit facilities from non-residents.

— Residents cannot obtain ringgit credit facilities from non-resident individuals.

Securities

— Ringgit securities must be deposited with authorised depositories.
— Ringgit securities held by non-residents must be transacted through an authorised depository for good delivery.
— All payments by non-residents or any security registered in Malaysia must be made in foreign currency or in ringgit from an external account.
— All proceeds in ringgit received by a non-resident from the sale of any resident security must be retained in an external account (subject to the conditions on such accounts). But, if the ringgit security is held for more than one year, proceeds from its sale can be:
  (1) immediately converted to foreign currency; or
  (2) credited to the external account.
— All payments to residents for any security registered outside Malaysia from non-residents must be made in foreign currency.

Import and export of currency notes, bills of exchange, assurance policies, etc.

— A resident traveller can import ringgit notes up to RM1,000, and any amount of foreign currencies.
— A resident traveller can export ringgit notes up to RM1,000 and foreign currencies up to the equivalent of RM10,000
— A non-resident traveller can import ringgit notes up to RM1,000, and any amount of foreign currencies.
— A non-resident traveller can export ringgit notes up to RM1,000 and foreign currencies up to the amount of foreign currencies brought into Malaysia.
— Approval is required for the import and export of ringgit notes and the export of foreign currency notes, other than as permitted above.
— Transitional provision: Up to 30 September 1998, travellers (resident and non-resident) can import any amount of ringgit on person or in baggage.

Labuan International Offshore Financial Centre

At the Labuan International Offshore Financial Centre, Offshore banks can no longer trade in ringgit instruments.

LEVY ON REPATRIATION OF PORTFOLIO CAPITAL

On 4 February 1999, Malaysia announced the imposition of a levy on portfolio capital repatriation to replace the 12-month holding period of foreign portfolio capital in Malaysia's equity market with effect from 15 February 1999. The levy was aimed at encouraging existing portfolio investors to take a longer term view on their investments in the country and discourage destabilising short-term flows.

The new policy would allow portfolio investors to repatriate their capital and profits as well as encourage new capital inflow into the country.

First Minister for Finance Daim told a press conference that there were two categories of funds — funds in Malaysia prior to 15 February 1999 and those that came in on and after the date.

He said the requirement to have capital control in Malaysia for at least 12 months from 1 September 1998 had contributed significantly to economic stability in the country.

The original capital brought into Malaysia before 15 February 1999 would be allowed to be repatriated, subject to a graduated levy based on the duration of investment. (See Table)

Dividends, interests and rentals were not subjected to any levy.

For purposes of control and monitoring, funds brought into Malaysia on or after 15 February 1999 would be placed in special external accounts to distinguish these funds from the existing external accounts (Toh *et al.*, 1999).

The Exit Tax

Principal as at	Repatriated	Levy (%)
Funds brought in before 15.2.99		
Principal		
1.9.98	31.3.99 (up to 7 months)	30
1.9.98	31.5.99 (7–9 months)	20

The Exit Tax: *(continued)*

Principal as at	Repatriated	Levy (%)
1.9.98	31.8.99 (9–12 months)	10
1.9.98	1.9.99 (>12 months)	0
Profits		
Repatriated before 12 months from the date they are made		no levy
Repatriated thereafter		10%
Funds brought in on or after 15.2.99		
Principal: No levy		
Profits		
Repatriated before 12 months from the date they are made		30%
Repatriated thereafter		10%

Source: *Business Times,* 5 February 1999.

PROPERTY EXEMPTED FROM EXIT TAX

On 18 February 1999, the Malaysian government exempted investments in property from its new exit tax regime as a further easing of the exchange control rules. It removed a double tax on gains from property sales by foreigners which arose after recent changes to the country's capital control measures (Diana Oon Abdullah, 1999).

For funds which came in before 15 February 1999, no levy was imposed upon the repatriation of the principal amount invested in properties, the statement added. For funds which came in from 15 February 1999, no levy was imposed on repatriated profits from investments in properties.

References

Butler, C., Dhillon, H. S. and Thiagarajah, L. (1991), *Guide to the Malaysian Capital Market,* Pelandok Publications and Institut Bank-Bank Malaysia, Kuala Lumpur.

Diana Oon Abdullah (1999), "Malaysia excludes property from exit tax regime", *Business Times*, 19 February 1999.

Pang, Johnson (1995), *Banking and Finance — Malaysia*, Federal Publications, Shah Alam, Malaysia.

Jaafar Ahmad (1993), "Adapting financial structures for accelerated development", in Tham Siew Yean and Muhammad Anuar Adnan (eds) *Financial Institution and Investment Opportunities in the Asia Pacific in the 1990s*, Penerbit Universiti Kebangsaan Malaysia, Bangi, pp.102–116.

Toh, E. and Meera Tharmaratnam (1998), "Offshore trading of ringgit banned, funds to be repatriated", *Business Times*, 2 September 1998.

Toh, E., Wong, R. and Diana Oon Abdullah, "KL's exit tax plan gets mixed reception", *Business Times*, 5 February 1999.

Bank Negara Malaysia website: www.bnm.gov.my (1999).

SINGAPORE

Introduction

In February 1998, the Monetary Authority of Singapore (MAS) announced several reforms to increase the competitiveness of Singapore as a financial centre. The two-fold strategic approach included the following:

— creating a more conducive regulatory environment,
— promoting the financial services industry.

New Financial Sector Promotion Department

Within the MAS itself, a new Financial Sector Promotion Department was formed to promote new activities, develop IT infrastructure and manpower and to introduce incentives for the finance sector.

THE REFORM PROCESS

The reforms were introduced as a result of the recommendations made by numerous special review committees which included many senior bankers.

The Financial Sector Review Group

The Financial Sector Review Group (FSRG) was formed in 1997 to look into the various aspects of the financial sector. It was chaired by Deputy Prime Minister Lee Hsien Loong.

THE FIVE COMMITTEES

In its discussion, the FSRG acknowledged the findings of an earlier group which was the *Finance and Banking Sub-Committee*, chaired by Mr Peter Seah, under Minister for Trade and Industry Mr Lee Yock Suan's Committee on Singapore's Competitiveness.

The FSRG set up three more committees to study specific areas in detail:

— Committee on Banking Disclosure chaired by Mrs Elizabeth Sam
— Corporate Finance Committee chaired by Mr Lim Yong Wah
— Stock Exchange of Singapore (SES) Review Committee chaired by Mr Lim Hua Min

The *Committee on Banking Disclosure* proposed ways to raise disclosure and accounting standards of banks to international best practice.

The *Corporate Finance Committee* reviewed the philosophy underlying the operation and supervision of capital markets. It looked at the roles of the MAS, SES and the Registry of Companies. It examined the rules and guidelines for corporate fund-raising and evaluate the efficiency of the fund-raising process and standards of corporate disclosure.

The *SES Review Committee* studied the traditionally protected business of stockbroking. It suggested ways to deregulate the industry, free brokerage commissions and open up access to the exchange. The Committee proposed that the minimum commission rates be progressively reduced, and that the industry be completely opened up within 5 years.

To follow up on broader issues, the government set up the *Committee on the Governance of the Exchanges* under the chairmanship of Mr Tharman Shanmugaratnam.

Committee on the Governance of the Exchanges

Although MAS provided the Chairman, the Committee tapped on expertise in the private sector. The Committee recommended how Singapore could reap the "first-mover" advantage to become a leading combined cash-derivatives exchange in Asia. It suggested the merger of SES and SIMEX, and to fully free up both commissions and access by January 2002.

Individually the proposals of each of the five committees were incremental, but collectively they have recommended a major reform for the financial sector in Singapore.

ADVISORY COUNCILS

In formalising private sector consultation, the MAS has set up two advisory councils.

Financial Sector Advisory Council

The Financial Sector Advisory Council (FSAC) will gather feedback and ideas from market participants in Singapore.

The objectives of the FSAC are to:

— provide MAS with feedback on regulatory issues,
— help MAS identify emerging market trends and new development opportunities for Singapore,
— gather and facilitate exchanges of views with market participants in Singapore and internationally, and promote the adoption of international best business practices.

International Advisory Panel

The International Advisory Panel (IAP) will give a global perspective from leading financial executives worldwide. It comprises about ten distinguished market participants, consultants and regulators.

Its objectives are to:

— advise MAS on trends in the global financial industry, emerging business lines and new growth opportunities,
— help MAS keep abreast of market developments and policy initiatives in major international centres,
— provide MAS with insights into international best practices in central banking and financial supervision.

The IAP is chaired by Mr J. Y. Pillay (MAS Board Member). The panel comprises top American, European and Japanese bankers.

IAP First Meeting

The panel had its first meeting in January 1999. It urged Singapore to push ahead with financial reforms. It emphasised that the most critical role that the MAS could play was to provide a conducive environment that would attract international intermediaries. It was crucial to have a banking sector that was open to full foreign participation. The challenge was to do so while nurturing strong local banks which would contribute to the depth and breadth of the financial centre.

The panel also supported the move to demutualise and merge the cash and derivatives exchanges (Stock Exchange of Singapore and Singapore International Monetary Exchange). It suggested that the new integrated exchange should explore strategic alliances with other regional exchanges (Source: MAS website www.mas.gov.sg/newspeeches).

Implementing the Recommendations

In implementing the numerous recommendations, the government has commissioned a financial sector strategy study by McKinsey and Company, and a complementary financial sector IT strategy study by Arthur D. Little.

SUMMARY OF THE RECOMMENDATIONS IMPLEMENTED

Source: MAS website
www.mas.gov.sg/singfinsec/singfinsec_finsecreview-c.htm

Banking

Raised Bank Disclosure Standards

— discontinue practice of maintaining hidden reserves
— provide details on loan loss provisions
— disclose off-balance sheet items in notes to acccounts
— disclose significant exposures

Clarified and liberalised guidelines on S$ loans for regionalisation projects

Lowered Minimum Cash Balance (MCB) from 6% to 3%

Raised limits on offhore banks' loans to resident from $200 to $300 million

Launched Real Time Gross Settlement System (RTGS) for Interbank Payments facilitated regulatory co-operation

— made it easier for foreign regulators to inspect Singapore branches of their banks
— allowed foreign banks to disclose information on credit facilities to their parent supervisory authorities

Insurance

Liberalised investment limits on Singapore general insurance and non-investment-linked life insurance fund

Put in place easier operating environment for captive insurers

— reduced paid up capital requirement from $1 million to $400,000
— captive insurers allowed to write prescribed non in-house risks

Enhance tax incentives

— extended 10-year tax exemption for Singapre-registered insurers in respect of income from offshore marine hull and liability business.

Fund Management

Committed to place out $25 billion of GIC funds and $10 billion of MAS funds over the next 3 years for external fund managers to manage.

Revamped CPF Investment Scheme

— Set new selection criteria for CPF-approved fund managers
— Set new investment guidelines and introduced disclosure requirements for CPF-approved unit trusts.

Liberalised guidelines for non-CPF unit trusts

— Introduced new investment, borrowing and advertising guidelines
— Removed minimum investment requirements for unit trust regular savings plans

— Removed entry requirements for foreign companies setting up as investment advisers in Singapore
— Reduced minimum global funds managed by parent company from $5 billion to $1 billion

Enhanced Tax Incentives

— Abolished withholding tax on unit trust distributors
— Extended tax exemption to unit holders' distributions made out of capital gains
— Exempted from tax fund managers who manage more than $5 billion in Singapore

Equity and Futures Markets

Eased conditions for foreign companies to list in S$ on the SES

Removed limit on investments in foreign currency-denominated shares by CPF-approved unit trusts

Launched new equity derivative contracts

— SIMEX launched MSCI Singapore stock index futures in September 1998 and Dow Jones Thailand stock index futures in November 1998.
— SIMEX relaunched MSCI Hong Kong stock index futures in November 1998.

Widened scope of activities for stockbrokers

— Reviewed SIMEX membership structure to allow SES members to apply for SIMEX membership so as to market and trade SIMEX's equity index contracts.
— Facilitated applications by stockbroking firms for investment adviser licences.

Introduced new best practice guide on audit committees and dealing in securities

Legalised share buy-backs

Commenced inspection of securities market intermediaries

Enhanced tax incentives

— Extended certain tax incentives for venture capital funds for a further 5 years beyond the current maximum of 10 years
— Renewed tax holiday for SIMEX for another 5 years
— Suspended stamp duty on securities transactions for one year with effect from 30 June 1998.

Bond Market

Increased government debt issues and announced a regular calendar of issues

— Issued $1.5 billion of 10-year Singapore Government Securities (SGS).

Increased issues by statutory boards like JTC, PUB, and HDB

— JTC launched $4 billion medium-term note programme.
— HDB announced plans to issue $2 billion worth of bonds.

Allowed foreign entities to issue S$-denominated bonds in Singapore

— International Finance Corporation launched the first triple-A S$ bond issued by a foreign borrower in October 1998.

Allowed banks to transact S$ repurchase agreements of up to $20 million with non-bank non-residents

Allowed banks to transact S$ currency and interest rate swaps with special purpose vehicles for securitising mortgages

Allowed CPF-approved unit trusts to invest in high grade bonds

Introduced tax incentives to encourage origination and trading of debt securities in Singapore

EXAMPLES OF SPECIFIC MEASURES

Merging SES and SIMEX

The government has accepted the recommendation to merge the SES and SIMEX. The process of merging has begun. The Pro-tem Committee on the new integrated exchange, headed by Mr J. Y. Pillay, is overseeing the process. (Refer Appendix)

Expanding Debt Capital Market

MAS has been issuing more Singapore Government Securities (SGS) to increase the free-float and deepen the bond market. It recently issued 10-year SGS to extend the long end of the yield curve.

Statutory boards such as Jurong Town Corporation and Housing & Development Board have taken the lead to issue bonds to fund long-term infrastructure and operational needs. Other statutory boards are expected to follow soon.

Revising the Singapore Dollar Internationalisation Policy

MAS has revised its Singapore dollar internationalisation policy, to allow supra-nationals and high-quality foreign corporations to tap the S$ bond market, while maintaining safeguards to discourage speculation in the S$.

The first bond issue, by the International Finance Corporation in October 1998, was well received, showing that there is strong international interest in issuing S$ bonds.

MAS has also been working with other government agencies to develop the legal, regulatory, tax and accounting frameworks to support mortgage and asset-backed securities markets. The development of these markets will broaden the range of debt instruments available, and create spin-offs for other market players, like rating agencies and financial guarantee insurers.

Reviewing Capital Adequacy Ratio

MAS has refined the Capital Adequacy Ratio (CAR) that local banks are required to maintain.

Singapore banks have since 1992 been required to maintain a CAR of 12%. This is much higher than the BIS standard of 8%.

Moreover, this 12% had to consist entirely of Tier 1 capital, i.e. equity, whereas of the BIS 8%, only 4% needs to be Tier 1. The remainder can consist of cheaper Tier 2 capital.

MAS has reviewed this requirement. From 1 December 1998, MAS will permit a change in the composition of this 12%. Of the 12%, banks should have at least 10% in Tier 1 capital. They can meet the remaining 2% with Upper Tier 2 capital.

Reviewing the Minimum Liquid Asset Requirement

The MAS is also refining the banks' Minimum Liquid Asset (MLA) requirement. The current MLA of 18% of banks' liabilities base is the highest in the world. This provides a substantial cushion for banks against potential liquidity difficulties, but it is not the most efficient way for banks to manage their liquidity needs.

The MAS will consider how to lower this across-the-board MLA requirement, and place more importance on banks' internal systems of liquidity management.

Banks with sound liquidity management systems will be given greater leeway to manage their needs, while banks which are assessed by MAS to have weaker systems will be required to maintain a higher level of liquid assets.

APPENDIX S–1

EXTRACTS FROM REPORT OF THE SUB-COMMITTEE ON FINANCE AND BANKING

(Source: Ministry of Trade and Industry website)

Terms of Reference

The Finance and Banking Sub-Committee, chaired by Mr Peter Seah, was formed in May 1997 as one of the five sub-committees of the Committee on Singapore's Competitiveness, chaired by Minister for Trade and Industry Mr Lee Yock Suan.

It had the following terms of reference:

- to review trends in banking and finance over the next 10 years,
- to identify new areas of growth,
- to recommend strategies to strengthen the competitiveness of Singapore's financial services.

Financial Trends

The financial services sector has grown steadily over the last 10 years. But growth has slowed down since 1993. The slower growth has been partly due to competition from other countries developing their own financial sector. Competition will intensify, not only from traditional competitors such as Hong Kong and Tokyo but also from financial centres in China, Malaysia, Thailand and Australia.

With globalisation and better technology, financial institutions may find it cheaper to operate from one financial centre in the same time zone. The race is on to be Asia's top financial centre. Singapore's competitors have large domestic economies which generate more business for their financial sector.

Singapore has a small domestic base. Its volume of financial activity depends on its capacity to provide high value-added services and to attract foreign institutions. To be a preferred financial centre, Singapore has to work on its strengths and reduce obstacles in developing its financial sector.

Having a large pool of educated, English-speaking workers highly skilled in IT applications is a big advantage. Singapore must use these strengths and build new ones.

Singapore has done well in offshore lending. According to data from the International Monetary Fund, Singapore ranks 9th in the world in terms of international lending. Singapore is also competitive in financial products such as derivatives and foreign exchange trading. A survey by the Bank for International Settlements (BIS) has shown that Singapore is the fourth largest in foreign exchange turnover and the fifth largest in derivatives turnover.

After the launch of the single European currency, the euro, on 1 January 1999, trading in eurocurrencies will decline. There will be a drop in foreign exchange transactions. Trading in other currencies, including Asian currencies, will increase.

Strategic Intent

Limited by its small domestic base, Singapore has lagged behind other Asian financial centres in developing its capital markets and in attracting international fund managers.

It has to position itself as a centre for syndications and cross-border project financing in the next decade. It has to attract fund management companies to manage discretionary funds, pension funds, insurance funds and other institutional funds.

It has to provide both the expertise and funds to boost fund management, corporate finance, debt and risk management activities.

In the next millennium, financial services will depend on technology, fast information and financial specialists.

Growth Areas

The Sub-Committee has identified seven growth areas and made specific recommendations for each of them:

(1) fund management
(2) treasury management
(3) equities market
(4) general debt issuance
(5) corporate finance & venture capital
(6) insurance and reinsurance
(7) cross-border electronic banking.

FUND MANAGEMENT

Singapore's fund management industry has grown rapidly in recent years but the growth still lags behind Hong Kong. One main reason is poor liquidity and the very strong preference for property investment. The best opportunity for developing liquidity is to bring new Singapore-based customers to the securities market.

Singapore has the advantage of a high national savings rate. These savings include government reserves, surplus funds of statutory boards and government-linked companies. These savings should be used more efficiently to raise the return of capital. (*Recommendation 1*)

Estate duty skews the allocation of capital towards property as a store of wealth. The present exemption rule should be reviewed to increase the flow of capital to more productive activities. (*Recommendation 2*)

Unit trusts provide the best means for small investors to manage the risks and to invest in stocks, shares and debt securities. Unit trusts should be actively promoted. (*Recommendations 3–5*).

An organised market for borrowing and lending of securities will help fund managers to hedge investment portfolios and to boost market liquidity. (*Recommendation 6*)

Capital gains on sale of securities should not be taxed unless the company trades in financial assets. (*Recommendation 7*)

Private pension and provident funds should be encouraged. (*Recommendations 8–9*)

The regulation of trust business should be rationalised to ensure flexibility. (*Recommendations 10–11*)

Recommendation 1

The pace at which public sector funds (including Singapore's foreign reserves) are allocated to the private sector should be increased, with at least 20% for management in three years by fund managers in Singapore. Fund managers should not have to guarantee principal as required by some government agencies.

Recommendation 2

Abolish estate duty as it no longer serves the purpose of wealth distribution. Alternatively, exemption from estate duty should be based on the gross value of the estate, regardless of asset class. The cut-off for estate duty exemption, currently at $9.6 million, should be increased.

Recommendation 3

3.1 Rationalise unit trust regulation and administration.
3.2 Reduce processing time for unit trust applications to 4–6 weeks.
3.3 Standardise trust deeds to expedite the approval process.
3.4 Separate prospectuses into two sections: a standard section containing regulatory information which is updated only when there are changes and the other containing "investor-friendly" information, relating to the investment objective and policy, fees, charges and risk factors as well as the track record of the fund manager.
3.5 Allow more flexibility in the promotion of unit trusts (both in respect of advertisements and in determining minimum investments).
3.6 A task force should be set up to identify other specific changes to improve the competitiveness of the industry.

Recommendation 4

4.1 Allow non-CPF funds to invest in CPF-approved unit trusts.
4.2 Give full discretion to:
   (a) fund managers of CPF-approved unit trusts which are managed by professional fund managers and there is a trustee, and

(b) managers of funds governed by the Trustees Act, to determine the geographical spread of investments, the investment instruments as well as the asset mix, to enhance returns for the trust funds while minimising risk. As a minimum, expand the scope of investments for CPF funds to all IFC developed countries. Regionally, since Thailand is included in the approved list of CPF investments, Indonesia, Philippines and China should also be included. Abolish the 40% cap on foreign assets and the 10% minimum liquid assets. Consider the following investment guidelines:
- Not more than 10% of fund assets may be invested in securities issued by the same group of companies.
- Securities in which more than 5% of fund assets are invested, should not in aggregate exceed 40% of total assets.
- For securities issued or guaranteed by governments and government-related bodies which are rated "AA" or better by international rating agencies, the 10% is raised to 35%, and the limit of 40% in aggregate value will not apply.
- Cash and Singapore Government Securities are excluded from these limits.

Recommendation 5

Withholding tax on distributions by unit trusts should be abolished.

Recommendation 6

Establish facilities for the borrowing and lending of securities quoted on the SES to provide liquidity.

Recommendation 7

Capital gains on sale of securities should not be taxed unless it is the business of the company to trade in financial assets.

The authorities in reviewing the issue should examine ways in which the revenue-enhancing side of business can be promoted rather than just focusing on the tax-levying side.

Recommendation 8

8.1 Revise CPF rules and regulations relating to private pension and provident funds to encourage their development. Private pension funds can be tailored to attract, motivate and retain key personnel.
8.2 Employees should be allowed to have their retirement funds placed with private pension funds rather than the CPF Board.

Recommendation 9

The tax treatment of funds managed by boutique fund managers should be clarified. As boutique fund managers are generally small operators, MAS should advise them of prospects for upgrading as licensed fund managers and the criteria required.

Recommendation 10

10.1 Allow approved trustee companies to establish trustee subsidiaries and holding companies in tax haven jurisdictions. The tax laws governing these subsidiaries should be reviewed, as under current provisions, such companies are deemed Singapore tax entities and are subject to Singapore taxation.
10.2 Rationalise the regulation and administration of trust business to ensure flexibility and transparency.
10.3 Provide secrecy provisions to preserve the confidentiality of trusts, unless in criminal investigation.
10.4 Trust administrators should not be required to submit trust deeds and related documents executed for foreign trusts to the IRAS and Commissioner of Stamp Duties. Allow trust duty to be paid by affixing revenue stamps to the trust deeds.
10.5 Allow licensed trustee companies to set up private trust companies and any special purpose holding companies in Singapore for offshore clients. These private trust companies should not be construed as Singapore tax entities, even if the administration is carried out in Singapore.
10.6 Provide fiscal incentives and implement regulatory measures to encourage the development of corporate trust services. In particular, tax incentives should be provided to attract expatriate staff with knowledge of specialised trust business such as corporate trustee of infrastructure projects, for example, by allowing expenses relating to expatriate staff to qualify for double tax deductions.

Recommendation 11

Revise the Trustees Act to be more in line with the regulatory framework provided under the US Employment Retirement Income Security Act, in order to better meet the objective of prudential management of trust assets.

TREASURY AND RISK MANAGEMENT

Singapore has achieved success in treasury activities including: credit intermediation, foreign exchange and derivatives trading, money market operations, underwriting new equity and debt issues, brokerage services, and futures trading.

However, it still lacks a critical mass of international fund managers and more vibrant equity and debt markets for sophisticated corporate finance and treasury activities.

Singapore should offer a comprehensive range of regional products to global investors, with market making and fixed income distribution capabilities and risk management solutions for all regional exposures. SIMEX should list a Singapore stock index and introduce other country stock indices.

Recommendation 12

12.1 Abolish withholding tax on debt papers issued in Singapore. This is currently approved on a case-by-case basis. There is no withholding tax on ACU deposits. Similarly, withholding tax should not be levied on longer-dated investments.

12.2 Provide tax incentives, for example, 10% concessionary tax rate, for targeted growth activities like specialised project finance, cross-border leasing and debt distribution with a view to promoting the development of these activities.

Recommendation 13

SIMEX should consider listing regional equity and interest rate products and their derivatives to facilitate fund managers' risk management and strengthen Singapore's position as a regional financial centre.

Recommendation 14

Introduce a Singapore stock index on SIMEX.

EQUITIES MARKET

Despite the efforts of the SES to attract foreign companies to list on the SES, the stock exchanges of Hong Kong and Malaysia have outgrown the SES, both in terms of market capitalisation and trading volume. One major factor has been the low trading volume. For example, in 1996, turnover on SES was US$63 billion, only a third of that transacted on the Hong Kong (US$182 billion) and Malaysian (US$184 billion) exchanges.

Recommendation 15

The SES should review its Listing Manual to encourage a more active market.

Recommendation 16

16.1 Singapore's fixed brokerage should be reviewed to ensure securities transaction costs are competitive. Free brokerage rates for institutional investors and review brokerage for retail investors.
16.2 GST exemptions should be reviewed to ensure a level playing field for fund managers in Singapore managing overseas funds.
16.3 Abolish stamp duty on all equity transactions.
16.4 Allow SES member firms to provide soft dollar commission as practised elsewhere.

Recommendation 17

When promoting Singapore as a base for operations, the agenda should include encouraging foreign companies to seek a listing on the SES.

Recommendation 18

18.1 Allow foreign shares listed on the SES or CLOB International to be traded in Singapore dollars, alternatively, allow dual currency listing.

18.2 Permit the use of CPF savings to buy foreign currency denominated securities listed on the SES.

Recommendation 19

A committee should be set up to review the structure of the equity options market to look at the shortcomings.

Recommendation 20

SIMEX should allow SES members to trade stock index futures and options on SIMEX.

Recommendation 21

21.1 The SES should introduce a wider range of derivative products to enhance liquidity.
21.2 Under the Securities Act, the definition of securities which may be traded on the SES should be broadened to include equity derivative products.
21.3 For SES to trade cash settled equity derivatives, the exemption provided by Section 58 of the Futures Trading Act should be extended to cover the SES.
21.4 Equity derivative products should be traded on the SES. This will keep the trading of derivatives together with the trading of their underlying cash instruments as it is expected that the users of these derivative products would be the same group of investors. This would provide end-users access to both cash and derivative instruments, in the same marketplace.

Recommendation 22

Multiple applications for IPO shares should be permitted. It is unnecessary to regulate the "luck of the draw" provided these applications are supported by sufficient funds.

Recommendation 23

Improve the Employee Stock Option Scheme to make it more attractive to employees. This will enable employers to retain key personnel by implementing the following:

23.1 Increase the maximum Employee Stock Option Schemes for companies listed on the Main Board to 10% of outstanding shares from 5%.

23.2 Treat any gains arising out of the exercise of stock options issued under the Employee Stock Option Scheme as capital gains and therefore not subject to tax. If not feasible, there should be a prescribed holding period, say five years, after which profit from the sale of the shares should be deemed capital gains. Alternatively, if tax on capital gains must be levied, it should be based on the profit arising at the point of sale of the shares rather than at the point of exercise of the option.

23.3 Amend the Companies Act to extend the life of the options to 10 years from the present 5 years.

23.4 Allow re-pricing of the exercise price of options, to adjust for market conditions.

Recommendation 24

Rules on the "window period", during which directors of the company and major shareholders are permitted to trade in the company's shares, are too restrictive. These parties are unnecessarily "locked-out" of the market. There are provisions on insider trading which provide sufficient protection for minority shareholders. The Model Code should be removed from the SES Listing Manual or amended.

Recommendation 25

Amend the Companies Act to permit share buy-backs by listed companies.

GENERAL DEBT ISSUANCE

Singapore's debt market is illiquid. This is because the government and statutory boards have huge surpluses to self-finance infrastructure projects. The corporate base is small and dominated by MNCs which do not depend on domestic sources of capital. To help develop the debt market, statutory boards and GLCs should borrow from the debt market.

Singapore must develop high value-added services like the financing of infrastructure projects and cross-border leasing which support economic development in the region. The legal framework and infrastructure are currently not conducive for such transactions and should be reviewed.

Recommendation 26

Encourage statutory boards and GLCs to borrow from the debt market to help its development.

Recommendation 27

The government should drive the yield curve by issuing longer term government bonds for benchmarking and to create depth in the market. Government securities are usually used for benchmarking because of credit quality and liquidity. There are no long-dated corporate bonds in Singapore.

Recommendation 28

Relax rules on the use of CPF savings for investment in approved debt instruments, including corporate bonds issued by Singapore companies.

Recommendation 29

29.1 Extend tax incentives to companies to promote Singapore as the domicile for locating relevant specialists, particularly in areas like specialised project finance and debt distribution.
29.2 Review tax laws and treaties and provide tax incentives to encourage cross-border leasing activities.
29.3 A task force consisting of industry players and regulators should be set up to review ways to develop the targetted activities.

Recommendation 30

The government should encourage Singapore professionals to do research on legal, tax and accounting practices in emerging economies like Laos, Myanmar and Cambodia. This will enhance information network and attract specialist finance teams to Singapore.

Recommendation 31

The SES should lead a consortium to establish a clearing house and regional custody facility for the trading of debt instruments issued by Asian entities and the government should provide tax incentives.

CORPORATE FINANCE / VENTURE CAPITAL

While Singapore has grown as a financial centre in Asia, Hong Kong is still the preferred choice for corporate finance activities. Major international investment banks locate their syndication teams in Hong Kong instead of Singapore.

Over the past decade, through the EDB, the government has provided support to develop the venture capital industry. Much more must be done if Singapore aims to become the regional hub for venture capital management.

Recommendation 32

Aggressively promote Singapore as RHQ. It has been observed that the capital and equity market professionals of investment banks are located where the regional headquarters are established. If Singapore can attract the regional headquarters of international, industrial, trading and services firms, financial business will follow.

Recommendation 33

The government should delegate to the MAS, the authority to administer all tax incentives granted to the financial services sector. This will be similar to the role of the EDB in relation to the manufacturing sector.

Recommendation 34

Allow IPOs to be issued on a book building basis with "green-shoe" option (which would help to secure the best price for the offer and reduces underwriting risk).

Recommendation 35

The SES should allow some flexibility when determining the placement and public issue mix of IPOs. SES should give the issuer and the merchant bank the flexibility to decide on the approach for each tranche. The SES could still exercise control by prescribing a minimum size (say 30%) for the public tranche.

Recommendation 36

Allow flexibility in share placements by allowing the company to borrow the shares from the promoters to facilitate the placement. The new shares, when approved, are returned to the promoters. This approach allows the issuer to take advantage of market conditions.

Recommendation 37

The SES should abolish the minimum spread of investors for bond and debt issues. Since the SES has already been exercising flexibility by not insisting on the 100 holders, on a case-by-case basis, this should be reflected in the SES Listing Manual. The minimum should be flexible, to be determined by negotiation between the SES and the investment bank.

Recommendation 38

The SES should review the approval procedures for IPOs and rights to streamline the process.

Recommendation 39

The SES should find ways to attract foreign companies listed on established exchanges either to seek quotation on CLOB International or listing on the SES by simplifying the procedures. Incentives should be given, e.g. waiver of listing fee for the first two years.

Recommendation 40

Tax relief should be considered for venture capital funds which are incorporated in Singapore but do not invest or provide seed money to Singapore companies, for example, allow gains on sale of venture capital investments carried in the company's books for, say more than 18 months, to be deemed as capital gains (and therefore not taxable) rather than as trading profit. The priority must be to entice venture capital funds and management to Singapore to achieve the critical mass to transform Singapore into a venture capital hub so that regional corporations would come to Singapore to raise venture capital funds.

Recommendation 41

EDB, as promoter of the venture capital business and the MAS which grants approval for managing venture capital funds, should form a task force to look into the various aspects of Singapore's corporate laws affecting the competitiveness of Singapore's venture capital industry.

INSURANCE AND REINSURANCE

The government's efforts to develop Singapore as an international reinsurance centre and a captive domicile have been creditable. Singapore is widely recognised as a premier reinsurance centre in the Asia-Pacific region.

But growth in the number of captive insurance has slowed, as has offshore business of professional reinsurers. New incentives are needed to accelerate this development. (*Recommendations 42–46*)

Specialised risks such as marine hull, oil and gas, etc., are not insured in Singapore because capacity and underwriting expertise are both limited. (*Recommendation 47*)

To stay ahead of the competition, Singapore must provide not only underwriting capacity, but also high value-added, one-stop reinsurance services such as IT network for reinsurance processing, risk management services, claims control and actuarial consultancy. (*Recommendations 48–49*)

Incentives should be provided to encourage reinsurers to write offshore risks and to write international business from Singapore. (*Recommendation 50*)

Insurance funds contribute substantially to the development of the fund management industry. More should be done to promote the life insurance by removing unnecessary constraints while providing incentives for Singaporeans to save. (*Recommendation 51*)

More should be done to attract reinsurance brokers which will help to compete for offshore reinsurance business. (*Recommendation 52*)

Special efforts should be made to encourage Singaporeans to save more (beyond the compulsory CPF contributions) to meet financial needs after retirement. A most effective way to achieve this objective is the deferred annuity sold by life insurers. (*Recommendation 53*)

Recommendation 42

To be competitive with other successful domiciles and to increase the number of captive insurers, captive insurers should be allowed to write second-party business.

Recommendation 43

Review the capitalisation requirements for captive insurers and adopt a more flexible approach such as a sliding scale; perhaps lowering capital requirements to say $250,000 for pure captives and $500,000 for second-party captives.

Recommendation 44

Review the current concessionary tax and be flexible to meet the needs of captive sponsors. Fix the corporate tax for captives at 26% but allow their sponsors to apply for a lower tax rate which could range from 0% to 25%.

Recommendation 45

To establish reciprocal law for allowing captives to move their corporate seats and business from other domiciles to Singapore without the need to liquidate the existing captives, and vice versa.

Recommendation 46

Income derived from managing foreign-owned captives should be taxed at the concessionary rate of 10% to encourage captive insurance managers to attract more clients to Singapore.

Recommendation 47

Allow double tax relief on premiums paid for marine cargo and hull insured locally to promote the insuring of marine cargo and hull risks locally. A tax holiday, say for 10 years, could be considered to enable Singapore-registered insurers to build up sufficient reserves to face overseas competition effectively.

Recommendation 48

Provide tax incentives to encourage reinsurance companies to locate an enhanced level of underwriting and risk management expertise in

Singapore, so as to increase the underwriting autonomy and territorial scope of their Singapore offices.

Recommendation 49

Professional reinsurers should be allowed to underwrite specialised pioneer products such as alternative risk-transfer products to promote further growth and enhance Singapore's competitiveness as a reinsurance centre.

Recommendation 50

Contingency reserves should be totally tax-deductible as an incentive for companies doing offshore business. For example, in the UK, such reserves are allowed at a percentage of the average of the last five years' net written premium, subject to the prescribed maximum limits.

Recommendation 51

There is a need to liberalise the current investment limits for insurance funds as they are no longer appropriate. Investment limits as percentages of the total insurance fund should be raised to 50% for equities, 50% for foreign assets and 30% for properties and property shares.

Recommendation 52

Income derived from the placement of offshore risks in Singapore should be taxed at a concessionary rate of 10% as an incentive to develop reinsurance broking in Singapore and to encourage reinsurance brokers to generate business for the Singapore reinsurance market.

Recommendation 53

To encourage savings, premiums paid for deferred annuities should be tax-deductible up to an annual maximum limit, the annuity funds be allowed to accumulate tax free and the annuity proceeds taxed only on maturity.

CROSS-BORDER ELECTRONIC BANKING

The Internet will support electronic commerce. The focus on electronic commerce will enhance Singapore's competitiveness in the global arena.

Recommendation 54

Expand NetTrust Initiative and align its development to ensure that Singapore-issued certificates are internationally accepted.

Recommendation 55

Continue to deregulate the industry and encourage innovation within the telecommunications industry to lead to more competitive pricing.

APPENDIX S–2

COMMITTEE ON GOVERNANCE OF THE EXCHANGES — MAJOR RECOMMENDATIONS

(Source: website: www.mas.gov.sg/whatsnew 18 January 1999)

The Committee on Governance of Exchanges submitted its report in January 1999. It acknowledges that the SES and SIMEX have done their jobs well. The SES has played an important role in developing Singapore's capital market. Its high prudential standards have enabled it to weather the Asian economic crisis. SIMEX is the most international derivatives exchange in the Asia-Pacific, offering a very wide range of Asian and global products.

The Committee has recommended the following:

— The two exchanges should re-assess their strategies to compete in an increasingly globalised environment.
— They improve their ownership and governance structures to operate as business entities.
— They combine resources and develop synergies between the cash and derivative markets.

Merging SES and SIMEX

After studying the trends in governance of other international exchanges, the Committee has also recommended that:

— SES and SIMEX be demutualised to separate ownership from participation, and merge into one exchange.
— The new exchange should be a private for-profit company with the same group of owners at the holding company level.
— The new company should aim for public listing within 5 years, providing an added incentive for owners to ensure its success.

Ownership of the New Exchange

On shareholding, the Committee has recommended the following:

— Existing SES and SIMEX members should be allocated shares in the new exchange because they have contributed to SES and SIMEX. Shareholding will encourage their commitment to the new company.
— The allocation of shares to members should be based on slight discounts to the imputed value of SES and SIMEX seats or shares currently. The discounts recognise the fact that seat values would have declined dramatically under the status quo, once commissions are liberalised and access to the exchanges opened up.

Value of the Shares

In value terms, the Committee has recommended the following:

— Each of the 33 SES members receive $6 million worth of shares in the new company. This is about 15% lower than the estimated current market value of $7 million for an SES seat.
— SIMEX members receive $115,000 worth of shares in the new company for each SIMEX share owned, and $170,000 worth of shares in the new company for each SIMEX seat owned. These correspond to seat and share values which are about 11% lower than the average for 1998.

The discount of 11% applied to SIMEX seat values is lower than the 15% discount applied above to SES seat values, since SIMEX's seat and share prices better reflect fair market value.

At preliminary valuation of $600–800 million for the combined entity, the recommended allocations translate into a 40%–50% combined shareholding for existing SES and SIMEX members. To broaden the shareholding base, the Committee recommends that the remaining shares of the integrated exchange be sold to new investors. A financial advisor will need to be appointed to value the new entity and price the shares fairly.

Balancing Different Interests

The Committee believes that the new exchange's success depends on the continued commitment of existing members. At the same time, it is also important to balance broker interests with broader financial sector and strategic interests.

The Committee has recommended that the aggregate broker shareholding should be subjected to a ceiling of 75% and a floor of 33% of the new entity. Until the new exchange is publicly listed, owners should be allowed to trade their shares privately. The ceiling and floor on aggregate broker ownership should remain until the IPO.

To ensure that the shareholder base is adequately diversified any shareholding of more than 5% in the integrated exchange should require MAS approval.

Inviting Strategic Investors

The Committee recommends that a pool of strategic investors, including local financial institutions and other institutions with long-term interest in Singapore's financial centre be invited to hold shares in the new entity. Strategic investors may be allowed to go beyond 5%, but MAS approval should also be required for holdings in excess of 10%.

Financial Sector Development Fund

The Committee proposes that proceeds from the sale of shares to new investors be placed in a new Financial Sector Development Fund. This will be used to develop skills and capabilities in Singapore's financial sector.

Organisation in the New Exchange

For the new exchange to benefit from the integration, the Committee has recommended that it should be organised as separate wholly-owned subsidiaries for trading, clearing, depository and IT systems services under a common parent holding company. In particular:

- SES and SIMEX trading operations will initially remain separate subsidiaries. Eventually, they may share a common trading engine when an integrated engine becomes available, and merge into a single trading subsidiary.
- Existing SES and SIMEX clearing functions could initially remain unchanged. But in future, there should be a stand-alone clearing subsidiary to enable cross-margining and more efficient use of collateral. The stand-alone clearing subsidiary could also pool resources and consider expanding into clearing services for the OTC and debt markets.
- Initially, there will be no change in SIMEX's Common Bond system. SIMEX clearing members should continue to earn clearing commissions and be adequately represented in the new entity's decision-making mechanism on admission of new clearing members.

Suitable "corporate veils" should be put in place to shield the holding company from subsidiary companies' legal liabilities and to prevent loss-migration between subsidiary companies.

Decision-making Mechanism

The Committee feels that the decision-making mechanism of the combined entity should ensure a diversity of financial sector interests. It should also give the exchange's top management some flexibility in operations. In particular:

- To balance broker and broader capital market participant perspectives, brokers should not comprise more than half of the Board, which will have 10 to 12 members. A minimum of 2 and up to 4 MAS-approved independent directors should be appointed, including the non-executive Board Chairman, to ensure balanced representation of interests favouring long-term financial centre development.
- The Board of Directors is responsible for providing strategic directions and appointing management executives. The top management of the new entity (Executive Committee — EXCO) should be responsible for operational decisions, business development and strategy formulation. The EXCO should include

existing SES and SIMEX top management, who will remain key members of the new top management team.

Regulatory Issues

The Committee proposes that in line with the SES Review Committee's recommendation that the brokerage industry should be fully liberalised within 5 years. Open access to the new integrated exchange should be phased in over 3 years. Completely open access should be in place by January 2002, by which time participation in the exchange would be fully divorced from ownership of the exchange.

The Committee also noted that MAS' regulatory framework and the exchanges' current bye-laws and regulations have to be reviewed. In the short term, existing legislation and bye-laws have to be amended. In the longer term, a thorough review of the regulatory framework has to be undertaken to:

— study if MAS' role in overseeing the new exchange has to be enhanced to ensure that there is no relaxation of current regulatory standards. There is also a need to state clearly the respective regulatory functions of MAS and the exchange; and
— study whether there should be a merging of current securities and futures legislation into a single "omnibus" legislation, to anticipate features such as common licensing for intermediaries operating in both markets, a shared trading platform for cash and derivatives, increased trading of hybrid cash-derivatives products and an integrated clearing house for both cash and derivatives clearing.

References

Monetary Authority of Singapore (1999), "Monetary policy operating procedures in Singapore", in Bank for International Settlements, *Monetary Policy Operating Procedures in Emerging Market Economies*, BIS Policy Papers, No. 5, March 1999, Bank for International Settlements, Basle, Switzerland, 218–29.

Montes, Manuel F. and Tan, Khee Giap (1999), "Developing the financial services industry in Singapore", in Masuyama, S., Vanderbrink, D. and Chia, S.Y. (eds.) *East Asia's Financial Systems: Evolution and Crisis*, Nomura Research Institute, Tokyo and Institute of Southeast Asian Studies, Singapore, 231–59.

Tan, Chwee Huat (1999), *Financial Markets and Institutions in Singapore*, 10 ed., Singapore University Press, Singapore.

THAILAND

Introduction — the Financial Crisis

In 1997, the Thai economy faced a severe financial crisis. According to a joint statement issued by the Ministry of Finance and the Bank of Thailand, the crisis was due to many causes, mainly related to the fundamental economic situation but also legal, institutional and information deficiencies, including a weak supervisory system.

The problems were due to excessive risk-taking in the private sector. Finance companies in particular had lent excessively for real estate development and speculative investments, and had financed long term loans with short term deposits. Many banks, finance companies and borrowers had taken on too many foreign currency debts.

Reform measures were introduced by the government. The exchange rate was allowed to float in July 1997 and a comprehensive economic package supported by the International Monetary Fund was put in place.

The program was designed to restore confidence to the financial system. This would allow credit to flow again and interest rates to normalise, both of which are preconditions for a reactivation of economic activity.

Reform Strategy

The strategy was to separate and suspend the weakest institutions and fully support the remaining ones, while dealing appropriately with each group. The following action was taken to strengthen the financial system. Financial institutions were encouraged to increase their capital and to refrain from dividend payment. Foreign majority participation was allowed for up to 10 years. Loan loss provisions were fully tax deductible.

A special Financial Institutions Development Fund (FIDF) was set up to support the institutions. It provides insurance cover for repayment of principal and interest to depositors and creditors of commercial banks, finance & securities companies and credit foncier companies.

The Commercial Banking Act and Finance Companies Act were amended to empower the Bank of Thailand to control institutions which had been poorly managed. It also empowered the BOT to write down the value of shares and made shareholders pay for the losses.

MEASURES TO RESTRUCTURE THE FINANCIAL SYSTEM

(Source: www.bot.or.th/research/public/MOF/ter.htm)

The two major measures to restructure the financial system were:

(1) the restructuring of the debt structure in the financial sector,
(2) the 14 August 1998 Financial Restructuring Package.

Financial Sector Restructuring

Thailand's financial sector restructuring had three main tracks:

(a) segregating viable and unviable financial institutions;
(b) strengthening the operation and regulation of the remaining institutions;
(c) reforming the capital market.

Segregating Viable and Unviable Financial Institutions

The Bank of Thailand segregated viable financial institutions from unviable ones to maintain the integrity of the financial system and to provide the basis for the subsequent reform measures.

Suspending Finance Companies

A total of 58 insolvent finance companies were suspended, 16 of them on 27 June 1997 and another 42 on 5 August 1997, leaving only 33 finance companies in operation.

To prevent bank runs and to restore public confidence, the Financial Institutions Development Fund (FIDF) provided guarantee for the remaining financial institutions.

Disposing Assets of the Closed Finance Companies

In October 1997, two important institutions were created as part of the financial restructuring:

— Financial Restructuring Authority (FRA),
— Asset Management Corporation (AMC).

Financial Restructuring Authority (FRA)

The FRA was set up on 24 October 1997 under the Emergency Decree on Financial Sector Restructuring BE 2540 (1997). It reviewed the plans submitted by shareholders and creditors of the suspended finance companies, and administered the public auction of finance company assets.

For example, it reviewed the rehabilitation plans of the 58 suspended finance companies and to oversee their liquidation. On 8 December 1997, FRA allowed only two of the 58 suspended companies to resume business: Kiatnakin Finance and Securities Public Company and Bangkok Investment Company. The remaining 56 were liquidated. Their assets were transferred to the FRA to be auctioned. The proceeds were used to pay the creditors.

As of November 1998, the FRA had auctioned assets worth 63 billion baht, comprising 36 billion baht in core assets (e.g. hire purchase loans, mortgage and commercial loans) and 27 billion baht in non-core assets (e.g. repossessed vehicles, equity and debt papers).

Asset Management Corporation (AMC)

The purchase of assets of these companies was done by the Asset Management Corporation (AMC) which was set up in October 1997 under the Emergency Decree on the Asset Management Corporation, dated 22 October BE 2540 (1997) as part of the financial sector restructuring program. Its initial capital of 1 billion baht was subscribed by the Thai Government. The shareholder is the Ministry of Finance.

The AMC ensured that the FRA was able to dispose of the non-performing assets it auctioned. The AMC only bought the troubled assets of the suspended finance companies. It would not buy bad assets from institutions operating normally. The private sector was encouraged to compete with the AMC in the purchase of assets. The AMC would manage, restructure and sell those assets in a way that minimised the long-run cost to government.

The AMC was responsible to bid for the lowest quality assets of the 56 closed finance companies. It acted as a buyer of last resort to prevent fire sale of assets, which in turn could undermine the collateral values in the financial system. The assets bought would be managed for resale later.

Setting up Radanasin Bank

The Radanasin Bank was originally set up as a good bank in January 1998. It had found its role somewhat modified in the light of the 14 August 1998 package. Radanasin subsequently merged with a small bank which had been unable to raise capital in line with its MOU signed with the authorities and was therefore intervened.

Loan Classification and Recapitalisation

For the remaining domestic financial institutions, the strategy was to strengthen their capital base through a combination of more realistic loan classification and provisioning (LCP) and private sector-led recapitalisation.

Foreign Ownership of Banks

In order to encourage recapitalisation, the restriction on foreign ownership in Thai financial institutions was relaxed. Foreign investors were allowed to acquire majority shareholding for up to 10 years. After that, they would be grandfathered as to the amount of shares held and would not be permitted to take up new shares until their ratio was brought down to 49%. This was substantially higher than the previous 25% limit.

Loan Classification and Provisioning (LCP)

To upgrade the LCP rules and accounting standard to the international level within the year 2000, the Bank of Thailand announced new asset classification and provisioning requirements.

Recognition of accrued interest income was shortened from 12 months to 6 months, and subsequently 3 months. Provisioning requirements were tightened in line with international practices according to the new asset categories of current, special mention, substandard, doubtful, doubtful of loss and losses.

The new rule provided for the gradual phased-in provisioning requirements of 5 accounting periods from the second accounting period (ending December 1998) to the last accounting period (ending December 2000).

The government realised that the new requirement would pose a burden on financial institutions in their negotiation with foreign and local partners, and in raising capital through public offer, especially in an environment of economic instability in the region. It introduced several measures to assist these institutions and strengthen their capital base. They included the following:

(a) On 14 August 1998, the government announced a package of capital support scheme to assist financial institutions to recapitalise, both for the tier 1 and tier 2 capital.
(b) A series of MOUs were signed between the BOT and the banks requiring the latter to maintain their capital adequacy ratio at a minimum of 8.5%.
(c) Issuing government bonds to restructure the liabilities of the FIDF.

By the end of 1998, bonds worth 400 billion baht had been issued, with a maturity ranging from 1 year to 10 years. These provided a benchmark yield curve for the corporate sector to re-access the capital market through the issuance of medium to long-term debentures.

Intervening Institutions Unable to Recapitalise

The government had hoped that by closing unviable institutions and strengthening supervision, it would permanently segregate the viable institutions from the unviable ones.

However, the worsening recession had created more non-performing loans. Solvent financial institutions could become unviable if they did not recapitalise quickly. The BOT had to intervene in a total of 6 banks and 12 finance companies in 1998.

Before the BOT injected new capital into these institutions through debt-to-equity swaps, it had to write down their registered capital and remove the management team. This action was based on the principle that existing shareholders had to bear losses and depositors would be fully protected if the integrity of the financial system was to be preserved.

Table: Intervened Banks and Finance Companies

	Banks		Finance Companies	
	Intervened	Total Remaining	Closed / Intervened	Total Remaining
End-1996	—	15	—	91
Dec 1997	—	15	56 closed	35
Jan 1998*	1	16	—	36
Feb 1998	3	16	—	36
May 1998	—	16	7 intervened	36
Aug 1998	2	16 (13 after consolidation is completed)	5 intervened	36 (24 after consolidation is completed)

* Cabinet approved the setting up of Radanasin Bank and its subsidiaries, Radanatun Finance and Radanasup Securities, in January 1998.
Radanasin Bank started operation on 16 March 1998 and Radanatun Finance on 23 February 1998.

OTHER REFORM MEASURES

Several medium-term actions were also taken to strengthen the financial system. These included a complete overhaul of supervisory practices as well as legal and regulatory reforms.

This program was supported by extensive technical assistance from the World Bank and the International Monetary Fund.

Other measures included the following:

— Improve the Bankruptcy Act so that creditors can collect the collateral faster.
— Modify the Banking Act and the Act on the Undertaking of Finance Businesses, Securities Businesses, and Credit Foncier Businesses to be in line with the current needs of the financial system.
— Improve the system of accounting and public disclosure to increase transparency.
— Improve the supervision of financial institutions.

AUGUST 14TH PACKAGE

On 14 August 1998, the government announced a restructuring package to strengthen the financial sector. The plan focused on 4 main aspects:

(1) consolidate bank and finance companies through additional intervention,
(2) encourage private investment in the banking system,
(3) provide public funds to recapitalise all remaining financial institutions, and
(4) develop a framework to create private asset-management companies.

With the above objectives, the restructuring strategy was focused on the following:

(1) commit funds to restructure viable banks and finance companies,
(2) incentives for accelerating corporate debt restructuring pari passu with recapitalisation,
(3) the efficient management of non-performing assets,
(4) the exit, merger, or sale of non-viable banks and finance companies,
(5) equitable loss-sharing arrangements, containment of public sector costs, and the avoidance of moral hazard,
(6) strengthen prudential supervision and accelerate adoption of international best practice,
(7) restructure and privatise state banks.

August 14th Package I — Capital Support Facilities

The capital support schemes provided funds to recapitalise the viable financial institutions, and to resume normal lending.

One scheme catalysed the entry of private capital. The other scheme provided incentives to restructure corporate debt and encourage new lending.

Tier 1 Capital Support Facility

Objectives

— the government helped to recapitalise financial institutions by catalysing the injection of private capital

— assisted in resuming normal lending practices.

Conditions and Safeguards

— adopt up-front the end-2000 LCP rules
— losses on the old portfolio to be borne by original shareholders
— new public and private capital to have preferred status
— government and new investor to have the right to change management
— institutions to provide their restructuring plans to FRAC and BOT

Form of Public Injection

— Tradeable government bonds with a maturity of 10 years

Amount of Public Injection

— the government would inject capital up to the amount provided by the private investor. However, if after full provisioning, the Tier 1 CAR fell below 2.5% the government would recapitalise the institution by itself up to this level before matching private funds.
— new investors had the option to buy back government shares
— no pre-determined limit per institution.

Tier 2 Capital Support Facility

Objectives

— recapitalise financial institutions
— facilitate corporate debt restructuring
— encourage new lending

Conditions and Safeguards

— legally binding debt restructuring agreement between the financial institution and the debtor
— debtor had to service the loan according to BOT regulations on troubled debt restructuring before Tier 2 capital was provided
— measurable increase was new lending

Form of Public Injection

— non-tradeable government bonds with a maturity of 10 years in exchange for subordinated debt instruments with matching maturing.

Amount of Public Injection

— up to 2% of each institution's risk weighted assets. The amount of Tier 2 support provided for new lending could exceed 1% of risk weighted assets.

Availability and Application Period

— Banks and finance companies could apply during 1 October 1998 to 1 November 2000
— the generiosity of the scheme would decline over time to encourage early debt restructuring.

August 14th Package II

In intervening the financial institutions, the government followed these principles:

— be cost efficient
— facilitate consolidation of the banking sector
— allow new domestic and foreign investment
— be credible and transparent
— enhance confidence in the whole banking system
— be consistent with the capital support facilities

With the above objectives, the following actions were taken:

Bangkok Metropolitan Bank (BMB) and Siam City Bank (SCIB):

In order to privatise these two banks, the end-2000 LCP rules were brought forward. The banks were recapitalised through a debt to equity conversion of outstanding FIDF lending. The new investors could bid for up to 100% of the entire bank, and absorb all assets and liabilities, including the non-performing assets.

However, the government would provide a loss-sharing or stop-loss guarantee on non-performing assets, as well as a guaranteed annual yield to service the liabilities. Potential investors had to specify in their bids the type of stop-loss and yield guarantee they required.

First Bangkok City Bank (FBCB)

The FBCB was absorbed by Krung Thai Bank (KTB). It was integrated with KTB because FBCB's branch network complemented that of KTB. The KTB also took over the staff and all FBCB branches and would have the right to rationalize staffing and the branch network.

Bangkok Bank of Commerce (BBC)

All performing assets and liabilities of BBC were transferred to KTB. The staff, branches and non-performing assets remained in BBC, which had been turned into a special financial institution, AMC, owned by FIDF. FIDF would determine the process of winding down BBC (by end-1999) with the aim to maximise loan recoveries, rationalise the staff and to sell off the branches.

Union Bank (UBB)

UBB and the newly intervened finance companies would be managed and eventually integrated with Krungthai Thanakit (KTT).

Laem Thong Bank (LTB)

LTB was integrated with Radanasin Bank.

CAPITAL MARKET DEVELOPMENT

The main objectives of capital market reform were to:

— promote transparency and
— promote direct financing or disintermediation.

The Securities and Exchange Act was amended to focus on disclosure of information.

The Ministry of Finance and the Bank of Thailand promoted the following:

— the primary market for domestic government bonds,
— a domestic secondary government bond market,
— a sustainable domestic bond market and comprehensive debt management capacity.

In June 1997, the Government set up the Secondary Mortgage Corporation (SMC) to securitise housing loans by issuing mortgage-backed securities of up to 40 billion baht. The Bank of Thailand had accorded SMC bonds — the instrument to be used in the exchange for mortgage loans — the same status as state enterprise bonds which would make them eligible for financial institutions to hold as reserve assets.

CORPORATE DEBT RESTRUCTURING ADVISORY COMMITTEE

In 1998, the Bank of Thailand set up a Corporate Debt Restructuring Advisory Committe (CDRAC). In August, the committee approved the following Framework for Corporate Restructuring in Thailand collectively with these organisations:

— Board of Trade,
— Federation of Thai Industries (representing debtor companies),
— Thai Bankers' Association,
— Association of Finance Companies,
— Foreign Banks' Association (representing the creditor groups).

The Bangkok Approach

(Source: www.bot.or.th/fsupv/public/cdraco/frame.htm)

The "Bangkok Approach" (modeled along the London Approach) is a framework for corporate debt restructuring in Thailand. Although it is non-statutory, it is expected to be adopted in corporate workouts involving multiple creditors.

Objective

The objective is to have an informal framework outside bankruptcy proceedings to restructure the corporate debt of viable entities to benefit creditors, debtors, employees, shareholders and the Thai economy by:

(a) minimising losses to all parties through a co-ordinated effort,
(b) helping companies to avoid being liquidated, thereby preserving jobs and production.

Principles

The framework outlined 19 principles:

1. Any corporate restructuring should achieve a business, rather than just a financial restructuring to further the long term viability of the debtor.
2. Priority must be given to rehabilitate assets to performing status in full compliance with Bank of Thailand regulations.
3. Each stage of the restructuring process must follow the schedule stated in Appendix I.
4. From the first debtor-creditor meeting, if the debtor's management is providing full and accurate information on the agreed schedule and participating in all creditor committee meetings, creditors shall "standstill" for a defined, extendable period to allow informed decisions to be made.
5. Both creditors and debtors must recognise the absolute necessity of active senior management involvement during the restructure.
6. A lead institution, and a designated individual within the lead institution, must be appointed early in the restructuring process to coordinate the entire process according to defined objectives and deadlines.
7. In major multi-creditor cases, a steering committee representative of a broad range of creditor interest should be appointed.
8. Decisions should be made on complete and accurate information which has been independently verified to ensure transparency.
9. In cases where accountants, attorneys and professional advisors are appointed, they must have requisite local knowledge, expertise and available dedicated resources.
10. Where it is normal practice to request the debtor to assume all the costs of professional advisors, lead institutions and creditors committees, creditors have direct economic interest, and hence a professional obligation, to help control such costs.
11. The Ministry of Finance and the Bank of Thailand should be kept informed on the progress of all debt restructuring to aid the review and regulatory framework and to facilitate restructuring.
12. The role of the Corporate Debt Restructuring Advisory Committee is to review and implement policies on restructuring for the public good. It may act as an independent intermediary in difficult cases or where other efforts have failed.
13. Creditors' existing collateral rights must continue.

14. New credit extended during the restructuring process above existing exposures as of the standstill date on reasonable terms in order that the debtor may continue operations must receive priority status based on title orientated security, inter-creditor agreement or indemnities.
15. Lenders should seek to lower their risk and hence their requisite returns, through an improved security package and profitability-based benefits rather than increased interest rates and imposition of restructuring fees.
16. Debt trading is appropriate under certain conditions but the selling creditor has the professional obligation to ensure the buyer does not have detrimental effect on the restructuring process.
17. Restructuring losses should be apportioned in an equitable manner which recognises legal priority between the parties involved.
18. Creditors retain the right to exercise independent commercial judgment and objectives but should carefully consider the impact of any action on the Thai economy, other creditors and potentially viable debtors.
19. Any of the principles or implementing policies contained in this framework can be waived, amended or superceded in any particular restructuring with the consent of all participating creditors.

Various Stages and Time Schedule

1. Call meeting of debtor, creditors and interested parties. This meeting may be called any time by debtor or creditor.
2. First creditors' meeting, appointment of Creditors' Committee or Lead Bank. (See Principles 6 and 7) and to establish a time frame. This should be done on 7 days' notice after Stage 1.
3. Creditors submit claims in writing to Creditors' Committee or Lead Bank. This should be done within 15 days of Stage 2.
4. At any creditors' meeting a debtor representative with decision-making authority must appear and answer all questions.
5. Within 7 days of Stage 2, the Debtor's "management" (i.e. directors or authorised officers) must submit the following information:
    (a) assets, liabilities and obligations the Debtor owes to third persons,
    (b) property given by the Debtor as security to creditors and the date given,

(c) property of other parties in the Debtor's possession,
(d) the Debtor's shareholdings in other companies or juristic persons,
(e) names, business and addrcsscs of all creditors,
(f) names, businesses and addresses of the Debtor's debtors,
(g) details of the property including paymens which the Debtor expects to receive in the future,
(h) all written consents for creditors to release to other creditors all information on the assets and liabilities of the Debtor (see also Principle 8).

6. The appointment of an independent accountant and other experts shall be carried out as requested by the creditors based on the agreed terms of reference. This should be done within 7 days of Stage 2.
7. Debtor submits all further information requested by creditors or independent accountant necessary to prepare plan (see also Principle 8). This should be done within 2 months of Stage 2, extendable up to a maximum of 1 month.
8. Plan submission by Creditors' Committee, Debtor and independent accountant to all creditors. This should be done within 3 months of Stage 2, extendable up to a maximum of 2 months.
9. Creditors' Meeting to discuss the plan. This is done 10 days after Stage 8.
10. Creditors propose amendments to the plan. This is done within 7 days of Stage 8.
11. If plan consideration is not completed, meeting will be adjourned to the next busines day.
12. New creditors meeting if request is approved to adjourn meeting to consider amendments to plan: Done 10 days after adjournment.
13. Decision on whether to privately reorganise, formally reorganise under the Bankruptcy Act or liquidate. This is done at creditors' meeting under Stage 9 or Stage 12 within 3 months from Stage 2.

PROGRESS OF CDRAC

On 13 October 1998, the CDRAC accepted 200 cases of debt workouts proposed by the member associations. These cases involved 353 companies with debts totaling 674 billion baht.

The Committee also closely monitored the progress on the amendments of the various tax and fee structures for the transfer of ownership of assets (underlying collateral) that would facilitate the process of debt restructuring.

Subsequently, the Joint Public-Private Sector Committee established debt restructuring forum at the provincial level to be chaired by provincial governors.

Separately, financial institutions creditors and debtors also negotiated simpler debt restructuring cases and reported the results to the authorities. At the end of October 1998, financial institutions had completed 660 cases of debt restructuring, totaling 36.6 billion baht (comprising of 9,707 million baht in the manufacturing sector, 3.4 billion baht in construction, 6.2 billion baht in real estate, 361 million baht in the exports sector, and 16.9 billion baht in other sectors). There were 2,390 other cases still in process of restructuring, totaling 569 billion baht.

Removing Tax Disincentives

The government facilitated corporate debt restructuring through tax and legal reforms. It removed tax disincentives by introducing temporary and permanent measures.

Temporary measures, expiring 31 December 1999 included the following:

— Deduct written-off debt from taxable income for the creditor.
— Eliminate or defer corporate income tax on written-off debt for the debtor.
— Eliminate all taxes on asset transfer from debtor to creditor (income tax, special business tax, stamp duties, and VAT).
— Eliminate taxes on accrued but unpaid interest, and the limitation of taxation on restructuring involving interest rate reductions by creditors.

The permanent measures were:

— Provision for tax-free mergers and non-cash acquisition of assets, in cases of 100% mergers.
— Elimination of income tax on short-selling transactions.
— Elimination of VAT and specific business tax on the transfer of assets to Special Purpose Vehicles (SPV).

Legal Amendment

Debt restructuring could only succeed if both debtors and creditors agreed to negotiate to find a solution. Thus, it was important to strengthen bankruptcy legislation and to reform judicial foreclosure proceedings. The following laws were amended:

- Bankruptcy Law: to facilitate corporate rehabilitation and debt restructuring
- Foreclosure proceedings (Code of Civil Procedures): to streamline court proceedings for settlement of claims.
- Foreclosure Law (Civil and Commercial Code): to increase the provision of secured credit.

SOCIAL SAFETY NET

Several social programs were also developed to minimise the impact of the crisis. They included job training and developing labour intensive projects.

The programs were supported by the World Bank, the ADB, and the Overseas Economic Cooperation Fund to provide two years of employment to those who became unemployed during the crisis. The programs also provided free medical treatment and improved rural health-care facilities.

The government also encouraged unemployed persons to become entrepreneurs through micro-credit programs and training program.

The reduction in incomes had caused the dropout rate in schools to increase. The government provided additional budget for the secondary education loan program to students whose families could no longer afford tuition payments. This program supplemented an existing grant program for primary education financed by the ADB. The school lunch program was expanded from 30% of all students to 35%.

The Social Investment Program (SIP) was aimed to help protect the unemployed, the underprivileged, and the poor from the emerging adverse social impacts. The SIP was a project loan from the World Bank and the OECF that financed 90% from loan disbursement and 10% from the national budget. Activities were also financed by UNDP and AusAid. The total cost of the SIP was about 22 billion baht. The program started in early 1999.

PRIVATISATION

As part of the market opening policy, the government began to privatise state enterprises to increase the role of the private sector in the economy.

Master Plan for State Enterprise Reform

The Master Plan for State Enterprise Reform which was approved by the Cabinet on 30 September 1998 set out the framework for privatisation of key sectors, principles of regulatory bodies, and sequencing of divestment. This plan served as the basic guideline for the reforms, and as a reference document for government agencies as well as the public sector.

The government also introduced a fast track schedule to sell shares of several state enterprises within 1999. The companies included Thai Airways International, Airport Authority of Thailand, ESSO (Thailand), and Ratchburi Power Plant.

In the energy sector, Petroleum Authority of Thailand (PTT) restructured its subsidiaries in preparation for privatisation in year 2000. PTT would become a national integrated oil and gas company after privatisation. PTT sold its stake in PTT Exploration and Production (Public) Co. Ltd. according to the Cabinet Resolution on 4 November 1997.

The Electricity Generating Authority of Thailand (EGAT) sold its stake in the Electricity Generating (Public) Co. Ltd. (EGCO).

Other state enterprises began to rationalise their organizational structure before implementing the privatisation program.

Public share offers for state enterprises were confined to those with corporate status. Therefore, there was a need to introduce a Corporatisation Law to transform the capital of state enterprises into shares, converting them into "Public Company Limited" under the Civil and Commercial Code.

The government would be the 100% shareholder to maintain rights and privileges of state enterprises in the early stage of transformation. The transformation process would not affect management structure and employee status.

The Cabinet approved the principle of Corporatisation Act on 2 June 1998. The 1954 Aviation Act was amended to permit Thai Airways International (Public) Co. Ltd. to sell its stake to domestic and foreign investors.

Foreign Ownership of Business Activities

On 18 August 1998, the Cabinet approved the amendment of the Alien Business Law to enhance competitiveness and to promote transparency with regard to increase liquidity in key sectors and to comply with international obligations.

The amendment had the following criteria:

- set up principle of freedom of business activities by foreigners except in those cases specifically restricted under two existing lists,
- further liberalise business activities, including brokerage services, wholesale and retail trade, construction, non-silk textile, garment, footwear, hotel, beverage production, auction business, etc.,
- reserve for Thai nationals (but open to foreign investment if approved by the Cabinet and Minister of Commerce) activities relating to:
  (1) national safety and security, culture, traditional folk handicraft, as well as national resources and environment; and
  (2) activities restricted because of specified and well justified strategic reasons.

Foreign Ownership of Real Estate

On 4 August 1998, the cabinet approved the amendments of Land Code and Condominium Act to eliminate restrictions on foreign ownership of property. The amendments were as follows:

- allow individual foreigners investing specified amounts in activities of productive interest for Thailand to own up to one rai (0.4 acre) of residential land,
- allow Thai citizens married to foreigners to own land,
- permit foreigners to purchase 100% of condominium buildings of 5 rai (2 acres) or less during the next five years,
- amend the lease provisions of the Civil and Commercial Code to provide personal right appretaining to real estate property instead of real right and the period of lease of selected real estate property has been limited to no less than 15 years but no more than 30 years, may be renewable for additional 30 years. The exact modalities will be defined in the law.

References

Financial Times (1995). *Banking in the Far East*, FT Financial Publishing, London.

Johnson, H. J. (1997). *Banking in Asia*, Lafferty Publications, Dublin.

KPMG (1991). *Banking and Finance in ASEAN*, KPMG, Singapore.

Kiriwat, Ekamol (1994), "Securities markets regulations and reforms in Thailand", in Faruqi, Shakil (ed.) *Financial Sector Reforms, Economic Growth and Stability: Experiences in Selected Asian and Latin American Countries*, World Bank, Washington, D.C., 139–44.

Vajragupta, Y. and Vichyanond, P. (1999), "Thailand's financial evolution and the 1997 crisis", in Masuyama, S., Vanderbrink, D. and Chia, S.Y. (eds.) *East Asia's Financial Systems: Evolution and Crisis*, Nomura Research Institute, Tokyo and Institute of Southeast Asian Studies, Singapore, 34–73.

Bank of Thailand website: www.bot.or.th

Corporate Debt Restructuring Advisory Committee: www.bot.or.th/fsupv/public/cdraco

HONG KONG

REFORMS IN THE 1980s

In Hong Kong, financial reforms were introduced in 1987. The main objectives were to strengthen the currency board arrangement and to maintain exchange rate stability.

1987: Removal of Interest Floor and Ceiling

The negative interest rate mechanism and the exemption of authorised institutions from the legal ceiling on lending rate of 60% in the Money Lenders Ordinance enabled interest rate to move in both directions without restriction to support the exchange rate of the Hong Kong dollar.

1988: Accounting Arrangement

In July 1988, under the Accounting Arrangement, the Hongkong & Shanghai Banking Corporation (HSBC, the Management Bank of the Clearing House of the Hong Kong Association of Banks) was required to maintain an account with the Exchange Fund, and to manage the net clearing balance of the other banks at a level not exceeding the balance in its account with the Exchange Fund, which was determined by the HKMA. After the Real Time Gross Settlement (RTGS) System was implemented in 1996, all banks in Hong Kong set up accounts directly with the HKMA. The HSBC ceased to be the Management Bank and the Accounting Arrangement was terminated.

REFORMS IN THE 1990s

1990: Exchange Fund Bills Program

This program was introduced in March 1990 to develop the local debt market. It increased the supply of Hong Kong dollar papers and set a benchmark yield curve for Hong Kong dollar debt. The program was expanded to Exchange Fund Notes in 1993.

1992: Liquidity Adjustment Facility (LAF)

The LAF was Hong Kong's version of a discount window. Banks could obtain liquidity assistance from the HKMA at the prescribed offer rate through a Sale and Repurchase Agreement involving eligible securities. They could also place excess liquidity with the HKMA through the LAF at the bid rate. The LAF was replaced by the Discount Window in September 1998.

1996: RTGS Interbank Payment System

With interbank transactions settled across the book of the HKMA, the Aggregate Balance was properly defined and was subject to the rule of currency board system.

1998: Publication of the Forecast Change in Aggregate Balance

The announcement of forecast change in Aggregate Balance enhanced the transparency of the linked exchange rate system and facilitated a more efficient and orderly interest rate adjustments in money market.

1998: Measures to Strengthen Currency Board System

Two major measures were the Convertibility Undertaking in respect of the Aggregate Balance and modifications to the Discount Window facility. These measures demonstrated a strong commitment to the linked exchange rate system and helped to dampen excessive and destabilising interest rate volatility.

RECENT REFORMS

(Source: Hong Kong Monetary Authority)
website: www.info.gov.hk/hkma dated 14 July 1999

Banking Sector Consultancy Study

The Banking Sector Consultancy Study was commissioned by the HKMA in March 1998 to evaluate the outlook of the banking sector over the next five years and to consider the effectiveness of its banking supervision. The findings were published in January 1999 for a three-month public consultation, which lasted until the end of March 1999.

Reform Package

After considering the views received during the public consultation period, on 14 July 1999, the HKMA announced a reform package for the banking sector and a time-table to implement these reforms. Two important features of this reform package are:

— deregulate the remaining interest rate rules
— enhance depositor protection in Hong Kong

Deregulate Interest Rate

Phase I of the deregulation will take place on 1 July 2000. Restrictions on the remaining regulated time deposits (i.e. those with a maturity of less than seven days) will be lifted. The interest rate rules on current and saving accounts will be deregulated in Phase II, or 12 months after Phase I.

Depositor Protection

On depositor protection, the HKMA received diverse views from market participants. In the first half of 2000, it plans to carry out a feasibility study on deposit insurance scheme or other forms of depositor protection in Hong Kong.

Other Measures

Other measures to strengthen the banking system include the following:

— improve disclosure framework for all authorised institutions
— develop a risk-based approach to banking supervision
— convert the current 3-tier to a 2-tier banking system
— relax one-branch policy for foreign banks
— allow restricted licensed banks to access the RTGS system.
— feasibility study on a credit register to provide information to lending institutions on the overall indebtedness of companies,
— promote better corporate governance among authorised institutions by strengthening their board of directors.

Relaxing the One-building Condition

In September 1999, the HKMA relaxed the one-building condition attached to the licences of foreign banks. Foreign banks are now allowed to maintain offices in a maximum of three separate buildings. This will allow foreign banks greater flexibility to locate their operations in a cost-effective way.

The restriction on the number of regional and back offices that foreign banks can maintain has also been lifted. The one-branch policy applied to overseas-incorporated banks authorised in and after 1978 and to overseas-incorporated restricted licence banks authorised in and after 1990.

RECENT DEVELOPMENT

Central Moneymarkets Unit Service

In 1990, the HKMA set up the Central Moneymarkets Unit (CMU) Service to provide computerised clearing and settlement facilities for Exchange Fund Bills and Notes.

The service was extended to other HK dollar debt securities in 1993 and to non-HK dollar debt securities in January 1996. The CMU is linked to international clearing systems such as Euroclear and Cedel. This link enables overseas investors to participate in Hong Kong dollar debt securities.

Since 1996, the CMU has been linked to the Real Time Gross Settlement (RTGS) interbank payment system to provide real-time and end-of-day Delivery Versus Payment (DVP) services to its members.

In December 1997, the CMU launched a Securities Lending Program for private sector securities to enhance their liquidity. It has also increased their attractiveness to investors by enhancing the yields for the lenders.

All debt instruments cleared through the CMU are either immobilised or dematerialised, and transfer of title is effected in computer book entry form. At the end of 1998, about 730 private debt issues, with a total nominal value of $224 billion were lodged with the CMU, an increase of 12.4% over 1997.

Bilateral Links

CMU is linked with several Central Securities Depositories (CSDs) in the Asia Pacific region to facilitate cross border trades in securities. These links help to reduce settlement risk by facilitating Delivery Versus Payment (DVP) settlement.

For example, in December 1997, the CMU linked up with the CSD in Australia. For this purpose, HKMA became a member of Reserve Bank Information and Transfer System (RITS) (for Australian government securities) and Austraclear (for private sector debt securities in Australia).

Similarly, in April 1998, the HKMA and the Reserve Bank New Zealand (RBNZ) set up a bilateral link between CMU and Austraclear New Zealand, a clearing system for both government and private sector debt issues operated by RBNZ.

In September 1999, CMU linked with the Korea Securities Depository (KSD) to provide clearing and settlement services for public and private debt securities in South Korea.

CMU has plans to link with the clearing system, Government Security Book-entry System (GSBS) in Mainland China.

DEVELOPING THE DEBT MARKET

Over the past decade, the HKMA has been actively promoting the debt market. Some of the measures introduced include the following:

- introduction of Exchange Fund Bills and Notes Program
- setting up a central clearing and custodian system for debt securities (Central Moneymarkets Unit or CMU) and linking it with Euroclear and Cedel and other central securities depositories
- implementing RTGS interbank payment system
- setting up Hong Kong Mortgage Corporation
- introducing the Securities Lending Program.

The Exchange Fund Bills and Notes Program was introduced in 1990. Over the years, the Program has expanded in size and tenor. The HKMA now issues 91-, 182- and 364-day bills, and 2-, 3-, 5-, 7- and 10-year notes. To facilitate the management of liquidity by the banks in the initial stage of the implementation of the RTGS, tap issues of 28-day bills have been issued since November 1996.

Secondary Market Liquidity

To stimulate secondary market liquidity, HKMA has appointed market makers to quote two-way prices for Exchange Fund papers. This arrangement has been extended to the notes of the Mass Transit Railway Corporation (MTRC), Airport Authority (AA), Kowloon-Canton Railway Corporation (KCRC) and the Hong Kong Mortgage Corporation (HKMC). As at December 1998, there were 28 market makers to promote liquidity in the secondary market.

There were also some changes in 1998 to the arrangements to provide liquidity to banks through using Exchange Fund paper and eligible securities as collateral in repos transactions with the HKMA. As part of the measures to strengthen the Currency Board arrangements, the HKMA tightened the provision of day-end liquidity through the Discount Window against debt securities not backed by foreign reserves. With effect from 7 September 1998, no new issues of paper other than Exchange Fund paper are now eligible for discounting under the Discount Window. Existing eligible issues will, however, continue to be accepted for Discount Window purposes until the paper matures.

Tax Exemption

To encourage the supply of Hong Kong dollar debt securities, profits tax exemption has been granted to income earned on Hong Kong dollar debt securities issued by 10 supranational organisations with top credit rating.

From May 1996, a concessionary tax rate equal to 50% of the profit tax rate has been granted to income earned on long-term Hong Kong dollar debt securities issued by corporations in Hong Kong which meet the rating and other requirements.

To fund its mortgage purchases, the HKMC set up a HK$20 billion Note Issuance Program (NIP) in January 1998 and a HK$20 billion

Debt Issuance Program (DIP) in June 1998. The NIP targets at financial institutions while the DIP targets at institutional investors. As at end-December 1998, the HKMC has issued HK$5.2 billion in unsecured debt under the two programs.

Mortgage-Based Securities

In 1999, HKMC launched a pilot scheme for mortgage-based securities (MBS). Under the scheme, HKMC purchased mortgages from banks and transferred the mortgage pool to a special purpose vehicle (SPV). The SPV issued MBS back to the banks with the HKMC as the guarantor for timely payment of principal and interest. The banks could then hold the MBS in their portfolio or sell to other investors.

Listing of EFNs on the SEHK

In August 1999, the CMU arranged for the SEHK Options Clearing House (SEOCH) and the HKFE Clearing Corporation to use Exchange Fund papers as common margin collateral for the trading in stock options and futures. A cross margining arrangement will reduce costs for the traders.

Both clearing houses will become Recognised Dealers of Exchange Fund papers and can settle these papers on behalf of their members. These members can then use Exchange Fund Bills and Notes as collateral in addition to cash. The adjustment of margin limits by SEOCH or HKCC can also be settled on a real time basis.

PART III

DIRECTORY OF FINANCIAL INSTITUTIONS IN SOUTHEAST ASIA AND HONG KONG

Brunei
Cambodia
Indonesia
Laos
Malaysia
Myanmar
Philippines
Singapore
Thailand
Vietnam
Hong Kong

BRUNEI DARUSSALAM

Local Bank

1. Islamic Bank of Brunei Berhad
   (formerly International Bank of Brunei Berhad)
   (formerly the Island Development Bank Berhad)

Foreign Banks

1. Citibank (USA)
2. Hongkong & Shanghai Banking Corp (Hong Kong)
3. Malayan Banking Berhad (Malaysia)
4. Overseas Union Bank (Singapore)
5. Standard Chartered Bank (UK)
6. United Malayan Banking Corp (Malaysia)

Finance Companies

1. Credit Corporation Berhad (Brunei)
2. IRB Finance Berhad (Brunei)
3. Mortgage and Finance Berhad (Brunei)

CAMBODIA

Central Bank

1. National Bank of Cambodia

State-owned Commercial Banks

1. Foreign Trade Bank
2. Municipal Bank

Commercial Banks

1. Agricultural & Commercial Bank of Cambodia
2. Bangkok Bank
3. Bank of National Wealth Cambodia
4. Banque Indonsuez
5. Cambodia Asia Bank
6. Cambodia Commercial Bank
7. Cambodia Development Bank
8. Cambodia Farmers Bank
9. Cambodia International Bank
10. Cambodia Mekong Bank
11. Cambodia Public Bank
12. Canada Bank
13. Chansavangwong Bank Corp
14. Emperor International Bank
15. First Overseas Bank
16. Global Commercial Bank
17. Great International Bank
18. Maybank
19. Krung Thai Bank
20. Pacific Commercial Bank
21. Phnom Penh City Bank
22. Royal Cambodia Bank
23. Siam City Bank
24. Singapore Banking Corp
25. Singapore Commercial Bank
26. Standard Chartered Bank
27. Thai Farmers Bank
28. Union Commercial Bank

State-owned Commercial Banks
(Name and Address)

1. **Foreign Trade Bank**
   24, Norodom Boulevard
   Phnom Penh, Cambodia
   Tel. (855) 232-5886

2. **Municipal Bank**
18, Ang Eng Street
Phnom Penh, Cambodia
Tel. (855) 232-5663

Commercial Banks
(Name and Address)

1. **Agricultural & Commercial Bank of Cambodia**
214 Samdach Pann Street
Phnom Penh, Cambodia
Tel. (855) 232-2272

2. **Bangkok Bank**
26, Norodom Boulevard
Phnom Penh, Cambodia
Tel. (855) 232-6593

3. **Bank of National Wealth Cambodia**
15, Street 214
Phnom Penh, Cambodia
Tel. (855) 018-81-0806

4. **Banque Indonsuez**
70, Norodom Boulevard
Phnom Penh, Cambodia
Tel. (855) 232-4772

5. **Cambodia Asia Bank**
252, Monivong Boulevard
Phnom Penh, Cambodia
Tel. (855) 232-6145

6. **Cambodia Commercial Bank**
26, Monivong Boulevard
Phnom Penh, Cambodia
Tel. (855) 232-6145

7. **Cambodia Development Bank**
6, Monivong Boulevard
Phnom Penh, Cambodia
Tel. (855) 232-6511

8. **Cambodia Farmers Bank**
4, Kampuchea Vietnam Road
Phnom Penh, Cambodia
Tel. (855) 232-2105

9. **Cambodia International Bank**
21, Road 12
Phnom Penh, Cambodia
Tel. (855) 232-7040

10. **Cambodia Mekong Bank**
1, Street Kramounsar
Phnom Penh, Cambodia
Tel. (855) 232-6525

11. **Cambodia Public Bank**
Street 114
Phnom Penh, Cambodia
Tel. (855) 232-6067

12. **Canada Bank**
63, Street 110
Phnom Penh, Cambodia
Tel. (855) 232-6046

13. **Chansavangwong Bank Corp**
145A, Street
Phnom Penh, Cambodia
Tel. (855) 232-7464

14. **Emperor International Bank**
9, Street 7 Khan Daun Penb
Phnom Penh,
Cambodia
Tel. (855) 232-6117

15. **First Overseas Bank**
36, Street 21
Phnom Penh, Cambodia
Tel. (855) 236-3888

16. **Global Commercial Bank**
337, Monivong Boulevard
Phnom Penh, Cambodia
Tel. (855) 236-4258

17. **Great International Bank**
25, Street 55
Phnom Penh, Cambodia
Tel. (855) 232-7087

18. **Maybank**
2, Norodom Boulevard
Phnom Penh, Cambodia
Tel. (855) 232-7590

19. **Krung Thai Bank**
149, Street 215
Phnom Penh, Cambodia
Tel. (855) 232-6587

20. **Pacific Commercial Bank**
350, Street 217
Phnom Penh, Cambodia
Tel. (855) 232-6888

21. **Phnom Penh City Bank**
20, Street 178
Phnom Penh, Cambodia
Tel. (855) 232-7354

22. **Royal Cambodia Bank**
94, Norodom Boulevard
Phnom Penh, Cambodia
Tel. (855) 232-6483

23. **Siam City Bank**
79, Kampuchea Vietnam Street
Phnom Penh, Cambodia
Tel. (855) 232-7199

24. **Singapore Banking Corp**
68, Street 214
Phnom Penh, Cambodia
Tel. (855) 232-7366

25. **Singapore Commercial Bank**
316, Monivong Boulevard
Phnom Penh, Cambodia
Tel. (855) 236-7471

26. **Standard Chartered Bank**
95, Sihannouk Boulevard
Phnom Penh, Cambodia
Tel. (855) 232-6685

27. **Thai Farmers Bank**
2, Street 118
Phnom Penh, Cambodia
Tel. (855) 232-4035

28. **Union Commercial Bank**
61, Street 130
Phnom Penh, Cambodia
Tel. (855) 232-7995

References

Brahm, L. J. (1992), *Banking and Finance in Indochina*, Woodhead — Faulkner, Hemel Hempstead, Hartfordshire.

Singapore Trade Development Board (1996), *Market Research Report — Cambodia*, Trade Development Board and Coopers & Lybrand, Singapore.

INDONESIA

State-owned Banks

1. Bank Indonesia (Central Bank)
2. Bank Bumi Daya
3. Bank Dagang Negara
4. Bank Ekspor Impor Indonesia
5. Bank Negara Indonesia 1946
6. Bank Pembangunan Indonesia (Bapindo)
7. Bank Rakyat Indonesia
8. Bank Tabungan Nasional

Foreign Banks

1. ABN-AMBRO Bank
2. American Express Bank
3. Bangkok Bank
4. Bank of America
5. Bank of Tokyo
6. Bank Perdania
7. Chase Manhattan Bank
8. Citibank
9. Deutsche Bank Asia
10. Hong Kong & Shanghai Bank
11. Standard Chartered Bank

Major Private National Banks

1. Bank Bali
2. Bank Buana Indonesia
3. Bank Bukopin
4. Bank Central Asia
5. Bank Dagang Nasional Indonesia
6. Bank Danamon
7. Bank Duta
8. Bank Indonesia Raya (Bank Bira)
9. Bank Indovest
10. Bank Internasional Indonesia
11. Bank Marshill Utama
12. Bank Niaga
13. Bank NISP
14. Bank Pacific
15. Bank Papan Sejahtera
16. Bank PDFCI
17. Bank Pikko
18. Bank Rama
19. Bank Surya
20. Bank Tiara Asia
21. Bank Umum Nasional
22. Ficorinvest Bank
23. Inter-Pacific Bank
24. Lippo Bank

25. Modern Bank
26. Overseas Express Bank
27. Pan Indonesia Bank (Panin)
28. Tamara Bank

State-owned Banks
(Name and Address)

1. **Bank Indonesia (Central Bank)**
   Jalan M. H. Thamrin 2
   Jakarta, Indonesia
   Tel. (021) 372408

2. **Bank Bumi Daya**
   Jalan Imam Bonjol 61
   Jakarta 10002, Indonesia
   Tel. (021) 333721

3. **Bank Dagang Negara**
   Jalan M. H. Thamrin 5
   Jakarta, Indonesia
   Tel. (021) 321707

4. **Bank Ekspor Impor Indonesia**
   Jalan Lapangan Setasiun 1
   Jakarta 11110, Indonesia
   Tel. (021) 42729

5. **Bank Negara Indonesia 1946**
   Jalan Jendral Sudirman
   Kavling 1
   Jakarta 10001, Indonesia
   Tel. (021) 570–1001

6. **Bank Pembangunan Indonesia (Bapindo)**
   Jalan R P Soerosa 2-4
   Jakarta, Indonesia
   Tel. (021) 321908

7. **Bank Rakyat Indonesia**
   Jalan Jendral Sudirman
   44-46
   Jakarta 10210, Indonesia
   Tel. (021) 570–3344

8. **Bank Tabungan Nasional**
   Jalan H R Rasuma Said
   Kavling C-17
   Jakarta Selatan, Indonesia
   Tel. (021) 578–1210

Foreign Banks
(Name and Address)

1. **ABN-AMBRO Bank**
   Jalan Ir. H. Juanda 23-24
   Jakarta 10001, Indonesia
   Tel. (021) 362309

2. **American Express Bank**
   Jalan H. R. Rasuna Said
   Kavling 3
   Jakarta, Indonesia
   Tel. (021) 521–6000

3. **Bangkok Bank**
   Jalan M. H. Thamrin 3
   Jakarta, Indonesia
   Tel. (021) 366008

4. **Bank of America**
   Jalan Medan Merdeka
   Selantan 17
   Jakarta 10011, Indonesia
   Tel. (021) 384–8031

5. **Bank of Tokyo**
   Jalan Jendral Sudirman
   Kavling 10-11
   Jakarta 10220, Indonesia
   Tel. (021) 570–6185

6. **Bank Perdania**
(no address available)

7. **Chase Manhattan Bank**
Jalan Jendral Sudirman
Kavling 21
Jakarta, Indonesia
Tel. (021) 578–2213

8. **Citibank**
Jalan Jendral Sudirman
Kavling 1
Jakarta 12930, Indonesia
Tel. (021) 578–2007

9. **Deutsche Bank Asia**
Jalan Imam Bonjol 80
Jakarta 10001, Indonesia
Tel. (021) 331092

10. **Hong Kong & Shanghai Bank**
Jalan Jendral Sudirman
Kavling 31
Jakarta 10001, Indonesia
Tel: (021) 571–0075

11. **Standard Chartered Bank**
Jalan M. H. Thamrin 53
Jakarta 10350, Indonesia
Tel. (021) 325008

Major Private National Banks
(Name and Address)

1. **Bank Bali**
Jalan Jendral Sudirman
Kav 27
Jakarta 12920, Indonesia
Tel. (021) 523–7914
Fax. (021) 250–0880
www.indoexchange.com/jsx/bali

2. **Bank Buana Indonesia**
Jalan Asemka 32-35
Jakarta, Indonesia
Tel. (021) 672901

3. **Bank Bukopin (Bank Umum Koperasi Indonesia)**
Gedung PT Bank Bukopin
Jalan M.T. Haryono Kav 50–51
Jakarta 12770 , Indonesia
Tel. (021) 798–9837
Fax. (021) 798–0625
ww.indoexchange.com.jsx/bukopin

4. **Bank Central Asia**
Jalan Jendral Sudirman
Kavling 22-23
Jakarta, Indonesia
Tel. (021) 671771

5. **Bank Dagang Nasional Indonesia**
Jalan Hayam Wuruk 8
Jakarta 10120, Indonesia
Tel. (021) 231–1221
Fax. (021) 380–5725
www.indoexchange.com/jsx/bdni

6. **Bank Danamon**
Jalan Kebon Sirih 15
Jakarta 10002, Indonesia
Tel. (021) 230–1926
Fax. (021) 231–0906
www.indoexchange.com/jsx/danamon

7. **Bank Duta**
Jalan Kebon Sirih 12
Jakarta 10110, Indonesia
Tel. (021) 380–0900
Fax. (021) 380–0901
www.indoexchange.com/jsx/duta

8. **Bank Indonesia Raya (Bank Bira)**
Wisma Metropolitan
Jalan Jendral Sudirman
Kav. 29-31
Jakarta 12920, Indonesia
Tel. (021) 251–2211
Fax. (021) 251–2208
www.indoexchange.com/jsx/bira

9. **Bank Indovest**
Gedung Asuransi Wahanaa Tata
Jalan H R Rasuna Said
Kav C-4
Jakarta 12920 Indonesia
Tel. (021) 526–2966
Fax. (021) 522–0448
www.indoexchange.com/jsx/indovest

10. **Bank Internasional Indonesia**
Jalan M. H. Thamrin
Kav 22
Jakarta 10350, Indonesia
Tel. (021) 230–0666
Fax. (021) 230–0777
www.indoexchange.com/jsx/bii

11. **Bank Marshill Utama**
Jalan Jendral Sudirman
Kav. 25
Jakarta 12920, Indonesia
Tel. (021) 522–1995
Fax. (021) 522–1985
www.indoexchange.com/jsx/masrshill

12. **Bank Niaga**
Jalan Jendral Sudirman 58
Jakarta 12190, Indonesia
Tel. (021) 250–5151
Fax. (021) 250–5205
www.indoexchange.com/jsx/niaga

13. **Bank NISP**
Jalan Gunung Sahari
No. 38,
Jakarta 10720, Indonesia
Tel. (021) 600–9037
Fax. (021) 649–2264
www.indoexchange.com/jsx/nisp

14. **Bank Pacific**
Jalan K H Samanhudi
17–19
Jakarta, Indonesia
Tel. (021) 376408

15. **Bank Papan Sejahtera**
Gedung Bank Papan Sejahtera
Jalan H R Rasuna Said
Kav C-1
Jakarta 12960, Indonesia
Tel. (021) 252–2919
Fax. (021) 252–2951
www.indoexchange.com/jsx/papan

16. **Bank PDFCI**
Private Development Finance Company
Gedung Bursa Efek Jakarta, Tower II
Jalan Jendral Sudirman Kav. 52-53
Jakarta 12190, Indonesia
Tel. (021) 515–1111
Fax. (021) 515–4572
www.indoexchange.com/jsx/pdfci

17. **Bank Pikko (formerly Bank Rahardja Makmur)**
Komplek Mangga Dua Plaza
Jalan Mangga Dua Raya
Jakarta 10730, Indonesia
Tel. (021) 612–0107
Fax. (021) 612–0114
www.indoexchange.com/jsx/pikko

18. **Bank Rama**
Jalan M. H. Thamrin 3
Jakarta 10110, Indonesia
Tel. (021) 231–3721
Fax. (021) 386–1203
www.indoexchange.com/jsx/rama

19. **Bank Surya**
Bank Surya Building
Jalan M. H. Thamrin Kav 9
Jakarta 10350, Indonesia
Tel. (021) 390–2540
Fax. (021) 390–2530
www.indoexchange.com/jsx/surya

20. **Bank Tiara Asia**
Jalan M T Haryono Kav 16
Jakarta 12810, Indonesia
Tel. (021) 831–0210
Fax. (021) 831–0250
www.indoexchange.com/jsx/tiara

21. **Bank Umum Nasional**
Gedung Bunas Center
Jalan Senen Raya 135
Jakarta 10410, Indonesia
Tel. (021) 231–2828
Fax. (021) 231–2929
www.indoexchange.com/jsx/bun

22. **Ficorinvest Bank**
Jalan H.R. Rasuna Said Kav. C-18
Jakarta 12940, Indonesia
Tel. (021) 829–8966
Fax. (021) 829–9321
www.indoexchange.com/jsx/ficorin

23. **Inter-Pacific Bank**
Wisma Metropolitan II
Jalan Jendral Sudirman Kav. 31
Jakarta 12920, Indonesia
Tel. (021) 571–1095
Fax. (021) 571–1084
www.indoexchange.com/jsx/interpac

24. **Lippo Bank**
Menara Asia
101 Diponegoro Boulevard
Lippo Karawaci 1200
Tengerang 15810, Indonesia

Tel. (021) 546–0301
Fax. (021) 546–0312
www.indoexchange.com/jsx/lippobank

25. **Modern Bank**
Plaza Permata Building
Jalan M. H. Thamrin No. 57
Jakarta 10350, Indonesia
Tel. (021) 390–3778
Fax. (021) 390–3286
www.indoexchange.com/jsx/modernbank

26. **Overseas Express Bank**
Jalan Pecenonga 84
Jakarta 10120, Indonesia
Tel. (021) 358103

27. **Pan Indonesia Bank (Panin)**
Panin Bank Centre
Jalan Jendral Sudirman, Senayan
Jakarta Pusat, Indonesia
Tel. (021) 270–0545
Fax. (021) 251–2578
www.indoexchange.com/jsx/paninbank

28. **Tamara Bank**
Jalan Asemka No. 31
Jakarta 11110, Indonesia
Tel. (021) 260–0091
Fax. (021) 260–0090
www.indoexchange.com/jsx/tamara

LAOS

Central Bank

1. Bank of the Lao DPR

Commercial Banks

1. Aloun Mai Bank
2. Foreign Commercial Bank of Lao DPR
3. Lane Xang Bank
4. Lao Mai Bank
5. Nakhoneluang Bank
6. Pak Thai Bank
7. Sethathilath Bank

Other Banks

1. Joint Development Bank (Lao-Thai JV)
2. Thai Military Bank (Rep Office)

MALAYSIA

(as of 31 July 1999)

Central Bank

1. Bank Negara Malaysia

Commercial Banks

1. ABN Amro Bank
2. Arab-Malaysian Bank
3. Ban Hin Lee Bank
4. Bangkok Bank
5. Bank Bumiputra Malaysia
6. Bank of America
7. Bank of Commerce
8. Bank of Nova Scotia
9. Bank of Tokyo-Mitsubishi
10. Bank Utama Malaysia
11. BSN Commercial Bank
12. Chase Manhattan Bank
13. Citibank
14. Deutsche Bank
15. EON Bank
16. Hock Hua Bank
17. Hong Leong Bank
18. HSBC Bank Malaysia
19. International Bank Malaysia
20. Malayan Banking
21. Multi-purpose Bank
22. Oriental Bank
23. OCBC Bank
24. Overseas Union Bank
25. Pacific Bank
26. Perwira Affin Bank
27. Phileo-Allied Bank
28. Public Bank
29. RHB Bank
30. Sabah Bank
31. Southern Bank
32. United Overseas Bank
33. Wah Tat Bank

Finance Companies

1. Advance Finance
2. Affin Finance
3. Amanah Finance Malaysia
4. Arab-Malaysia Finance
5. Asia Commercial Finance
6. BBMB Kewangan
7. BSN Finance
8. Bolton Finance
9. Cempaka Finance
10. City Finance
11. Credit Corporation Malaysia
12. Delta Finance
13. EON Finance
14. Hong Leong Finance
15. Interfinance

16. Kewangan Bersatu
17. Mayban Finance
18. MBf Finance
19. Oriental Finance
20. Perdana Finance
21. Perkasa Finance
22. Public Finance
23. Sabah Finance
24. Sime Finance
25. United Merchant Finance

Merchant Banks

1. Amanah Merchant Bank
2. Arab-Malaysian Merchant Bank
3. ASEAM Bankers Malaysia
4. BSN Merchant Bank
5. Bumiputra Merchant Bankers
6. Commerce International Bankers
7. Malaysian Int'l Merchant Bankers
8. Perwira Affin Merchant Bank
9. Perdana Merchant Bankers
10. RHB Sakura Merchant Bankers
11. Sime Merchant Bankers
12. Utama Merchant Bank

Commercial Banks
(Name and address)

1. **ABN Amro Bank Bhd**
Level 25, Tower 2,
MNI Twins
11, Jalan Pinang
Kuala Lumpur 50450
Malaysia
Tel: 262-7888
Fax: 262-5693

2. **Arab-Malaysian Bank Bhd**
Level 18, Menara Dion
Jalan Sultan Ismail
Kuala Lumpur 50250
Malaysia
Tel: 206-3939
Fax: 206-6855

3. **Ban Hin Lee Bank Bhd**
Menara BHL Bank
51 Jalan Sultan Ahmad Shah
Pulau Penang 10050
Malaysia
Tel: (04) 227-7882

4. **Bangkok Bank Bhd**
105, Jalan Tun H S Lee
Kuala Lumpur 50923
Malaysia
Tel: 232-4552
Fax: 238-8569

5. **Bank Bumiputra Malaysia Bhd**
Menara Bumiputra
Jalan Melaka
Kuala Lumpur 50913
Malaysia
Tel: 298-1011
Fax: 298-7135

6. **Bank of America Malaysia Bhd**
Wisma Goldhill
Jalan Raja Chuan
Kuala Lumpur 50200
Malaysia
Tel: 202-1133
Fax: 201-9087

7. **Bank of Commerce (M) Bhd**
   6, Jalan Tun Perak
   Kuala Lumpur 50050
   Malaysia
   Tel: 293-1722
   Fax: 298-6628

8. **Bank of Nova Scotia Bhd**
   Menara Bousted
   69 Jalan Raja Chulan
   Kuala Lumpur 50734
   Malaysia
   Tel: 241-0766
   Fax: 241-2160

9. **Bank of Tokyo-Mitsubishi (M) Bhd**
   1, Lebuh Ampang
   Kuala Lumpur 50931
   Malaysia
   Tel: 238-9100
   Fax: 232-1024

10. **Bank Utama (Malaysia) Bhd**
    363, Jalan Kulas
    Kuching 93740
    Malaysia
    Tel: (082) 41-9294
    Fax: (082) 42-4954

11. **BSN Commercial Bank (M) Bhd**
    Tingat 27, Putra Place
    100 Jalan Putra
    Kuala Lumpur 50350
    Malaysia
    Tel: 443-6466
    Fax: 441-3703

12. **Chase Manhattan Bank (M) Bhd**
    Aras 26, Menara Dion
    Jalan Sultan Ismail
    Kuala Lumpur 50250
    Malaysia
    Tel: 270-4111
    Fax: 270-4110

13. **Citibank Bhd**
    28 Medan Pasar
    Kuala Lumpur 50904
    Malaysia
    Tel: 232-8585
    Fax: 202-1101

14. **Deutsche Bank (M) Bhd**
    Level 18 Menara IMC
    8 Jalan Sultan Ismail
    Kuala Lumpur 50250
    Malaysia
    Tel: 202-1163
    Fax: 201-9822

15. **EON Bank Bhd**
    Wisma Cyclecarri
    288 Jalan Raja Laut
    Kuala Lumpur 50350
    Malaysia
    Tel: 294-1188
    Fax: 294-9588

16. **Hock Hua Bank Bhd**
    Wisma Hock Hua
    15 Jalan Pulau
    Sibu 96000
    Malaysia
    Tel: (084) 33-3888
    Fax: (084) 33-7888

17. **Hong Leong Bank Bhd**
Wisma Hong Leong
18 Jalan Perak
Kuala Lumpur 50450
Malaysia
Tel: 264-2828
Fax: 925-8623

18. **HSBC Bank Malaysia Bhd**
2, Leboh Ampang
Kuala Lumpur 50912
Malaysia
Tel: 230-0744
Fax: 232-1146

19. **International Bank Malaysia Bhd**
Wisma Uoa Damansara
50 Jalan Dungun
Kuala Lumpur 50490
Malaysia
Tel: 253-2699
Fax: 253-9266

20. **Malayan Banking Bhd**
Manara Maybank
100 Jalan Tun Perak
Kuala Lumpur 50936
Malaysia
Tel: 230-8833
Fax: 230-2611

21. **Multi-Purpose Bank Bhd**
Manara Multi-purpose
8 Jalan Munshi Abdullah
Kuala Lumpur 50100
Malaysia
Tel: 294-8800
Fax: 294-6727

22. **Oriental Bank Bhd**
Bangunan Oriental Bank
1 Jalan Hang Leku
Kuala Lumpur 50100
Malaysia
Tel: 202-4600
Fax: 202-4267

23. **OCBC Bank (M) Bhd**
Wisma Lee Rubber
Jalan Melaka
Kuala Lumpur 50100
Malaysia
Tel: 292-0344
Fax: 298-4363

24. **Overseas Union Bank (M) Bhd**
OUB Building
Lebuh Pasar Besar
Kuala Lumpur 50050
Malaysia
Tel: 230-5005
Fax: 230-9696

25. **Pacific Bank Bhd**
Wisma Genting
Jalan Sultan Ismail
Kuala Lumpur 50730
Malaysia
Tel: 261-4822
Fax: 264-3482

26. **Perwira Affin Bank Bhd**
Wisma SPK
Jalan Sultan Ismail
Kuala Lumpur 50250
Malaysia
Tel: 241-0000
Fax: 241-9922

27. **Philleo Allied Bank (M) Bhd**
Aras 22, Menara Phileo
189, Jalan Tun Razak
Kuala Lumpur 50400
Malaysia
Tel: 266-3388
Fax: 266-3500

28. **Public Bank Bhd**
Menara Public Bank
146, Jalan Ampang
Kuala Lumpur 50947
Malaysia
Tel: 263-8888
Fax: 232-0607

29. **RHB Bank Bhd**
Tower 2, RHB Centre
Jalan Tun Razak
Kuala Lumpur 50400
Malaysia
Tel: 987-8888
Fax: 987-9000

30. **Sabah Bank Bhd**
Wisma Tun Fuad Stephens
Jalan Tuaran
Kota Kinabalu 88100
Malaysia
Tel: (088) 21-8911
Fax: (088) 23-1184

31. **Southern Bank Bhd**
Wisma Genting
Jalan Sultan Ismail
Kuala Lumpur 50772
Malaysia
Tel: 263-7000
Fax: 232-5008

32. **United Overseas Bank (M) Bhd**
Menara UOB
P O Box 11212
Kuala Lumpur 50738
Malaysia
Tel: 292-4511
Fax: 294-0617

33. **Wah Tat Bank Bhd**
15 Jalan Bank
Sibu Sarawak 96007
Malaysia
Tel: (084) 33-6733
Fax: (084) 33-2803

Finance Companies in Malaysia
(Name and Address)

1. **Advance Finance Bhd**
Lot 180, Seksyen 12
KTLD Jalan Haji Taha
Kuching, Sarawak 93400
Malaysia
Tel (082) 23-3999
Fax (082) 23-9716

2. **Affin Finance Bhd**
Bangunan LTAT
Jalan Bukit Bintang
Kuala Lumpur 55100
Malaysia
Tel: 284-7766
Fax: 242-3448

3. **Amanah Finance Malaysia Bhd**
Bangunan Amanah Capital
82 Jalan Raja Chuan
Kuala Lumpur 50200
Malaysia
Tel: 261-4155
Fax: 261-7748

4. **Arab-Malaysia Finance Bhd**
Bangunan Arab-Malaysia
Peti Surat 12540
Kuala Lumpur 50450
Malaysia
Tel: 238-2100
Fax: 230-8108

5. **Asia Commercial Finance Bhd**
Suite 10-01 Menara Lion
165 Jalan Ampang
Kuala Lumpur 50450
Malaysia
Tel: 261-3033
Fax: 262-6878

6. **BBMB Kewangan Bhd**
Menara Promet
Jalan Sultan Ismail
Kuala Lumpur 50250
Malaysia
Tel: 242-6111
Fax: 248-2184

7. **BSN Finance Bhd**
Central Plaza
34 Jalan Sultan Ismail
Kuala Lumpur 50800
Malaysia
Tel: 243-2288
Fax: 245-9311

8. **Bolton Finance Bhd**
Kompleks Cambell
98 Jalan Dand Wangi
Kuala Lumpur 50100
Malaysia
Tel: 291-8989
Fax: 298-3877

9. **Cempaka Finance Bhd**
Wisma TAS
21 Jalan Melaka
Kuala Lumpur 50100
Malaysia
Tel: 230-1304
Fax: 230-6210

10. **City Finance Bhd**
UOA Centre
19 Jalan Pinang
Kuala Lumpur 50450
Malaysia
Tel: 264-6470
Fax: 264-6458

11. **Credit Corp Malaysia Bhd**
Menara Bank Pembangunan
Jalan Sultan Ismail
Kuala Lumpur 50919
Malaysia
Tel: 291-6688
Fax: 292-9260

12. **Delta Finance Bhd**
85 Jalan Kampong Nyabor
Sibu Sarawak 96007
Malaysia
Tel: (084) 33-3079
Fax: (084) 31-6312

13. **EON Finance Bhd**
Wisma Cyclecarri
288 Jalan Raja Laut
Kuala Lumpur 50350
Malaysia
Tel: 294-8888
Fax: 298-8618

14. **Hong Leong Finance Bhd**
Wisma Hong Leong
18 Jalan Perak
Kuala Lumpur 50450
Malaysia
Tel: 264-3939
Fax: 264-2814

15. **Interfinance Bhd**
Bangunan Satok
Jalan Satok
Kuching Sarawak 93400
Malaysia
Tel: (082) 25-1323
Fax: (082) 41-5340

16. **Kewangan Bersatu Bhd**
Wisma MCIS
Jalan Barat
Petaling Jaya 467200
Malaysia
Tel: 755-8477
Fax: 756-5445

17. **Mayban Finance Bhd**
1 Medan Tuaku Satu
Kuala Lumpur 50300
Malaysia
Tel: 293-1255
Fax: 291-7620

18. **MBf Finance Bhd**
Plaza MBf
8 Jalan Yap Kwan Seng
Kuala Lumpur 50450
Malaysia
Tel: 261-1177
Fax: 262-4780

19. **Oriental Finance Bhd**
Menara Olympia
8 Jalan Yap Kwan Seng
Kuala Lumpur 50450
Malaysia
Tel: 261-1177
Fax: 262-4780

20. **Perdana Finance Bhd**
44 Jalan Telawi
Bangsar Baru
Kuala Lumpur 59100
Malaysia
Tel: 283-2988
Fax: 283-2925

21. **Perkasa Finance Bhd**
Bangunan Safuan
7 Jalan Raja Abdullah
Kuala Lumpur 50300
Malaysia
Tel: 292-8033
Fax: 298-3394

22. **Public Finance Bhd**
Bangunan Public Bank
6 Jalan Sultan Sulaiman
Kuala Lumpur 50000
Malaysia
Tel: 274-1788
Fax: 230-4266

23. **Sabah Finance Bhd**
84 Jalan Gaya
Kota Kinabalu, 88838
Sabah, Malaysia
Tel: (088) 21-6663
Fax: (088) 21-5761

24. **Sime Finance Bhd**
42 Jalan Tun Perak
Kuala Lumpur 50050
Malaysia
Tel: 238-0077
Fax: 232-4207

25. **United Merchant Finance Bhd**
20 Mui Plaza
Jalan P Ramlee
Kuala Lumpur 50250
Malaysia
Tel: 241-1155
Fax: 248-0607

Merchant Banks
(Name and Address)

1. **Amanah Merchant Bank Bhd**
Bangunan Amanah Capital
82 Jalan Raja Chulan
Kuala Lumpur 50200
Malaysia
Tel: 261-0155
Fax: 261-5770

2. **Arab-Malaysian Merchant Bank Bhd**
Bangunan Arab-Malaysia
55 Jalan Raja Chulan
Kuala Lumpur 50200
Malaysia
Tel: 238-2633
Fax: 238-2644

3. **ASEAM Bankers Malaysia Bhd**
Menara Maybank
100 Jalan Tun Perak
Kuala Lumpur 50050
Malaysia
Tel: 238-4211
Fax: 238-4194

4. **BSN Merchant Bank Bhd**
Wisma Genting
Jalan Sultan Ismail
Kuala Lumpur 50744
Malaysia
Tel: 201-7011
Fax: 201-8022

5. **Bumiputra Merchant Bankers Bhd**
Menara Aetna Universal
84 Jalan Raja Chulan
Kuala Lumpur 50200
Malaysia
Tel: 261-5266
Fax: 261-5051

6. **Commerce International Bankers Bhd**
Commerce Square
Jalan Samantan
Kuala Lumpur 50490
Malaysia
Tel: 253-6688
Fax: 253-5522

7. **Malaysian International** Merchant Bankers Bhd
Bangunan MIDF
195A Jalan Tun Razak
Kuala Lumpur 50400
Malaysia
Tel: 261-1200
Fax: 264-7593

8. **Perwira Affin Merchant Bank Bhd**
Menara Bousted
69 Jalan Raja Chulan
Kuala Lumpur 50744
Malaysia
Tel: 242-3700
Fax: 241-7701

9. **Perdana Merchant Bankers Bhd**
Wisma Genting
Jalan Sultan Ismail
Kuala Lumpur 50250
Malaysia
Tel: 232-4188
Fax: 232-2964

10. **RHB Sakura Merchant Bankers Bhd**
Tower 3, RHB Centre
426 Jalan Tun Razak
Kuala Lumpur 50400
Malaysia
Tel: 937-3888
Fax: 987-8000

11. **Sime Merchant Bankers Bhd**
Bangunan Sime Bank
Jalan Sultan Sulaiman
Kuala Lumpur 50000
Malaysia
Tel: 201-2022

12. **Utama Merchant Bank Bhd**
Plaza Central
Jalan Sultan Ismail
Kuala Lumpur 50250
Malaysia
Tel: 243-8888
Fax: 243-0304

References

Bank Negara Malaysia
www.bnm.gov.my/fin_sys

MYANMAR

State-owned Banks

1. Central Bank of Myanmar
2. Myanma Agricultural and Rural Development Bank
3. Myanma Economic Bank
4. Myanma Foreign Trade Bank
5. Myanma Investment and Commercial Bank

State-owned Insurance Company

1. Myanma Insurance

Domestic Private Banks

1. Asia Wealth Bank
2. Asian Yangon International Bank
3. First Private Bank
4. Cooperative Bank
5. Kanbawza Bank (Taunggyi)
6. Myanmar Citizens Bank
7. Myanmar May Flower Bank
8. Myanmar Oriental Bank
9. Myanmar Universal Bank
10. Myawaddy Bank
11. Prime Commercial Bank
12. Tun Foundation Bank
13. Yadanabon Bank (Mandalay)
14. Yangon City Bank
15. Yoma Bank

Foreign Banks

1. ABN-AMRO Bank (Netherlands)
2. Arab Bangladesh Bank (Bangladesh)
3. Bangkok Bank (Thailand)
4. Bank of Ayudhya (Thailand)
5. Bank of Commerce (Malaysia)
6. Bank of Tokyo (Japan)
7. Banque Francaise du Commerce Exterieur (France)
8. Banque Indosuez (France)
9. Banque Nationale de Paris (France)
10. DBS Bank (Singapore)

11. Global Commercial Bank (Cambodia)
12. Hongkong and Shanghai Bank (Hong Kong)
13. Keppel Tat Lee Bank (Singapore)
14. Krung Thai Bank (Thailand)
15. Malayan Banking (Malaysia)
16. Overseas Chinese Banking Corp (Singapore)
17. Overseas Union Bank (Singapore)
18. Panin Bank (Indonesia)
19. Public Bank (Malaysia)
20. Siam City Bank (Thailand)
21. Societe Generale (France)
22. Standard Chartered Bank (UK)
23. Thai Farmers Bank (Thailand)
24. Thai Military Bank (Thailand)
25. United Overseas Bank (Singapore)

State-owned Banks
(Name and address)

1. **Central Bank of Myanmar**
   24/26, Sule Pagoda Road
   P.O Box 184,
   Yangon, Myanmar
   Tel: 83665

2. **Myanma Agricultural & Rural Development Bank**
   1/7, Latha Street
   Yangon, Myanmar
   Tel: 83653

3. **Myanma Economic Bank**
   564, Merchant Street
   Yangon, Myanmar
   Tel: 83610

4. **Myanma Foreign Trade Bank**
   80/86, Maha Bandoola
   Garden Street
   P.O. Box 203
   Yangon, Myanmar
   Tel: 83622

5. **Myanma Investment and Commercial Bank**
   526/532, Kon The Lan
   P.O. Box 442
   Yangon, Myanmar
   Tel: 83659

State-owned Insurance Company
(Name and address)

1. **Myanma Insurance**
   163/167, Pansodan Street,
   P.O. Box 204
   Yangon, Myanmar
   Tel: 83656

State-Owned Economic Enterprises

Ministry of Agriculture

— Myanma Agriculture Service
— Myanma Farms Enterprise

Ministry of Forests

— Myanma Timber Enterprise

Ministry of Livestock Breeding and Fisheries

— Livestock, Feedstuff and Milk Products Enterprise
— Myanma Fisheries Enterprise

Ministry of Mines

— No. 1 Mining Enterprise
— No. 2 Mining Enterprise
— No. 3 Mining Enterprise
— Myanma Gems Enterprise
— Myanma Pearl Enterprise
— Myanma Salt and Marine Chemical Enterprise

Ministry of Industry

— Myanma Ceramic Industries
— Myanma Foodstuff Industries
— Myanma Jute Industries
— Myanma General and Maintenance Industries
— Myanma Paper and Chemical Industries
— Myanma Pharmaceutical Industries
— Myanma Textile Industries
— Myanma Heavy Industries

Ministry of Energy

— Myanma Electric Power Enterprise
— Myanma Oil and Gas Enterprise
— Myanma Petrochemical Enterprise
— Myanma Petroleum Products Enterprise

Ministry of Construction

— Public Works

Ministry of Transport

— Inland Water Transport
— Myanma Airways
— Myanma Five Star Line
— Myanma Port Authority
— Myanma Shipyards
— Road Transport

Ministry of Communications, Posts & Telegraphs

— Myanma Posts and Telecommunications

Ministry of Rail Transportation

— Myanma Railways

Ministry of Information

— Motion Picture Enterprise
— News and Periodicals Enterprise
— Printing and Publishing Enterprise

Ministry of Finance and Revenue

— Central Bank of Myanmar
— Myanma Agricultural and Rural Development Bank
— Myanma Economic Bank
— Myanma Foreign Trade Bank
— Myanma Insurance

- Myanma Investment and Commercial Bank

Ministry of Trade

- Construction and Electrical Stores Trading
- General Merchandise Trading
- Inspection and Agency Services
- Myanma Agricultural Produce Trading
- Myanma Department Stores
- Myanma Export and Import Services
- Medicines and Medical Equipment Trading
- Stationery Printing and Photographic Stores
- Vehicles, Machinery and Equipment Trading
- Companies Registration Office

Ministry of Hotels and Tourism

- Myanma Hotels and Tourism Services
- Restaurant and Beverage Enterprise

List of Chambers of Commerce

- The Union of Myanmar Chamber of Commerce and Industry
- The Myanmar Rice Millers Association
- Union of Myanmar Aquatic Trade Technicians Association
- Union of Myanmar Muse/Namkhan Border Trade
- Myanmar Printers and Publishers Association
- Mandalay Chamber of Commerce and Industry
- Sagaing Division Chamber of Commerce and Industry
- Mon State Chamber of Commerce and Industry
- Kayin State Chamber of Commerce and Industry
- Union of Myanmar Myawaddy Border Trade Chamber of Commerce
- Rakhine State Chamber of Commerce and Industry
- Union of Myanmar Bu Thi Taung — Maung Daw Border Trade Chamber of Commerce and Industry
- Magwe Division Chamber of Commerce and Industry
- Union of Myanmar Myeik/Kawthaung Border Trade Chamber of Commerce
- Union of Myanmar Tachileik Border Trade Chamber of Commerce
- Bago Division Chamber of Commerce and Industry
- Northern Shan State Chamber of Commerce and Industry
- Ayeyarwady Division Chamber of Commerce and Industry
- Southern Shan State Chamber of Commerce and Industry
- Kachin State Chamber of

Commerce and Industry
- Tanintharyi Division Chamber of Commerce and Industry
- Union of Myanmar Konlon Hawpan Chin Shwe Haw Border Trade Chamber of Commerce
- Union of Myanma Kalay / Tamu Border Trade Chamber of Commerce
- Kayah State Chamber of Commerce and Industry
- Chin State Chamber of Commerce & Industry
- Myanma Pulses Beans and Sesamum Traders
- Yangon Division Chamber of Commerce & Industry

References

Myat Kyaw (1996), "Myanmar's Banking and Financial System" in Tan, T.M., Low, A.M., Williams, J. and Plumnin, I. P. (eds) *Business Opportunities in Myanmar*, Prentice Hall, Singapore, 195-204.

Foo, T. W., Goh, Y. H., Tan, A. T., and Tham, Y. H. (1996), "Banking and Finance in Myanmar" in Tan, T.M., Low, A.M., Williams, J. and Plumnin, I. P. (eds) *Business Opportunities in Myanmar*, Prentice Hall, Singapore, 195-204.

Website:
www.myanmar.com.gov

PHILIPPINES

Central Bank

1. Bangko Sentral ng Pilipinas

Commercial Banks

1. Allied Banking Corporation
2. Asia Trust Development Bank
3. Asian Bank Corporation
4. Banco de Oro Commercial Bank
5. Bank of Commerce
6. Bank of the Philippine Islands
7. China Banking Corporation
8. Citytrust Banking Corporation
9. East-West Banking Corporation
10. Equitable Banking Corporation
11. Far East Bank & Trust
12. First Philippine International Bank
13. Metropolitan Bank & Trust
14. PDCP Development Bank
15. Philippine Bank of Communications
16. Philippine Banking Corporation
17. Philippine Commercial International Bank
18. Philippine National Bank
19. Philippine Savings Bank
20. Philippine Trust
21. Philippine Veterans Bank
22. Pilipinas Bank
23. Planters Development Bank
24. PNB Republic Bank
25. Prudential Bank & Trust
26. Rizal Commercial Banking Corporation
27. Security Bank and Trust
28. Security Bank Corporation
29. Solidbank Corporation
30. Traders Royal Bank
31. Union Bank of the Philippines
32. United Coconut Planters Bank
33. Urban Bank
34. Westmont Bank

Specialised Government Development Banks

1. Development Bank of the Philippines
2. Land Bank of the Philippines
3. Philippine Amanah Bank

Foreign Banks

1. ANZ Banking Group
2. Bangkok Bank
3. Bank of America
4. Bank of Tokyo-Mitsubishi
5. Chemical Bank
6. Citibank
7. Deutsche Bank
8. Development Bank of Singapore
9. Fuji Bank
10. Hongkong & Shanghai Banking Corp
11. ING Bank
12. International Commercial Bank of China
13. Korea Exchange Bank
14. Standard Chartered Bank

Offshore Banking Unit

1. American Express Bank
2. Bank of California
3. Bank of Credit & Commercial International
4. Bank of Nova Scotia
5. Bankers Trust
6. Banque Indosuez
7. Banque Nationale de Paris
8. Barclays Bank
9. Chase Manhattan Bank
10. Credit Lyonnais
11. First Interstate Bank of California
12. First National Bank of Boston
13. First National Bank of Chicago
14. International Bank of Singapore
15. Manufacturers Hanover Trust
16. Security Pacific Bank
17. Societe Generale

Commercial Banks
(Name and Address)

1. **Allied Banking Corporation**
Allied Bank Center
6754 Ayala Avenue
Makati, Philippines
Tel. 816–3311
Fax. 816–1669

2. **Asia Trust Development Bank**
Quezon Avenue
Quezon City, Philippines
Tel. 922–9018
Fax. 922–2121

3. **Asian Bank Corporation**
Asian Plaza
Sen. Gil. Puyat Avenue
Corner Tordesillas Street
Makati, Philippines
Tel. 819–0611

4. **Banco de Oro Commercial Bank**
12 ADB Avenue
Ortigas Center
Mandaluyong City, Philippines
Tel. 636–0513

5. **Bank of Commerce**
Bankers Center Building
6764 Ayala Avenue
Makati, Philippines
Tel. 817–4906

6. **Bank of the Philippine Islands**
BPI Building
6765 Ayala Avenue
Makati, Philippines
Tel. 813–5561
Fax. 818–8801
www.bpi.com.ph

7. **China Banking Corporation**
China Bank Building
Paseo de Roxas, corner Villar Streets
Makati, Philippines
Tel. 817–7981
Fax. 892–0232

8. **Citytrust Banking Corporation**
Citytrust Bank Building
379 Sen. Gil. J. Puyat Avenue
Makati, Philippines
Tel. 818–0411

9. **East–West Banking Corporation**
349 Sen. Gil. Puyat Avenue
Makati, Philippines
Tel. 892–2050

10. **Equitable Banking Corporation**
262 Juan Luna Street, Binondo
Manila, Philippines
Tel. 242–7101
Fax. 241–5984

11. **Far East Bank & Trust**
Far East Bank Building
Sen. Gil. Puyat Avenue
Makati, Philippines
Tel. 845–9888
Fax. 891–5216
www.febtc.com.ph

12. **First Philippine International Bank**
8737 Paseo de Roxas
Makati, Philippines
Tel. 815–8536

13. **Metropolitan Bank & Trust**
Metrobank Plaza Building
Sen. Gil. Puyat Avenue
Makati, Philippines
Tel. 810–3311
Fax. 817–6248
www.sequel.net/metrobank

14. **PDCP Development Bank**
PDCP Development Bank Building
8737 Paseo de Roxas
Makati, Philippines
Tel. 815–8536
Fax. 819–5376

15. **Philippine Bank of Communications**
214 Juan Luna Street,
Binondo
Manila, Philippines
Tel. 242–8701
Fax. 242–1868

16. **Philippine Banking Corporation**
Philbanking Building
6797 Ayala Avenue
Makati, Philippines
Tel. 817–0901
Fax. 817–0892

17. **Philippine Commercial International Bank**
PCI Bank Towers,
Makati Avenue
Corner H. V. de la Costa Street
Makati, Philippines
Tel. 840–7000
Fax. 817–6984
www.pcib.com.ph

18. **Philippine National Bank**
PNB Financial Center
Roxas Boulevard
Manila, Philippines
Tel. 891–6021
Fax. 833–1241
www.philnabank.com.ph

19. **Philippine Savings Bank**
PS Bank Tower,
Sen. Gil. Puyat Avenue
corner Tindalo Street
Makati, Philippines
Tel. 813–1468
Fax. 810–1568

20. **Philippine Trust Company**
Philtrust Building
1000 United Nations Avenue
Corner San Marcellino Street
Manila, Philippines
Tel. 524–9061
Fax. 521–7309

21. **Philippine Veterans Bank**
PVB Building
101 dela Rosa Street
Makati, Philippines
Tel. 813–5311

22. **Pilipinas Bank**
ACT Tower
135 Sen. Gil. Puyat Avenue
Makati, Philippines
Tel. 819–1931

23. **Planters Development Bank**
314 Buendia Avenue Extension
Makati, Philippines
Tel. 812–9221

24. **PNB Republic Bank**
Legaspi Towers 300
Roxas Boulevard
Corner Vito Cruz Street
Manila, Philippines
Tel. 57-38-51

25. **Prudential Bank & Trust**
Prudential Bank Building
Ayala Avenue
Makati, Philippines
Tel. 817–8981
Fax. 817–5146
ww.prudentialbank.com.ph

26. **Rizal Commercial Banking Corporation**
RCBC Building
333 Sen. Gil. Puyat Avenue
Makati, Philippines
Tel. (632) 894–9000
Fax. (632) 894–9958
www.rcbc.com.ph

27. **Security Bank and Trust**
SBTC Building
6778 Ayala Avenue
Makati, Philippines
Tel. 818–7677

28. **Security Bank Corporation**
Security Bank Building
6776 Ayala Avenue
Makati, Philippines
Tel. 867–6788
Fax. 813–2069

29. **Solidbank Corporation**
Solidbank Building
777 Paseo de Roxas
corner Sedeno Street
Makati, Philippines
Tel. 894–8888
Fax. 813–3962
www. solidbank.com.ph

30. **Traders Royal Bank**
TRB Tower
Roxas Boulevard
Pasay City, Philippines
Tel: 831–2821

31. **Union Bank of the Philippines**
Sarmiento Building
Ayala Avenue,
Corner Herrera Street
Makati, Philippines
Tel. 811–3566
Fax. 893–8593

32. **United Coconut Planters Bank**
UCPB Building
Makati Avenue
Makati, Philippines
Tel. 818–8361

33. **Urban Bank**
Urban Bank Center,
Urban Avenue
corner Sen. Gil. Puyat Avenue
Makati, Philippines
Tel. 843–0831
Fax. 816–4668
ww.urbanvirtualbank.com.ph

34. **Westmont Bank**
411 Quintin Paredes Street
Binondo
Manila, Philippines
Tel. 243–0951

References

KPMG (1991) Banking and Finance in ASEAN.
FT Financial Publishing (1995), Banking in the Far East.

SINGAPORE

Local Banks
(All local banks are full licence banks)

1. Bank of Singapore
2. Chung Khiaw Bank
3. Development Bank of Singapore
4. Far Eastern Bank
5. Industrial & Commercial Bank
6. Keppel TatLee Bank
7. Oversea-Chinese Banking Corp
8. Overseas Union Bank
9 United Overseas Bank

Foreign Banks
(Full Licence)

1. ABN AMRO Bank
2. Ban Hin Lee Bank
3. Bangkok Bank
4. Bank Negara Indonesia
5. Bank of America
6. Bank of China
7. Bank of East Asia
8. Bank of India
9. Bank of Tokyo-Mitsubishi
10. Chase Manhattan Bank
11. Citibank
12. Credit Agricole Indosuez
13. HL Bank
14. Hongkong and Shanghai Banking Corporation
15. Indian Bank
16. Indian Overseas Bank
17. Kwangtung Provincial Bank
18. Malayan Banking Berhad
19. Sakura Bank
20. Sime Bank Berhad
21. Standard Chartered Bank
22. UCO Bank

Foreign Banks
(Restricted Licence)

1. American Express Bank
2. Banca Commerciale Italiana
3. Banque Nationale de Paris
4. Bayerische Landesbank Girozentrale
5. Chiao Tung Bank
6. Credit Suisse First Boston
7. Deutsche Bank
8. Dresdner Bank

9. First Commercial Bank
10. Habib Bank
11. Korea Exchange Bank
12. Moscow Narodny Bank
13. Sumitomo Bank

Foreign Banks
(Offshore Licence)

1. ABSA Bank
2. Agricultural Bank of China
3. Allied Irish Banks
4. Arab Bank
5. Arab Banking Corporation
6. Asahi Bank
7. Australia & New Zealand Banking Group
8. Banca Di Roma, Societa' Per Azioni
9. Banca Monte Dei Paschi Disiena
10. Banca Nazionale Del Lavoro
11. Banco Do Brasil
12. Banco Santander
13. Bank Austria AG
14. Bank Austria Creditanstalt International
15. Bank Brussels Lambert
16. Bank Bumiputra Malaysia
17. Bank Ekspor Impor Indonesia
18. Bank of Communications
19. Bank of Hawaii
20. Bank of Montreal
21. Bank of New York
22. Bank of New Zealand
23. Bank of Nova Scotia
24. Bank of Taiwan
25. Bank of Yokohama
26. Bankboston
27. Bankers Trust
28. Banque Internationale A Luxembourg
29. Banque Worms
30. Barclays Bank
31. Bayerische Vereinsbank
32. BHF-Bank AG
33. Canadian Imperial Bank of Commerce
34. Cariplo-Cassa Di Risparmio Delle Provincie Lombarde
35. Chang Hwa Commercial Bank
36. China Construction Bank
37. Cho Hung Bank
38. Christiania Bank
39. Commercial Bank of Korea
40. Commerzbank
41. Commonwealth Bank of Australia
42. Compagnie Financiere De CIC Et De L'Union Europeenne
43. Credit Lyonnais
44. Credit Suisse
45. Creditanstalt
46. Credito Italiano
47. Dai-ichi Kangyo Bank
48. Daiwa Bank
49. Den Danske Bank
50. Den Norske Bank
51. First National Bank of Chicago
52. Fuji Bank
53. Hang Seng Bank
54. Hanil Bank
55. Hua Nan Commercial Bank
56. Industrial & Commercial Bank of China
57. Industrial Bank of Japan
58. ING Bank

59. International Commercial Bank of China
60. Istituto Bancario San Paolo De Torino
61. KBC Bank
62. Korea Development Bank
63. Korea First Bank
64. Korea Long Term Credit Bank
65. Krung Thai Bank
66. Llyods Bank
67. Long Term Credit Bank of Japan
68. Meespierson
69. Merita Bank
70. Mitsubishi Trust & Banking Corporation
71. Mitsui Trust & Banking Co.
72. Morgan Guaranty Trust Company of New York
73. Natexis Banque
74. National Australia Bank
75. National Bank of Kuwait
76. National Westminster Bank
77. Nationsbank
78. Norddeutsche Landsbank Girozentrale
79. Norinchukin Bank
80. Northern Trust Company
81. Paribas
82. Philippine National Bank
83. Rabobank
84. Raiffeisen Zentralbank Osterreich
85. Republic National Bank of New York
86. Royal Bank of Canada
87. Royal Bank of Scotland
88. Sanwa Bank
89. SGZ-Bank Sudwestdeutsche Genossenschafts-Zentralbank
90. Siam Commercial Bank
91. Skandinaviska Enskilda Banken
92. Societe Generale
93. State Bank of India
94. Sudwestdeutsche-Landesbank Girozentrale
95. Sumitomo Trust & Banking Co.
96. Svenska Handelsbanken
97. Thai Farmers Bank
98. Tokai Bank
99. Toronto Dominion Bank
100. Toyo Trust & Banking Co
101. UBS
102. Unibank of Denmark
103. Union De Banques Arabes Et Francaises
104. Westdeutsche Landesbank Girozentrale
105. Westpac Banking Corporation

Merchant Banks

1. ABN AMRO Asia Merchant Bank
2. AFC Merchant Bank
3. Allied Irish Merchant Bank
4. ANZ Singapore
5. Asian-American Merchant Bank
6. Asian Finance & Investment Corp
7. Bank Austria Creditanstalt
8. Bank Brussels Lambert
9. Bank of Montreal Asia
10. Bank of Nova Scotia Asia
11. Bankamerica Singapore
12. Bankers Trust International
13. Banque Internationale A Luxembourg Bil

14. Barclays Private Bank Asia
15. BNP Prime Peregrine
16. CBA Asia
17. CEF Singapore
18. Chase Manhattan (SEA)
19. CIBC Asia
20. Citicorp Investment Bank
21. Commerzbank (SEA)
22. Coutts Bank (Schweiz)
23. Credit Agricole Indosuez Merchant Bank
24. Credit Lyonnais Merchant Bankers
25. Credit Suisse First Boston
26. Daiwa Merchant Bank
27. Daiwa Singapore
28. De Nationale Investeringsbank Asia
29. Deutsche Capital Singapore
30. DKB Merchant Bank
31. DNB Asia
32. Dresdner (SEA)
33. Fuji International Finance
34. HSBC Investment Bank
35. IBJ Merchant Bank
36. Ichiyoshi Merchant Bank
37. ING Merchant Bank
38. KDB International
39. Kexin International
40. Kookmin Bank
41. Kredietbank
42. Klyods Merchant Bank
43. LTCB Merchant Bank
44. Meespierson Asia
45. Meritanordbanken Merchant Bank
46. Merrill Lynch International Bank
47. N M Rothschild & Sons
48. National Australia Merchant Bank
49. National Bank of Canada
50. NDC Merchant Bank
51. Nedship Merchant Bank
52. New Japan Merchant Bank
53. Nikko Merchant Bank
54. Nomura Singapore
55. Paribas Merchant Banking
56. Rabobank Asia
57. Republic National Bank of New York
58. Royal Bank of Canada
59. Royal Trust Bank
60. Sakura Merchant Bank
61. Sanwa Singapore
62. Sanyo Merchant Bank
63. SB Merchant Bank
64. Schroder International Merchant Bankers
65. Skandinaviska Enskilda Banken
66. Soceite Generale Asia
67. Standard Chartered Merchant Bank
68. Sumitomo Trust Merchant Bank
69. SVE Asia Ltd
70. Tokyo-Mitsubishi International
71. Toronto Dominion (SEA)
72. UBS (East Asia)
73. United Merchant Bank
74. Wako Merchant Bank
75. West Merchant Bank
76. WestLB Asia Pacific
77. Westpac Singapore
78. Yamaichi Merchant Bank

Finance Companies

1. DBS Finance
2. Far East Finance Organisation
3. Focal Finance

4. Golden Castle Finance
5. Hong Leong Finance
6. Keppel Finance
7. Mayban Finance
8. Nanyang Finance
9. OCBC Finance
10. Overseas Union Trust
11. Public Finance
12. Sime Finance
13. Sing Investments & Finance
14. Singapore Finance
15. Singapura Building Society
16. United Overseas Finance
17. Wayfoong Mortgage & Finance

Local Banks
(Name and Address)

1. **Bank of Singapore**
101 Cecil Street #01-02
Tong Eng Building
Singapore 069533
Tel. (65) 223–9266
Fax. (65) 535–3768

2. **Chung Khiaw Bank**
80 Raffles Place
UOB Plaza One 6th Storey
Singapore 048624
Tel. (65) 222–8622
Fax. (65) 226–2848

3. **Development Bank of Singapore (DBS Bank)**
6 Shenton Way
DBS Building Tower One
Singapore 068809
Tel. (65) 220–1111
Fax. (65) 221–1306
www.dbs.com.sg

4. **Far Eastern Bank**
80 Raffles Place
UOB Plaza One 6th Storey
Singapore 048624
Tel. (65) 221–9055
Fax. (65) 539–3345

5. **Industrial & Commercial Bank**
80 Robinson Road
Singapore 068898
Tel. (65) 221–1711
Fax. (65) 225–9777

6. **Keppel TatLee Bank**
10 Hoe Chiang Road
Keppel Towers
Singapore 089315
Tel. (65) 222–8222
Fax. (65) 225–2256
www.keppelbank.com.sg

7. **Oversea-Chinese Banking Corp (OCBC)**
65 Chulia Street,
OCBC Centre
Singapore 049513
Tel. (65) 535–7222
Fax. (65) 533–7955
www.ocbc.com.sg

8. **Overseas Union Bank**
1 Raffles Place, OUB Centre
Singapore 048616
Tel. (65) 533–8688
Fax. (65) 533–2293
www.oub.com.sg

9. **United Overseas Bank**
80 Raffles Place
UOB Plaza One

Singapore 048624
Tel. (65) 533–9898
Fax. (65) 534–2334
www.uob.com.sg

Foreign Banks
(Name and address)

1. **ABN AMRO Bank** (Netherlands)
63 Chulia Street
Singapore 049514
Tel. (65) 231–8888
Fax. (65) 532–3108
www.abnamro.nl

2. **Ban Hin Lee Bank** (Malaysia)
39 Robinson Road #01-02
Robinson Point
Singapore 068911
Tel. (65) 532–1318
Fax. (65) 535–536

3. **Bangkok Bank** (Thailand)
180 Cecil Street
Bangkok Bank Building
Singapore 069546
Tel. (65) 221–9400
Fax. (65) 225–5852
www.bbl.co.th

4 **Bank Negara Indonesia** (Indonesia)
158 Cecil Street #01-00
Dapenso Building
Singapore 069545
Tel. (65) 225–7755
Fax. (65) 225–4757
www.bni.co.id

5. **Bank of America** (US)
9 Raffles Place #18-00
Republic Plaza Tower One
Singapore 048619
Tel. (65) 239-3888
Fax. (65) 239-3068
www.bankamerica.com

6. **Bank of China** (China)
4 Battery Road
Bank of China Building
Singapore 049908
Tel. (65) 535–2411
Fax. (65) 534–3401
www.bank-of-china.com

7. **Bank of East Asia** (Hong Kong)
137 Market Street
Bank of East Asia Building
Singapore 048943
Tel. (65) 224–1334
Fax. (65) 225–1805
www.hkbea.com

8. **Bank of India** (India)
138 Robinson Road
Hong Leong Centre
Singapore 068906
Tel. (65) 222–0011
Fax. (65) 225–4407
www.bankofindia.com

9. **Bank of Tokyo-Mitsubishi** (Japan)
9 Raffles Place
Republic Plaza
Singapore 048619
Tel. (65) 538–3388
Fax. (65) 538–8083
www.btm.co.jp

10. **Chase Manhattan Bank** (US)
150 Beach Road
Gateway West Building
Singapore 189720
Tel. (65) 291–1298
Fax. (65) 290–1756
www.chase.com

11. **Citibank** (US)
5 Shenton Way
UIC Building
Singapore 068808
Tel. (65) 224–2611
Fax. (65) 224–8172
www.citibank.com.sg

12. **Credit Agricole Indosuez** (France)
6 Raffles Quay #17-00
John Hancock Tower
Singapore 048580
Tel. (65) 535–4988
Fax. (65) 532–2422
www.credit-agricole.fr

13. **HL Bank** (Malaysia)
20 Collyer Quay #01-02
Tung Centre
Singapore 049319
Tel. (65) 535–2466
Fax. (65) 533–9340
www.hlb.hongleong.com.my

14. **Hongkong & Shanghai Banking Corporation** (Hong Kong)
21 Collyer Quay #01-00
HongkongBank Building
Singapore 049320
Tel. (65) 530-5000
Fax. (65) 225-0663
www.hongkongbank.com

15. **Indian Bank** (India)
3 Raffles Place
Bharat Building
Singapore 048617
Tel. (65) 534–3511
Fax. (65) 533–1651
www.indian-bank.com

16. **Indian Overseas Bank** (India)
64 Cecil Street
IOB Building
Singapore 049711
Tel. (65) 225–1100
Fax. (65) 224–4490
www.iob.com

17. **Kwangtung Provincial Bank** (China)
60 Cecil Street
KPB Building
Singapore 049709
Tel. (65) 223–9622
Fax. (65) 225–9970

18. **Malayan Banking** (Malaysia)
50 Raffles Place
Singapore Land Tower
Singapore 048623
Tel. (65) 535–2266
Fax. (65) 532–7909
www.jaring.my/maybank

19. **Sakura Bank** (Japan)
16 Raffles Quay #01-04
Hong Leong Building
Singapore 048581
Tel. (65) 220–9761
Fax. (65) 225–0962
www.sakura.co.jp

20. **Sime Bank** (Malaysia)
150 Cecil Street #01-00
AXA Life Building
Singapore 069543
Tel. (65) 225–3111
Fax. (65) 224–7871

21. **Standard Chartered Bank** (UK)
6 Battery Road
Singapore 049909
Tel. (65) 225–8888
Fax. (65) 789–3756
www.stanchart.com

22. **UCO Bank** (India)
3 Raffles Place #01-01
Bharat Building
Singapore 048617
Tel. (65) 532–5944
Fax. (65) 532–5044
www.ucobank.com

Foreign Banks — Restricted Licence
(Name and Address)

1. **American Express Bank** (US)
16 Collyer Quay
Singapore 049318
Tel. (65) 538–4833
Fax. (65) 534–3022
www.aeb-eg.com

2. **Banco Commerciale Italiana** (Italy)
9 Raffles Place #51-01
Republic Plaza
Singapore 048619
Tel. (65) 220–1333
Fax. (65) 225–2004
www.bci.it

3. **Banque Nationale de Paris** (France)
20 Collyer Quay
Tung Centre
Singapore 049319
Tel. (65) 224-0211
Fax. (65) 224-3459
www.bnp.fr/english

4. **Bayerische Landesbank Girozentrale** (Germany)
300 Beach Road #37-01
The Concourse
Singapore 199555
Tel. (65) 293–3822
Fax. (65) 293–2151
www.blb.de

5. **Chiao Tung Bank** (Taiwan)
80 Raffles Place #23-20
UOB Plaza Two
Singapore 048624
Tel. (65) 536–6311
Fax. (65) 536–0680
www.ctnbank.com.tw

6. **Credit Suisse First Boston** (Switzerland)
80 Raffles Place #49-01
UOB Plaza One
Singapore 048624
Tel. (65) 538–6322
Fax. (65) 531–2708
www.csfb.com

7. **Deutsche Bank** (Germany)
6 Shenton Way #15-08
DBS Building Tower Two
Singapore 068809
Tel. (65) 225–6955
Fax. (65) 225–9442
www.deutsche-bank.de

8. **Dresdner Bank** (Germany)
20 Collyer Quay #22-00
Tung Centre
Singapore 049319
Tel. (65) 222–8080
Fax. (65) 224–4008
www.dresdner-bank.de

9. **First Commercial Bank** (Taiwan)
76 Shenton Way #01-02
Singapore 079119
Tel. (65) 221–5755
Fax. (65) 225–1905

10. **Habib Bank** (Pakistan)
3 Phillip Street #01-03
Commerce Point
Singapore 048693
Tel. (65) 438–0055
Fax. (65) 438–0644

11. **Korea Exchange Bank** (South Korea)
2 Finlayson Green #01-00
Asia Insurance Building
Singapore 049247
Tel. (65) 224–1633
Fax. (65) 224–3701
www.koexbank.co.kr

12. **Moscow Narodny Bank** (UK)
50 Robinson Road
MNB Building
Singapore 068882
Tel. (65) 220–9422
Fax. (65) 225–0140

13. **Sumitomo Bank** (Japan)
6 Shenton Way #27-08
DBS Building Tower Two
Singapore 068809
Tel. (65) 220–1611
Fax. (65) 225–9647
www.sumitomobank.co.jp

Reference

Monetary Authority of Singapore (1997), *Directory of Financial Institutions in Singapore*, Monetary Authority of Singapore. MAS website: www.mas.gov.sg

FINANCIAL INSTITUTIONS IN SINGAPORE

Type of Institution	1996	1997	1998
Commercial Banks	143	152	151
Local (All local banks are full banks)	12	12	11
Foreign	131	140	140
— Full Banks	22	22	22
— Restricted Banks	13	13	13
— Offshore Banks	96	105	105
Merchant Banks	79	79	75
Representative Offices of Banks	57	67	69
Institutions with Asian Currency Units	214	223	219
Finance Companies	20	19	18
Money Brokers	8	8	8
Dealers	85	90	85
— SES Members	33	33	33
— Non-SES Members	52	57	52
Investment Advisers	154	159	151
SIMEX Members	77	75	68
— Corporate Clearing Members	38	36	35
— Corporate Non-Clearing Members	27	28	22
— Commercial Associate Members	12	11	11
Insurance Companies	144	151	163
— Direct Insurers	58	58	61
— Life Insurers	8	8	8
— General Insurers	44	44	47
— Composite Insurers	6	6	6
Professional Reinsurers	37	44	50
— Life Reinsurers	2	3	2
— General Reinsurers	28	32	38
— Composite Reinsurers	7	9	10
Captive Insurers	49	49	52
Representative Offices of Insurers and Professional Reinsurers	17	16	13

Source: Monetary Authority of Singapore

THAILAND

Domestic Banks

1. Bangkok Bank
2. Bank of Asia
3. Bank of Ayudhya
4. Krung Thai Bank
5. Nakornthon Bank
6. Radhanasin Bank
7. Siam Commercial Bank
8. Thai Danu Bank
9. Thai Farmers Bank
10 Thai Military Bank

The following banks were intervened by the authorities in 1998. Some have merged with other banks.

1. Bangkok Bank of Commerce
2. Bangkok Metropolitan Bank
3. First Bangkok City Bank
4. Laem Thong Bank
5. Siam City Bank
6. Union Bank of Bangkok

Foreign Banks

1. ABN-AMRO Bank (Netherland)
2. Bank of America (USA)
3. Bank of China (China)
4. Bank of Tokyo-Mitsubishi (Japan)
5. Banque Indosuez (France)
6. Banque National de Paris (France)
7. Bharat Overseas Bank (India)
8. Chase Manhattan Bank (USA)
9. Citibank (USA)
10. Dai-Ichi Kangyo (Japan)
11. Deutsche Bank (Germany)
12. Dresdner Bank (Germany)
13. Hongkong and Shanghai Bank (UK)
14. Industrial Bank of Japan (Japan)
15. Int'l Commercial Bank of China (Taiwan)
16. Oversea Chinese Banking Corp (Singapore)
17. Sakura Bank (Japan)
18. Sime Bank (Malaysia)
19. Standard Chartered Bank (UK)
20. Sumitomo Bank (Japan)

New Foreign Banks
(with International Banking Facility Licence)

1. American Express (USA)
2. Bank of Nova Scotia (Canada)
3. Bank of New York (USA)
4. Bankers Trust (USA)
5. Credit Lyonnais (France)
6. DBS Bank (Singapore)
7. Fuji Bank (Japan)
8. Generale Bank (Belgium)
9. Internationale Naderlanden Netherland
10 Korea Development Bank
11. Korea Exchange Bank
12. Long-Term Credit Bank of Japan
13. National Australia Bank
14. Overseas Union Bank (Singapore)
15. Royal Bank of Canada
16. Sanwa Bank (Japan)
17. Societe Generale (France)
18. Tokai Bank (Japan)
19. United Overseas Bank (Singapore)

Domestic Banks

1. **Bangkok Bank**
333, Silom Road
Suriwongse, Bangrak
Bangkok 10500, Thailand
Tel. (662) 231–4333
Fax. (662) 236–8281

2. **Bank of Asia**
191 South Sathorn Road
Yannawa, Sathorn
Bangkok 10120, Thailand
Tel. (662) 287–2211
Fax. (662) 213–2652

3. **Bank of Ayudhya**
1222 Rama V Road,
Bangpongpang, Yannawa
Bangkok 10120, Thailand
Tel. (662) 296–2000
Fax. (662) 683–1484

4. **Krung Thai Bank**
35 Sukhumvit Road,
Klongtoey
Bangkok 10110, Thailand
Tel. (662) 255–2222
Fax. (662) 255–9380

5. **Nakornthon Bank**
90 North Sathorn Road
Silom, Bangrak
Bangkok 10500, Thailand
Tel. (662) 233–2111
Fax. (662) 236–1968

6. **Radhanasin Bank**
Italthai Tower
2034 New Petchaburi Road
Bangkapi Huaykwang
Bangkok 10320, Thailand
Tel. (662) 716–0700

7. **Siam Commercial Bank**
9 Rachadapisek Road,
Ladyao, Jatujak
Bangkok 10900, Thailand
Tel. (662) 544–5678
Fax. (662) 937–7454

8. **Thai Danu Bank**
393 Silom Road,

Suriwongse, Bangrak
Bangkok 10500, Thailand
Tel. (662) 233–9160
Fax. (662) 237–1648

9. **Thai Farmers Bank**
1 Soi Thai Farmer
Radburana Road
Bangkok 10140, Thailand
Tel. (662) 470–1122
Fax. (662) 470–1144

10. **Thai Military Bank**
3000 Paholyothin Road
Ladyao, Jatujak
Bangkok 10900, Thailand
Tel. (662) 299–1111,
Fax. (662) 273–7121

List of Credit Foncier Companies

(These companies were not intervened by the authorities)
Source: www.bot.or.th

1. Asia Credit Foncier Co Ltd
2. Bangkok Home Co Ltd
3. Credit Foncier Unico Housing Co Ltd
4. Land and Houses Credit Foncier Co Ltd
5. LPN Credit Foncier Co Ltd
6. Sahaviriya Credit Foncier Co Ltd
7. Sinkahakan Credit Foncier Co Ltd
8. Tarakorn Credit Foncier Co Ltd
9. Thai Keha Credit Foncier Co Ltd
10. Thai Saving Promotion Credit Foncier Co Ltd
11. Thanapat Credit Foncier Co Ltd
12. Vanit Credit Foncier Co Ltd

Credit Foncier Companies
(Name and address)

1. **Asia Credit Foncier Co Ltd**
292 Soi Siam Square 4,
Rama I Road
Patumwan, Bangkok 10330, Thailand
Tel. (662) 252–9196

2. **Bangkok Home Limited**
14/57-58 Moo 2,
Srinakarin Road, Nongbon, Pravet
Bangkok 10260, Thailand
Tel. (662) 393–9420
Fax. (662) 393–9431

3. **Credit Foncier Unico Housing Ltd**
29/1 Unico House Building, Lungsuan
Ploenjit, Lumpini, Patumwan
Bangkok 10330, Thailand
Tel. (662) 251–7126
Fax. (662) 251–7471

4. **Land and Houses Credit Foncier Co Ltd**
38 Q House Convent Building
Convent Road, Silom, Bangrak
Bangkok 10500, Thailand
Tel. (662) 237–8866
Fax. (662) 237–8860

5. **L P N Credit Foncier Co Ltd**
127/149 Rama III Road, Chongnonsi
Yannawa, Bangkok 10120, Thailand
Tel. (662) 295–1911
Fax. (662) 284–0432

6. **Sahaviriya Credit Foncier Co Ltd**
1921/48, Rama IV Road, Lumpini, Patumwan
Bangkok 10330, Thailand
Tel. (662) 252–3238

7. **Sinkahakan Credit Foncier Co Ltd**
55 Sinkahakarn Building, Rachadapisek Dindaeng,
Bangkok 10310, Thailand
Tel. (662) 246–0096
Fax. (662) 246–2554

8. **Tarakorn Credit Foncier Co Ltd**
173 Bureau of Crown Property
Ratchasima Road, Dusit
Bangkok 10300, Thailand
Tel. (662) 282–8328

9. **Thai Keha Credit Foncier Co Ltd**
123 Thai Life Insurance Building 1
Rajadapisek Road, Dindaeng
Bangkok 10310, Thailand
Tel. (662) 246–9665

10. **Thai Saving Promotion Credit Foncier Co Ltd**
42 Songserm Insurance Building
Surawongse Road, Sipraya, Bangrak
Bangkok 10500, Thailand
Tel. (662) 266–4670
Fax. (662) 237–5951

11. **Thanapat Credit Foncier Co Ltd**
4-6 Happyland Plaza, Ladprao, Klongjun
Bangkapi, Bangkok 10240, Thailand
Tel. (662) 377–5336

12. **Vanit Credit Foncier Co Ltd**
1126/1 Vanit Building
New Petchburi Road, Makkasun
Bangkok 10400, Thailand
Tel. (662) 250–1051

List of Finance and Securities Companies

(These companies were not intervened by the authorities)

1. AIG Finance (Thailand) PCL
2. Asec Finance and Securities Co Ltd
3. Asia Finance PCL
4. Ayudhya Investment and Trust PCL
5. Bangkok First Investment and Trust PCL

6. Book Club Finance and Securities PCL
7. BTM Finance and Securities (Thailand) Ltd
8. Citicorp Finance and Securities (Thailand) Ltd
9. Ekachart Finance & Securities PCL
10. HSBC Finance & Securities (Thailand) Ltd
11. Kiatnakin Finance and Securities PCL
12. Krungthai Thanakit PCL
13. National Finance Co Ltd
14. National Finance and Securities PCL
15. Ocean Securities and Finance Co Ltd
16. Peregrine Nithi Finance Securities Ltd
17. Phatra Thanakit PCL
18. Radhantun Finance PCL
19. SG Asia Credit PCL
20. Siam Sanwa Industrial Crdit PCL
21. Thai Investment and Securities PCL
22. Thai Capital Finance and Securities Co Ltd
23. Thai Sakura Finance and Securities Co Ltd
24. Thaksin Finance Co Ltd

The following companies were intervened by the authorities

Intervened on 14 May 1998

1. Bangkok Asian Finance Co Ltd
2. Erawan Trust Co Ltd
3. Ksit Finance and Securities PCL
4. Mahatun Finance Co Ltd
5. Nava Finance and Securities PCL
6. Progressive Finance Co Ltd
7. Union Asia Finance PCL

Intervened on 14 August 1998

1. Dhana Siam Finance and Securities PCL
2. First City Investment PCL
3. IFCT Finance and Securities PCL
4. Thai Summit Finance and Securities Co Ltd
5. Vajiradhanathun Finance Co Ltd

Finance and Securities Companies
(Name and address)

1. **AIG Finance**
   102 Sukhumvit 26,
   Sukhumvit Road,
   Klongtoey
   Bangkok 10110, Thailand
   Tel. (662) 259–0063
   Fax. (662) 259–7390

2. **Asec Finance and Securities**
   728/10 Sukhumvit Road,
   Bangplasroy,
   Muang, Chonburi 20000,
   Thailand
   Tel. (038) 273–423
   Fax. (038) 272–336
   Tel. (662) 676–5788
   (Bangkok Branch)

3. **Asia Finance**
54 Harintorn Building
North Sathorn Road, Silom
Bangkok 10500, Thailand
Tel. (662) 267–3740
Fax. (662) 267–3746

4. **Ayudhya Investment and Trust**
898 Ploenjit Tower
Ploenjit, Lumpini, Patumwan
Bangkok 10330, Thailand
Tel. (662) 263–0355
Fax. (662) 263–0388

5. **Bangkok First Investment and Trust**
300 Silom Road, Silom, Bangrak
Bangkok 10500, Thailand
Tel. (662) 237–6097
Fax. (662) 237–6736

6. **Book Club Finance and Securities**
1060 Siam Commercial Bank Building 2
Petchburi Road, Rajatavee
Bangkok 10400, Thailand
Tel. (662) 251–5555
Fax. (662) 255–1666

7. **BTM Finance and Securities**
54 Harinthorn
North Sathorn Road, Silom
Bangkok 10500, Thailand
Tel. (662) 266–3070
Fax. (662) 266–3080

8. **Citicorp Finance & Securities**
82 Saengthongthani Building
North Sathorn Road, Silom
Bangkok 10500, Thailand
Tel. (662) 232–2100
Fax. (662) 232–2484

9. **Ekachart Finance & Securities**
444 MBK Tower
Phayathai, Wangmai, Patumwan
Bangkok 10330, Thailand
Tel. (662) 217–9922
Fax. (662) 216–6909

10. **HSBC Finance & Securities**
287 Liberty Square Building
Silom Road, Silom
Bangkok 10500, Thailand
Tel. (662) 631–1590
Fax. (662) 631–1580

11. **Kiatnakin Finance and Securities**
500 Amarin Tower
Ploenjit, Lumpini, Patumwan
Bangkok 10330, Thailand
Tel. (662) 256–9122
Fax. (662) 256–9933

12. **Krungthai Thanakit PCL**
159 Sermmitr Tower
Sukhumvit 21, Klongtoey
Bangkok 10110, Thailand
Tel. (662) 261–7373
Fax. (662) 261–7447

13. **National Finance**
503 KSL Tower
Sri Ayudhaya Road, Phayathai
Bangkok 10400, Thailand
Tel. (662) 642–6131
Fax. (662) 642–6140

14. **National Finance and Securities**
444 MBK Tower Building
Phayathai Road, Wangmai, Patumwan
Bangkok 10330, Thailand
Tel. (662) 217–9595
Fax. (662) 217–9642

15. **The Ocean Securities and Finance**
163 Thaisamoot, Surawong Road
Suriyawongse, Bangrak
Bangkok 10500, Thailand
Tel. (662) 234–7500
Fax. (662) 238–4151

16. **Peregrine Nithi Finance Securities**
Building No. 66/66-68
Tivanont Road, Taladkwan, Muang
Nontaburi 11000, Thailand
Tel. (662) 580–0937
Fax. (662) 580–0915

17. **Phatra Thanakit**
252/6 Muang Thai-Phatra Building
Rachadapisek Road, Huaykwang
Bangkok 10310, Thailand
Tel. (662) 265–1000
Fax. (662) 275–3666

18. **Radhantun Finance**
2034/124 New Petchburi Road
Bangkapi, Huaykwang
Bangkok 10310, Thailand
Tel. (662) 716–1600
Fax. (662) 716–1730

19. **SG Asia Credit**
320 Rama IV Road, Mahapruetaram
Bangkok 10500, Thailand
Tel. (662) 235–1477
Fax. (662) 238–4722

20. **Siam Sanwa Industrial Credit**
130-132 Sinthorn Tower 2
Wittayu Road, Lumpini
Bangkok 10330, Thailand
Tel. (662) 263–2100
Fax. (662) 263–2045

21. **Thai Investment and Securities**
48/2 TISCO Tower
North Sathorn Road
Bangkok 10500, Thailand
Tel. (662) 633–6000
Fax. (662) 633–6800

22. **Thai-Capital Finance & Securities**
19 SCB Building 3, Park Plaza
Floor 12, Rachadapisek Road
Ladyao, Jatujak

Bangkok 10900, Thailand
Tel. (662) 937–9400
Fax. (662) 937–9370

23. Thai Sakura Finance & Securities
952 Ramaland Building
Rama IV Road,
Suriyawongse
Bangkok 10500, Thailand
Tel. (662) 632–9700
Fax. (662) 632–9711

24. Thaksin Finance
9/2 Shi-Utit Road, Hadyai
Songkla 90110, Thailand
Tel. (074) 244301

List of Securities Companies
(as of 4 February 1998)
Website: www.sec.or.th

1. Adkinson Securities PCL
2. Afco Securities Co Ltd
3. Amsteel Securities (Thailand) PCL
4. Asia Securities Trading PCL
5. Asset Plus Securities Co Ltd
6. BZW-KT Securities Co Ltd
7. Capital Nomura Securities PCL
8. Cathay Capital Co Ltd
9. Deutsche Morgan Grenfell Securities (Thailand) Co Ltd
10. Dhana Siam Securities Co Ltd
11. Jardine Fleming Thanakok Securities Ltd
12. National Securities Co Ltd
13. Nava Securities Co Ltd
14. Nithipat Capital & Securities Co Ltd
15. Phatra Securities Co Ltd
16. SBC Warburg Premier Securities Co Ltd
17. SCB Securities Co Ltd
18. Seamico Securities PCL
19. Securities One PCL
20. Sri Dhana-DBS Securities Co Ltd
21. TSFC Securities Ltd
22. Union Securities Co Ltd
23. United Securities PCL
24. Vajira Securities Ltd

Securities Companies
(Name and address)
Website: www.sec.or.th

1. Adkinson Securities PCL
Sindhorn Tower, 132
Wireless Road
Bangkok 10330, Thailand
Tel. (662) 252–0215

2. Afco Securities Co Ltd
Harindhorn Buidling,
North Sathorn Road
Bangkok 10500, Thailand
Tel. (662) 632–0400
Fax. (662) 632–0420

3. Amsteel Securities (Thailand) PCL
Thai CC Tower,
South Sathorn Road
Bangkok 10120, Thailand
Tel. (662) 210–0400
Fax. (662) 210–0500

4. **Asia Securities Trading PCL**
Sathorn City Tower
175 South Sathorn Road
Bangkok 10120, Thailand
Tel. (662) 285–1666
Fax. (662) 285–1900

5. **Asset Plus Securities Co Ltd**
Lake Rachada Building
193/111 Rachadapisek Road
Bangkok 10110, Thailand
Tel. (662) 661–9999

6. **BZW-KT Securities Co Ltd**
Amarin Tower, 500
Ploenchit Road
Bangkok 10330, Thailand
Tel. (662) 256–9883
Fax. (662) 256–9796

7. **Capital Nomura Securities PCL**
Thai-Wah Tower, 21/3
South Sathorn Road
Bangkok 10120, Thailand
Tel. (662) 285–0096

8. **Cathay Capital Co Ltd**
Cathay Trust Building, 1016
Rama 4 Road
Bangkok 10500, Thailand
Tel. (662) 238–3334
Fax. (662) 236–5800

9. **Deutsche Morgan Grenfell Securities (Thailand) Co Ltd**
208 Building,
208 Wireless Road
Bangkok 10330, Thailand
Tel. (662) 651–5400
Fax. (662) 651–5420

10. **Dhana Siam Securities Co Ltd**
Sindhorn Tower
132 Wirless Road
Bangkok 10330, Thailand
Tel. (662) 250–0250

11. **Jardine Fleming Thanakok Securities Ltd**
Silom Complex Building,
191 Silom Road
Bangkok 10500, Thailand
Tel. (662) 231–3777
Fax. (662) 231–3797

12. **National Securities Co Ltd**
MBK Tower,
444 Phyathai Road
Bangkok 10330, Thailand
Tel. (662) 217–9622
Fax. (662) 217–9642

13. **Nava Securities Co Ltd**
422 Navathanakit Building,
Phyathai Road
Bangkok 10330, Thailand
Tel. (662) 215–0969

14. **Nithipat Capital & Securities Co Ltd**
52 Thaniya Plaza Building,
Silom Road
Bangkok 10500, Thailand
Tel. (662) 231–2431

15. **Phatra Securities Co Ltd**
Muang Thai-Phatra Building

252/6 Rachadapisek Road
Bangkok 10320, Thailand
Tel. (662) 275–0888

16. **SBC Warburg Premier Securities Co Ltd**
Diethelm Towers B, 93/1
Wireless Road
Bangkok 10330, Thailand
Tel. (662) 651–5700
Fax. (662) 651–5730

17. **SCB Securities Co Ltd**
Sindhorn Tower,
132 Wireless Road
Bangkok 10330, Thailand
Tel. (662) 263–3500
Fax. (662) 263–3801

18. **Seamico Securities PCL**
Liberty Square Building
287 Silom Road
Bangkok 10500, Thailand
Tel. (662) 631–1600
Fax. (662) 631–1709

19. **Securities One PCL**
Golden Pavillian Building
Rajdamri Road
Bangkok 10330, Thailand
Tel. (662) 652-1234

20. **Sri Dhana-DBS Securities Co Ltd**
Srivikorn Building
18/8 Sukhumvit 21 Road
Bangkok 10110, Thailand
Tel. (662) 661–6055
Fax. (662) 661–6044

21. **TSFC Securities Ltd**
Ploenchit Tower
898 Ploenchit Road
Bangkok 10330, Thailand
Tel. (662) 263–0666
Fax. (662) 263–0760

22. **Union Securities Co Ltd**
P.S. Tower,
Sukhumvit 21 Road
Bangkok 10110, Thailand
Tel. (662) 261-1850

23. **United Securities PCL**
Grand Amarin Tower
1550 New Petchburi Road
Bangkok 10310, Thailand
Tel. (662) 207–0038

24. **Vajira Securities Ltd**
Grand Amarin Tower
1550 New Petchburi Road
Bangkok 10310, Thailand
Tel. (662) 207–0139
Fax. (662) 652–8754

List of Asset Management Companies
As of 23 February 1998

1. Ayudhya Jardine Fleming Asset Management Ltd
2. BBL Asset Management Co Ltd
3. FBCB Asset Management Co Ltd
4. GS Assets Management Co Ltd
5. The Mutual Fund Public Co Ltd

6. Nokornthon Schroder Asset Management Ltd
7. One Asset Management Ltd
8. SCB Asset Management Co Ltd
9. Siam City Asset Management Co Ltd
10. SITCA-BMB International Asset Management Co Ltd
11. Thai Asia Mutual Fund Co Ltd
12. Thai Capital Management Co Ltd
13. Thai Farmers Asset Management Co Ltd
14. Thai Trust Fund Management Co Ltd
15. TMB Asset Management Co Ltd

LIST OF ASSET MANAGEMENT COMPANIES

As of 23 February 1998

1. **Ayudhya Jardine Fleming Asset Management Ltd**
   Ploenchit Tower, 898
   Ploenchit Road
   Bangkok 10330, Thailand
   Tel. (662) 263–0200
   Fax. (662) 263–0199

2. **BBL Asset Management Co Ltd**
   Bangkok Bank Building
   333 Silom Road
   Bangkok 10500, Thailand
   Tel. (662) 231–4955
   Fax. (662) 231–4884

3. **FBCB Asset Management Co Ltd**
   Q-House Tower,
   South Sathorn
   Tung Mahamek
   Bangkok 10210, Thailand
   Tel. (662) 679–2030
   Fax. (662) 679–1820

4. **GS Assets Management Co Ltd**
   Ploenchit Tower,
   Ploenchit Road
   Bangkok 10330, Thailand
   Tel. (662) 263–0800
   Fax. (662) 263–0811

5. **The Mutual Fund Public Co Ltd**
   Lake Ratchada Building,
   193 Ratchadaphisek Road
   Bangkok 10110, Thailand
   Tel. (662) 661–9000
   Fax. (662) 661–9100

6. **Nokornthon Schroder Asset Mgt Ltd**
   Sathornthani Tower 1
   North Sathorn Road
   Bangkok 10500, Thailand
   Tel. (662) 236–6133
   Fax. (662) 234–1812

7. **One Asset Management Ltd**
   Kaysorn Place Building
   Ploenchit Road
   Bangkok 10330, Thailand
   Tel. (662) 656–1200
   Fax. (662) 656–1250

8. **SCB Asset Management Co Ltd**
Sindhorn Building
3, Wireless Road
Bangkok 10330, Thailand
Tel. (662) 263–2800
Fax. (662) 263–4004

9. **Siam City Asset Management Co Ltd**
Ploenchit Center Tower,
Sukhumvit Road
Bangkok 10110, Thailand
Tel. (662) 656–9111
Fax. (662) 656–9119

10. **SITCA-BMB International Asset Management Co Ltd**
1908 Phetchaburi Road,
Bangkapi
Bangkok, Thailand
Tel. (662) 318–9488
Fax. (662) 718–1490

11. **Thai Asia Mutual Fund Co Ltd**
Rajanakarn Building
183 South Sathorn Road
Bangkok 10120, Thailand
Tel. (662) 676–5654
Fax. (662) 676–5675

12. **Thai Capital Management Co Ltd**
Kamolsukosol Building
317 Silom Road
Bangkok 10500, Thailand
Tel. (662) 631–1000
Fax. (662) 238–1224

13. **Thai Farmers Asset Management Co Ltd**
Muang Thai-Phatra Office
Tower 1,
252/38 Ratchadaphisek
Road
Bangkok 10310, Thailand
Tel. (662) 693–2300
Fax. (662) 693–2320

14. **Thai Trust Fund Management Co Ltd**
Sindhorn Building,
Wireless Road
Bangkok 10330, Thailand
Tel. (662) 263–3882
Fax. (662) 256–6223

15. **TMB Asset Management Co Ltd**
Abdul-Rahim Tower,
Rama 4 Road
Bangkok 10500, Thailand
Tel. (662) 636–1818
Fax. (662) 636–1820

References

KPMG (1991), Banking and Finance in ASEAN.

Financial Times (1995), Banking in the Far East,

Bank of Thailand website: www.bot.or.th

VIETNAM

(as of August 1997)

State-owned Banks (Hanoi)

1. Industrial & Commercial Bank of Vietnam
2. Vietcombank
3. Vietnam Bank for Agriculture & Rural Development
4. Vietnam Bank for Investment & Development

Foreign Banks (Hanoi)

1. ABN-AMRO Bank
2. ANZ Bank
3. Bangkok Bank
4. Bank of America
5. Banque National de Paris
6. Chase Manhattan Bank
7. Ching Fong Commercial Bank
8. Citibank
9. Credit Lyonnais
10. Firstvina Bank
11. Fuji Bank
12. Hong Kong Bank
13. ING Bank
14. May Bank
15. Standard Chartered
16. VID Public Bank (JV Bank)

State-owned Banks (Ho Chi Minh City)

1. Industrial and Commercial Bank of Vietnam
2. Vietcombank
3. Vietnam Bank for Agriculture & Rural Development
4. Vietnam Bank for Investment & Development

Foreign Banks (Ho Chi Minh City)

1. ABN-AMRO Bank
2. ANZ Bank
3. BFCE Bank
4. Bangkok Bank
5. Bank of America
6. Banque National de Paris
7. Credit Agricole Indosuez

8. Credit Lyonnais
9. Chinfon Commercial Bank
10. Cho Hung Bank
11. Deutsche Bank
12. Firstvina Bank
13. Fuji Bank
14. Hong Kong Bank
15. Indovina Bank
16. International Bank of Asia
17. International Commercial Bank of China
18. ING Bank
19. May Bank
20. Shinhan Bank
21. Thai Military Bank
22. Tokyo Mitsubishi Bank
23. United Overseas Bank
24. Vinasiam Bank
25. VID Public Bank

State-owned Banks (Hanoi)

1. **Industrial & Commercial Bank of Vietnam**
   16 Phan Dinh Phung
   Hanoi, Vietnam
   Tel. 823–2008
   Fax. 823–3452

2. **Vietcombank**
   198 Tran Quang Khai
   Hanoi, Vietnam
   Tel. 826–9950
   Fax. 824–1395

3. **Vietnam Bank for Investment & Development**
   194 Tran Quang Khai
   Hanoi, Vietnam
   Tel. 826–6963
   Fax. 826–6959

4. **Vietnam Bank for Agriculture & Rural Development**
   4 Pham Ngoc Thach
   Hanoi, Vietnam
   Tel. 852-5374
   Fax. 852-5376

Foreign Banks (Hanoi)

1. **ABN–AMRO Bank**
   3rd floor, Deaha Business Centre
   Hanoi, Vietnam
   Tel. 831–5250
   Fax. 831–5275

2. **ANZ Bank**
   14 Le Thai To Street
   Hanoi, Vietnam
   Tel. 825–8190
   Fax. 825–8188

3. **Bangkok Bank**
   41-B Ly Thai To Street
   Hanoi, Vietnam
   Tel. 826–0886
   Fax. 826–7397

4. **Bank of America**
   27 Ly Thuong Kiet
   Hanoi, Vietnam
   Tel. 824–9316
   Fax. 824–9322

5. **Banque National de Paris**
   8 Trung Hung Dao
   Hanoi, Vietnam
   Tel. 825–3175
   Fax. 826–6982

6. **Chase Manhattan Bank**
31 Hai Ba Trung
Hanoi, Vietnam
Tel. 822–9534
Fax. 822–9603

7. **Ching Fong Commercial Bank**
55 Quang Trung
Hanoi, Vietnam
Tel. 825–0555
Fax. 825–0566

8. **Citibank**
17 Ngo Quyen,
Hanoi, Vietnam
Tel. 825–1950
Fax. 825–3960

9. **Credit Lyonnais**
10 Trang Thi
Hanoi, Vietnam
Tel. 825–8102
Fax. 826–0080

10. **Firstvina Bank**
Daehea Business Centre
Hanoi, Vietnam
Tel. 831–5130
Fax. 831–5134

11. **Fuji Bank**
International Centre
17 Ngo Quyen
Hanoi, Vietnam
Tel. 826–6553
Fax. 826–6365

12. **Hong Kong Bank**
8 Trang Hung Dao
Hanoi, Vietnam
Tel. 269994
Fax. 269941

13. **ING Bank**
17 Ngo Quyen
Hanoi, Vietnam
Tel. 824–6888
Fax. 826–9216

14. **May Bank**
74 Ngo Quyen
Hanoi, Vietnam
Tel. 824–1788
Fax. 824–1799

15. **Standard Chartered**
27 Ly Thai To
Hanoi, Vietnam
Tel. 825–8970
Fax. 825–8880

16. **VID Public Bank (Joint Venture Bank)**
2 Ngo Quyen
Hanoi, Vietnam
Tel. 826–6953
Fax. 826–8228

State-owned Banks
(Ho Chi Minh City)

1. **Industrial and Commercial Bank of Vietnam (Incombank)**
79A Ham Nghi, District 1
Ho Chi Minh City, Vietnam
Tel. 829–7266
Fax. 829–5342

2. **Vietcombank**
29 Chuong Duong, District 1
Ho Chi Minh City, Vietnam
Tel. 823–0310
Fax. 829–7228

3. **Vietnam Bank for Agriculture & Rural Development**
50 Chuong Duong, District 1
Ho Chi Minh City, Vietnam
Tel. 829–3516
Fax. 829–4063

4. **Vietnam Bank for Investment & Development**
134 Nguyen Cong Tru, District 1
Ho Chi Minh City, Vietnam
Tel. 823–0125
Fax. 829–8862

Foreign Banks
(Ho Chi Minh City)

1. **ABN-AMRO Bank**
162 Pasteur, District 1
Ho Chi Minh City, Vietnam
Tel. 822–2992
Fax. 829–7240

2. **ANZ Bank**
11 Me Linh Square, District 1
Ho Chi Minh City, Vietnam
Tel. 829–9319
Fax. 829–9316

3. **Bank Francaise du Commerce Exterieur (BFCE)**
11 Me Linh Square, District 1
Ho Chi Minh City, Vietnam
Tel. 822–2830
Fax. 829–9126

4. **Bangkok Bank**
117 Nguyen Hue, District 1
Ho Chi Minh City, Vietnam
Tel. 822–3416
Fax. 822–3421

5. **Bank of America**
1 Phung Khac Khoan, District 1
Ho Chi Minh City, Vietnam
Tel. 829–9928
Fax. 829–9942

6. **Banque National de Paris**
2 Thi Sach, District 1
Ho Chi Minh City, Vietnam
Tel. 829–9504
Fax. 823–0490

7. **Credit Agricole Indosuez**
Regency Chancellor Court
21 Nguyen Thi Minh Khai, District 1
Ho Chi Minh City, Vietnam
Tel. 829–6061
Fax. 829–6065

8. **Credit Lyonnais**
4th Han Nam Building
65 Nguyen Du, District 1
Ho Chi Minh City, Vietnam
Tel. 829–9226
Fax. 829–6465

9. **Chinfon Commercial Bank**
27 Tu Xuong, District 3
Ho Chi Minh City, Vietnam
Tel. 822–0888
Fax. 820–2431

10. **Cho Hung Bank**
3rd floor, Yoco Building
Nguyen Thi Minh Khai,
District 1
Ho Chi Minh City, Vietnam
Tel. 822–8515
Fax. 822–8534

11. **Deutsche Bank**
174 Nguyen Dinh Chieu,
District 3
Ho Chi Minh City, Vietnam
Tel. 822–2747
Fax. 822–2760

12. **Firstvina Bank**
3 Ho Tung Mau, District 1
Ho Chi Minh City, Vietnam
Tel. 829–1566
Fax. 829–1583

13. **Fuji Bank**
OSIC Building
8 Nguyen Hue, District 1
Ho Chi Minh City, Vietnam
Tel. 824–3195
Fax. 824–3194

14. **Hong Kong Bank**
New World Hotel Annex
75 Phan Hong Thai, Dist. 1
Ho Chi Minh City, Vietnam
Tel. 829–2288
Fax. 823–0530

15. **Indovina Bank**
36 Ton That Dam, District 1
Ho Chi Minh City, Vietnam
Tel. 822-4995
Fax. 823-0131

16. **International Bank of Asia**
58 Dong Khai, District 1
Ho Chi Minh City, Vietnam
Tel. 829–2554
Fax. 829–2508

17. **International Commercial**
Bank of China Building
5B Ton Duc Thang, Dist. 1
Ho Chi Minh City, Vietnam
Tel. 822–5697
Fax. 822–5698

18. **ING Bank**
136 Nam Ky Khoi Nghia,
District 1
Ho Chi Minh City, Vietnam
Tel. 824–1500
Fax. 824–1502

19. **May Bank**
183 Nguyen Van Troi,
Phu Nhuan
Ho Chi Minh City, Vietnam
Tel. 845–8241
Fax. 844–4132

20. **Shinhan Bank**
7th floor, Yoco Building
Nguyen Thi Minh Khai,
District 1
Ho Chi Minh City, Vietnam
Tel. 823–0012
Fax. 823–0009

21. **Thai Military Bank**
11 Ben Chuong Duong,
District 1
Ho Chi Minh City, Vietnam
Tel. 822–2218
Fax. 823–0045

22. **Tokyo Mitsubishi Bank**
8th Landmark Building
5B Ton Duc Thang,
District 1
Ho Chi Minh City, Vietnam
Tel. 823–1560
Fax. 823–1559

23. **United Overseas Bank**
OSIC Building
8 Nguyen Hue, District 1
Ho Chi Minh City, Vietnam
Tel. 825–1424
Fax. 825–1423

24. **Vinasiam Bank**
2 Pho Duc Chinh, District 1
Ho Chi Minh City, Vietnam
Tel. 821–0557
Fax. 821–0585

25. **VID Public Bank**
15A Ben Chuong Duong,
District 1
Ho Chi Minh City, Vietnam
Tel. 822–3583
Fax. 822–3612

HONG KONG

Website: www.info.gov.hk/hkma/eng/bank/index.htm

Licensed Banks Incorporated in Hong Kong
(as of 31 March 1999)

1. Asia Commercial Bank
2. Bank of America (Asia)
3. Bank of East Asia
4. Chekiang First Bank
5. Chiyu Banking Corp
6. Citic Ka Wah Bank
7. DAH Private Bank
8. Dah Sing Bank
9. Dao Heng Bank
10. First Pacific Bank
11. Hang Seng Bank
12. Hongkong & Shanghai Banking Corp
13. Hongkong Chinese Bank
14. HSBC Investment Bank
15. Hua Chiao Commercial Bank
16. International Bank of Asia
17. Jardine Fleming Bank
18. Jian Sing Bank
19. Kwong On Bank
20. Liu Chong Hing Bank
21. Nanyang Commercial Bank
22. Overseas Trust Bank
23. Po Sang Bank
24. Shanghai Commercial Bank
25. Tai Sang Bank
26. Tai Yau Bank
27. Union Bank of Hong Kong
28. United Chinese Bank
29. Wayfoong Finance
30. Wing Hang Bank
31. Wing Lung Bank

Licensed Banks Incorporated Outside Hong Kong
(as of 31 March 1999)

1. ABN Amro Bank
2. Agricultural Bank of China
3. American Express Bank
4. Argentaria, Caja Postal Y Banco Hipotecario
5. Asahi Bank
6. Australia & New Zealand Banking Group
7. Baden-Wurttembergische Bank
8. Banca Commerciale Italiana

9. Banca di Roma
10. Banca Nazionale del Lavoro
11. Banco Central Hispanoamericano
12. Banco di Napoli
13. Banco Santander
14. Bangkok Bank
15. Bank Austria
16. Bank Austria Creditanstalt International
17. Bank Brussels Lambert
18. Bank Melli Iran
19. Bank of America
20. Bank of China
21. Bank of Communications
22. Bank of Fukuoka
23. Bank of India
24. Bank of Montreal
25. Bank of New York
26. Bank of Nova Scotia
27. Bank of Scotland
28. Bank of Taiwan
29. Bank of Tokyo-Mitsubishi
30. Bank Boston
31. Bankers Trust Company
32. Banque Nationale de Paris
33. Banque Worms
34. Barclays Bank
35. Bayerische Hypo-und Vereinsbank
36. Bayerische Landesbank Girozentrale
37. Bhf-Bank
38. Canadian Imperial Bank of Commerce
39. Cariplo
40. Chang Hwa Commercial Bank
41. Chase Manhattan Bank
42. Chiba Bank
43. China & South Sea Bank
44. China Construction Bank
45. China State Bank
46. Chugoku Bank
47. Chung Khiaw Bank
48. Chuo Trust & Banking
49. Citibank
50. Commerzbank
51. Commonwealth Bank of Australia
52. Rabobank Nederland
53. Coutts Bank
54. Credit Agricole Indosuez
55. Credit Commercial de France
56. Credit Lyonnais
57. Credit Suisse First Boston
58. Dai-Ichi Kangyo Bank
59. Daishi Bank
60. Daiwa Bank
61. Den Danske Bank
62. Deutsche Bank
63. Development Bank of Singapore
64. DG Bank
65. Dresdner Bank
66. Eighteenth Bank
67. Equitable Banking Corporation
68. Erste Bank der oesterreichischen Sparkassen
69. First Commercial Bank
70. First National Bank of Chicago
71. Fuji Bank
72. Generale Bank
73. Generale Belgian Bank
74. Hachijuni Bank
75. Hamburgische Landesbank Girozentrale

76. Hanvit Bank
77. Hua Nan Commercial Bank
78. Indian Overseas Bank
79. Industrial and Commercial Bank of China
80. Industrial Bank of Japan
81. ING Bank
82. Iyo Bank
83. Juroku Bank
84. KBC Bank
85. Kincheng Banking Corporation
86. Korea Exchange Bank
87. Kwangtung Provincial Bank
88. Long-Term Credit Bank of Japan
89. Malayan Banking
90. Mitsubishi Trust and Banking Corp
91. Morgan Guaranty Trust Company
92. Natexis Banque
93. National Australia Bank
94. National Bank of Canada
95. National Bank of Pakistan
96. National Commercial Bank
97. National Westminster Bank
98. NationsBank
99. Nishi-Nippon Bank
100. Norwest Bank Minnesota
101. Ogaki Kyoritsu Bank
102. Oversea-Chinese Banking Corp
103. Overseas Union Bank
104. PARIBAS
105. Philippine National Bank
106. PT Bank Negara Indonesia
107. Republic National Bank of New York
108. Royal Bank of Canada
109. Sakura Bank
110. San-in Godo Bank
111. Sanwa Bank
112. Seoul Bank
113. Shiga Bank
114. Shizuoka Bank
115. Sin Hua Bank
116. Skandinaviska Enskilda Banken
117. Societe Generale
118. Standard Chartered Bank
119. State Bank of India
120. State Street Bank and Trust
121. Sumitomo Bank
122. Sumitomo Trust & Banking
123. Svenska Handelsbanken
124. Tokai Bank
125. Toronto-Dominion Bank
126. Toyo Trust and Banking
127. UBS
128. UCO Bank
129. Unibank
130. Unicredito Italiano Societa' per Azioni
131. United Overseas Bank
132. Westdeutsche Landesbank Girozentrale
133. Westpac Banking Corp
134. Yamaguchi Bank
135. Yasuda Trust & Banking
136. Yien Yieh Commercial Bank
137. Zenshinren Bank

Restricted Licence Banks Incorporated in Hong Kong
(as of 31 March 1999)

1. ABSA Asia
2. Allied Capital Resources
3. Ansbacher (HK)
4. BA Asia
5. BNP International Financial Services
6. BOCI Capital Limited
7. Canadian Eastern Finance
8. CCIC Finance
9. Chase Manhattan Asia
10. Chase Manhattan Card
11. Citicorp Commercial Finance
12. Citicorp International
13. DKB Asia
14. East Asia Finance
15. Fuji International Finance
16. GE Capital Finance
17. H & CB Finance
18. Hang Seng Finance
19. Indover Asia
20. Industrial & Commercial International Capital
21. ING Barings Asia
22. KDB Asia
23. Kincheng-Tokyo Finance
24. Lehman Brothers Finance
25. Nedcor Asia
26. N. M. Rothschild & Sons
27. ORIX Asia
28. Public Bank
29. Sanwa International Finance
30. Schroders Asia
31. Shinhan Finance
32. Societe Generale Asia
33. SPC Credit
34. Tokyo-Mitsubishi International
35. UBAF

Restricted Licence Banks Incorported Outside Hong Kong
(as of 31 March 1999)

1. Bank Bumiputra Malaysia
2. Bank of Ayudhya
3. Bank of Bermuda
4. Bank of Hawaii
5. Bank of Butterfield & Son
6. Bankers Trust Australia
7. Chinatrust Commercial Bank
8. Citibank International
9. Emirates Bank International
10. First Union National
11. Hana Bank
12. Industrial Bank of Korea
13. International Bank of Taipei
14. Keppel TatLee Bank
15. Kleinwort Benson
16. KorAm Bank
17. Lloyds Bank
18. MeesPierson
19. Pacific Bank
20. Pacific Finance
21. PT Bank Pembangunan Indonesia
22. Siam Commercial Bank
23. Thai Farmers Bank
24. Thai Military Bank
25. Union Bank of California

Deposit-taking Companies
(as of 31 March 1999)

1. ACB Finance
2. Argo Enterprises

3. Asahi Finance
4. Avco Financial Services
5. BA Finance
6. Bali International Finance
7. BCA Finance
8. BCOM Finance
9. BDNI Finance
10. BII Finance
11. BNS International
12. BPI International Finance
13. BRI Finance
14. BT Asia
15. Bumi Daya International Finance
16. C.F. Finance
17. Charoen Pokphand Finance
18. Chau's Brothers Finance
19. Che Hsing Finance
20. Chiao Yue Finance
21. Chiyu Finance
22. Cho Hung Finance
23. Chung Nan Finance
24. Chuo Trust Asia
25. Commonwealth Finance Corp
26. Corporate Finance
27. Cosmos Finance
28. Credit Lyonnais Hongkong
29. Dah Sing Finance
30. Daiwa Overseas Finance
31. Danamon Finance
32. Dao Heng Finance
33. Delta Asia Credit
34. Dharmala International Finance
35. Duta International Finance
36. East Asia Credit
37. Edward Wong Credit
38. First Metro International Investment
39. First Union HKCB
40. Five Rams Finance
41. Fukuoka City Finance
42. Fukuoka Finance International
43. Gunma Finance
44. Habib Finance International
45. Hachijuni Asia
46. Hana Finance
47. Hanvit Finance
48. Hang Seng Credit
49. HBZ Finance
50. Henderson International Finance
51. Hung Kai Finance
52. IBA Credit
53. IBU International Finance
54. Inchroy Credit Corp
55. Indo Hong Kong International Finance
56. Iyo Finance
57. JCG Finance
58. Juroku International Finance
59. Ka Wah International Merchant Finance
60. KEB (Asia) Finance
61. Kexim Asia
62. Kincheng Finance
63. KLB Asia Finance
64. Kookmin Finance
65. Korea First Finance
66. Kwong On Finance
67. Liu Chong Hing Finance
68. Mashreq Asia
69. Michinoku Finance
70. Mitsubishi Trust Finance
71. Nanyang Finance
72. Niaga Finance
73. Nishi-Nippon Finance
74. Orient First Capital
75. OUB Finance

76. Philtrust Finance
77. PNB International Finance
78. Po Fung Finance
79. RCBC International Finance
80. Sakura Finance
81. Shacom Finance
82. Sin Hua Finance
83. Staco International Finance
84. Standard London
85. Sumitomo Trust Finance
86. Takugin International
87. Toyo Trust
88. Union Finance
89. Vietnam Finance
90. W.I. Carr Indosuez Capital
91. Wayfoong Credit
92. Wing Hang Finance
93. Wing Lung Finance
94. Yasuda Trust Asia Pacific
95. Yien Yieh Finance

PART IV

ABBREVIATIONS OF FINANCIAL TERMS USED IN SOUTHEAST ASIA AND HONG KONG

ABBREVIATIONS

AA	Airport Authority
AA	Articles of Association
AAB	Authorised agent bank
AAF	ASEAN Automotive Federation
AAIIBP	Al-Amanah Islamic Investment Bank of the Philippines
AASC	Auditing and Accounting Services Company (Vietnam)
AAT	Airport Authority of Thailand
ABC	Automated Banking Consortium (Malaysia)
ABI	Approved Bond Intermediary (Singapore)
ABN	Asian Business News Network
ABS	Association of Banks in Singapore
ABS	Asset-backed securities
ABV	Agricultural Bank of Vietnam
A/C	Account
ACG	Asia Pacific Central Securities Depository Group
ACH	Automated Clearing House
ACP	Airport Core Program (Hong Kong)
ACT	Approved Cyber Trader Scheme (Singapore)
ACU	Asian Currency Unit
ADA	Authorised Depository Agent (Malaysia)
ADB	Asian Development Bank
AEI	Association of Indonesian Securities Issuers
AFCRA	ASEAN Forum of Credit Rating Agencies
AFES	Association of Financial Engineering (Singapore)
AFFM	Australian Financial Futures Market
AFS	Automation Feasibility Study Scheme (Singapore)
AFTA	ASEAN Free Trade Area
AGL	Assurances Generales du Lao

Agribank	Vietnam Bank for Agriculture and Rural Development
AI	Authorised Institution
AIA	Association for Insurance Advancement (Singapore)
AIBD	Association of International Bond Dealers
AIS	Approved International Shipping Enterprise Scheme (Singapore)
AIS	Approved Investment Scheme (Singapore)
AIT	Approved International Trader Scheme (Singapore)
AKKI	Indonesian Credit Card Association
ALM	Asset liability management
ALPPIA	Asosiasi Lembaga Pembiayaan Pembangunan Indonesia (Indonesian Association of Development Financial Institutions)
ALS	Automation Leasing Scheme (Singapore)
ALS	Area Licensing Scheme (Singapore)
AMC	Asset Management Company
AMC	Asset Management Corporation
Amcorp	Arab-Malaysian Corporation (Malaysia)
AMETIAP	Association of Maritime Education and Training Institutions in the Asia Pacific
AMEX	American Stock Exchange
AMMB	Arab-Malaysian Merchant Bank Berhad (Malaysia)
AMU	Asset Management Unit
AMUT	Arab-Malaysian Unit Trusts Berhad
ANNA	Association of National Numbering Agencies
AOT	Approved Oil Trade Scheme (Singapore)
APBN	Indonesian acronym for State Budget
APEC	Asia Pacific Economic Cooperation
APEI	Indonesian Association of Securities Underwriters
APINDO	Employers Association of Indonesia
APMT	Asia Pacific Mobile Telecommunication Satellite project
APR	Annualised Percentage Rate
APRC	Asia Pacific Regional Committee of IOSCO
APT	Asset Privatisation Trust (Philippines)
ARF	Additional Registration Fee (Singapore)
ARF	ASEAN Regional Forum
ARM	Adjustable Rate Mortgage

ASAC	Asian Securities Analysts Council
ASAF	Asian Securities Analysts Federation
ASAP	Association of Securities Analysts of the Philippines
ASB	Amanah Saham Bumiputera Scheme (Malaysia)
ASC	Accounting Society of China
ASC	Approved Securities Company (Singapore)
ASCM	Association of Stockbroking Companies Malaysia
ASEAN	Association of Southeast Asian Nations
ASEAN CCI	ASEAN Chamber of Commerce and Industry
ASEI	Asuransi Ekspor Indonesia (Indonesian export insurance company)
ASIA	Asian Securitisation and Infrastructure Assurance Pte Ltd (Singapore)
ASKRINDO	Asuransi Kredit Indonesia (Indonesian credit insurance company)
ASME	Association of Small and Medium Enterprises (Singapore)
ASN	Amanah Saham Nasional (Malaysia)
ASSET	Automated Trading System for the Stock Exchange of Thailand
ASX	Australian Stock Exchange
ATC	Authorised Trading Centre (Singapore)
ATC	Agreement on Textile and Clothings
ATF	ASEAN Tourism Forum
ATI	Account transfer instruction
ATM	Automated teller machine
AWAS	Advanced Warning and Surveillance Unit (Malaysia)
AWS	Annual wage supplement (Singapore)
B/A	Banker's Acceptance
BAAC	Bank of Agriculture & Agricultural Cooperatives (Thailand)
BACS	Bankers' Automatic Clearing Services Ltd (Hong Kong)
BAFIA	Banking and Financial Institutions Act (Malaysia)
BAN	Badan Arbitrase Nasional (Indonesia) (National Arbitration Board)
Bao Viet	Vietnamese state-owned insurance company
BAP	Bankers Association of the Philippines

BAPEPAM	Badan Pengawas Pasar Modal (Indonesia) (Capital Market Supervisory Agency)
BAPETI	Indonesian Commodity Exchange Executive Agency
BAPPENAS	National Development Planning Board (Indonesia)
Bapindo	Bank Pembangunan Indonesia (Indonesian Development Bank)
BAS	Bureau of Agricultural Statistics (Philippines)
BBC	Bangkok Bank of Commerce
BBD	Bank Bumi Daya (Indonesia)
BBMB	Bank Bumiputra Malaysia Berhad
BCA	Bank Central Asia (Indonesia)
BCC	Business Cooperation Contract
BCCS	Board of Commissioners of Currency of Singapore
BCD	Building Control Division (Singapore)
BCDA	Bases Conversion Development Authority (Philippines)
BCEL	Banque pour le Commerce Exterrior Lao (Foreign Commercial Bank of Lao PDR)
BCP	Business Collaboration Program (Singapore)
BDB	Bank Dagang Bali (Indonesia)
BDC	Bond Dealing Centre (Thailand)
BDN	Bank Dagang Negara (Indonesia)
BDNI	Bank Dagang Nasional Indonesia
BDS	Business Development Scheme (Singapore)
BE	Bonus ekspor (export bonus)
Becamex	Song Be Export Import Trading Company (Vietnam)
BEJ	Bursa Efek Jakarta (Jakarta Stock Exchange)
Bernama	Pertubuhan Berita Nasional Malaysia
BES	Bursa Efek Surabaya (Surabaya Stock Exchange)
BESS	Book Entry Settlement System (Indonesia)
BFI	Brokers' Fidelity Insurance Scheme
BHC	Bank holding company
Bhd	Berhad
BHQ	Business Headquarters Program (Singapore)
BHS	Bank Harapan Sentosa (Indonesia)
BI	Bank Indonesia (Central Bank)
BIBF	Bangkok International Banking Facility
BIBOR	Baht Interbank Offer Rate
BIDA	Batam Industrial Development Authority

BIDP	Bintan Integrated Development Project (Indonesia)
BIDV	Bank for Investment and Development of Vietnam
BII	Bank Internasional Indonesia
BIMAS	Bimbingan Massal (Indonesia) (Mass guidance program)
BIMB	Bank Islam Malaysia Berhad
BIMB	Bank Industri Malaysia Berhad
BIMP-EAGA	Brunei, Indonesia, Malaysia and Philippines East Asia Growth Area
BIP	Batamindo Industrial Park (Indonesia)
BIS	Bank for International Settlements
BIS	Basic Investment Scheme (Singapore)
BKK	Badan Kredit Kecamatan (Indonesia)
BKPM	Badan Koordinasi Penanaman Modal (Investment Coordinating Board)
B/L	Bill of lading
BLR	Base lending rate
BLS	Bridging Loan Scheme (Singapore)
BLT	Build, lease and transfer
BMB	Bangkok Metropolitan Bank
BMC	Biro Maklumat Cek (Malaysia)
BMF	Bumiputera Malaysia Finance Berhad
BMI	Bank Mua'malat Indonesia
BMTA	Bangkok Mass Transit Authority
BN	Barisan Nasional
BNI	Bank Negara Indonesia
BNM	Bank Negara Malaysia (Central Bank of Malaysia)
BOA	Bank of America
BOA	Bank of Asia (Thailand)
BOC	Bank of China
BOC	Bureau of Customs (Philippines)
BOI	Board of Investments
BOL	Bank of Lao PDR
BOL	Bill of lading
BOO	Build, operate and own
BOOT	Build, own, operate and transfer
BOP	Balance of payments
BOT	Bank of Thailand
BOT	Build, operate and transfer
Bp	Basis point

Bpd	Barrels per day
BPD	Bank Pembangunan Daerah (Indonesia) (Local development bank)
BPEN	National Export Development Agency (Indonesia)
BPG	Best Practice Guide
BPI	Bank of the Philippine Islands
BPK	State Audit Board (Indonesia)
BPPN	Badan Penyehatan Perhankan Nasional (Indonesian Bank Restructuring Agency, IBRA)
BPR	Bank Perkreditan Rakyat (Indonesia) (People's Lending Banks, rural banks)
BPS	Central Bureau of Statistics
BPULN	Badan Penyelesaian Utang dan Lelang Negara (Indonesia's State Debt Recovery Agency)
BQS	Bond Quotation System (Singapore)
BRI	Bank Rakyat Indonesia
BRM	Bank Rahardja Maksur (Indonesia)
BSDC	Bangkok Stock Dealing Center
BSE	Bumiputera Stock Exchange
BSKL	Bursar Saham Kuala Lumpur (Kuala Lumpur Stock Exchange)
BSN	Bank Simpanan Nasional (Malaysia) National Savings Bank (Malaysia)
BSP	Bangko Sentral ng Pilipinas (Central Bank of the Philippines)
BTN	Bank Tabungan Negara (Indonesia)
BTO	Bank taken over
BTr	Bureau of Treasury (Philippines)
BT-SRI	Business Times Singapore Regional Index
BTT	Board of Trade of Thailand
BUKOPIN	Bank Umum Koperasi Indonesia (Indonesian Cooperative Bank)
BULOG	Buro Logistik (Indonesia) (National Logistics Agency)
BUMD	Badan Usaha Milik Daerah (Indonesia) (Provincial-owned government enterprise)
BUMN	Badan Usaha Milik Negara (state-owned enterprise)
BUN	Bank Umum Nasional (Indonesia)
BUPLN	Badan Urusan Piutang dan Lelang Negara (Indonesia)

	(Agency for State Receivables and Auctions)
BUS	Bank Umum Servitia (Indonesia)
BWK	Bank Windu Kencana (Indonesia)
CA	Collective agreement
CAA	Civil Aviation Authority (Vietnam)
CAAS	Civil Aviation Authority of Singapore
CAHB	Commerce Asset Holding Berhad (Malaysia)
call	Cum all
CAMEL	Capital adequacy, Asset quality, Management, Earnings, Liquidity
CAMINCO	Cambodian National Insurance Company
CAPS	Capital augmented preferred shares (Singapore)
CAR	Capital Adequacy Ratio
CAT	Communication Authority of Thailand
CB	Central bank
CBA	Currency Board Arrangement (Cambodia)
CBC	China Banking Corporation (Philippines)
CBD	Central business district
cbi	Cum bonus issue
CBM	Central Bank of Myanmar
CBOE	Chicago Board Options Exchange
CBOT	Chicago Board of Trade
CBP	Central Bank of the Philippines
CCASS	Central Clearing and Settlement System (Hong Kong)
CCIC	Chemical Construction Installation Company (Vietnam)
CCPI	Composite consumer price index
CCPS	Convertible cumulative preference share
cd	Cum dividend
CD	Certificate of deposit
CDC	Cambodia Development Council
CDF	Cluster Development Fund (Singapore)
CDP	Central Depository Pte Ltd (Singapore)
CDRAC	Corporate Debt Restructuring Advisory Committee (Thailand)
CDRC	Consolidated Daily Report of Condition (Philippines)
CDRC	Corporate Debt Restructuring Committee (Malaysia)

CDS	Central Depository System (Malaysia)
CEDEL	Centrale de Livraison de Valeurs Mobilieres
CEO	Chief Executive Officer
CEPT	Common Effective Preferential Tariff
CERTAS	Certification Assistance Scheme (Singapore)
CESTI	Centre for Science and Technology Information (Vietnam)
CFA	Chartered Financial Analyst
CFO	Chief Financial Officer
CFP	Certified Financial Planner
CFTC	Commodities Futures Trading Commission
CGC	Credit Guarantee Corporation (Malaysia)
CHAPS	Clearing House Automated Payment System
CHATS	Clearing House Automated Transfer System
CHIPS	Clearing House Inter-bank Payment System
CHOGM	Commonwealth Heads of Government Meeting
CI	Certificate of indebtedness
CIA	Cambodia International Airlines
CIB	Cambodia Investment Board
CIC	Capital Issues Committee (Malaysia)
CIEM	Central Institute of Economic Management (Vietnam)
CIF	Costs, insurance and freight
CIO	Chief Information Officer
CISA	Certified Investment and Securities Analyst (Thailand)
CITIC	China International Trust and Investment Corporation
CKD	Completely knocked-down
CLF	Countryside Loan Fund (Philippines)
CLOB	Central Limit Order Book (Singapore)
CME	Chicago Mercantile Exchange
CMNP	Citra Marga Nusaphala Persada (Indonesia)
CMPP	PT Centris Multi Persada Pratama (Indonesia)
CMS	Capital Market Society of Indonesia
CMU	Central Moneymarkets Unit (Hong Kong)
COE	Certificate of Entitlement (Singapore)
COINS	Corporate Information Superhighway
COIT	Committee on International Trade (Singapore)
COL	Cost of living
COMEX	Commodity Exchange (New York)

COMMEX	Commodity and Monetary Exchange of Malaysia
COO	Chief Operation Officer
COP	Committee on Privatisation (Philippines)
COP	Committee on Productivity (Singapore)
CPC	Committee for Planning and Cooperation (Laos)
CPF	Central Provident Fund (Singapore)
CPFIS	CPF Investment Scheme (Singapore)
CPI	Consumer price index
CPKO	Crude palm kernel oil
CPO	Crude palm oil
CPP	Cambodian People's Party
CPP	Chamber of Pawnbrokers of the Philippines
CRAC	Corporate Restructuring Advisory Committee (Indonesia)
CRC	Cost Review Committee (Singapore)
cri	Cum rights issue
CRR	Cash reserve requirement
CSBSOE	Central Steering Board for State-owned Enterprises (Vietnam)
CSD	Central Securities Depository
CSIE	Consolidated Statement of Income and Expense (Philippines)
CSIS	Centre for Strategic and International Studies (Indonesia)
CSOC	Consolidated Statement of Condition (Philippines)
CSP	Comprehensive Shipping Policy
CSPI	Composite Share Price Index (Indonesia)
CSRC	China Securities Regulatory Commission
CTB	Chamber of Thrift Banks (Philippines)
CTC	Commodities Trading Commission (Malaysia)
CTO	Commodities Trading Ordinance (Hong Kong)
CULS	Convertible unsecured loan stock
D/A	Documents Against Acceptance
DAI	Indonesian Insurance Council
Dana	Islamic-based unit trust (Malaysia)
Danareksa	National Investment Trust (Indonesia)
DBAP	Development Bankers Association of the Philippines
DBP	Development Bank of the Philippines
DBR	Disclosure-based regulation

DBS	Development Bank of Singapore
DCF	Discounted cash flow
DCPP	Direct Computer Package Program (Singapore)
DD	Designated dealer (Thailand)
DD	Demand Draft
DEM	Deutschemark
DFAS	Design for Automation Scheme (Singapore)
DFI	Development finance institutions
DGP	Development Guide Plan
DGPT	Directorate General of Posts & Telecommunications (Vietnam)
DIP	Debt Issuance Program
DJIA	Dow Jones Industrial Average
DMB	Deposit money banks (Philippines)
DNI	Negative Investment List (Indonesia)
DOE	Department of Education
DOE	Department of Environment
Doi moi	renovation or renewal (Vietnam)
DOLE	Department of Labour and Employment (Philippines)
DOSRI	Directors, officers or stockholders and their related interests (Philippines)
DOT	Department of Tourism
DOT	Department of Trade
D/P	Documents Against Payment
DP	Devisa pelangkap (Indonesia) (complementary foreign exchange market)
DPA	Dewan Pertimbangan Agung (Indonesia) (Supreme Advisory Council)
DPR	Dewan Perwakilan Rakyat (Indonesia) (Indonesia's House of Representatives)
DPLK	Financial institution pension fund (Indonesia)
DPPK	Employer pension fund (Indonesia)
DPRDI	Indonesian acronym for Provincial House of Representatives
DPRDII	Indonesian acronym for District or Municipal House of Representatives
DPS	Dependants' Protection Scheme (Singapore)
DRI	Dollar rate of interest
DSM	Department of Standards Malaysia
DTA	Double taxation agreement

DTC	Deposit-taking company
DTC	Deposit-taking Cooperative
DTD	Double Taxation Deduction Scheme (Singapore)
DTROP	Drug Traffiking (Recovery of Proceeds) Ordinance (Hong Kong)
DVEZ	Dinh Vu Economic Zone (Vietnam)
DVP	Delivery versus Payment
DVP	Design Ventures Program (Singapore)
EAB	East Asia Commercial Joint Stock Bank (Vietnam)
EAEC	East Asian Economic Caucus
EAGA	East ASEAN Growth Area
EBC	Equitable Banking Corporation (Philippines)
EC	Electronic commerce
EC	European Community
ECA	Export credit agency
ECH	Electronic Commerce Hotbed
ECIC	Export Credit Insurance Corporation
ECICS	Export Credit Insurance Corporation of Singapore
ECN	Electronic communication network
ECR	Export Credit Refinancing Scheme (Malaysia)
ECU	European Currency Unit
EDB	Economic Development Board
EDF	Entrepreneur Development Fund (Singapore)
EDI	Electronic data interchange
EDL	Electricite du Laos (Electricity Authority of Laos)
EEA	European Economic Area
EEC	European Economic Community
EEF	Exchange Equalisation Fund
EERI	Effective Exchange Rate Index
EFAC	Exchange Fund Advisory Committee (Hong Kong)
EFB	Exchange Fund Bill
EFIL	Exchange Fund Investment Ltd (Hong Kong)
EFN	Exchange Fund Note
EFTA	European Free Trade Area
EFTPOS	Electronic fund transfer at point of sale
EGAT	Electricity Generating Authority of Thailand
EGCO	Electricity Generating Public Co Ltd (Thailand)
EIS	Enhanced Investment Scheme (Singapore)
EIU	Economic Intelligence Unit

EKB	Expanded commercial banks (Philippines)
ELDISTRA	Electronics long distance trading system
EMAS	Exchange Main Board Share Index (Malaysia)
EMEAP	Executives' Meeting of East Asia and Pacific Central Banks
EMS	European Monetary System
EMU	European Monetary Union
EO	Executive Order (Philippines)
EPC	Employment Promotion Center (Laos)
EPC	Enterprise Promotion Center (Singapore)
EPF	Employees' Provident Fund (Malaysia)
EPS	Earning per share
EPTE	Entrepot Produksi untuk Tujuan Ekspor (Indonesia) (export production unit)
EPTL	Enterprise des Posts et Telecommunications Lao
EPU	Economic Planning Unit (Malaysia)
EPZ	Export processing zone
ERB	Energy Regulatory Board (Philippines)
ERF	Enterprise Rehabilitation Fund (Malaysia)
ERM	Exchange Rate Mechanism
ERP	Electronic Road Pricing (Singapore)
ERTA	Expressway and Rapid Transit Authority (Thailand)
ESA	Electronic Share Application (Singapore)
ESAF	Enhanced Structural Adjustment Facility (Laos)
ESPC	Entrepreneur Skills Development Centre (Malaysia)
ETC	Electronic Teller Card
ETL	Enterprise des Telecommunications Lao
ETO	Express Transportation Organisation (Thailand)
ETRS	Electronic Trade Related Services
EU	European Union
EURAP	European Union Reintegration Assistance Program (Vietnam)
EuroCP	Euro commercial paper
EVN	Electricity Vietnam

FAA	Federal Aviation Administration
FACTS	Fully Automated Computer Trading System
FAMA	Federal Agriculture and Marketing Agency (Malaysia)

FAO	Food and Agriculture Organisation
FASA	Federation of ASEAN Shipping Associations
FATF	Financial Action Task Force (Hong Kong)
FBCB	First Bangkok City Bank (Thailand)
FCA	Foreign currency account
FCAG	Financial Centre Advisory Group (Singapore)
FCC	First Capital Corporation (Singapore)
FCDU	Foreign Currency Deposit Unit
FD	Fixed deposit
FDC	Franchise Development Centre (Singapore)
FDI	Foreign direct investment
FDIC	Federal Deposit Insurance Corporation
FDSS	Fixed Delivery and Settlement System
FEAS	Federation of Euro-Asian Stock Exchanges
FEB	Far East Bank (Philippines)
FEBC	Foreign exchange bearer certificate
FEBTC	Far East Bank and Trust Company (Philippines)
FEC	Foreign Exchange Certificates
FELDA	Federal Land Development Authority (Malaysia)
FETC	Foreign Exchange Trading Centre (Vietnam)
FGLID	Factories and General Labour Inspection Department (Myanmar)
FIBV	International Federation of Stock Exchanges (Federation Internationale des Bourses de Valeurs)
FIC	Foreign Investment Committee
FID	Foreign Investment Department (Vietnam)
FIDF	Financial Institution Development Fund (Thailand)
FIES	Family Income and Expenditure Survey (Philippines)
FIL	Foreign Investment Law
FIMC	Foreign Investment Management Committee
FIO	Forest Industry Organisation (Thailand)
FIPF	Financial Institution Pension Fund (Indonesia)
FLSRO	Front-line self-regulatory organisation
FMCG	Fast moving consumer goods
FMO	Fish Marketing Organisation (Thailand)
FMUTM	Federation of Malaysian Unit Trust Managers
FOB	Free on board
FOMC	Federal Open Market Committee
FOREX	Foreign exchange
FOSCO	Foreign Service Corporation (Vietnam)

FRA	Forward Rate Agreement
FRA	Financial Restructuring Authority (Thailand)
FRAC	Financial Restructuring Advisory Committee (Thailand)
FRANDAS	Franchise Development Assistance Scheme (Singapore)
FRB	Federal Reserve Board
FRB	Fixed rate bond
FRCD	Floating rate certificate of deposit
FRIM	Forest Reseearch Institute of Malaysia
FRN	Floating rate note
FSAC	Financial Sector Advisory Council (Singapore)
FSOC	Financial Sector Outline Committee (Indonesia)
FSR	Financial sector reform
FSRG	Financial Sector Review Group (Singapore)
FTA	Free trade agreement
FTA	Free trade area
FTC	Finance and Treasury Centre Scheme (Singapore)
FTI	Federation of Thai Industries
FTZ	Free trade zone
FWS	Flexible wage system (Singapore)
FX	Foreign exchange
FXRN	Fixed Rate Note
FY	Fiscal year
G7	Group of Seven
GAAP	Generally accepted accounting principles
GATS	General Agreement on Trade and Services
GATT	General Agreement on Tariffs and Trade
GBHN	Indonesian acronym for Guidelines of State Policy
GCOP	Government Committee on Organisation and Personnel (Vietnam)
GDC	General Department of Customs (Vietnam)
GDP	Gross domestic product
GDR	General Department of Rubber (Vietnam)
GDR	Global depository receipt
GDS	General Department of Statistics (Vietnam)
GDT	General Department of Tourism (Vietnam)
GES	Gold Exchange of Singapore
GES	Good Enterprise System (Thailand)
GFI	Government financial institutions (Philippines)

GGS	General Guarantee Scheme (Malaysia)
GHB	Government Housing Bank (Thailand)
GIA	General Insurance Association (Singapore)
GIC	Government Investment Certificate (Malaysia)
GIC	Government Investment Corporation (Singapore)
GII	Government Investment Issue (Malaysia)
GITIC	Guangdong International Trust and Investment Corporation
GKN	Indonesian acronym for National Partnership Movement
GLC	Government-linked companies (Singapore)
GLO	Government Lottery Office (Thailand)
GNP	Gross national product
GOCC	Government owned and controlled corporation (Philippines)
Golkar	Golongan Karya (Indonesia) (functional groups)
GPA	Gross Problematic Assets
GPC	Government Pricing Commission (Vietnam)
GPM	Graduated payment mortgage
GPO	Government Pharmaceutical Organisation (Thailand)
GRA	General revenue account
GSB	Government Savings Bank (Thailand)
GSBS	Government Securities Book-entry System
GSIS	Government Service Insurance System (Philippines)
GSM	Global System for Mobile Communications
GSM	Government securities market
GSP	Generalised System of Preferences
GST	Goods and services tax
GTC	Good-till-cancel order
GTD	Good-till-date order
GUN	Grantor underwritten note
HACTL	Hong Kong Air Cargo Terminals Ltd
HCMC	Ho Chi Minh City
HCMC P&T	Ho Chi Minh City Post and Telecommunications
HCS	Health Corporation of Singapore
HDB	Housing & Development Board (Singapore)
HEPZA	Ho Chi Minh City Export Processing Zone Authority

HIBOR	Hong Kong Inter Bank Offer Rate
HIECC	HCMC International Exhibition and Convention Centre (Vietnam)
HITC	Hanoi International Technology Centre
HKAB	Hong Kong Association of Banks
HKCC	HKFE Clearing Corporation Ltd (Hong Kong)
HKD	Hong Kong dollar
HKFE	Hong Kong Futures Exchange
HKFGC	Hong Kong Futures Guarantee Corporation
HKIA	Hong Kong International Airport
HKICL	Hong Kong Interbank Clearing Ltd
HKIFA	Hong Kong Investment Funds Association
HKMA	Hong Kong Monetary Authority
HKMC	Hong Kong Mortgage Corporation
HKNPL	Hong Kong Note Printing Limited
HKSAR	Hong Kong Special Administrative Region
HKSCC	Hong Kong Securities Clearing Co Ltd
HKSI	Hong Kong Securities Institute
HKUTA	Hong Kong Unit Trust Association
HNW	High net worth
HOS	Home Ownership Scheme (Singapore)
HP	Hire purchase
HPIS	Home Protection Insurance Scheme (Singapore)
HSAI	Hang Seng Asia Index
HSBC	Hong Kong Shanghai Banking Corporation
HSCCI	Hang Seng China-Affiliated Corporations Index
HSCEI	Hang Seng China Enterprises Index
HSI	Hang Seng Index
HSMCI	Hang Seng Midcap 50 Index
HTZ	High Technology Zone
HWBC	Hanoi Water Business Company (Vietnam)
IADP	Industry-wide Automation Development Program (Singapore)
IAI	Ikatan Akuntan Indonesia (Association of Indonesian Accountants)
IAL	Investment Adviser Licence (Singapore)
IAP	International Advisory Panel (Singapore)
IAS	Investment Allowance Scheme (Singapore)
IASC	International Accounting Standards Committee
IBAS	International Bidding Assistance Scheme (Singapore)

IBBM	Institut Bank-Bank Malaysia (Institute of Bankers Malaysia)
IBCL	Interbank call loan
IBF	Institute of Banking & Finance (Singapore)
IBF	International banking facility
IBI	Indonesian Banker Institute
IBRA	Indonesian Banking Restructuring Agency
IBRD	International Bank for Reconstruction and Development
IBS	International Bank of Singapore
ICBV	Industrial and Commercial Bank of Vietnam
ICCH	International Commodities Clearing House
ICEB	Indonesian Commodity Exchange Board
ICFA	Institute of Chartered Financial Analysts
ICO	International Coffee Organisation
ICORC	International Committee on the Reconstruction of Cambodia
ICPAS	Institute of Certified Public Accountants of Singapore
ICS	Insurance Corporation of Singapore
ICTC	International Research, Consulting and Training Centre for Foreign Economic Relations (Vietnam)
ICU	Implementation Coordination Unit (Malaysia)
IDD	International direct dial
IDFC	Indonesian Development Finance Corporation
IDR	Indonesian Depository Receipt
IDR	Indonesian rupiah
IDR	International Depository Receipt
IDS	Innovation Development Scheme (Singapore)
IEAT	Industrial Estate Authority of Thailand
IFBS	Interest free banking system
IFC	International Finance Corporation
IFCT	Industrial Finance Corporation of Thailand
IFDAS	International Fairs Development Assistance Scheme (Singapore)
IFS	International financial statistics
IFTS	Inter-bank Fund Transfer System
IHAP	Investment Houses Association of the Philippines
IIPS	Institute for Industry Policy and Strategy (Vietnam)
IKPI	Induk Koperasi Perikanan Indonesia (Indonesian Fisheries Cooperative)

IKPN	Induk Koperasi Pergawai Negeri (Indonesia) (Civil Servants' Cooperative)
ILP	Industrial Linkage Program (Malaysia)
IMAS	Investment Management Association of Singapore
IMF	International Monetary Fund
IMM	PT Indosat Multi Media (Indonesia)
IMM	International Monetary Market
IMO	International Maritime Organisation
IMS-GT	Indonesian Malaysian Singapore Growth Triangle
IMT-GT	Indonesian Malaysian Thailand Growth Triangle
Incombank	Industrial and Commercial Bank of Vietnam
Indosat	Indonesian Satellite Corporation
INDRA	Indonesian Debt Restructuring Agency
INKOPAD	Induk Koperasi Angkatan Darat (Indonesia) (National Army Cooperative)
INKOPAL	Induk Koperasi Angkatan Laut (Indonesia) (National Navy Cooperative)
INKOPAU	Induk Koperasi Angkatan Udara (Indonesia) (National Air Force Cooperative)
INKOPPOL	Induk Koperasi Kepolisian (Indonesia) (National Police Cooperative)
INKOVERI	Induk Koperasi Veteran RI (Indonesia) (National Veterans Cooperative)
Inpres	Presidential decree (Indonesia)
INRO	International Natural Rubber Organisation
INST	Institute of Nuclear Science and Technology (Vietnam)
IOBC	International Offshore Banking Centre
IOCR	Incremental Output capital ratio
IOFC	International Offshore Financial Centre
IOIT	Institute of Information Technology (Vietnam)
IOSCO	International Organisation of Securities Commissions
IPA	Issue and payment agent
IPE	International Petroleum Exchange
IPEJ	Jakarta Securities Brokers Club
IPO	Initial public offer
IPP	Independent power producer
IPP	Investments Priority Plan (Philippines)
IPTN	Industri Pesawat Terbang Nusantara (Indonesia) (State-owned Nusantara Aircraft Industry)

IPTW	Insentif Pembayaran Tepat Waktu (Indonesia)
IRA	Interest rate agreement
IRAS	Inland Revenue Authority of Singapore
IRR	Interest rate rule (Hong Kong)
IRR	Internal rate of return
ISDN	Integrated services digital network
ISIN	International Securities Identification Numbers for Malaysian Securities
ISO	International Standards Organisation
ISP	Internet service provider
IT	Information technology
ITIC	International Trust and Investment Corporation
ITM	In the money
IVB	Indovina Bank (Vietnam)
IZ	Industrial Zone
Jabotabek	Jakarta, Bogor, Tanerang and Bekasi (Indonesia)
Jamsostek	Indonesian acronym for Workers' Social Security
JATS	Jakarta Automated Trading System
JCI	Jakarta Composite Index
JETCO	Joint Electronic Teller Company (Hong Kong)
JETRO	Japan External Trade Organisation
JIBOR	Jakarta Interbank Offer Rate
JIC	Jakarta Investors Club
JIT	Just in time
JKR	Jabatan Kerja Raya (Malaysia) (Public Works Department)
JPA	Johor Port Authority (Malaysia)
JPY	Japanese yen
JSX	Jakarta Stock Exchange
JSX LQ45	Jakarta Stock Exchange LQ45 Index
JTC	Jurong Town Corporation (Singapore)
JTM	Jabatan Telecom Malaysia
JUB	Indonesian acronym for Amount of circulating money
JV	Joint venture
JVC	Joint venture company
KADA	Kemubu Agricultural Development Authority (Malaysia)
KADIN	Kamar Dagang dan Industri Indonesia (Indonesian Chamber of Commerce & Industry)

KB	Commercial bank (Philippines)
KCRC	Kowloon Canton Railway Corporation
KCT	Kelang Container Terminal Berhad (Malaysia)
KDU	Indonesian acronym for Rural cooperatives
KDEI	PT Kliring Deposit Efek Indonesia (Indonesian Securities Clearing and Depository Corporation)
Kepres	Presidential Instruction (Indonesia)
KIK	Kredit Investasi Kecil (Indonesia) (Small investment loan)
KKMB	Komplek Kewangan Malaysia Berhad
KKPA	Kredit Kepada Koperasi Primer Untuk Anggotanya (Indonesia)
KKUD	Kredit Kepada Koperasi Unit Desa (Indonesia) (Credit to Rural Unit Cooperatives)
KLACH	Kuala Lumpur Automatic Clearing House
KLBI	Indonesian acronym for Bank Indonesia Liquidity Credit
KLCC	Kuala Lumpur City Centre
KLCCH	Kuala Lumpur Commodity Clearing House
KLCE	Kuala Lumpur Commodity Exchange
KLCI	Kuala Lumpur Composite Index
KLIA	Kuala Lumpur International Airport
KLIBOR	Kuala Lumpur Interbank Offer Rate
KLOFFE	Kuala Lumpur Options and Financial Futures Exchange
KLSE	Kuala Lumpur Stock Exchange
KMKP	Kredit Modal Kerja (Indonesia) (Permanent working capital loan)
Kopemkei	Koperasi Pemodal Pemodal Kecil Indonesia (Small Investors Cooperative of Indonesia)
KPEI	Indonesian Stock Clearing and Guarantee Corporation
KPR	Indonesian acronym for Housing credit provided by Indonesian banks
KRW	Korean won
KSD	Korea Securities Depository
KSEI	Indonesian Stock Central Custodian Corporation
KSM	Kelompok Swadaya Masyarakat (Indonesia) (Local self-help group)
KSO	Indonesia acronym or "Joint operating scheme"

	in telecommunications
KTB	Krung Thai Bank (Thailand)
KTM	Kretapi Tanah Melayu (Malaysian Railway)
KTT	Krung Thai Thanakit PCL (Thailand)
KUD	Kooperasa Unit Desa (Indonesia) (Village cooperative unit)
KUK	Kredit Usaha Kecil (Indonesia) (Small scale credit program)
KUKMI	Indonesian acronym for Indonesian Small and Medium Business Association
KULBER	KLSE Bernama Real-time Information Services (Malaysia)
Kupedes	Kredit Umum Pedesaan (Indonesia) (General purpose village loan)
KUT	Kredit Usaha Tani (Indonesia) (General lending scheme for farmers)
LABOR	Labuan Interbank Offer Rate
LAF	Liquidity Adjustment Facility
LAR	Liquid asset requirement
LAS	Leasing Association of Singapore
LB	Licensed bank
LBO	Leveraged buyout
LBP	Land Bank of the Philippines
LC	Letter of credit
LCP	Loan classification and provisioning
LDP	Loan deposit ratio
LDTC	Licensed deposit taking company
LEAP	Local Enterprise Accounting Program (Singapore)
LECP	Local Enterprise Computerisation Program (Singapore)
LEFS	Local Enterprise Finance Scheme (Singapore)
LESCO	Lao Employment Services Company
LETAS	Local Enterprise Technical Assistance Scheme (Singapore)
LFETO	Leveraged Foreign Exchange Trading Ordinance (Hong Kong)
LFHPT	Loan Fund for Hawkers and Petty Traders (Malaysia)
LFI	Law on Foreign Investment
LG	Letter of guarantee

LGU	Local government unit (Philippines)
LIA	Life Insurance Association (Singapore)
LIAM	Life Insurance Association of Malaysia
LIBID	London Interbank Bid Rate
LIBOR	London Interbank Offer Rate
LIDAS	Licensing Development Assistance Scheme
LIFFE	London International Financial Futures Exchange
LIFFOE	London International Financial Futures & Options Exchange
LIMA	Langkawi International Maritime and Aerospace Exhibition (Malaysia)
LIMEAN	London interband mean
LIPCO	Lao Investment Promotion Company
LIUP	Local Industry Upgrading Program (Singapore)
LKP	Indonesian acronym for Clearing and guarantee institution
LLL (L3)	Legal lending limit
LME	London Metals Exchange
LMW	Licensed Manufacturing Warehouse (Malaysia)
LNCD	Long-term negotiable certificate of deposit
LNG	Liquefied natural gas
Loteco	Long Binh Techno Park Development Company (Vietnam)
LPDR	Lao People's Democratic Republic
LPG	Liquefied petroleum gas
LPP	Indonesian acronym for Settlement and custody institution
LPSM	Indonesian acronym for Self-help development institution
LRO	Local representative office
LRT	Light Rail Transit
LSE	London Stock Exchange
LTA	Land Transport Authority (Singapore)
LTAB	Indonesian acronym for Transaction statement used in the stock exchange
LTAT	Lembaga Tabung Angkatan Tentera (Malaysia)
LTB	Laem Thong Bank (Thailand)
LTCA	Labuan Trust Companies Act (Malaysia)
LURC	Land Use Rights Certificate (Vietnam)
LURO	Land Use Rights Owner (Vietnam)
LUTH	Lembaga Urusan dan Tabung Haji (Malaysia)

LVR	Loan-to-value ratio
LYON	Liquid yield option note
MA	Memorandum of Association
MA	Monetary Authority
MA	Moving average
MAA	Malaysian Assurance Alliance Berhad
M&A	Merger and acquisition
MAC	Myanmar Accountancy Council
MADA	Muda Agricultural Development Authority (Malaysia)
MAEI	Malaysian American Electronics Industries Association
MAERS	Market average exchange rate system
MAFI	Ministry of Agriculture and Food Industry (Vietnam)
MARA	Majlis Amanah Rakyat (Malaysia) (Council of Trust for Indigenous People)
MARC	Malaysian Rating Corporation Berhad
MARCAP	Market capitalisation
MARD	Ministry of Agriculture and Rural Development (Vietnam)
MARDB	Myanmar Agricultural & Rural Development Bank
MARDI	Malaysian Agriculture Research & Development Institute
MART	Money Market Association of the Philippines
MAS	Malaysian Airlines System
MAS	Monetary Authority of Singapore
MASET	Malaysian Airlines System Electronic Ticketing
MASTIC	Malaysian Science and Technology Information Centre
MAT	Management action trigger limit
MATRADE	Malaysian External Trade Development Corporation
Maybank	Malayan Banking Berhad
MB	Metropolitan Bank (Philippines)
MB	Monetary Board (Philippines)
MBHC	Multibank holding company
MBS	Mortgage backed securities
MBSB	Malaysia Building Society Berhad
MBTC	Metropolitan Bank and Trust Company (Philippines)

MCB	Malaysian Coconut Board
MCB	Minimum cash balance
MCCM	Malay Chamber of Commerce Malaysia
MCD	Malaysian Central Depository
MCOT	Mass Communication Organisation of Thailand
MDAS	Manpower Development Assistance Scheme (Singapore)
MDC	Multimedia Development Corporation
MDCH	Malaysian Derivatives Clearing House Berhad
MEA	Metropolitan Electricity Authority (Thailand)
MEB	Myanmar Economic Bank
MEER	Ministry of External Economic Relations (Laos)
MEFP	Memorandum of Economic and Financial Policies (Indonesia)
MEGA	Management of Economic Group Assistance program (Singapore)
MEPE	Myanmar Electric Power Enterprise
MEPF	Ministry of Economy, Planning and Finance (Laos)
MEPS	MAS Electronic Payment System
MEPZ	Mactan Export Processing Zone (Philippines)
MERC	Chicago Mercantile Exchange
MFA	Ministry of Foreign Affairs
MFA	Multi Fiber Agreement
MFC	Multi-finance corporation (Indonesia)
MFCC	Malaysian Futures Clearing Corporation
MFN	Most favoured nation
MFORR	Malaysian Futures and Options Registered Representative
MFSL	Myanmar Five Star Line
MFTB	Myanmar Foreign Trade Bank
MGS	Malaysian Government Securities
MGS	Multimedia Super Corridor Research & Development Grant Scheme (Malaysia)
MHPI	Malaysian Housing Price Index
MHT	Ministry of Hotels and Tourism
MIA	Malaysian Institute of Accountants
MIA	Missing in action
MIC	Myanmar Investment Commission
MICB	Myanmar Investment and Commercial Bank
MICCI	Malaysian International Chamber of Commerce & Industry

MICE	Meetings, incentives, conventions and exhibitions
MICR	Magnetic ink character recogition
MIDAS	Market and Investment Development Assistance Scheme (Singapore)
MIDF	Malaysian Industrial Development Finance Berhad
MIDFCCS	MIDF Consultancy and Corporate Services Sdn Bhd
MIDFIH	MIDF Investment Holdings Sdn Bhd
MIER	Malaysian Institute of Economic Research
MIFE	Manila International Futures Exchange
MIGA	Multilateral Investment Guarantee Agency
Miliar	Billion (Indonesia)
MIMB	Malaysian International Merchant Bankers
MIMOS	Malaysian Institute of Microelectronic Systems
MINDEF	Ministry of Defence (Singapore)
MISC	Malaysian International Shipping Corporation
MITA	Malaysian Income Tax Act
MITA	Ministry of Information and the Arts (Singapore)
MITI	Ministry of International Trade and Industry
MkSE	Makati Stock Exchange
MLA	Minimum liquid asset
MLR	Minimum lending rate
MLLE	Maximum Limit of Loan Extension
MLSW	Ministry of Labour and Social Welfare (Laos)
MM	Metro Manila
MMA	Myanmar Mines Authorities
MMDA	Money market deposit account
MME	Malaysian Monetary Exchange
MMO	Money market operation
MNC	Multinational corporation
MND	Ministry of National Development (Singapore)
MNE	Multinational enterprise
MNFP	Malaysian National Focal Point
MNI	Malaysian National Insurance Sdn Bhd
MNRB	Malaysian National Reinsurance Berhad
MO	Marketing Organisation (Thailand)
MOA	Ministry of Agriculure
MOC	Ministry of Construction
MOCI	Ministry of Culture and Information (Vietnam)
MOE	Ministry of Education
MOET	Ministry of Education and Training (Vietnam)
MOF	Marketing Organisation for Farmers (Thailand)

MOF	Ministry of Finance
MOFF	Multiple options funding facility
MOGE	Myanmar Oil and Gas Enterprise
MOH	Ministry of Health
MOHI	Ministry of Heavy Industries (Vietnam)
MOHR	Ministry of Human Resources
MOI	Ministry of Industry
MOL	Ministry of Labour
MOLISA	Ministry of Labour, War Invalids and Social Affairs (Vietnam)
MOM	Ministry of Manpower
MOMP	Ministry of Marine Products (Vietnam)
MOR	Manual of Regulations (Philippines)
MORC	Memorandum of Regulatory Cooperation
MOST	Ministry of Science & Technology
MOSTE	Ministry of Science, Technology and Environment
MOT	Ministry of Trade
MOTC	Ministry of Transport and Communications
MOU	Memorandum of understanding
MPA	Marine and Port Authority (Singapore)
MPA	Myanmar Port Authority
MPC	Multipurpose card
MPDF	Mekong Project Development Facility (Vietnam)
MPI	Ministry of Planning and Investment (Vietnam)
MPOPC	Malaysian Palm Oil Promotion Council
MPR	Majelis Permusyswaratan Rakyat (Indonesia) (People's Consultative Assembly)
MRCB	Malaysian Resources Corporation Berhad
MRPI	Maybank-RAM Property Index
MRR	Manila Reference Rate
MRRDB	Malaysian Rubber Research and Development Board
MRT	Mass Rapid Transit
MRTA	Metropolitan Rapid Transit Authority (Thailand)
MRTC	Mass Rapid Transit Corporation
MRTP	Mortgage Reducing Term Policy
MSC	Multimedia Super Corridor (Malaysia)
MSCI	Morgan Stanley Capital International
MSCII	Morgan Stanley Capital Investment Index
MSE	Manila Stock Exchange
MSLE	Myanmar Small Loans Enterprise

MSRS	Malaysian Share Registration Services Sdn Bhd
MSS	Minimum Sum Scheme (Singapore)
MT	Mail Transfer
MTACS	Malaysian Trade Allocation and Confirmation System
MTDC	Malaysian Technology Development Corporation
MTI	Ministry of Trade and Industry
MTN	Medium term note
MTN	Multilateral Trade Negotiations
MTP	Marine Transport Department (Vietnam)
MTPB	Malaysian Tourism Promotion Board
MTR	Mass transit railway
MTRC	Mass Transit Railway Corporation (Hong Kong)
MTUC	Malaysian Trades Union Congress
MUI	Malayan United Industries Berhad
MWA	Metropolitan Waterworks Authority (Thailand)
MYR	Malaysian ringgit
NA	National Assembly (Vietnam)
NACCS	National Automatic Cheque Clearing System (Malaysia)
NAFTA	North American Free Trade Agreement
NAPCO	New Airport Projects Coordination Office (HK)
NASD	National Association of Securities Dealers (US)
NASDAQ	NASD Automated Quotation System
NAV	Net asset value
NBB	National Bank of Brunei
NBC	National Bank of Cambodia
NBFI	Non-bank financial intermediary
NCB	National Computer Board (Singapore)
NCCIM	National Chamber of Commerce & Industry of Malaysia
NCD	Negotiable certificate of deposit
NCI	Net capital inflow
NCM	Non-clearing member
NCR	National Capital Region (Philippines)
NDA	Net domestic assets
NDP	National Development Policy (Malaysia)
NEA	National Electrification Administration (Philippines)
NEAC	National Economic Action Council (Malaysia)

NECC	National Electronic Commerce Committee (Malaysia)
NEDA	National Economic and Development Authority (Philippines)
NEER	Nominal effective exchange rate
NEM	New Economic Mechanism (Laos)
NEP	New Economic Policy (Malaysia)
NEPC	National Energy Policy Committee (Laos)
NEPC	National Energy Policy Council (Thailand)
NERP	National Economic Recovery Plan (Malaysia)
NESDB	National Economic & Social Development Board (Thailand)
NETS	Network For Electronic Transfers
NEU	National Economics University (Vietnam)
NGO	Non-government organisation
NHA	National Housing Agency (Thailand)
NHMFC	National Home Mortgage Finance Corporation (Philippines)
NID	Negotiable instrument of deposit
NIE	National Institute of Education (Singapore)
NIE	New Industrialising Economy
NIF	New Investment Fund (Malaysia)
NIF	Note issuing facility
NII	Net interest income
Nikkei	Nihon Keizai Shimbun
NIM	Net interest margin
NIP	Note Issuance Program
NIR	Net international reserves
NISTPAS	National Institute for Science and Technology Policy and Strategy Studies (Vietnam)
NITC	National Information Technology Council (Malaysia)
NOP	Net open position
NOW	Negotiable order of withdrawal
NPAT	Net profit after tax
NPB	National Productivity Board (Singapore)
NPBT	Net profit before tax
NPC	National Petroleum Corp (Thailand)
NPC	National Power Corporation (Philippines)
NPC	National Productivity Centre (Malaysia)
NPD	Nuclear Power Department (Vietnam)

NPFDB	National Population & Family Development Board (Malaysia)
NPL	Non-performing loan
NPV	Net present value
NRCPS	Non-redeemable convertible preference shares
NRCPSS	Non-redeemable convertible cumulative preference share
NSB	National Savings Bank
NSC	National Securities Commission (Vietnam)
NSC	National Science Centre (Malaysia)
NSC	National Statistical Center (Laos)
NSO	National Statistical Office (Philippines)
NSTB	National Science and Technology Board (Singapore)
NSTP	New Straits Times Press Berhad (Malaysia)
NT	Nota transaksi (Indonesia) (stock exchange transaction note)
NTA	Net tangible assets
NTB	Nakornthon Bank (Thailand)
NTB	Non-tariff barriers
NTD	New Taiwan dollar
NTP	National Telecommunication Policy (Malaysia)
NTP	National Technology Plan (Singapore)
NTUC	National Trades Union Congress (Singapore)
NWC	National Wages Council
NYCE	New York Cotton Exchange
NYFE	New York Futures Exchange
NYMEX	New York Mercantile Exchange
NZFOE	New Zealand Futures and Options Exchange
OBA	Offshore Banking Act (Malaysia)
OB/OS	Over bought / over sold index
OBM	Original brand manufacturer
OBSA	Off balance sheet activity
OBU	Offshore banking unit
OCBC	Oversea-Chinese Banking Corporation (Singapore)
OCOI	Operating cost on operating income
OD	Overdraft
ODA	Official Development Assistance Program (Vietnam)
ODM	Original design manufacturer

ODRCF	One-day rolling currency futures
OECD	Organisation for Economic Cooperation & Development
OECF	Overseas Economic Cooperation Fund
OEI	Overseas Enterprise Incentive (Singapore)
OEM	Original equipment manufacturer
OFCL	On-shore foreign currency loan
OHQ	Operational Headquarters
OIA	Offshore Insurance Act (Malaysia)
OIC	Omnibus Investment Code (Philippines)
OII	Overseas Investment Tax Incentive (Singapore)
OMC	Open Market Committee (Bank Indonesia)
OMO	Open market operation
OPC	Off Peak Car scheme (Singapore)
OPE	Office of Project Evaluation (Vietnam)
OPEC	Organisation of Petroleum Exporting Countries
OPP 1	First Outline Perspective Plan (Malaysia)
OPP 2	Second Outline Perspective Plan (Malaysia)
OPT	Operasi Pasar Terbuka (Indonesia) (Open market operations)
OSE	Office of State Enterprises (Thailand)
OTC	Over-the-counter
OTC-FIS	Over-the-counter Fixed Income Service (Indonesia)
OTM	Out of the money
OUB	Overseas Union Bank (Singapore)
PAB	Philippine Amanah Bank
PAF	Patent Application Fund (Singapore)
PAFC	Philippine Association of Finance Companies
PAFTAD	Pacific Trade and Development Conference
Pakdes	Paket Desember 1988 (Indonesia) (December 1998 Package)
Pakfeb	Paket Februari (Indonesia) (February Package)
Pakmei	Paket Mei (Indonesia) (May Package)
Pakto	Paket Oktober 1988 (Indonesia) (October 1988 Package)
P&L	Profit and loss
Pancasila	Five principles of the State (Indonesia)
PAS	Performance Agreement System (Thailand)

PASBDI	Philippine Association of Securities Brokers and Dealers Inc
PAQ	Productive Asset Quality
PAT	Port Authority of Thailand
PAYE	Pay as you earn
PBC	Philippine Banking Corporation
PBCom	Philippine Bank of Communications
PBOC	People's Bank of China
PCB	Printed circuit board
PCCCI	Philippine Commercial Credit Card Inc
PCD	Philippine Central Depository Inc
PCHC	Philippine Clearing House Corp
PCDI	Philippine Central Depository Inc
PCI	Philippine Composite Index
PCIB	Philippine Commercial International Bank
PCL	Public company limited (Thailand)
PD	Perusahaan Dagang (Indonesia) (trading company)
PD	Presidential Decree (Philippines)
PDAS	Product Development Assistance Scheme (Singapore)
PDB	Port Development Board (Hong Kong)
PDCP	Private Development Corporation of the Philippines
PDIC	Philippine Deposit Insurance Corporation
PDP	Planters Development Bank (Philippines)
PDS	Philippine Dealing System
PDS	Private debt securities
PE	Price earning ratio
PEA	Provincial Electricity Authority (Thailand)
PEBT	Pemberitahuan Ekspor Barang Tertentu (Indonesia) (Certificate of export for special products)
PECC	Pacific Economic Cooperation Council
PEFINDO	Peringkat Efek Indonesia (Indonesia's securities rating agency)
PEFLGC	Philippine Export & Foreign Loan Guarantee Corp
Pelita V	Fifth Five-year Development Program (Indonesia)
PEN	Privatisation Exchangeable Notes
Perbanas	Perhimpunan Bank-Bank Umum Nasional Swasta (Indonesia) (National Private Bank Association)

PERC	Political and Economic Risk Consultancy
Perjan	Perusahaan Jawatan (Indonesia) (government agency)
Perum	Perusahaan Umum (Indonesia) (public corporation)
Perumka	Indonesian acronym for Indonesian state railway company
PERTAMINA	Perusahaan Pertambangan Minyak dan Gas Bumi Negera (Indonesia) (State-owned Indonesian petroleum and natural gas company)
Petrolimex	National Petroleum Import Export Corporation (Vietnam)
Petronas	Petrolium Nasional (Malaysia)
PGS	Principal Guarantee Scheme (Malaysia)
PHBK	Indonesian acronym for Bank and Self-help Group Link Project
PHILCOM	Philippine Global Communications Inc
PHILSLA	Philippine League of Savings and Loan Associations
PHP	Philippine peso
PIAM	Persatuan Insuran Am Malaysia
PIBF	Provincial International Banking Facility (Thailand)
PILTEL	Pilipino Telephone Corp
PIN	Personal identification number
PIO	Protection of Investors Ordinance (Hong Kong)
PIR	Perusahan Inti Rakyat (Indonesia)
PISO	Public Information Services Office
PIT	Personal income tax
PJP-I	First Long Term Development Program (1969–94) (Indonesia)
PJB	PT Pembangkit Listrik Jawa Bali (Indonesia)
PKM	Proyek Kredit Mikro (Indonesia) (Micro Credit Project)
PKNS	Perbadanan Kemajuan Negeri Selangor (Malaysia) (Selangor State Development Corporation)
PKT	Proyek Kemitraan Terpadu (Indonesia)
PKT	Indonesian acronym for Integrated Partnership Program
PLAS	Public Listing Assistance Scheme (Singapore)
PLDT	Philippine Long Distance Telecommunication

PLE	Promising Local Enterprise (Singapore)
PLMO	Property Loan Management Organisation (Thailand)
PLN	Perusahaan Listrik Negara (Indonesia) (State-owned electric company)
PLUS	Projek Lebuhraya Utara-Selatan (Malaysia)
PMA	Pernanaman Modal Asing (Indonesia) (foreign investment)
PMDN	Indonesian acronym for Domestic investment
PMP	Privatisation Master Plan (Malaysia)
PMVD	Indonesian acronym for Local venture capital company
PN	Perusahan Negara (Indonesia) (state corporation)
PNB	Permodalan Nasional Berhad (Malaysia)
PNB	Philippine National Bank
PNR	Philippine National Railways
PNSL	Perbadanan Nasional Shipping Line Berhad (Malaysia)
PORIM	Palm Oil Research Insititute of Malaysia
PORLA	Palm Oil Registration and Licensing Authority (Malaysia)
POSB	Post Office Savings Bank
PP	Perusahaan Persaorangan (Indonesia) (sole proprietorship)
PP	Private placement
PPA	Philippines Ports Authority
PPAW	Provision for Productive Asset Write-off
PPD	Policy and Planning Division (Laos)
PPH	Indonesian acronym for Ownership notification form (used in the stock exchange)
PPI	Producer Price Index
PPUE	Perserikatan Perdagangan Uang dan Efek-Efek (Indonesia) (Association of Money and Securities Traders)
PPUK	Proyek Pengembangan Usaha Kechil (Indonesia) (Small Enterprise Development Project)
PQP	Prevailing Quota Premium (Singapore)
Pribumi	Indigenous Indonesian
PROTON	Perusahaan Otomobil Nasional Berhad (Malaysia)
PRT	People-mover Rapid Transit

PSA	Port of Singapore Authority
PSB	Philippine Savings Bank
PSB	Productivity and Standards Board (Singapore)
PSC	Production sharing contract
PSDC	Penang Skill Development Centre (Malaysia)
PSE	Philippine Stock Exchange
PSEFI	PSE Foundation Inc (Philippines)
PSEI	Parallel Stock Exchange of Indonesia
PSIC	Philippine Standard Industrial Classification
PT	Perseroan Terbatas (Indonesia) (limited liability company)
PTA	Preferential trade agreement
PTM	PT Timar Putra Nasional (Indonesia)
PTN	PT Perusahaan Listrik Negara (Indonesia)
PTT	Petroleum Authority of Thailand
PUB	Public Utilities Board (Singapore)
PVBP	Price Value Basis Point
PVP	Payment versus Payment
PWA	Provincial Waterworks Authority (Thailand)
PWO	Public Warehouse Organisation (Thailand)
RAC	Royal Air Cambodge
RADD	Real aggregate domestic demand
R&D	Research and development
RAM	Rating Agency Malaysia Berhad
RAS	Requirement Assessment Service
RAS	Rubber Association of Singapore
RASIS	Real-time Analysis Stock Information Service
RB	Rural bank (Philippines)
RBAP	Rural Bankers Association of the Philippines
RBI	Reserve Bank of India
RBNZ	Reserve Bank of New Zealand
RCB	Registry of Companies and Businesses (Singapore)
RCBC	Rizal Commercial Banking Corporation (Philippines)
RCCPS	Redeembale convertible cumulative preference share
RCF	Revolving credit facility
RCPS	Redeemable cumulative preference share
RDAS	Research and Development Assistance Scheme
RDTC	Registered deposit taking company

RE	Retained earnings
REDAS	Real Estate Developers Association of Singapore
REER	Real effective exchange rate
Reksadana	Indonesian acronym for pension mutual funds
RENTAS	Real Time Electronic Transfer of Funds and Securities
RENSTRA	Indonesian acronym for Strategic Plan of Bank Indonesia
Repelita	Rencana pengembangan lima tahun (Indonesia) (Five-year plan)
Repo	Repurchase agreement
REX	Research Exchange Program (Singapore)
RFP	Request for proposal
RHB	Rashid Hussain Berhad (Malaysia)
RIC	Regional Investment Company Fund (Singapore)
RIIAM	Research Institute of Investment Analysts Malaysia
RISC	Research Incentive Scheme for Companies (Singapore)
RITS	Reserve Bank Information and Transfer System
RITST	Research Institute for Technological and Scientific Transportation (Vietnam)
RKT	Indonesian acronym for Annual work plan
RLB	Restricted licence bank
RM	Malaysian riggit
RM	Reserve Money
RMB	Renminbi
ROA	Return on assets
ROC	Registrar of Companies
ROCA	Risk management, operations, compliance, asset quality
ROE	Return on equity
ROI	Return on investment
ROL	Rehabilitate, operate and lease
ROM	Rehabilitate, operate and maintain
ROV	Registry of Vehicles (Singapore)
ROVR	Repatriation Opportunities for Vietnamese Returnees
R/P	Repurchase Agreement
RRIM	Rubber Research Institute of Malaysia
RR/P	Reverse Repurchase Agreement
RSA	Rate sensitive asset

RSE	Research scientist and engineer
RSI	Relative strength index
RSL	Rate sensitive liability
RTGS	Real Time Gross Settlement System
RTS	Regionalisation Training Scheme for Overseas Employees (Singapore)
RUF	Revolving Underwriting Facility
RVF	Regional Venture Fund Incentive (Singapore)
RWA	Risk weighted asset
RWCR	Risk weighted capital ratio
RZ	Restricted Zone (Singapore)
SAA	Securities Analysts Association (Thailand)
SAARC	South Asia Association for Regional Cooperation
SAB	State Agricultural Bank (Myanmar)
SAC	Singapore Accreditation Council
SAC	Structural Adjustment Credits (Laos)
SAF	Structural Adjustment Facility (Laos)
SAN	Shared ATM Network (Malaysia)
SAR	Special Administrative Region
S&L	Savings and loan
S&P	Standard & Poor's
SBAP	Savings Bankers Association of the Philippines
SBI	Sertifikat Bank Indonesia (Bank Indonesia Certificate)
SBL	Single borrower's limit
SBMA	Subic Bay Metropolitan Authority (Philippines)
SBPU	Surat Berhaga Pasar Uang (Indonesia) (Money market securities)
SBS	Singapore Bus Services Ltd
SBV	State Bank of Vietnam
SC	Securities Commission (Malaysia)
SCA	Securities Commission Act (Malaysia)
SCANS	Securities Clearing Automated Network Services (Malaysia)
SCC	Sabah Credit Corporation (Malaysia)
SCCI	State Committee for Cooperation and Investment (Vietnam)
SCCP	Securities Clearing Corporation of the Philippines
SCI	Singapore Confederation of Industries
SCIB	Siam City Bank (Thailand)

SCMP	South China Morning Post
SCORE	System on Computerised Order Routing and Execution
SDC	Share Depository Center (Thailand)
SDDS	Special Data Dissemination Standards (Hong Kong)
SDF	Skills Development Fund (Singapore)
Sdn Bhd	Sendirian Berhad (Malaysia)
SDP	Strategic Development Plan (Singapore)
SDR	Special Drawing Rights
SEACEN	Southeast East Asian Central Banks
SEATS	Stock Exchange Automated Trading System
SEAVI	Southeast Asia Venture Investment
SEBI	Securities and Exchange Board of India
SEC	Securities and Exchange Commission (Philippines)
SEC	Securities Exchange Commission (Thailand)
SEDC	State Economic Development Corporation (Malaysia)
SEE	State Economic Enterprises
SEHK	Stock Exchange of Hong Kong
SEIS	Stock Exchange Information Services Ltd (Hong Kong)
SEM	Single European Market
SEOCH	SEHK Options Clearing House
SEPC	State Enterprise Policy Commission (Thailand)
SERC	State Enterprise Reform Commission (Thailand)
SERTS	SCANS Electronic Registration and Transfer Service (Malaysia)
SES	Stock Exchange of Singapore
SESDAQ	SES Dealing and Automated Quotation System
SET	Secure Electronic Transaction
SET	Stock Exchange of Thailand
SEZ	Special Economic Zone
SFCHK	Securities and Futures Commission of Hong Kong
SFE	Sydney Futures Exchange
SG	Shipping guarantee
SGD	Singapore dollar
SGS	Singapore Government Securities
SHIFT	System for Handling Interbank Fund Transfer
SIA	Securities Industry Act (Malaysia)
SIB	Securities and Investment Board (Hong Kong)
SIBA	Singapore Insurance Brokers' Association

SIBOR	Singapore Interbank Offer Rate
SIC	Securities Industry Council (Singapore)
SICDA	Securities Industry (Central Depositories) Act (Malaysia)
SICOM	Singapore Commodity Exchange
SIDC	Securities Industry Development Centre (Malaysia)
SIF	Singapore International Foundation
SIFA	Singapore International Franchising Association
SIFC	Small Industries Finance Corporation (Thailand)
SIFO	Small Industries Finance Office (Thailand)
SIFS	Small Industries Finance Scheme (Singapore)
SIG	Singapore Insurance Group
SII	Singapore Insurance Institute
SIJORI	Singapore, Johor, Riau Province
SIMEX	Singapore International Monetary Exchange
SIMPEDES	Simpanan Pedesaan (Indonesia) (Rural savings program)
SIMSCI	MSCI Singapore stock index futures contract
SingTel	Singapore Telecom
SIP	Social Investment Program (Thailand)
SIP	State Investment Plan (Laos)
SIPFI	Securities Investors Protection Fund Inc (Philippines)
SISIR	Singapore Institute of Standards & Industrial Research
SITC	Singapore Insurance Training Centre
SITDDEC	South Investment, Trade and Development Data Exchange Centre (Malaysia)
SKAPI	Standar Khusus Akuntansi Perbankan Indonesia (Special Standard for Application of Banking Accounting in Indonesia)
SKEJ	Jakarta Electronic Clearing System
SLA	Savings and Loan Association
SLI	Small local investors
SLORC	State Law and Order Restoration Council (Myanmar)
SLR	Statutory liquidity ratio
SLS	Special Loan Scheme
SMA	Singapore Manufacturers Association
SMART	Singapore Mint Advance Reservation Scheme
SMBA	Singapore Merchant Bankers Association
SMC	San Miguel Corporation

SMC	Secondary Mortgage Corporation (Thailand)
SME	Small and medium enterprise
SMF	Secondary Mortgage Facility
SMI	Small and medium industry
SMIDEC	Small and Medium Industries Development Corporation (Malaysia)
SMILE	Singapore Myanmar Investment and Leisure Enterprise
SMM	Secondary Mortgage Market
SMO	State Management Organisation (Laos)
SNCD	Short-term negotiable certificate of deposit
SNEF	Singapore National Employers Federation
SO	Securities Ordinance (Hong Kong)
SOCSO	Social Security Organisation (Malaysia)
SOE	State-owned enterprise
SOFFEX	Swiss Options and Financial Futures Exchange
SOHO	Small home office
S-ONE	Securities One (Thailand)
SOSA	Strength of support assessment
SOTUS	Share Ownership Top Up Scheme (Singapore)
SP	Singapore Power
SPAN	Sistem Penjelasan Automatick Nasional (Malaysia)
SPC	State Planning Committee
SPDC	State Peace Development Council (Myanmar)
SPEEDS	Sistem Pemindahan Elektronik untuk Dana dan Sekuriti
SPI	Stock price index
SPP	Small power producer
SPTF	Skim Perbankan Tanpa Faedah (Malaysia) (Interest free banking scheme)
SPTS	Saigon Post and Telecommunications Services (Vietnam)
SPV	Special Purpose Vehicle
SRB	Self-regulating banking
SRO	Self-regulatory organisation
SRQ	Strategic Response Quotient
SRR	Statutory Reserve Requirement
SRT	State Railways of Thailand
SSB	Shari'ah Supervisory Board (Indonesia)
SSC	State Securities Commission (Vietnam)
SSE	Small scale enterprise

SSN	Social safety net
SSRI	Singapore Securities Research Institute
SSS	Social Security System (Philippines)
SSTS	Scripless Securities Trading System
SSX	Surabaya Stock Exchange
STAQS	Securities Trading Automated Quotation System (China)
STAR	Sistem Transit Aliran Ringan (Malaysia)
STARS	Singapore Titles Automated Registration System
STB	Singapore Tourism Board
STET	Submission through electronic transmission
STI	IMF-Singapore Regional Training Institute
STK	Satuan Tugas Khusus (Indonesia) (bad debt work-out team)
STM	Syarikat Telecom Malaysia Berhad
STMY-GS	Short-term yielding government securities (Philippines)
STPB	Singapore Tourist Promotion Board
SUBC	Singapore-United States Business Council
SVC	Stored value card
SVP	Shipping Venture Facility (Malaysia)
SWIFT	Society for Worldwide Interbank Financial Telecommunications
TABANAS	Tabungan Nasional (Indonesia) (nation-wide saving scheme in Indonesia)
TAM	Trade Associated Member
TAMADES	Tambungan Masyarakat Pedesaan (Indonesia) (Village Savings Program)
TAS	Telecommunication Authority of Singapore
TB	Treasury bill
TB	Thrift bank (Philippines)
TBA	Thai Bankers' Association
TBP	Total Business Planning Program (Singapore)
TC	Traveller's cheque
TCC	Thai Chamber of Commerce
TDZ	Trade development zone
TDB	Thai Danu Bank
TDB	Trade Development Board (Singapore)
TDC	Township Trade Dispute Committee (Myanmar)
TDMC	Tourism Development Management Committee (Myanmar)

TDRI	Thailand Development Research Institute
TEU	Twenty-foot equivalent unit
TFB	Thai Farmers Bank
TGF	Trade Guarantee Fund (Philippines)
THAI	Thai Airways International
THB	Thai baht
TIBOR	Tokyo inter bank offer rate
TIC	Tipya Insurance Co Ltd (Thailand)
TIDY	Trade Input Driven System
TIFFE	Tokyo International Financial Futures Exchange
TMB	Thai Military Bank
TNB	Tenaga Nasional Berhad (Malaysia)
TOB	Taken-over bank
TOP	Panel on Takeovers and Mergers (Malaysia)
TOPS	Traded Options System (Hong Kong)
Topix	Tokyo Stock Exchange price Index
TOT	Telephone Organisation of Thailand
TPF	Teachers Provident Fund (Malaysia)
TPI	Thai Petrochemical Industry
TPKP	Indonesian acronym for Corporate employee housing savings scheme in Indonesia
TPN	PT Timor Putra Nasional (Indonesia)
TR	Trust receipt
TRIS	Thai Rating and Information Services
TSD	Thailand Securities Depository
TSE	Tokyo Stock Exchange
TSR	Transferable subscription rights
TT	Telegraphic transfer
TTAT	Thai Telephone & Telecommunications
TTM	Thailand Tobacco Monopoly
TTO	Thai Textile Organisation
TTZ	Tan Thuan Export Processing Zone (Vietnam)
TWSC	Township Workers' Supervisory Committee (Myanmar)
UBB	Union Bank of Bangkok
UBC	Unit business cost
UBP	Union Bank of the Philippines
UCP	Uniform Customs & Practice for Documentary Credits
UDA	Urban Development Authority (Malaysia)
UDESCO	Urban Development Service Company (Vietnam)

UEM	United Engineers (Malaysia) Berhad
ULC	Unit labour cost
UNDP	United Nations Development Program
Unibank	PT United City Bank (Indonesia)
UNIDO	United Nations Industrial Development Organisation
UOB	United Overseas Bank (Singapore)
UPUK	Small Business Development Unit (Indonesia)
URA	Urban Redevelopment Authority (Singapore)
US-AEP	United States-Asia Environment Partnership
USAID	United States Agency for International Development
USD	US dollar
VA	Value added
VACC	Vietnam American Chamber of Commerce
VACM	Vietnam Association of Cigarette Manufacturers
VACO	Vietnam Auditing Company
VAR	Value at risk
VARNET	Vietnam Academic Research and Education Network
VASCO	Vietnam Air Service Company
VAT	Value added tax
VBA	Vietnam Bank of Agriculture
VBARD	Vietnam Bank for Agriculture and Rural Development
VC	Venture capital
VCA	Vietnam Computer Association
VCC	Vietnam Cement Corporation
VCCI	Vietnam Chamber of Commerce and Industry
VEAM	Vietnam Engineering & Agriculture Machinery Corp.
VEFAC	Vietnam Exhibition and Trade Fair Center
VEIC	Vietnam Electronics and Informatics Corporation
VIA	Vietnam International Assurance Company
VIAC	Vietnam International Arbitration Center
VIAS	Vietnam Investment Advisory Service
VICOFA	Vietnam Cocoa and Coffee Association
VICT	Vietnam International Container Terminal
VID Bank	Vietnam Investment and Development Bank
Vietcochamber	Chamber of Commerce and Industry of Vietnam

Vietcombank	Bank for Foreign Trade Bank of Vietnam
Vietindebank	Bank for Investment and Development of Vietnam
Viglacera	Vietnam Corporation of Ceramics & Construction Glass
VILC	Vietnam International Leasing Company
Vinacafe	Vietnam National Coffee Corporation
Vinachem	Vietnam Chemical Corporation
Vinacoal	Vietnam National Coal Company
Vinafor	Vietnam Forestry Product Company
Vinalines	Vietnam National Maritime Corporation
Vinamarine	Vietnam National Maritime Bureau
Vinamilk	Vietnam National Milk Company
Vinapco	Vietnam Air Petrol Co.
Vinapico	Vietnam National Alcohol, Beer & Beverage Corporation
Vinaplat	Vietnam Plastic Imports & Exports
Vinare	Vietnamese Reinsurance Company
Vinataba	Vietnam National Tobacco Corporation
Vinatex	Vietnam Naional Textile and Garment Corporation
Vinatom	Vietnam Atomic Energy Commission
VLCC	Very large crude carrier
VMY	Visit Myanmar Year
VNA	Vietnam Airlines
VNAPIEC	Vietnam National Agricultural Produce Import Export Corporation
VNAT	Vietnam National Administration of Tourism
VND	Vietnamese dong
VNPT	Vietnam Post and Telecommunication Corp
VOC	Vereenigde Oostindische Compagnie (Dutch East India Company)
VOSCO	Vietnam Ocean Shipping Company
VPS	Vietnam Postal Services
VQS	Vehicle Quota System (Singapore)
VRB	Variable rate bond
VRU	Vietnam Railway Union
VSC	Vietnam Steel Corporation
VSIP	Vietnam Singapore Industrial Park
VSTTC	Vietnam Singapore Technical Training Centre
VTA	Vietnam Tourism Administration
VTGC	Vietnam Textile and Garment Corporation
VTV	National Vietnam Television

VUEIE	Vietnam Union of Electronic and Informatic Enterprises
WEC	Week End Car scheme (Singapore)
wef	With effect from
WEF	World Economic Forum
WEFA	Wharton Econometric Forecasting Associates Inc
WGC	World Gold Council
WHT	Withholding tax
WPI	Wholesale price index
Wrts	Warrants
WSIP	Wuxi Singapore Industrial Park
WTO	World Trade Organisation
WWF	World Wildlife Fund
WWMO	Waste Water Management Organisation (Thailand)
WWW	World wide web
xall	Ex all
xbi	Ex bonus issue
xd	Ex dividend
xri	Ex rights issue
xw	Ex warrant
YA	Year of assessment
YOY	Year-on-year
YTC	Yield to call
YTM	Yield to maturity
ZNCD	Zero-coupon negotiable certificate of deposit

PART V

LEXICON OF FINANCIAL TERMS USED IN SOUTHEAST ASIA AND HONG KONG

LEXICON OF FINANCIAL TERMS

(SOUTHEAST ASIA AND HONG KONG)

Abandoned Housing Project Fund (Malaysia)
A special fund set up by the Malaysian government to revive viable housing projects abandoned during the 1986 recession.

Advanced Warning and Surveillance Unit (AWAS) (Malaysia)
A system in the Kuala Lumpur Stock Exchange to alert the Exchange regarding brokers and listed companies facing problems. (See also: Kuala Lumpur Stock Exchange.)

Agreement on Textile and Clothings (ATC)
In 1994, the ATC replaced the former MFA (Multi Fibre Agreement) following the evolution of WTO from GATT after the Uraguay Round of meetings.

Agribank
See Vietnam Bank for Agriculture and Rural Development; and Vietnam Bank for Agriculture.

Airport Core Program
See Hong Kong International Airport

Al-Amanah Islamic Investment Bank of the Philippines (AAIIBP)
The AAIIBP is a government bank set up under a special law to provide banking and investment facilities to promote economic development in the Autonomous Region of Muslim Mindanao. Its operations are based on Islamic banking concepts. (See also: Islamic bank.)

All-Ordinaries index
A share price index of 230 companies listed on the Australian Stock

Exchange. It includes the All-Industrials index and the All-Resources index.

Allied Banking Corporation (Philippines)
Allied Banking Corporation is a financial institution listed on Philippine Stock Exchange. It started in 1977 after the acquisition of General Bank & Trust Company. During the initial years, the bank served mainly the financial needs of local Chinese merchants. The bank is part of the Lucio Tan Group of Companies, which is one of the largest conglomerates in the Philippines, with interests in tobacco, brewery, hotel and airline industries. After obtaining the expanded commercial banking licence in 1981, the bank expanded its services and has diversified into merchant banking activities. Its major banking-related subsidiaries include: Allied Bank Philippines (UK) Plc, Allied Leasing & Finance Corp, First Allied Savings Bank.

Amanah Saham Bumiputera (ASB) scheme
Amanah Saham Bumiputera (ASB) in Malaysia provides an opportunity for Bumiputera individuals to invest in a unit trust scheme which has a fixed transaction price.

Amanah Saham Nasional Berhad (ASN)
This is Malaysia's national unit trust company set up by the Permodalan Nasional Berhad (PNB) as a wholly-owned subsidiary to sell its portfolio of shares to the Bumiputera community. (See also: Bumiputera Investment Foundation, Permodalan Nasional Berhad.)

American Depository Receipt for DBS Bank
In 1980, Morgan Guaranty Trust of New York established a facility whereby American Depository Receipts (ADRs) were issued for the shares of DBS Bank of Singapore. Under this arrangement, American investors can trade in DBS shares. This was the first time that the depository receipt of a Singapore company was issued abroad.

The underlying shares backing the ADRs are deposited by brokers with banks acting as custodians for Morgan Guaranty. The New York office of Morgan Guaranty acts as the depository for the issue and cancellation of the ADRs. The DBS Bank is the custodian for the shares deposited in Singapore against the issue of such ADRs. (See also: depository receipt.)

Ankatan Bersenjata Republik Indonesia (ABRI)
Indonesian Armed Forces

Annual Assay Commission (Singapore)
The Annual Assay Commission is set up by the Board of Commissioners of Currency (Singapore) to test, examine, and determine whether the coins struck by the Singapore Mint are in accordance with the specifications and standards set by law.

Approved Bond Intermediary (ABI)
As announced in the 1999 Singapore Budget, under the new Approved Bond Intermediary scheme, debt securities lead-managed by ABIs qualify for tax exemption on interest.

Approved Cyber Trader scheme (Singapore)
The Approved Cyber Trader (ACT) scheme was introduced in 1999 and administered by Singapore Trade Development Board. Its objective is to promote Singapore as the region's e-commerce hub. With effect from 1999, ACT companies enjoy a concessionary tax incentive on offshore income derived from transactions over the Internet.

Approved Contract Manufacturer and Trader scheme (Singapore)
As announced in the 1999 Singapore Budget, under the new Approved Contract Manufacturer and Trader scheme, qualifying firms get GST exemption.

Approved International Shipping Enterprise Scheme (Singapore)
The Approved International Shipping Enterprise Scheme (AIS) is administered by Singapore's Trade Development Board (TDB) to promote Singapore as an international maritime centre. A company with AIS status gets tax exemption on income from the operation of their ships in international waters. Tax exemption period is for an initial period of 10 years subject to a 5-yearly review. The qualifying income covers income from operation of non-Singapore-flag vessels outside Singapore and qualifying dividends from approved subsidiaries and associated companies. The company should be a significant owner and operator of a fleet of vessels. It has a directly attributable total business spending in Singapore of at least S$4 million a year. It has at least 10% of its fleet in terms of number (minimum one vessel) registered under the Singapore flag.

Approved International Trader Scheme (Singapore)
The Approved International Trader (AIT) scheme is administered by Singapore's Trade Development Board (TDB) to promote Singapore as a global trading centre. A company with the AIT status is taxed at

a concessionary rate of 10% on income derived from offshore international trading activities in approved commodities.

The qualifying incomes include profits from trading, commissions from brokering, profits from trading in approved futures exchanges and foreign exchange gains incidental to these transactions. The trader should have an annual turnover in Singapore of at least US$100 million. It should have a directly attributable total business spending in Singapore of at least S$2 million a year.

Approved Oil Trader Scheme (Singapore)

The Approved Oil Trader (AOT) scheme is administered by Singapore's Trade Development Board (TDB) to promote Singapore as an international oil trading centre. A company with AOT status is taxed at a concessionary rate of 10% on income derived from international trading activities in approved oil products. The qualifying income is broad-based, encompassing various aspects of oil trading. The trader must be an established international oil trading company with a worldwide network and a good track record. It should have an annual turnover in Singapore of at least US$100 million. It should have directly attributable total business spending in Singapore of at least S$2 million a year.

Approved Securities Company (Singapore)

A securities company which has been granted the Approved Securities Company (ASC) status by the Singapore government enjoys incentives as announced by the Minister for Finance in his Budget Statement 1994.

The incentives which are granted to ACUs (Asian Currency Units) and ASCs are meant to encourage the growth of international derivatives trading and arbitrage activities and the trading of regional securities in Singapore.

An ACU or an ASC enjoys a concessionary tax rate of 10% on income derived from lending and borrowing foreign securities with another ACU, ASC or a non-resident person. The fee income derived by approved fund managers from arranging securities lending and borrowing transactions on behalf of foreign investors will also qualify for the concessionary tax rate.

Tax exemption also applies to the securities lending fee, manufactured dividend and interest paid by the ACU or ASC to a non-resident person. Unless it is a bank or a branch of a bank, the non-resident person must not have any permanent establishment in

Singapore. These changes took effect from Year of Assessment 1995. With effect from March 1994, the Singapore government does not levy stamp duty on documents executed under seal and agreements in respect of such securities lending and borrowing transactions.

Previously, the tax exemption scheme for syndicated offshore credit and underwriting facilities was only open to ACUs. As non-bank institutions, such as securities companies, have become important players in arranging and participating in syndicated facilities, the Minister decided to extend the scheme to ASCs with effect from 1 March 1994. The objective is to encourage securities companies to expand their operations in Singapore. (See also: Asian Currency Units.)

Arab-Malaysian Unit Trusts Berhad (AMUT)
A joint venture between the Arab-Malaysian Banking Group and Australia's investment bank Macquarie Bank.

Armed Forces Fund
Malaysia's Armed Forces Fund (Tabung Angkatan Tentera) was set up in 1973 to provide superannuation benefits to servicemen in the armed forces.

Articles of Association (Singapore)
To be registered as a limited liability company in Singapore, a business enterprise must submit a Memorandum of Association and Articles of Association to the Registry of Companies and Businesses (RCB).

The Memorandum of Association (or MA) is the company's constitution and defines the business activities the company is set up for. The Articles of Association (or AA) contain the company's internal regulations. They must not have any provisions forbidden by the Companies Act. By paying a fee to the RCB, any member of the public can inspect the Memorandum and Articles of Association of any registered company.

ASB-Loan Scheme for Bumiputera Hardcore Poor
The scheme was launched in 1992 by the Malaysian government as part of its effort to eradicate poverty. A family with monthly income of less than RM175 can borrow up to RM5,000 for investment in ASB unit trust. The fund is provided by the Central Bank and managed by the Permodalan Nasional Berhad (PNB). An investor is entitled to a return of 4% of the dividend declared by the PNB with the remaining

dividend income used to repay the loan principal. (See also: Amanah Saham Bumiputera scheme, Amanah Sahan Nasional Berhad.)

ASEAN Forum of Credit Rating Agencies (AFCRA)
AFCRA is an association of regional credit rating agencies. It facilitates the exchange of information and ideas about credit rating and the bond market throughout Asia.

Asian Commercial Paper
The Asian Commercial Paper (ACP) is a financial instrument first introduced in the Asian Dollar Market in 1979. It is a short term unsecured promissory note issued by a non-bank company to raise working capital. This instrument enables well-known companies to raise relatively cheap short term funds in the market. It differs from an ordinary bill of exchange that it is not originated from a trade transaction. The first ACP was issued by the Bermuda-incorporated C. Itoh (International) and was guaranteed by its parent company, C. Itoh (Hong Kong), which in turn was a subsidiary of the C. Itoh group of Japan.

Asian Currency Unit (ACU)
The Asian Currency Unit (ACU) is a unit within a bank which has been granted such a licence by the Monetary Authority of Singapore (MAS) to deal in the Asian Dollar Market. The unit has to maintain separate accounting records for its transactions. This is to ensure that the flow of funds to and from the Asian Dollar Market will not disrupt domestic monetary management.

The first ACU was started in 1968 by the Singapore branch of the Bank of America. The bank was granted permission by the Singapore Government to set up a currency unit similar to its Eurocurrency Unit in London. The objective was to attract Asian non-resident deposits to fund the bank's Asian lending activities. Since then, many other institutions have been granted ACU licences.

The ACU is supervised by the MAS and is subject to Singapore banking legislation. However, it is exempted from some provisions of the Banking Act. For instance, it is not required to maintain a minimum cash balance with the MAS. It does not have to comply with statutory liquidity requirements.

The ACU is allowed to accept external non-resident deposits without reference to the exchange control authorities. It may deposit with or lend to another ACU and non-residents. It may lend to residents subject to approval.

The ACU may engage in the opening and advising of letters of credit, the discounting of bills, and the issuing of guarantees in dealings with non-residents. It may engage in investment in foreign currency securities, and foreign exchange transactions with non-residents. No reports on the individual deposits or loans are required. (See also: Asian dollar market.)

Asian Currency Unit and foreign bank
In order to obtain an ACU licence, the head office of a foreign bank must provide an undertaking to the Monetary Authority of Singapore (MAS) that it will make available, on demand, specified currencies in case of unforeseen liquidity or other shortfalls in the unit's assets. The activities of an ACU are limited by the maximum size of assets/liabilities stipulated by the MAS. (See also: Asian Currency Unit.)

Asian dollars
These are US dollars circulating in Asian financial markets. When the same US dollars circulate in European financial markets, they are known as Eurodollars. The distinction between Asian dollars and Eurodollars is geographical rather than in substance. The Asian dollar market also deals in other hard currencies such as German mark and Japanese yen. (See also: Asian Currency Unit; Asian dollar market; Eurodollar market.)

Asian Dollar Bond
An Asian dollar bond is an international bond denominated in US dollars. It may be denominated in other hard currencies such as the Japanese yen or German mark. It has the following features:

(1) it is listed on the Singapore Stock Exchange;
(2) Singapore financial institutions are represented in the management, underwriting, and selling groups;
(3) the placement of the issue is mainly in Asia.

Asian Dollar Bond — secondary market
The secondary market for Asian dollar bonds comprises financial institutions which buy and sell on their own accounts as well as on behalf of their cleints. Asian bonds are listed on the Stock Exchange of Singapore. Deals may be effected through the Exchange or through over-the-counter market by telephone or fax among the dealers and brokers.

The dealing and settlement procedures are patterned after the rules of the Association of International Bond Dealers. As locational distribution of the markets makes physical delivery of the securities difficult and expensive, settlement is provided by two clearing systems — Euroclear in Brussels and Cedel in Luxembourg. (See also: Cedel; Euroclear.)

Asian Dollar Market
The Asian Dollar Market is the Asian counterpart of the Eurodollar market. It is a financial market in Asia where institutions accept deposits of major currencies (US$, yen, deutschemark, sterling pound, Swiss franc) outside their countries of issue. These funds are then lent out for investment purposes in Asia. The market is so called because the most important currency traded is the US dollar.

Major participants in the market are commercial banks, monetary authorities of governments (such as central banks, government agencies), multinational corporations, international organisations, other financial institutions, and wealthy individuals. Most of the deals in the Asian Dollar Market are for deposits of less than one-year maturity. The long term counterpart is the Asian Bond Market.

Financial institutions in Singapore are given special ACU licences (Asian Currency Unit) by the Monetary Authority of Singapore to trade in the Asian Dollar Market. These ACUs are eligible for tax incentives offered by the Singapore government. (See also: Asian Currency Unit, Asian Bond Market.)

Asiatrust Development Bank Inc (Philippines)
Asiatrust Development Bank was incorporated as Quezon City Development Bank in 1960. It is one of the first private development banks in the Philippines and its main objective is to finance entrepreneurs and high-growth small and medium enterprises.

Askrindo
See Asuransi Kredit Indonesia

Asosiasi Lembaga Pembiayaan Pembangunan Indonesia (ALPPIA)
See Indonesian Association of Development Financing Institutions.

Asset Management Unit (AMU) Indonesia
AMU is a unit set up by the Indonesian Bank Restructuring Authority in 1998. It serves as the main recovery agency for loans booked in

banks which have failed. (See also: Indonesian Bank Restructuring Authority.)

Asset Management Company (AMC) Malaysia
AMC is a Malaysian government agency set up in 1998 with a capital of RM25 billion. Its objective is to take over non-performing loans (NPLs) in the Malaysian financial sytem. It would relieve banks of the tedious loan recovery process, allowing them to concentrate on their core business of lending to productive sectors. It would buy the NPLs of financial institutions at market prices, revive them and sell them at a profit.

Asset Management Corporation (AMC) Thailand
The Asset Management Corporation (AMC) in Thailand was set up in October 1997 under the Emergency Decree on the Asset Management Corporation, dated 22 October BE 2540 (1997) as part of the financial sector restructuring program. The role of this state agency is to administer the assets of 58 finance companies whose operations were suspended by the order of the Finance Minister on 26 June 1997 (16 companies) and on 5 August 1997 (42 companies). Its initial capital of 1 billion baht has been subscribed by the Thai Government. The shareholder is the Ministry of Finance. (See also: Financial Sector Restructuring Authority — Thailand.)
(www.bot.or.th / govnr / public / news / be.htm)

Association for Insurance Advancement (Singapore)
The Association for Insurance Advancement (AIA) in Singapore was formed in 1983 to take over from the Insurance Trust Fund the responsibility of funding the activities of the former Singapore Insurance Training Centre (SITC). Funds come from subscriptions made by the General Insurance Association of Singapore, the Life Insurance Association of Singapore, the Singapore Reinsurers' Association and the Singapore Insurance Brokers' Association. (See also: Singapore Insurance Training Centre.)

Association of International Bond Dealers (AIBD)
A Zurich-based association established in 1969. It recommends rules and regulations for bond dealing and publishes quotes and yields for the eurobond market.

Association of Securities Analysts of the Philippines (ASAP)
The Association of Securities Analysts of the Philippines (ASAP) was

formed to promote the professional growth of securities analysts. It was incorporated on 9 October 1996. [Address: 4/F, PCCI Corporate Centre, 118 Alfaro St, Salcedo Village, Makati City, Philippines. Tel: (632) 893-3920. Website: http://www.asap.com.ph

Assurances Generales du Lao (AGL)
An insurance joint venture between the Government of Lao DPR and Assurances Generales de France. It began operations in 1992 and was granted a monopoly by the government on condition that it provided a full range of insurance services.

Astra International
Indonesia's largest automotive maker. It is also the agent for a wide range of cars including Toyota, Daihatsu, Peugot, BMW, Isuzu and Nissan. Astra also operates in many sectors including plywood, agribusiness, heavy equipment, electronics and financial services.

Asuransi Ekspor Indonesia (ASEI)
An Indonesian state-owned credit insurance company which provides export insurance and export credit guarantee.

Asuransi Kredit Indonesia (Askrindo)
An Indonesian credit insurance company which provides credit guarantee cover to banks for financing small and medium industries.

Australian Stock Exchange (ASX)
The Australian Stock Exchange was formed in 1987. It combines the six stock exchanges in Australia and includes the options market in Sydney and the Australian Financial Futures Market in Melbourne.

Authorised Trading Centre (Singapore)
After the massive floatation of Singapore Telecom shares in 1993, the number of shareowners in Singapore increased significantly. In order to cope with the increased volume of trade, the Stock Exchange of Singapore (SES) set up Authorised Trading Centres (ATCs) located at bank branches and stockbroking firms.

Investors do not need a trading account to buy and sell shares at ATCs. They only need a CDP (Central Depository) securities account to hold their shares and an ATM (automatic teller machine) card to pay for their shares.

Automated Trading System for the Stock Exchange of Thailand (ASSET)
ASSET is a computerised trading system introduced at the Stock Exchange of Thailand (SET) in 1991 to cope with the expanded trading volume. The system automatically matches transactions with immediate confirmation to the buying and selling brokers.

Automation Leasing Scheme (Singapore)
The Automation Leasing Scheme (ALS) is a low cost financing program offered by Singapore's Economic Development Board and to encourage companies to upgrade their operations by investing in automation equipment. It offers leasing, hire purchase and mortgage loans.

Bad cheque blacklisting
See Biro Maklumat Cek (Malaysia)

Bad debt work-out team (Satuan Tugas Khusus or STK)
In 1994, in order to tackle problem loans, Bank Indonesia (Central Bank) identified a group of banks with severe loan portfolio difficulties. It required each of them to form a bad debt work-out team (STK) to be headed by a member of its board of directors. The STK would work on the loan problem and report monthly to BI. The STK was a temporary arrangement and would dissolve once the bad debt problem was under proper control.

Badan Koordinasi Penanaman Modal
See Investment Coordinating Agency (Indonesia)

Badan Kredit Kecamatan (BKK) (Indonesia)
The BKK program was set up in the 1970s by the Central Java government to provide credit to villagers who were short of business capital.

Badan Pemeriksa Keuangan (Indonesia)
Supreme Audit Board in Indonesia. It controls the accountability of public finance, has investigatory powers and is independent of the Executive branch of the government. It reports to the Dewan Perwakilan Rakyat (DPR, or House of Representatives). (See also: Dewan Perwakilan Rakyat.)

Badan Pengawas Pasar Modal (BAPEPAM)
BAPEPAM is Indonesia's Capital Market Supervisory Agency which was formed in 1976. It supervises the Jakarta and Surabaya stock exchanges. While BAPEPAM is not an independent agency, it has substantial responsibilities for carrying out the day-to-day supervision of the market, issuers, and for licensing underwriters, brokers, dealers, and investment managers. It has both regulatory and investigative powers and can take legal action through the Ministry of Finance. (See also: Capital Market Law.)

Badan Penyehatan Perbankan Nasional
See Indonesian Bank Restructuring Authority

Badan Urusan Logistik (BULOG)
See Board of Logistic Affairs (Indonesia)

Badan Usaha Malik Negara (BUMN)
State-owned enterprise in Indonesia. (See also: Indonesian state-owned enterprise.)

Baht Interbank Offer Rate (BIBOR)
The rate used among banks in Thailand to settle their transactions.

Banco Espanol-Filipino de Isabel
Set up in 1851, Banco Espanol-Filipino de Isabel was the first commercial bank in the Philippines and in Southeast Asia. It is now known as the Bank of the Philippine Islands. (See also: Bank of the Philippine Islands.)

Bangko Sentral ng Pilipinas (BSP)
See Central Bank of the Philippines

Bangkok Metropolitan Bank
Bangkok Metropolitan Bank (BMB) started operations in 1950 as the 12th commercial bank of Thailand. Its founders were Phraya Tonavanik Montri, Ng Zi Liang and Udane Tejapaibul. In 1993, Bangkok Metropolitan Bank became a Public Company Limited and its capital was increased to 10 billion baht.

During the 1997–98 financial crisis, BMB and numerous other banks ran into difficulty and were intervened by the Bank of Thailand. The BMB was offered for privatisation.

Bangkok International Banking Facility (BIBF)
The BIBF was introduced in 1992. Banks with BIBF licences can set up offshore banking units (OBUs) to attract foreign capital to finance economic development. Incentives are provided for OBUs. Income is taxed at 10% instead of the normal 30%. Municipal taxes and stamp duty are waived.

Bangkok Stock Dealing Center (BSDC)
The BSDC was set up in 1995 in accordance with the Securities Act. It is Thailand's secondary market besides the Stock Exchange of Thailand (SET). It has 74 finance and securities companies as its founding members. It is a self-regulatory organisation and non-profit organisation supervised by the Securities and Exchange Commission (SEC). One of its objectives is to provide a market for small and medium enterprises to rise funds for expansion. Computerised trading takes place in six different boards. The boards have different rules and trade in different securities. They are: Main Board, Dealing Board, Big Lot Board, Foreign Board, Odd Lot Board and Private Placement Board. (Website: www.bsdc.or.th)

Bank for Agriculture and Agricultural Cooperatives (BAAC) (Thailand)
The BAAC provides financial facilities to farmers, farmer associations and agricultural cooperatives. It also provides deposit services of a commercial bank. It is a decentralised organisation with more than 600 branches and about 800 district field offices throughout Thailand. (Website: www.baac.mof.go.th)

Bank for Foreign Trade of Vietnam (Vietcombank)
Vietcombank is one of the state-owned commercial banks in Vietnam. It was set up in 1963 and has about 20 branches in Vietnam. It is authorised to deal in foreign exchange and international banking business. About 80% of Vietnam's foreign trade passes through Vietcombank. It has a subsidiary Vietnam Finance Co Ltd in Hong Kong. It has established a joint venture bank with Korea's Daewoo Securities and Korea First Bank.

Bank for International Settlements (BIS)
The BIS was established in 1930, originally to facilitate the payments to countries still owed First World War reparations by Germany. Since then it has evolved into a central bank for many central banks.

Countries regularly represented at the BIS meetings are those belonging to the International Monetary Fund (IMF) Group of Ten. Other countries represented from time to time include the remaining members of the European Union, some Eastern European countries and other countries such as Saudi Arabia, as required.

The BIS takes deposits and makes loans and plays a role in international finance, especially when speculative transactions are involved. Directors of the BIS hold a monthly meeting at the bank's head office in Basle, Switzerland. Its board includes representatives of the central banks of the UK, France, Germany, Belgium, Italy, Switzerland, the Netherlands and Sweden. (See also: Bank for International Settlement Guidelines.)

Bank for International Settlements Guidelines

In 1988, in a move to increase the financial soundness of the global banking system, the Bank for International Settlements (BIS, generally regarded as the central bank of all central banks) introduced guidelines requiring banks which operate internationally to have capital equivalent to at least 8% of their risk-weighted assets by the end of 1992. Of the capital, at least 4% must be core or Tier 1 capital, which includes shareholders' funds and minority interests. Tier 2 capital comprises subordinated debt, loan-loss provisions, and 45% of unrealised profits on securities holdings. In many countries, central banks require their banks to comply with BIS guidelines.

Bank for Investment and Development of Vietnam (BIDV)

BIDV was formerly the Bank for Construction and Development. It finances mainly infrastructure and commercial projects for the government and state-owned enterprises. VID Public Bank is its joint venture bank with the Public Bank Berhad from Malaysia.

Bank Indonesia

Bank Indonesia (BI) is the central bank of Indonesia. Its functions include note and coin issue, maintenance of liquidity, regulation of money and credit expansion. It regulates all financial institutions except insurance companies. Supervision is done through the issue of regulations and guidelines and inspecting financial reports and operations. It provides lender-of-last-resort facilities to banks.

Bank Indonesia Certificates (Sertifikat Bank Indonesia or SBI)

These are discount financial instruments issued by Bank Indonesia for short term investment by banks.

Bank Industri Malaysia Berhad (BIMB)
Bank Industri Malaysia Berhand or the Industrial Bank of Malaysia was set up 1979 to provide long-term financing beyond the normal maturity offered by other financial institutions.

Bank Industri Negara
State Industrial Bank (Indonesia)

Bank Islam Malaysia Berhad (BIMB)
BIMB is Malaysia's first Islamic bank which was set up in 1983. Its activities are based on Islamic banking principles and conform with the Syariah. In 1996, as part of its expansion, BIMB set up a Syariah-based Consumer Financing Centre which focuses on retail banking such as motor vehicle financing, education financing and personal finance.

Bank Muamalat Indonesia
An Indonesian commercial bank which operates on Islamic banking principles. It also participates in the collection of alms and tithes and provides finance for pilgrimage.

Bank Negara Malaysia (BNM)
Bank Negara is the central bank of Malaysia, established in 1959. It formulates and implements Malaysia's monetary and credit policies. It regulates and supervises the financial system under the Central Bank of Malaysia Ordinance, the Bank and Financial Institutions Act, the Islamic Banking Act, the Insurance Act and the Takaful Act.

Bank of England
The UK central hank, founded in 1694. It is also known as the Old Lady of Threadneedle Street (its location in the City of London).

Bank of Lao PDR (BOL)
Bank of Lao PDR is the central bank of Laos. It maintains monetary control and promotes the development of financial markets. The main objective of monetary control is to reduce inflationary rate while recognising the need for continued credit growth to finance the development needs of the country. The objective is achieved through high interest rate structure (to absorb excess liquidity and encourage savings) and using monetary policy instruments such as reserve requirement ratio, credit and discount window, and the issue of treasury bills.

A non-state bank must deposit USD 5 million with the BOL as start-up capital once its licence is approved. The bank may draw down on this deposit after operations have begun, provided it maintains a deposit of 10% of the capital with BOL at all times. All banks are required to provide information to the BOL on a regular basis.

Bank of Thailand (BOT)
The Bank of Thailand (BOT) is the Central Bank of Thailand. It was first set up in 1939 as the Thai National Banking Bureau attached to the Ministry of Finance. Its operations then were limited to only some central banking functions such as the issue of government bonds, taking deposits from and lending to the government, government agencies and commercial banks and transferring fund between the central region and the other parts of the country. In 1941, the Bureau started to operate the exchange control.

After the Second World War, the Bureau was upgraded to a central bank. Its functions include the following: formulate monetary policy and recommend economic policy to the government; provide banking facilities to the government, state enterprises and financial institutions; supervise financial institutions and develop the financial system issue bank notes; manage the country's assets and liabilities; represent Thailand in international organisations and cooperate with other central banks; provide economic and financial information in Thailand and abroad. (Website: www.bot.or.th)

Bank of the People of Cambodia
See National Bank of Cambodia

Bank of the Philippine Islands (BPI)
The Bank of the Philippine Islands is the oldest bank in the Philippines and in South East Asia. It started as Banco Espanol–Filipino de Isabel in 1851. It is the Philippines' third biggest domestic bank in terms of assets. Its operations cover three core businesses which are institutional banking, investment banking and consumer banking. The parent bank handles institutional banking while its wholly owned subsidiary, BPI Capital Corporation deals with investment banking and BPI Family Bank caters to consumer banking. The bank has 350 branches nationwide. Other wholly-owned subsidiaries include BPI Agricultural Development Bank Inc, BPI Leasing Corp, BPI Express Card Corp, BPI Securities Corporation and BPI International Finance Ltd in Hong Kong. (See also: Filipino Fund Inc.)
(Website: www.bpi.com.ph)

Bank Pembangunan Daerah (BPD)
Indonesian state-owned regional development banks which extend medium and long term loans for development projects.

Bank Pembangunan Semesta
Universal Development Bank (Indonesia)

Bank Perkreditan Rakyat (BPR)
An Indonesian rural credit bank such as a market bank, employee bank, village bank and paddy bank. It accepts savings and extends loans to traders in market places and villages. The operation of this type of bank is limited to the villages.

Bank Supervision in Singapore
All banks in Singapore are supervised by the Monetary Authority of Singapore (MAS) whcih ensures that they comply with the Banking Act and other guidelines. The MAS carries out field inspection, issues guidelines and notices, and reviews reports which all banks are required to submit. It also monitors the foreign exchange position of the banks and gives guidance on management and internal control.

Bank Tabungan Negara (BTN)
Indonesian state-owned savings bank. It collects savings such as the National Development Savings Scheme (Tabungan Pembangunan Nasional, or Tabanas), Time Insurance Savings Scheme (Tabungan Asuransi Berjanka or Taska) and savings for the downpayment in house ownership credit scheme.

Bank Tabungan Himpunan
A privately owned savings bank in Indonesia

Bank Tabungan Persiun Nasional
A privately owned savings bank in Indonesia

Banking Disclosure Panel (Singapore)
This is one of the three committees within the Financial Sector Reivew Group which was set up by the Singapore government in 1997 to review the financial sector. It studied disclosure practices for Singapore banks with a view to attaining the standards disclosure of developed countries. (See also: Corporate Finance Committee, Financial Sector Review Group, SES Review Committee.)

Banks in Indonesia
In 1968, there were about 200 banks in Indonesia. In an effort to consolidate the banking industry, the monetary authorities forced many of them to merge. By the early 1970s, there were about 100 banks. In 1988 after the monetary authorities deregulated the banking industry, the number of banks rose to about 240. Many of these banks have capital of less than Rp 50 billion (US$21 million). The authorities are urging them to merge.

Banks (state-owned) (Indonesia)
There were 7 state-owned banks in Indonesia: BNI (Bank Negara Indonesia), BTN (Bank Tabungan Negara), Bank Exim (Export and Import Bank), BDN (Bank Dagang Negara), BBD (Bank Bumi Daya), BRI (Bank Rakyat Indonesia), and Bapindo (Bank Pembangunan Indonesia).

In 1998, the Indonesian government consolidated the state banks by merging four of them to form part of Bank Rakyat Indonesia (BRI): Bank Dagang Negara (BDN), Bank Ekspor Impor Indonesia (EXIM), Bank Bumi Daya (BBD) and Bank Pembangunan Indonesia (Bapindo).

Bankard Inc (Philippines)
Bankard Inc is a financial service institution listed on the Philippine Stock Exchange. It was started by the PCIBank in 1981 as the Philippine Commercial Credit Card Inc (PCCCI) to operate domestic credit card business. In 1991, PCIBank was granted a licence by MasterCard International to issue credit cards in the Philippines. PCIBank then signed an agreement with Bankard Inc designating the latter to manage its PCIBank MasterCard international credit card operations. In 1992, PCCCI changed its name to Bankard Inc.
(Website: www.bankard.com)

Banking and Financial Institutions Act (BAFIA) (Malaysia)
The Banking and Financial Institutions Act was passed by the Malaysian Parliament in 1989. It has replaced the Banking Act 1973 and the Finance Companies Act 1969. The Act provides a comprehensive legislative framework for the licensing and regulation of all financial institutions.

It provides a framework for the supervision of three broad categories of financial institutions: the licensed institutions, scheduled institutions and the non-scheduled institutions.

Licensed institutions are those involved in banking and in the money and foreign exchange markets. They include commercial banks, merchant banks, finance companies, discount houses and money brokers. *Scheduled institutions* are non-bank institutions such as credit and charge card companies, building societies, factoring, leasing companies and development finance institutions. *Non-scheduled institutions* include statutory bodies and persons involved in the provision of finance.

Bankruptcy Law (Indonesia)
In 1998, the Indonesian government introduced a new Bankruptcy Law to replace an outdated bankruptcy law passed in 1905. Under the new law, a person or institution with debts owed to two or more creditors can be declared bankrupt by a court order if there is a default on at least one of the debts. All bankruptcy matters are handled by a new commercial court.

A creditor or a government prosecutor can petition the court to declare the debtor a bankrupt. For a debtor bank, the petition must come from the central bank, Bank Indonesia. For public listed companies, the petition must come from the Bapepam (the Capital Market Supervisory Board).

The court must set a hearing date within 48 hours after the petition is registered, hold the hearing within 20 days and make a ruling within 30 days. Eight days after the court's ruling, the parties may appeal to the Supreme Court which will make its ruling within 30 days after the appeal has been registered.

The new law allows a plaintiff or government prosecutor to apply to the court to seize the debtor's assets. The court may appoint a receiver to manage the debtor's business or oversee payments to the creditors.

Bao Minh
Bao Minh was formerly a branch of Vietnam's State Insurance Company (Bao Viet) in Ho Chi Minh City. In 1995, it became a separate insurance company.

Bao Viet
Vietnamese state-owned insurance company

Barings Crisis
In February 1995, the financial world was shocked when the well known British Barings PLC suddenly went bankrupt. Its Singapore-based futures trader Nicholas Leeson made US$1.3 billion losses on the Nikkei 225 futures contracts and on Japanese long bonds. Barings PLC was eventually bought over by Dutch banking group, ING in March 1995.

Base lending rate (BLR)
A bank's lending rate based on its cost of fund.

Batamindo Industrial Park (BIP)
An industrial park located on Indonesia's Batam Island. It is jointly developed by the Singapore and Indonesian governments. The park was officially opened in 1992. By 1996, BIP has attracted about 80 companies which employed about 44,000 Indonesians.

Berhad
Malay word for limited — denoting a limited liability company in Malaysia

Bernama
Malaysia's national news agency

Beta
A statistical measure which shows the movement of a share's price in relation to the market index. A beta of more than one shows that the share price moves more than the index.

Beta Mekong Fund
A closed-end investment fund listed on the Dublin Stock Exchange. It is managed by Indochina Asset Management Ltd.

Beta Vietnam Fund
A closed-end investment fund listed on the Dublin Stock Exchange. It is managed by Indochina Asset Management Ltd.

Bhd
Short form for the Malay word berhad (limited). (See also: berhad, sendirian berhad.)

Bimbingan Masal (BIMAS) (Indonesia)
BIMAS (mass guidance program) is Indonesia's nation-wide agricultural credit program.

Biro Maklumat Cek
It is a bureau within Bank Negara Malaysia (Central Bank of Malaysia) set up to monitor bad cheques. Under the rules of the bureau, any person who issues a bad cheque (i.e. without sufficient fund in the account) three times within 12 months will be blacklisted. The bank

account will be closed and the customer will be prohibited to operate any bank account in Malaysia for six months. The prohibition period will be longer for subsequent blacklisting of the same account.

Board of Commissioners of Currency of Singapore (BCCS)
The Board of Commissioners of Currency of Singapore (BCCS, more popularly called the Currency Board) was formed in 1967. Historically, it may be traced back to 1899 when Singapore was part of the Straits Settlements (which comprised Penang, Malacca and Singapore). In 1952, it was known as the Board of Commissioners of Currency, Malaya, and British Borneo.

The present Currency Board came into existence after Singapore became an independent republic in 1965. Its main function is to issue and redeem currency notes and coins. Legislation governing the issue of the Singapore currency is set out in the Currency Act. The main objectives of the BCCS are to ensure that: the demand of currency notes and coins is met; the highest degree of protection for the Board's assets and prudent management of the Currency Fund and the Currency Reserve Fund. (See also: Currency Act; Currency Fund.)

Board of Investments (BOI) Philippines
The Board of Investments (BOI) in the Philippines is a government agency in the Department of Trade & Industry. It promotes investments in the Philippines. Its One-stop Action Center offers prospective investors what they need to know about investing in the Philippines. Its annual Investment Priorities Plan indicates the preferred areas needed for economic development. It has representative offices in London, Bonn, San Francisco and Tokyo.

Board of Logistic Affairs (BULOG)
An Indonesian government agency that conducts market operation by releasing and buying stocks to stabilise prices of main commodities such as rice and sugar.

Bond Quotation System
This is an automatic order matching system for bond trading introduced by the Stock Exchange of Singapore in 1995. Trading is done through market-makers which quote both bid and offer prices.

Borneo Development Corporation
The Borneo Development Corporation was set up in 1958 as a subsidiary of the Commonwealth Development Corporation. In 1975,

it was purchased by the Sabah and Sarawak state government. Its main objective is to promote industrial and commercial development in the states of Sabah and Sarawak.

Bridging Loan Scheme (Singapore)
During the financial crisis in 1998, the Singapore government introduced the Bridging Loan Scheme to assist CPF (Central Provident Fund) members in servicing their housing loans. The objective was to meet shortfalls in their instalment payments as a result of the government's decision to reduce employers' CPF contribution by 10 percentage point.

Bucket shop
An organisation that solicits orders but not execute them on a recognised futures exchange. It is illegal in most countries.

Bumiputera Industrial Fund
The Bumiputera Industrial Fund was set up in 1993 by the Malaysian government to encourage the Bumiputera community to participate in industrial development. The objective is assist small and medium Bumiputera enterprises in improving their products, upgrading their technology and marketing their products.

Bumiputera Investment Foundation
This foundation was set up by the Malaysian government in 1978 to promote the ownership of share capital by Bumiputera in the corporate sector of Malaysia, in line with the New Economic Policy. (See also: Amanah Saham Nasional Berhad, Permodalan Nasional Berhad.)

Bursa Efek Surabaya
Surabaya Stock Exchange

Bursa Efek Jakarta (BEJ)
Jakarta Stock Exchange Inc, the company that manages the Jakarta Stock Exchange. It was transferred to the private sector in 1992. It is owned by about 200 brokerage firms which constitute the members and the shareholders of the exchange.

Bursa Paralel Indonesia
Indonesian over-the-counter market set up in 1991. It merged with the Surabaya Stock Exchange in 1995.

Bursa Saham Kuala Lumpur
See Kuala Lumpur Stock Exchange

Business Collaboration Program (Singapore)
Singapore's Business Collaboration Program (BCP) is administered by the Economic Development Board (EDB) to encourage local companies to collaborate in areas like bulk purchasing, facility sharing and joint marketing. The company receives grants to engage consultants to develop such concepts, conduct feasibility studies, draw up action plans, and help to implement. The amount of grant is on case-by-case basis.

Business Cooperation Contract (BCC) (Vietnam)
BCC is an investment contract whereby a foreign investor signs a contract with a Vietnamese partner to do business, and share the cost and the profit. No legal entity is formed, liability of either party is not limited to the investment contributed.

Business Development Scheme (Singapore)
Singapore's Business Development Scheme (BDS) is administered by the Economic Development Board (EDB) to help local firms to offset costs incurred in identifying opportunities in international markets. It provides grants to cover the costs of studies or overseas visits to explore new technologies or markets, to establish new business contacts, to pursue joint-venture arrangements, to participate in approved business development seminars. BDS covers: (a) up to 50% of airfare and overseas allowance; (b) up to 50% of the cost of acquiring reports, data and intelligence on markets, new technologies and joint-venture partners; (c) up to 70% of the seminar fees.

Business Headquarters Program (Singapore)
Singapore's Business Headquarters Program was introduced by Economic Development Board (EDB) in 1994 to attract foreign companies to use Singapore as a base to expand their services to the region. Such services include product development, logistics, merchandising, customer support, financial management and procurement. It is an extension of the Operational Headquarters (OHQ) program which the EDB introduced in 1986 to encourage companies to use Singapore as their headquarters to manage their subsidiaries in the region.

BHQ incentives include: (a) pioneer service status (up to 10 years of tax exemption); (b) export of service (tax exemption on 90% of chargeable income for the qualifying portion of export services, for up to 10 years); (c) warehousing & servicing (tax exemption on 50% of chargeable income for the qualifying portion of export sales or services, for up to 10 years).

Companies awarded the BHQ status can also apply for: Investment Allowance; Initiatives for New Technologies (INTECH) grants; approved royalties, fees and development contributions; tax exemption on offshore dividend income; double deduction for R&D expenses.

Business Times — Singapore Regional Index (BT-SRI)
BT-SRI is a stock index launched by the Stock Exchange of Singapore (SES) and the Singapore Press Holdings Ltd in 1996. The value-weighted index is constructed using the Paasche formula, which immunises the index level from any changes in the capitalisation of the component stocks.

It covers 38 stocks of Singapore and foreign companies listed on the SES. These companes are from 11 industrial sectors, ranging from airlines to telecommunication. Most of them have substantial exposure in the region. Examples are Acer Computer, Cerebos Pacific, Hong Kong Land, Jardine Matheson, Pacific Carriers, Singapore Airlines and Singapore Telecom, Thakral and Want Want Holdings.

Cagamas
Cagamas Berhad is the national mortgage corporation of Malaysia. It was set up in 1987 as an intermediary between primary lenders of housing loans and investors in long term funds. The role of Cagamas is to purchase housing loans from the originators of these loans and to issue fixed rate bearer bonds for investors. The bonds have a maturity ranging from 3 to 5 years.

Cagamas Bonds (Malaysia)
These are securitised mortgaged-backed bonds issued by Malaysia's national mortgage corporation, Cagamas Berhad.

Call Options Market — Singapore
The call options market was first introduced in the Stock Exchange of Singapore (SES) in 1977. After some active trading during the initial years, the market was dormant. Trading of options was re-introduced by the SES in 1993.

Cambodia Commercial Bank

The first joint venture bank set up by the National Bank of Cambodia and the Siam Commercial Bank.

Cambodia Finance Bank

A joint venture bank set up in 1992 by the National Bank of Cambodia and a Thai-Cambodia group.

Cambodia Gold and Trust Corporation

The only official corporation authorised by the National Bank of Cambodia to deal in gold bars.

Cambodia International Airlines (CIA)

Thai-owned Cambodian airline. In 1994, with the inauguration of national carrier Royal Air Combodge, CIA ceased operations. (See also: Royal Air Cambodge.)

Cambodian National Insurance Company (CAMINCO)

Cambodian National Insurance Company is a government-owned insurance company. It deals mainly with marine cargo insurance. Another firm, Indochine Insurance Union provides a wide range of insurance cover including fire, theft, motor vehicle and health insurance.

CAMEL Supervision Approach

An assessment based on components such as Capital adequacy, Asset quality, Management, Earnings and Liquidity.

Camintel

Camintel is a telecommunications joint venture between Cambodia's Ministry of Posts and Telecommunications and Indonesian company PT Indosat which owns a 49% stake.

Capital adequacy — banks

Banks are required by their central banks to comply with the minimum capital adequacy guidelines set by the Bank of International Settlements (BIS). (See also: Bank of International Settlements Guidelines.)

Capital Augmented Preferred Shares (CAPS)

CAPS are a combination of preferred shares and subordinated debt.

Capital Issues Committee (CIC)

Malaysia's Capital Issues Committee was formed in 1968 to supervise the issue of securities by public companies. It issued guidelines to provide a set of criteria for new issues of securities. In 1993, the functions of the CIC and the Panel of Takeovers and Mergers were absorbed by the newly formed Securities Commission. (See also: Kuala Lumpur Stock Exchange, Securities Commission.)

Capital market

A capital market is a financial market which deals in long-term financial instruments or a market where equity capital or bond issues may be floated. The term is often used in contrast with money market which deals mainly in short-term financial instruments. (See also: money market.)

Capital Market Law (Indonesia)

Indonesia's Capital Market Law (No. 8/1995) came into effect in January 1996. It has replaced the 1952 Emergency Law to provide a comprehensive legal framework to develop Indonesia's capital market. Its main objective is to create an orderly, fair and efficient capital market. It ensures that the interest of investors are protected. It empowers the Capital Market Supervisory Agency (BAPEPAM) to investigate any person or institution suspected of violating the Capital Market Law. (See also: Capital Market Supervisory Agency.)

Capital Market Society of Indonesia (CMS)

CMS is a non-profit private sector organisation launched in 1996. It promotes the Indonesian capital market by providing information and education support. It organises seminars, training sessions and research. It conducts courses and helps individuals in obtaining licences for BAPEPAM, the market watchdog.

Capital Market Supervisory Agency

See BAPEPAM (Badan Pengawas Pasar Modal).

Cash reserve ratio

In most Southeast Asian, commercial banks are required to maintain a minimum cash balance with their respective central banks. This cash reserve ratio is a percentage of the bank's liabilities base. The central bank is enpowered to vary this ratio from time to time to regulate bank liquidity.

Cash-settled gold futures
Cash-settled gold futures contract is traded at the Singapore International Monetary Exchange (SIMEX). It has replaced the former gold futures contract which was inactive for several years as traders found it unattractive.

This contract is cash-settled based on the Loco-London morning fix on the last day of the contract. This feature allows the investors to avoid the cost of taking physical delivery. But those who wish to take delivery of physical gold can do so by executing an Exchange for Physical (EFP) through a SIMEX corporate member. (See also: gold fixing; SIMEX.)

Cedel
Based in Luxembourg, Cedel is a clearing system to settle international financial instruments such as bonds. (See also: Asian bonds; Euroclear.)

Central bank intervention
Action taken by a central bank to influence monetary conditions. Intervention can be by direct control such as ceiling on interest rates, limit on the volume of bank lending, exchange control inhibiting cross-border currency flows or through open-market operation and informal discussion. The open-market operation could involve purchase or sale by the central bank in the domestic financial markets or in the foreign exchange market.

Central Bank of Myanmar (CBM)
The aim of the Central Bank of Myanmar is to preserve the internal and external value of the Kyat. It formulates and implements monetary policy to foster monetary, credit and financial conditions conducive to orderly, balanced and sustained economic development.

Central Bank of Myanmar Law
The Central Bank of Myanmar Law was enacted in 1990 to replace the old Bank Law of 1975. It confers upon the Central Bank of Myanmar powers to operate with relative independence and to exercise supervisory and regulatory authority over financial institutions both state-owned and private banks.

Central Bank of the Philippines
The Central Bank of the Philippines (Bangko Sentral ng Pilipinas BSP)

administers the monetary, banking and credit system of the Philippines. Its functions include the maintaining of monetary stability, preserving the value and convertibility of the peso into other currencies. It fosters monetary, credit and exchange conditions conducive to a balanced and sustainable growth of the Philippine economy.

Its powers are exercised through the Monetary Board chaired by the Central Bank governor. The seven board members include the Secretary of Finance, the Director General of the National Economic and Development Authority, the chairman of the Board of Investments, and Secretary of the Budget. Two other members are from the private sector, appointed by the President of the Philippines.

Central Depository Pte Ltd (CDP)

The Central Depository Pte Ltd (more popularly called CDP) is a wholly-owned subsidiary of the Stock Exchange of Singapore (SES). It is a central depository for all share certificates. All investors must have a securities account with CDP. The account is like a bank current account where all transactions are recorded. Under the scripless trading system, there is no physical movement of share certificates or scrips. CDP sends statements to investors to inform them of the transactions and the balance in their accounts. The scripless system is a fast and convenient means of settling transactions. CDP operates as a central nominee and all securities at the CDP are registered in its name. However, it has no rights to the registered securities as it only holds the securities on behalf of investors.

Central Depository System (CDS)

A scripless securities clearing and settlement system

Central Provident Fund

The Central Provident Fund (CPF) was introduced in Singapore on 1 July 1955 as a compulsory savings scheme to which both the employees and their employers make monthly contributions. It covers all employees in Singapore except those of pensionable establishment in the Civil Service and those who contribtue to other approved provident funds. Since 1992, self-employed persons are also required to contribute to their CPF Medisave accounts. (See also: CPF accounts; Medisave.)

The objective of the CPF scheme is to provide funds to employees when they retire or when they are physically or mentally unable to work. The Fund also provides for the nominated beneficiary of employees in the event of their death before withdrawing from the Fund.

Since 1968, CPF members may use their savings to buy flats built by the government. In subsequent years, members were also allowed to buy other types of properties, to invest in shares and for other approved purposes.

Central Provident Fund (CPF) Board

The Central Provident Fund (CPF) Board is a statutory board which administers Singapore's compulsory savings scheme under which all employees and their employers make monthly contributions. Since its establishment in 1955, the CPF Board has mobilised large amounts of savings which can be withdrawn by members when they reach retirement age, or for buying properties, investing in shares and other approved uses. The Board invests its surplus funds mostly in long term government securities. The Board pays interest and credits them to the members' accounts. (See also: CPF — interest rate; CPF rates of contribution.)

CPF accounts — ordinary, special and medisave

Each CPF member has three accounts with the CPF: ordinary, special and medisave. Each of these can only be used for specific purposes, as follows:

Ordinary account — housing, approved investments, CPF insurance, education and topping-up parents' Retirement Accounts.

Special account — old age and contingency purposes.

Medisave account — pay hospitalisation and medical expenses.

CPF Investment Scheme

The CPF Investment Scheme is the merger of the CPF Basic Investment Scheme (BIS) and the CPF Enhanced Investment Scheme (EIS) with effect from January 1997.

The investment options available to CPF members are:

- S$ shares and loan stocks of approved trustee companies listed on the SES main board and SESDAQ
- S$ shares and loan stocks of non-trustee companies on the SES main board and SESDAQ (subject to a sub-limit of 20% of investible funds)
- approved unit trusts

— gold (subject to a sub-limit of 10%), gold certificates, gold saving accounts and physical gold held by approved banks
— Scripless Singapore government bonds
— S$ deposits with approved banks (minimum initial amount of S$10,000; minimum maturity period of one year)
— fund management accounts (minimum initial: S$200,000. Fund managers can only invest in approved CPF investments).
— endowment insurance plans (the life insured must be that of the CPF member; maturity date must not be later than 60th birthday; policy cannot be pledged or assigned).

CPF — rates of contribution

When the CPF scheme was first introduced in 1955, employees contributed 5% of their monthly salary, to be matched by another 5% from their employer. The long-term combined contribution rate is 40% for employees below 55 years old with equal contributions from the employee and his employer. For employees between age 55 and 59, the combined rate is 25%, for the 60–64 age group the rate is 15% and for those 65 years old and above, the rate is 10%. The purpose of the reduced rates is to encourage the continued employment of older workers.

Table: CPF — Contributions rates, 1955–99

Effective	Rate of Contribution (%)		
Date	Employer	Employee	Total
Jul 1955	5	5	10
Sep 1968	6.5	6.5	13
Jan 1970	8	8	16
Jan 1971	10	10	20
Jul 1972	12	12	24
Jul 1973	13	13	26
Jul 1974–76	15	15	30
Jul 1977	15.5	15.5	31
Jul 1978	16.5	16.5	33
Jul 1979	20.5	16.5	37
Jul 1980	20.5	18	38.5
Jul 1981	20.5	22	42.5
Jul 1982	22	23	45
Jul 1983	23	23	46
Jul 1984–85	25	25	50
Apr 1986–87	10	25	35

Table: *(Continued)*

Effective Date	Rate of Contribution (%) Employer	Employee	Total
Jul 1988	12	24	36
Jul 1989	15	23	38
Jul 1990	16.5	23	39.5
Jul 1991	17.5	22.5	40
Jul 1992	18	22	40
Jul 1993	18.5	21.5	40
Jul 1994–98	20	20	40
Jan 1999	10	20	30

Source: Central Provident Fund.

Table: CPF rates of contribution for old employees

Employee's age	Employer pays	Employee pays	Total
55-59	7.5 %	12.5 %	20 %
60-64	7.5 %	7.5 %	15 %
65 & above	5.0 %	5.0 %	10 %

Source: Central Provident Fund.

CPF trustee stocks
These are specially designated shares which investors may use their CPF money to buy under the CPF investment scheme.

CPF — withdrawal under section 15
Section 15 of Central Provident Fund Act allows withdrawal to be made for any of the following reasons:

(a) the member has attained the age of 55 years;
(b) not being a citizen of Singapore, intends to depart permanently from Singapore and West Malaysia;
(c) is certified to be physically or mentally unable to continue in any employment;
(d) is found to be of unsound mind;
(e) death;
(f) being a Malaysian citizen, intend to depart permanently from Singapore.

Central Steering Board for State-owned Enterprises (CSBSOE)
The central equitisation board in Vietnam. Its members comprise cabinet ministers. It drafts regulations for state-owned enterprises to abide when they are equitised (privatised).

Certification Assistance Scheme — Singapore
The Certification Assistance Scheme (CERTAS) is a scheme to help local Singapore companies to get international certification (e.g. ISO 9000) as required by their overseas buyers. It pays 50% of the company's preliminary assessment and application fees for the international certification. Companies must meet the minimum requirements under ISO 9000 before applying for certification.

Chartered Financial Analyst
The Chartered Financial Analyst (CFA) examination is administered by the Institute of Chartered Financial Analysts (ICFA) in the USA. Subjects covered in the CFA examination include: ethics and securities law, financial accounting, quantitative analysis, economics, techniques of fixed income and equity analysis, and portfolio management. The primary mission of ICFA, established in 1962, is to enhance professional standards of those involved in investment decision-making. The ICFA has several affiliated associations in Asia, including the Singapore chapter of the International Society of Financial Analysts.

Chek Lap Kok Airport
See Hong Kong International Airport.

Chicago Board of Trade (CBOT)
The largest commodity exchange in the world. The Chicago Board of Trade was established in 1848 and accounts for 51% of the turnover in futures contracts in the US and the bulk of the world's grain futures trading. The CBOT offers contracts in a variety of commodities, ranging from soybeans to long-term US government bonds.

Chicago Mercantile Exchange (CME)
CME is the second largest commodity exchange in the world. It is also known as "the Merc". Contracts are available in a wide range of commodities, such as live hogs, frozen pork bellies and frozen skinned hams. Through its division known as the International Monetary Market (IMM), the CME trades currencies and financial instruments.

China Banking Corporation (Philippines)
China Banking Corporation is a commercial bank listed on the Philippine Stock Exchange. It started operations in 1920. It was the first bank in the Philippines to have on-line computerized operations as well as the first bank to have telephone banking, known as Tellerphone. The bank ranks among the biggest banks offering a wide range of banking services. Its subsidiaries include ASEAN Finance Corporation Ltd, CBC Finance Inc and CBC Venture Capital Corporation.

China Securities Regulatory Commission (CSRC)
The CSRC was formed in 1992 by the State Council of the People's Republic of China as an executive agency of the State Council Securities Policy Committee (SCSPC). The CSRC administers and supervises the securities markets and industry, and formulates regulations.

CIA
See Cambodia International Airlines

CISA
See Certified Investment and Securities Analyst (See also: Securities Analysts Association — Thailand.)

Civil Code of the Socialist Republic of Vietnam
Vietnam's Civil Code was adopted by the National Assembly on 28 October 1995. It was promulgated on 9 November 1995 and came into effect on 1 July 1996. The Civil Code is the most important legislation since 1975. It has gone through numerous drafts and took legislators fourteen years before a final version was accepted. The Code covers a wide scope and attempts to ensure the legal rights and interests of individuals and organisations, the interests of the State and the interests of the public, to ensure legal safety and equality in civil relations and to promote economic development.

Clearing House
It is an organisation that maintains records of the trading of securities. The clearing house has a separate entity from the exchange although it may be owned by the exchange.

Clearing House Automated Payment System (CHAPS)
CHAPS is a payment system available nationwide in Britain. It is

operated by settlement banks which communicate through computers. Payments sent through the system are guaranteed and cleared on the same day.

Clearing House Interbank Payment System (CHIPS)
CHIPS is a computerized network used in the United States for the transfer of international payments. Members may be "settling" or "non-settling". A non-settling member maintains an account with a settling member to effect settlement on its behalf.

CLOB Trading System
The Central Limit Order Book (CLOB) system is used for trading shares at the Singapore Stock Exchange (SES). It maintains an order book and matches buy and sell orders. Each order in the book has a limit price. This is the highest price for a buy order or the lowest price for a sell order at which the order can be executed. The bid and ask prices are established from the orders.

Upon receiving a buy or sell order from a client, the broker will enter the order into his computer terminal. Once the order has been recorded in the CLOB system, the SES central computer checks the order book and matches it with other orders for that particular stock acccording to time priority. If the order can be matched, the deal is executed immediately. If the order cannot be matched, it will be added to the list of orders already in CLOB until a matching is successful. At the close of the trading day, unmatched orders lapse automatically. An order may be withdrawn before it has been matched.

Cluster Development Fund (CDF) — Singapore
The CDF is a special S$1 billion fund set up in 1993 under the management of Economic Development Board. The objective is to enable companies in the same sector to work together to create a "critical mass" for expansion. Its aims is to attract high technology companies to Singapore, to accelerate the development of promising local enterprises (PLE), and to form strategic partnerships between MNCs and PLEs.

Commercial bill
A non-bank bill of exchange (loan) generated by merchant banks and companies. The bill is evidence of the borrower's debt and commitment to repay at the due date as marked on the bill.

Commercial Law of Vietnam
The Commercial Law came into effect on 1 January 1998. It governs the formation of contracts, agency bidding, branches, and representative offices, sales promotion, commercial advertising, commercial paper, remedies and commercial disputes.

Commercial paper
A short-term promissory note issued as evidence of debt. Promissory notes, commercial bills and corporate bonds are forms of commercial paper.

COMMEX Malaysia
See Commodity and Monetary Exchange of Malaysia

Commodities Trading Act — Malaysia
See Futures Industry (Amendment & Consolidation) Act 1997 — Malaysia.

Commodities Trading Commission (CTC) — Malaysia
In 1998, the Commodities Trading Commission (CTC) merged with the Securities Commission as a result of the Futures Industry (Amendment & Consolidation) Act 1997 which came into effect on 16 April 1998 and repealed the Commodities Trading Act 1985. The Act brought the regulation of the commodity futures market under the ambit of the Futures Industry Act 1993, thus rationalising the regulation of the futures market in Malaysia. It also authorises the merger of the Commodities Trading Commission (CTC) with the Securities Commission.

Commodity and Monetary Exchange of Malaysia (COMMEX Malaysia)
In 1998, the Kuala Lumpur Commodity Exchange (KLCE) changed its name to the Commodity and Monetary Exchange of Malaysia (or COMMEX Malaysia) and merged with its subsidiary Malaysian Monetary Exchange (MME). (See also: Kuala Lumpur Commodity Exchange KLCE, Kuala Lumpur Options and Financial Futures Exchange KLOFFE and Malaysian Monetary Exchange MME.) (Website: www.klce.com.my)

Commodity Exchange of New York (COMEX)
Founded in 1933, COMEX is the third largest commodity exchange

in the world. It trades mainly metals and is best known for gold and silver futures trading.

Commodity Futures Act — Singapore
The Commodity Futures Act (Singapore) contains provisions to regulate futures trading in rubber and other commodities.

Commodity Futures Trading Commission (CFTC)
The CFTC is a US federal agency formed in 1975 to regulate commodities trading.

Communications Authority of Thailand (CAT)
CAT is a state enterprise set up in 1977 under the Ministry of Transport and Communications. It operates postal and telecommunications services in Thailand. It is also the owner of Thailand's telecommunication infrastructure, investor in submarine and satellite network. (Website: www.cat.or.th)

Consolidated Daily Report of Condition (CDRC)
The Consolidated Daily Report of Condition enables the Central Bank of the Philippines to determine whether or not a bank is complying with the required capital-to-risk assets ratio and with the required reserves on deposits. (See also: Consolidated Statement of Condition.)

Consolidated Insurance Company Inc (Philippines)
Consolidated Insurance Co. Inc is an insurance company listed on the Philippine Stock Exchange. It provides non-life insurance coverage for fire, marine, motor car, casualty and bonds.

Consolidated Statement of Condition (CSOC)
The Consolidated Statement of Condition (CSOC) and the Consolidated Statement of Income and Expense (CSIE) enable the Central Bank of the Philippines to monitor banks's asset quality and to establish trends and generate relevant balance sheet and operating ratios of every bank for comparison with other banks. (See also: Consolidated Daily Report of Condition.)

Consumer Price Index (CPI)
The Consumer Price Index (CPI) measures the price movements of a specific basket of goods and services purchased by a typical

household in a country. The items include food, clothing, housing, utilities, transport and miscellaneous. The index is usually computed by a national statistics department. It typically uses the Laspeyre's formula with fixed weights for the items and a specific base year. In a large country, there may be separate CPIs for the various regions within the country. In some countries, (e.g. Singapore), there may also be separate CPIs computed for various income groups such as low income, middle income and high income households to reflect the spending behaviour of the respective groups.

Consumer Price Index (Philippines)
The Philippine Consumer Price Index measures changes in the average retail prices of goods and services consumed by all income households in the country. The index uses 13 regional market baskets, one for every region. The number of items ranges from 384 to 651 with corresponding weights derived from the 1985 Family Income and Expenditure Survey conducted by the National Statistical Office (NSO) and updated to 1988 levels through the use of relative price movements. The CPI is computed, using the Laspeyre's formula with fixed weights and with 1988 as the base year. CPI series are computed for the Philippines by region. There is a CPI for the National Capital Region (NCR) and CPIs for areas outside the NCR. The NSO does the CPI computation while both the NSO and the Bureau of Agricultural Statistics are involved in price data collection.

Contract Development Incentive Scheme (Singapore)
The Contract Development Incentive Scheme was introduced by the Singapore International Monetary Exchange (SIMEX) in 1994 to encourage local members to commit themselves to SIMEX's newer contracts.

The incentives include rebates on clearing fees and on trading permits as well as discounts and priority in securing new SIMEX seats for those locals trading a minimum volume in designated contracts. Designated contracts comprise currency contracts, Euromark, high sulphur fuel oil, Japanese government bond and MSCI-Hong Kong index contracts.

Copyright Agreement Between US and Vietnam
The Copyright Agreement Between the US and Vietnam Governments on the Establishment of Copyright Relations was signed on 27 June

1997 during US Secretary of State Madeline Albright's visit to Vietnam. The Copyright Agreement provides a legal basis for protecting the copyrightable works of American companies and individuals in Vietnam and the copyrights of Vietnamese in the US. It is expected to improve prospects for increased transfer of technology to Vietnam.

Corporate Debt Restructuring Committee (CDRC)
CDRC is a committee set up by the Malaysian government to help viable companies from being forced into liquidation.

Corporate Finance Committee (Singapore)
This is one of the three committees within the Financial Sector Reivew Group which was set up by the Singapore government in 1997 to review the financial sector. It looked into the framework of rules and guidelines for corporate fund-raising that would foster innovation and entrepreneurship. It also examined the roles of the Stock Exchange of Singapore, Monetary Authority of Singapore and the Registry of Companies. It recommended new activities to meet the financing need of corporations, and the rules to promote such activities. (See also: Banking Disclosure Panel, Financial Sector Review Group, SES Review Committee.)

Corporate Information Superhighway (COINS) (Malaysia)
COINS is a Malaysian nation-wide broad band network which supports multiprotocol and multimedia applications.

Credit foncier company
The main activity of a credit foncier company in Thailand is to finance the purchase of immovable properties.

Credit Guarantee Corporation Malaysia Berhad (CGC)
The CGC was set up in 1972 to provid guarantee cover to commercial banks for loans extended to small enterprises. The objective is to ensure that small enterprises have access to credit from the commercial banks. It has launched several schemes to assist small enterprises including the Principal Guarantee Scheme and the Loan Fund for Hawkers and Petty Traders. (See also: Principal Guarantee Scheme, Loan Fund for Hawkers and Petty Traders.)

Credit POSB Pte Ltd

Credit POSB Pte Ltd is a wholly-owned subsidiary of the POSBank in Singapore. It provides the following services:

— mortgage loans to individuals to buy residential and commercial properties
— grants renovation and furnishing loans
— administers the Tuition Fee Scheme for the National University of Singapore and the Nanyang Technological University
— manages staff housing loan scheme for the Civil Service, statutory boards and government-linked companies
— manages and provides funds for staff renovation, vehicle and micro-computer loan scheme for the Ministry of Finance, statutory boards and some government-linked companies
— offers a financing scheme to help Housing Development Board (HDB) tenants to buy their HDB shops

Currency Act — Singapore

The Currency Act governs the issue of the Singapore currency by the Board of Commissioners of Currency of Singapore (BCCS). The Act provides that the Singapore currency will be fully backed by external assets including gold, sterling and foreign currencies. Under the Currency (Amendment) Act 1990, the BCCS has set up a Currency Reserve Fund to cushion against fluctuations in the Currency Fund arising from volatile foreign exchange rates.

Currency Board

See Board of Commissioners of Currency of Singapore.

Currency Board (Brunei)

The Brunei Currency Board was set up in 1967. It issues the Brunei currency and controls its circulation. It also licenses and monitors all the banks and finance companies.

Currency Fund (Singapore)

The Board of Commissioners of Currency of Singapore maintains a Currency Fund Income Account for all income and profit earned from the foreign investment of the Currency Fund reserves. Expenses incurred by the Board in issuing and redeeming currency are charged to this account. At the end of the year, any surplus or deficit is transferred to the Consolidated Revenue Account of the Government.

(See also: Board of Commissioners of Currency of Singapore; Currency Act.)

Cyberview Sdn Bhd (Malaysia)
Cyberview is the developer of the 2,800 hectare flagship zone in Cyberjaya. One of its major stakeholders is the Multimedia Development Corporation.

Daimyo bond
A security launched to offset the problem of lack of liquidity in the samurai bond market. Introduced in 1987 by the World Bank, the daimyo is a bearer bond sold in Japan and in the euromarket.

Dana Islam
Islamic-based unit trust

Danaharta (Malaysia)
Danaharta (or Pengurusan Danaharta Nasional Berhad) is a Malaysian wholly-owned government company set up during the 1998 financial crisis. It serves as the national asset management company to deal with non-performing loans of banks.

Danamodal (Malaysia)
Danamodal is a company owned by Bank Negara Malaysia (central bank) to serve as an interim funding institution for banks which could not raise capital directly during the financial crisis.

DCB-RHB Mudharabah Fund
An Islamic-based unit trust launched in 1996 by DCB-RHB Unit Trust Management in Malaysia.

Dealer representative
Person with a dealer representative licence granted under the Securities Industry Act of Singapore and authorised to deal in securities.

Dealers and Remisiers
At the Stock Exchange of Singapore (SES), trading of shares is done not only by stockbroking members, but also by dealers and remisiers in the respective broking firms. Only persons who have passed the Dealer's Representative Examination conducted by the Institute of Banking and Finance can be dealers or remisiers.

Dealers are employees of broking firms. They buy or sell shares for their clients as well as the firms' clients. They are paid a fixed salary plus bonus. Remisiers are not employees of broking firms. Their income depends on the commission earned from buying and selling shares for their clients. (See also: remisiers.)

Delta
A measure of the amount an option price is expected to change for a unit change in the price of the underlying instrument. (See also: Gamma, Rho, Theta, Vega.)

Dependants' Protection Scheme (DPS) (Singapore)
The Dependants' Protection Scheme (DPS), a low cost life and accident insurance scheme for Central Provident Fund (CPF) members, was implemented in 1989. Under the scheme, CPF members below 55 are provided $30,000 coverage against premature death or permanent disability. The scheme is voluntary and members may opt out of the scheme. Premiums, which vary with members' age, are deducted from members' CPF savings. The insurance scheme is renewed automatically every year. The premiums are relatively lower than a commercial insurance because of the large base and minimal administrative costs.

Depository receipt
A depository receipt is a financial instrument whereby investors in one country can buy, hold or sell the securities issued by companies in another country. The depository receipt is a certificate on which is indicated the following information: name of the issuing company in the foreign country, name of the registered holder, the number of depository shares held representing ordinary shares of a specified par value of the company; the name of the custodian and that of the local depository. It also contains a summary of the depository agreement, and the benefits and responsibilities of the holder.

Depository receipts are issued by virtue of a depository ageeement between the foreign company and the local depository. They are issued by the local depository upon proof that the ordinary share certificates of the foreign company has been deposited with a foreign custodian appointed by the local depository as its agent in the foreign country.

Under the depository receipt system the local depository is the sole registered holder of the ordinary shares but the depository receipt holder is the actual investor and owner of those shares. The custodian has been appointed to act as proxy of the local depository and to safeguard the interests of the depository receipt holders. One important feature of the depository receipt is that it is governed by the laws of the depository holder's domicile, while the original shares are regulated by the law of the foreign country.

Deposit-taking company (DTC)
A deposit-taking company in Hong Kong must have a minimum paid-up capital of HK$25 million. It may only take deposit of HK$100,000 or more with a maturity term of not less than 3 months.

Design for Automation Scheme (DFAS)
This scheme is administered by the Economic Development Board in Singapore. It encourages companies to design products for more automation. The project should involve significant redesigning and provide significant improvement in the production process. The EDB grants up to 70% of approved costs (consultant fees, salaries, airfare, overseas living allowance).

Design Ventures Program
This program is administered by Trade Development Board's Export Institute of Singapore. It encourages local manufacturers to invest in product design and packaging. It pays part of the design project costs, including consultancy fee, data collection and analysis, and prototype production. It grants up to 75% of the costs, subject to a ceiling of S$100,000.

Derivative products
These are products constructed from existing products such as options, swaps or forwards. The opposite of 'vanilla' or 'straightforward' products.

Development Bank of Singapore
The Development Bank of Singapore (DBS Bank) was set up in 1968 by the Singapore Government to take over the industrial financing function of the Economic Development Board which was formed to spearhead Singapore's industrialisation plan. As stated in its first annual report, the original objective was to provide industrial financing and to assist in setting up new industries.

In the 1980s, the Development Bank of Singapore began to project itself as a commercial bank. In 1983, it adopted a new corporate identity to highlight its commercial emphasis rather than the stereotyped development bank image. Since then, "DBS Bank" has been used as its new signature for marketing purposes.

The most important shareholder is the Singapore Government which owns substantial capital through its holding companies such as Temasek and MND Holdings. DBS shares are listed on the Stock Exchange of Singapore. Since 1992, DBS Bank (Foreign) shares have been traded in the United States through a sponsored ADR (American Depository Receipt) program.

In 1992, DBS Bank acquired a 10% shareholding in Wing Lung Bank in Hong Kong, in line with its plan to selectively expand its presence and establish strategic alliances with financial institutions in the region. In Indonesia, it has a joint venture commercial bank, PT DBS Buana Tat Lee Bank. In Thailand, it has acquired a 3.4% shareholding in the Thai Danu Bank and a 19% stake in the TSD Leasing Ltd.

In 1998, DBS Bank acquired the Post Office Savings Bank (POSBank) of Singapore.

DBS Bank and Euroclear

The DBS Bank is Euroclear's depository in Singapore for bonds. In 1991 it was appointed Euroclear's depository for the clearing of Singapore equities. The Bank accepts all physical deliveries made in Singapore for the account of Euroclear participants. (See also: Euroclear clearing system.)

DBS(CPF) Stock Index

The DBS(CPF) Stock Index assists investors to monitor the performance of CPF-approved trustee stocks under the CPF Investment Scheme.

Development Bank of the Philippines (DBP)

The Development Bank of the Philippines (DBP) was set up in 1946 under the name of Rehabilitation Finance Corporation. It provided credit facilities for the rehabilitation and development of agriculture and industry and the reconstruction of war-damaged properties. Its activities have expanded and now allocates government funds to all sectors of the economy. It is managed by a board of directors appointed by the President of the Philippines.

Development finance institutions — Malaysia

These are institutions owned largely by the public sector and provide medium and long term funds to complement the development effort of the Malaysian government. Examples are the Bank Industri Malaysia Berhad, Malaysian Industrial Development Finance Berhad (MIDF), the Agriculture Bank and the Development Bank of Malaysia.

Dewan Perwakilan Rakyat — House of Representatives (Indonesia)
It is the legislative branch of the State. It has 500 members: 100 nominated by the President (from the Armed Forces, reduced to 75 in 1997), and 400 directly elected. The Dewan approves all statutes and debates on government policies.

Dewan Pertimbangan Agung (DPA) (Indonesia)
Indonesia's Supreme Advisory Council. It assists the President, who chooses its members from political parties, functional groups and prominent persons.

Dewan Perwakilan Rakyat (DPR) (Indonesia)
Indonesia's House of Representatives

Direct Computer Package Program (DCPP)
This program is arranged by EDB's Enterprise Promotion Centre (EPC) to promote information technology to local enterprises at competitive costs. EPC arranges for bulk purchase of computer hardware and software directly from manufacturers.

Discount house
The basic function of a discount house is to accept short-term funds from commercial banks and other financial institutions. Banks deposit their funds with discount houses, usually on an overnight or callable basis whereby the funds could be withdrawn when needed. For the commercial banks, these deposits with discount houses are considered as liquid assets for the purpose of meeting their statutory liquidity requirement imposed by the central bank or monetary authority. The discount houses invest these funds in short-term instruments such as treasury bills, bills of exchange, short-term government securities and NCDs.

Discount market
A discount market is a short-term money market for the purchase and discounting of trade and bankers' acceptance, bills of exchange, and other commercial papers. It is also a market for government securities such as treasury bills and government bonds.

Double Deduction for Overseas Investment Development Expenditure (DD)

This is one of the tax incentives announced in the 1993 Singapore Budget Statement. The purpose is to encourage local enterprises to explore overseas investment opportunities. It allows double deduction against income of approved expenditures incurred in developing investments outside Singapore. Qualifying activities include: (i) feasibility studies, site visits, investment missions, due diligence studies; (ii) maintaining overseas project offices. The overseas project office must be exclusively for developing investment opportunities.

Double Taxation Deduction Scheme (DTD)

This is a tax deduction scheme to encourage manufacturers to export Singapore-made goods (at least 25% Singapore content). It allows a company to deduct against its taxable income twice the eligible expenses incurred in the following activities: participating in overseas trade fairs, missions either as a group or individually; participating in approved local trade fairs; setting up overseas trade offices; engaging in export market development activities; advertising in approved Singapore export publications; printing product brochures or catalogues. The company must be a resident company or has a permanent establishment in Singapore. It should also not be enjoying any tax relief under the Economic Expansion Incentives (Relief from Income Tax) Act.

Dow Jones Industrial Average (DJIA)

DJIA is a share price index of shares traded on the New York stock market. It is named after Charles Dow and Eddie Jones who first teamed up in 1882 to report stockmarket news to New York's financial community. The decision by the two men to launch a reporting firm distributing stockmarket news, analysis and gossip from a small Wall Street office sowed the seed of the Wall Street Journal, of which Charles Dow was the first editor. The DJIA takes the average of the closing prices of 30 representative stocks from industries such as chemicals and steel.

Dutch tender method

This is one of the two methods to tender in a public share offer in Singapore. Under the Dutch method, successful applicants will pay the price they tendered for. (See also: Single strike price method.)

Economic Committee (Singapore) — Recommendations
During the 1970s and early 1980s, the Singapore economy had continuous high growth desptie the oil crisis and world recession. In 1985, growth slowed down significantly and the Singapore economy had its first major recession with a negative growth rate. The government set up a special Economic Committee chaired by Brigadier General Lee Hsien Loong, the then Minister of State for Trade and Industry to examine Singapore's economic problems, to identify new growth areas and to define new economic strategies.

The Committee gave a wide range of recommendations dealing with all aspects of the economy. For the financial sector, it identified seven areas of growth: risk management, fund management, capital markets, unlisted securities market, financial and commodity futures, financing third-country trading and reinsurance.

Economic Court (Vietnam)
Vietnam's Economic Court was set up in 1993 as a division of the People's Court system. The Economic Court decides on disputes relating to commercial contracts. These are contracts between two legal entities (a company, a state-owned enterprise, a licensed foreign enterprise), or between a legal entity and an individual with business registration. It also decides on disputes between a company and its owners. Other disputes dealt by the Court include the purchase and sales of shares and stocks.

Economic Development Board (Brunei)
The Economic Development Board in Brunei was set up in 1976 to assist in industrial growth under the Five Year National Development Plan. The EDB is also in charge of tourism and is responsible for licensing travel agents. It also administers the law concerning third party motor vehicle insurance.

Economic Development Board (Singapore)
The Economic Development Board in Singapore was set up in 1961. It formulates and implements economic and industrial development strategies for Singapore. Its mission is to develop Singapore into a global hub of knowledge-driven industries.

Eldistra
See Electronic Long Distance Trading system

Electronic Banking
Transfer fund or conduct banking transactions through electronic means.

Electronic Commerce Hotbed (ECH) program
A program which promotes the use of electronic commerce.

Electronic Long Distance Trading system (Eldistra)
A trading system used at the Surabaya Stock Exchange in Indonesia. (See also: Surabaya Stock Exchange.)

Electronic share application
Applying for new share issues by electronic means. One example is to use a ATM card to apply and transfer the subscription fund.

Electronic Share Application — Singapore
In 1993, in cooperation with several banks, the Stock Exchange of Singapore (SES) introduced the electronic share application (ESA) facility whereby investors can apply for shares with their automated teller machine (ATM) cards. They do not have to buy cashier's orders nor submit share application forms. A receipt is issued and funds deducted directly from the applicant's account.

ESA is a one-stop application and payment system. It reduces the processing time for banks during money settlement as all information is captured in the computer system, requiring no further data entry. Refunds for unsuccessful applications are also faster as the applicant's account is credited directly — no cheques need to be posted as in the case of physical share applications.

Electronic Trade Related Services (ETRS)
These services enable trade documents to be transmitted electronically. The documents include purchase orders, packing lists, invoices, letters of credit and shipping documents.

EMAS index — Malaysia
EMAS (Exchange Main Board Share Index) is the main board all-shares price index at the Kuala Lumpur Stock Exchange in Malaysia.

Employees' Provident Fund
Employees' Provident Fund (EPF) is Malaysia's social security organisation set up in 1951 initially for members' old age protection. Over the decades, its range of benefits has been extended to include pre-retirement and withdrawal for house ownership. In 1991, the Act was amended to give EPF more flexibility in managing its portfolios

to obtain better yields. The requirement for the Fund to invest in Malaysian Government Securities was reduced. New avenues of investment include promissory notes, bills of exchange, real property, joint venture, and participation in privatisation programs. In January 1993, the contribution rate was increased to 22% of an employee's monthly wage, with the employer and employee contributing 12% and 10% respectively.

Emergency (Essential Powers) Act, 1979 Essential (Protection of Depositors) Regulations 1986 (Malaysia)
The Act gives the Central Bank the powers to investigate the affairs of any person it suspects or has reason to believe is a deposit-taker. It empowers the Bank to freeze the properties of the deposit-taker and other persons associated with the deposit taker, assume control over the deposit-taker, and to appoint receivers and managers. The Act also enumerates the powers of the managers, provisions on priority of payment and cost.

Enterprise des Telecommunications Lao (ETL)
ETL is Lao's national telecommunication carrier. It was formerly part of the Enterprise des Post et Telecommunications Lao (EPTL). In 1996, ETL signed a master contract with Thailand's Shinawatra International for the provision of telecommunication service in Laos.

Enterprise Rehabilitation Fund (Malaysia)
The Enterprise Rehabilitation Fund was set up by the Malaysian government during the 1985–86 recession to assist ailing bumiputera enterprises with viable on-going projects and good recovery prospects.

Entrepreneur Development Fund (EDF) — Singapore
EDF is a scheme administered by the Economic Development Board. It provides loans to Singapore entrepreneurs and key management staff to own shares in their companies. (See also: Regional Investment Company fund.)

Entrepreneur Skills Development Centre (ESPC) — Malaysia
The ESPC is located in Kuala Lumpur Malaysia. It is a centre within the Federation of Malaysian Manufacturers and is recognised by Malaysia's Human Resource Devleopment Fund. Employers can

claim part of their costs of sending their employees to be trained at the ESPC. (See also: Federation of Malaysian Manufacturers.)

Equitable Banking Corporation (Philippines)
Equitable Bank was established in 1950 and was the first commercial bank to be licensed by the Bangko Sentral ng Pilipinas. The bank's initial focus was to provide banking services to the Chinese-Filipino community. It has since diversified its services with a nationwide network of branches. Its major banking-related subsidiaries include EBC Investments Inc, Equitable Savings Bank, Equitable Finance Ltd and EBC Insurance Brokerage Inc.

Equitise
Vietnam term for Privatise

Euroclear clearing system
Based in Brussels, Euroclear is a clearing system to settle international financial instruments such as Asian dollar bonds, Eurodollar bonds, certificates of deposit and other securities. It was formed in 1972. It acts as the safekeeping centre for the securities.

Euroclear runs a worldwide network of depository offices. When a member of Euroclear trades with another member, there is no need for securities to be physically transferred. Instead, a book entry is made at Euroclear in Brussels.

Eurokiwi
New Zealand dollars held outside New Zealand

Eurokiwi bonds
Bonds denominated in $NZ and issued in the euromarkets, generally to non-New Zealand investors.

Exchange Banks' Association
See Hong Kong Association of Banks

Exchange control
Regulations imposed by a government to control the flow of currencies into and out of the country.

Exchange Control Act (Malaysia)
The Act restricts dealings in gold and foreign currencies, payments to and from residents, issuance of securities outside Malaysia, imports

and exports and settlements. The Act empowers the Controller for Foreign Exchange to grant permissions and consent on the foregoing and to enforce the provisions of the Act.

Exchange control in Singapore
Exchange control was introduced to the Colony of Singapore in 1939. After independence, the Exchange Control Act of 1970 came into effect and was administered by the Monetary Authority of Singapore (MAS). Since the 1970s, the Singapore Government has liberalised control measures in stages in order to enhance the republic's growth as a financial centre. By 1978, Singapore has completely liberalised its exchange control regulations.

Exchange Fund (Hong Kong)
In Hong Kong, the Exchange Fund is managed by the Hong Kong Monetary Authority. It issues and redeems Certificates of Indebtedness which give authority to the note-issuing banks to issue banknotes. The amount of banknotes that each bank is allowed to issue depend on the amount of Certificate of Indebtedness that it holds. In 1990, Exchange Fund Bills of 91, 182 and 364-day were introduced. In 1995, notes of 2, 3, 5, 7 and 10-year maturities were introduced. The Exchange Fund Ordinance empowers the Financial Secretary to control the Fund in consultation with Exchange Fund Advisory Committee.

Exchange Main Board Share Index (EMAS) (Malaysia)
EMAS refers to the share price performance of all KLSE's main board companies. (See also: Kuala Lumpur Composite Index.)

Expanded Commercial Bank (Philippines)
It is Philippine commercial bank which has been authorised by the Central Bank to perform functions in addition to those of a commercial bank. It can function as an investment house and invest in the equity of non-allied companies and own up to 100% of the equity of a financial institution, other than a commercial bank.

Export Credit Insurance Corporation of Singapore Ltd (ECICS)
The Export Credit Insurance Corporation of Singapore Ltd (ECICS) was set up in 1976 with an authorised capital of S$ 300 million. Half of the initial paid-up capital of S$ 30 million was contributed by the Government and the other half came from commercial banks and

insurance companies. Singapore thus became the fourth Asian country to have such a scheme, the other three being Japan, Hong Kong and Taiwan.

On 1 June 1992, the name "Export Credit Insurance Corporation of Singapore Ltd" was changed to "ECICS Holdings Ltd". The new name reflects the change from a company set up in 1975 as part of an economic activation program (to cater for the credit insurance needs of Singapore exporters) to a holding company with subsidiaries in financing, credit insurance, venture capital, property investment and information technology.

Fannie Mae

Fannie Mae is a security issued by the Federal National Mortgage Association of the US (FNMA, hence Fannie Mae) an independent US agency whose main business is to buy mortgages from banks, mortgage companies, savings and loan associations and insurance companies, and to help these lenders in their home financing. (See also: Ginnie Mae.)

Far East Bank and Trust Company (Philippines)

Far East Bank and Trust Company (FEBTC) was incorporated in 1960. It is one of the largest and most diversified universal banks in the Philippines. It has a wide network of branches and international offices. Its major banking-related subsidiaries include FEB Investments Inc, FEB Leasing & Finance Corp, FEB Stock Brokers Inc and FEB Exchange Inc. (Website: www.febtc.com)

Fed

Short form for Federal Reserve System

Federal National Mortgage Association of the US

See Fannie Mae

Federal Reserve System (Fed)

The Fed is the US central bank, established in 1913. It comprises the Federal Reserve Board, Federal Open Market Committee and the twelve Federal Reserve banks, of which the New York Fed is the most important for financial markets.

Federation of Euro-Asian Stock Exchanges (FEAS)

The FEAS was established in 1995 at the initiation of the Istanbul Stock

Exchange. The founding members were 12 stock exchanges in emerging markets in Europe and Asia at different stages of development. As of 1998, there were 22 member exchanges. (Website: www.feas.org)

Federation of Malaysian Unit Trust Managers (FMUTM)
FMUTM is an association which represents unit trust management companies in Malaysia.

Filipino Fund Inc.
Filipino Fund Inc. is a financial service company listed on the Philippine Stock Exchange. It is a closed-end investment company incorporated in 1991. Its focus is on long-term capital appreciation through investment in high-growth Philippine listed equity securities. The investment manager of the fund is BPI Investment Management Inc, a wholly-owned subsidiary of the Bank of the Philippine Islands. (See also: Bank of the Philippine Islands.)

Finance and Treasury Centre Scheme
The Finance and Treasury Centre (FTC) scheme was introduced by the Monetary Authority of Singapore in 1993 to attract international companies to locate their treasuries in Singapore. It provides a concessionary tax rate of 10% and other tax benefits for income derived from treasury activities.

Finance Companies
The main business of finance companies is to collect fixed deposits from the public and to give loans for the purchase of consumer durable goods, vehicles and properties. Some finance companies provide account receivable financing, factoring and leasing. In most countries, finance companies complement the role of commercial banks.

Finance Companies in Singapore
Finance companies in Singapore are supervised by the Monetary Authority of Singapore under the Finance Companies Act. There are two groups of finance companies: independent and bank-related. The major independent finance companies are Hong Leong Finance and Singapore Finance. Bank-related finance companies include DBS Finance, Keppel Tat Lee Finance, United Overseas Finance, and Overseas Union Trust.

Financial Centre Advisory Group (FCAG) (Singapore)
The FCAG was set up by the Singapore government in March 1999 to advise the Monetary Authority of Singapore. Chaired by banker and former cabinet minister Mr S Dhanabalan, the 12-member group of top banking, insurance and stockbroking leaders will assist the MAS in further developing Singapore as a key financial centre.

Its objectives are to:

— provide MAS with feedback on regulatory and supervisory issues;
— help MAS identify emerging market trends and new development opportunities for Singapore;
— promote skills development within the financial sector;
— gather and facilitate exchanges of views with market participants in Singapore and internationally; and
— promote in Singapore the adoption of international best practices in banking and finance.

The FCAG will complement its International Advisory Panel (IAP) which provides MAS with global perspectives on financial sector developments.

The FCAG has set up sub-committees on commercial banking, treasury activities, securities and asset management, and insurance.

Financial derivative
A financial derivative is a financial instrument whose value is "derived" from and thereby depends upon a more fundamental instrument such as a bond or a share of stock. For example, the value of a stock option depends on the value of the underlying stock. The value of a Nikkei futures contract depends on the value of the Nikkei 225 or Nikkei 300 stock average.

Financial Guarantee Insurance — MAS Regulations
Financial guarantee insurance provides guarantee insurance for bonds — including infrastructure bonds and asset-backed securities — issued by Asian borrowers to finance infrastructure projects in emerging markets.

The first such insurer, Aisan Securitisation and Infrastructure Assurance Pte Ltd (ASIA) made it debut in Singapore in 1995. ASIA is a joint venture between the Government of Singapore Investment

Corporation (GIC), Asian Development Bank, US-based CapMac Holdings and some private sector shareholders.

In 1998, the Monetary Authority of Singapore (MAS) introduced new regulations to govern financial guarantee insurance operations in Singapore. The insurer must have a minimum paid up capital of US$75 million and a claims-paying ability rating in the top three classifications awarded by an international credit rating agency.

The insurer must transfer at least 50% of its net profits to a Reserve Fund each year if the fund has less than 50% of its paid up capital. This fund has to be maintained in addition to the loss reserves and unearned premium reserves. This amount is reduced to 25% when the fund level reaches between 50 and 100% of the insurer's paid up capital. When the fund level exceeds 100% of paid up capital, the insurer is required to transfer only 5% of net profits to the Reserve Fund.

The insurers are allowed to underwrite obligations issued to finance construction, maintenance, improvement of expansion of physical infrastructure regardless of whether such obligaitons are payable or guaranteed by a government unit. These insurers may underwrite obligations that are backed by assets, cash flows or market values associated with income-producing real property, as well as obligations related to corporate bonds or promissory notes issued by a corporation.

The insurers must maintain at all times a minimum qualified capital of 1% of the aggregate new exposure to asset-backed obligations; 1.3% for infrastructure obligations, government obligations and real estate obligations; 2% for other secured obligations and 4% for unsecured obligations. Qualified capital refers to the insurer's paid up capital, share premium reserves, retained earnings, capital on call and the Reserve Fund.

Financial Institutions Development Fund (FIDF) — Thailand

FIDF is a fund set up by the Bank of Thailand (central bank) to assist financial institutions during the financial crisis in 1997. It provides insurance cover for repayment of principal and interest to depositors and creditors of commercial banks, finance & securities companies and credit foncier companies.

Financial Institutions of Myanmar Law

Under the old Bank Law of 1975, only state-owned banks were allowed to operate in Myanmar. In 1990, the Financial Institutions of

Myanmar Law was enacted to allow the setting up of private financial institutions, subject to the approval from the Central Bank of Myanmar.

Financial instrument
A document such as a bill of exchange, bond, treasury note or promissory note.

Financial Reporting Act 1997 (Malaysia)
The Financial Reporting Act 1997 establishes the Financial Reporting Foundation and the Malaysian Accounting Standards Board. Under this Act, the Financial Reporting Foundation functions as the overseeing organisation in the standard setting structure while the Malaysian Accounting Standards Board will issue, approve and review accounting standards.

Financial Reporting Foundation
See Financial Reporting Act 1997 (Malaysia)

Financial Sector Resturcturing Authority — Thailand
The Financial Sector Restructuring Authority (FRA) in Thailand was set up on 24 October 1997 under the Emergency Decree on Financial Sector Restructuring BE 2540 (1997). It is an independent body to oversee the rehabilitation of 58 finance companies whose operations were suspended by the order of the Finance Minister on 26 June 1997 (16 companies) and 5 August 1997 (42 companies) and to safeguard the interest of depositors and investors. The administration of the purchase of assets of these companies is done by the Asset Management Corporation which was also set up in October 1997. (See also: Asset Management Corporation — Thailand.) (Website: www.fra.or.th)

Financial Sector Review Group (Singapore)
The Financial Sector Review Group was set up by the Singapore government in 1997 to review the financial sector. Chaired by Deputy Prime Minister Lee Hsien Loong, the group formed three committees each of which examined one specific aspect of financial sector.

The SES Review Committee studied a conceptual framework that would make Singapore's capital market more international and competitive. It also reviewed the rules and by-laws of the Stock Exchange of Singapore (SES) and the Securities Industry Act. The

Corporate Finance Committee looked into the framework of rules and guidelines for corporate fund-raising that would foster innovation and entrepreneurship. It also examined the roles of the SES, Monetary Authority of Singapore and the Registry of Companies. The Banking Disclosure Committee studied disclosure practices for Singapore banks with a view to attaining the standards disclosure of developed countries. (See also: Banking Disclosure Panel, Corporate Finance Committee, SES Review Committee.)

First Abacus Financial Holdings Inc (Philippines)
The First Abacus Financial Holdings Inc is a financial service company listed on the Philippine Stock Exchange. The company, formerly known as 7 Seas Oil Exploration & Resources Inc was incorporated with the purpose of oil exploration. It has diversified and acquired equity interests in real estate, restaurant and family entertainment through the Philippine Racing Club Inc and Fun Time Pizza, USA. In 1996, with the acquisition of a 100% equity stake in Abacus Capital & Investments Corporation, it changed its name to First Abacus Financial Holdings Inc. The company's financial services include underwriting, stock broking and investment banking.

First Bangkok City Bank Public Company Limited (FBCB)
The First Bangkok City Bank was set up in 1934 as the Tan Peng Choon Bank. It was an extension of a trading company and provided a channel for overseas Chinese in Thailand to remit money to China. After World War II, the bank expanded its activities to serve the banking needs in Thailand. In 1960, the name was changed to Thai Development Bank. In 1977, the name was changed again to First Bangkok City Bank to avoid the misconception that it was government-related as the term "development" might have implied. It was listed on the Stock Exchange of Thailand in 1987. It offered a whole range of banking services. It was affected by the 1997 financial crisis and was absorbed by Krung Thai Bank.
(Website: www.fbcb.co.th)

First Outline Perspective Plan (OPP1)
Under Malaysia's First Outline Perspective Plan which covered the 1971–90 period, the government implemented four development plans (the Second Malaysian Plan 1971–75 to the Sixth Malaysian Plan 1986–90). These were implemented in line with the New Economic Policy (NEP) to eradicate poverty and to restructure society so as to

eliminate the identification of race with economic function. (See also: New Economic Policy, Second Outline Perspective Plan OPP2.)

Fixed Delivery and Settlement System (FDSS)
The Fixed Delivery and Settlement System is used in some stock exchanges. For example, in the Kuala Lumpur Stock Exchange, it is based on a T+5 rolling settlement. Under a fixed rolling settlement system, all trades are scheduled for settlement the same number of days after the trade date. It allows trades to settle on all business days of the week. For example, in a T+5 rolling settlement, Monday trades are settled by the following Monday (five business days hence).

Fixed price method
When a company floats a share issue for subscription by the public, the price is normally fixed by the issuing company. In recent years, in Singapore, a share issue may be offered in two tranches: one at a fixed price and another by tender. (See also: tender method.)

Floor trader
The person on the floor of an exchange, such as futures exchange or stock exchange, who executes orders on behalf of clients.

Footsie FT-SE
London Financial Times Stock Exchange Index which lists the 100 largest public company shares traded on the London Stock Exchange.

Foreign currency deposit unit (FCDU)
A Philippine bank with a foreign currency deposit unit is authorised by the Central Bank of the Philippines to engage in foreign currency denominated transactions.

Foreign Exchange Certificates (Myanmar)
The Central Bank of Myanmar issues Foreign Exchange Certificates (FECs) in denominations of 1 unit, 5 units and 10 units (equivalent to US$1, US$5 and US$10 respectively) for the convenience of tourists and foreign currency account holders. The FECs are exchangeable with US dollars.

Foreign Exchange Control (Myanmar)
Foreign exchange control is administered by the Central Bank of Myanmar in accordance with instruction from the Ministry of Finance

and Revenue. Travellers may bring in foreign currency up to US$2,000 without any declaration.

Foreign Exchange Trading Centre (FETC) (Vietnam)
FETCs were set up by the State Bank of Vietnam in Hanoi and Ho Chi Minh City to channel foreign exchange through the banking system. Participants in the FETCs include Vietnamese commercial banks with foreign exchange licences, major licensed trading companies including joint venture with foreign companies. The FETC is run by a Board of Management with representatives from the State Bank and commercial banks. It helps to set the official exchange rate of Vietnamese dong (VND) and the US dollar. It provides an organised market where buyers and sellers of foreign exchange can meet to strike deals with one another.

At the start of each session, the FETC obtains bids from buyers and sellers. Negotiations take place under the supervision of the Board of Management to strike a rate which then applies to all deals done in that session. The closing rate at each session then becomes the official market exchange rate. Between the closed session and the following session, all banks are required to sell at a rate within 0.5% of the fixed rate and buy at the fixed rate.

Foreign Exchange — Vietnam
See Foreign Exchange Trading Centre

Foreign Investment Committee (FIC) (Malaysia)
The FIC is a committee formed in 1974 to implement the Malaysian government's guidelines on regulation of acquisition of assets or interests, mergers or takeovers of companies and major issues pertaining to foreign investment. (See also: Securities Commission.)

Foreign Investment Department (FID) (Vietnam)
The FID is a department within the Vietnam's Ministry of Planning and Investment (MPI). It advises foreign investors on current legislation, introduces projects wanted by the government, receives investment documents (such as application, company charter, feasibility study report, contract between the foreign investor and its Vietnamese partner), prepares opinion for the Office of Project Evaluation in Hanoi and delivers the licence to the investor. Its representative office in HCM city: 178 Nguyen Dinh Chieu Street, District 3, HCMC. Tel: 848-822-3905, Fax: 848-829-9413. (See also: Ministry of Planning and Investment.)

Foreign Investment Law (Myanmar)
The Foreign Investment Law in Myanmar was enacted in 1988. It provides incentives for the inflow of foreign direct investment. The important features of this Law include non-nationalisation, tax holiday of up to three years and 100% foreign ownership. The law also guarantees the repatriation in foreign currency the rightful entitlement of the foreign investor. Foreign investors may incorporate enterprise on a 100% ownership basis.

Foreign ownership of local banks — Singapore
Foreign ownership of local Singapore banks was liberalised in 1990. The ceiling on foreign shareholding of Singapore-incorporated banks was raised from 20 to 40%. Within the higher 40% limit, however, a sub-limit of 5% was imposed on the holdings of any single or related group of foreign shareholders.

Foreign Service Corporation (Vietnam)
A state-owned company which assists foreign companies to recruit local staff.

Forest Research Institute of Malaysia (FRIM)
The main objectives of FRIM are to generate knowledge and develop appropriate technology for the conservation, management, development and use of forest resources. (Website: www.frim.gov.my)

Forward market
A market where traders and speculators can take out contracts for the purchase or sale of commodities at a future date in specified volumes and at specified prices. Futures trading is an example of a forward market. (See also: forward rate, spot, swaps.)

Forward rate
The price for a commodity, such as a foreign currency, for delivery some time more than two days hence. Forward rates in currencies comprise the spot rate plus or minus a forward margin. (See also: forward margin.)

Forward rate agreement (FRA)
An agreement between two parties seeking to protect themselves against a future interest-rate movement in a particular currency, for a specified period and at an agreed contract rate. Settlement is effected

between the two parties for the difference between the contract rate and the interest settlement rate.

Franchise Development Assistance Scheme — Singapore
In Singapore, the Franchise Development Assistance Scheme (FRANDAS) is administered by the Productivity and Standards Board to help local companies franchise their successful business. It covers 50% of the costs of franchise development and marketing overseas. (See also: Franchise Development Centre.)

Franchise Development Centre — Singapore
Singapore's Franchise Development Centre at the Productivity and Standards Board helps local companies in similar trades to cooperate in order to achieve economies of scale in developing a franchise. It helps to (a) identify business opportunities for economic grouping; (b) conduct market surveys and feasibility studies; (c) develop business plans, operation manuals, corporate image-building, intellectual property protection program, training and marketing programs for the franchise.

Full licence bank — Singapore
Full licence banks in Singapore transact the whole range of banking business, both personal and corporate. These include current, savings, and fixed deposit accounts, trade financing, the transfer of funds, commercial letters of credit, trust receipts, traveller's cheques and currencies. They may also give advice on trade and investment, foreign exchange regulations, and may furnish credit reports and trade information.

Included in this category are all the 9 locally incorporated banks and 22 foreign banks, most of which have been in Singapore for many years. Most of the full licence banks have also been granted the Asian Currency Unit (ACU) licence to deal in the Asian Dollar Market.

Fund For Food (Malaysia)
The RM 700 million fund was set up in 1993 by Bank Negara Malaysia (Central Bank) to provide low interest term loans to promote investment in primary food production and distribution (including fisheries, animal husbandry, vegetables and fruits).

Participating financial institutions include commercial banks, finance companies and Bank Pertanian Malaysia Berhad, Bank Pembangunan Malaysia Berhad, Bank Industri Malaysia Berhad and Bank Islam Malaysia Berhad. Malaysian companies, Malaysian citizens, small and medium primary food production projects are eligible to apply for such loans through the financial institutions.

Fund for Reviving and Developing the System of Financial Institutions (Thailand)
This is a fund of which all financial institutions in Thailand must become members and contribute up to 0.5% of their year-end deposits. The fund may be used to help any financial difficulty in order to maintain the economic stability of Thailand.

Fund for Small and Medium Scale Industries (Malaysia)
The RM1.5 billion fund was set up in 1998 to promote small and medium scale industries (SMI) in manufacturing, agro-based and supporting services. SMIs must fulfill the following conditions:- Shareholders' fund of not exceeding RM10 million, Malaysian-owned companies (at least 51% ownership) registered under the Companies Act 1965, the Co-operative Societies Act 1996, entrepreneurs registered under the Registrar of Business and citizens residing in Malaysia.

Fund Management — Liberalisation of CPF Funds
In 1995, the Singapore government liberalised rules to allow CPF account holders to invest in overseas stock. This was done in three stages:

Stage 1 From 1 January 1995, the investment scope of CPF unit trusts and fund management accounts was expanded:

— CPF unit trusts were allowed to invest in foreign stocks and bonds traded on the Stock Exchange of Singapore (SES). The proportion of foreign currency denominated investments was limited to 20% of the value of the fund, to prevent over-exposure to currency risks.
— CPF fund management accounts were allowed to invest in foreign stocks and bonds on SES. In addition, they could invest in regional markets such as Malaysia, Thailand, Hong Kong, South Korea and Taiwan. Fund management accounts could have wider latitude because only CPF members with investible balances of above S$200,000 could open such accounts. They were considered sophisticated investors.

Stage 2 From 1 January 1997, the investment scope of unit trusts was expanded to include stocks listed in the regional capital markets. The limit on foreign currency denominated investments was raised from 20% to 40%.

Stage 3 From 1 January 1999, the investment scope for unit trusts and fund management accounts was expanded to include capital markets outside Asia, such as US, Germany and Japan. The limit on foreign currency denominated investments was raised to 50% of the value of the fund.

Futures contract
An agreement to buy or sell a standard quality commodity — such as gold, US$ or bank bills of exchange — on specific future date at an agreed price determined at the time the contract is traded on the futures exchange.

Futures Industry (Amendment & Consolidation) Act 1997 — Malaysia
The Futures Industry (Amendment & Consolidation) Act 1997 came into effect on 16 April 1998 and repealed the Commodities Trading Act 1985. It brought the regulation of the commodity futures market under the ambit of the Futures Industry Act 1993, thus rationalising the regulation of the futures market in Malaysia. It also authorises the merger of the Commodities Trading Commission (CTC) with the Securities Commission.

Futures Trading Act — Singapore
The Futures Trading Act 1986 authorises the Monetary Authority of Singapore (MAS) to monitor the futures market and approve the setting up or termination of a futures exchange. A licence is needed for a futures broker, representative, trading adviser or representative, or a futures pool operator.

Auditors of futures companies must report to the MAS, if they detect irregularities which jeopardise the funds of clients or if they are unable to confirm whether claims of creditors are covered by assets. Futures brokers must keep customers' funds in separate bank accounts, and furnish clients with separate written risk disclosures.

The Act imposes heavy penalty on shaky deals in the futures market. Offences include false trading, bucketing or falsely claiming to have carried out an order, spreading rumours about false trading, manipulating prices or attempting to corner the market in any commodity which is subject to a futures contract, engaging in fraud or deceptive devices, making statements knowing them to be false, misleading or deceptive. Heavy fines of $100,000 or jail sentence of up to 7 years may be imposed.

Gamma
A measure of the amount "delta" is expected to change in response to a unit change in the price of the underlying instrument. (See also: Delta, Vega, Theta, Rho.)

General Insurance Association of Singapore
The objectives of the General Insurance Association (GIA) of Singapore are to enable companies transacting fire, marine, motor and workmen's compensation insurance business to take joint action in matters affecting the common interest and welfare of the companies.

Ginnie Mae
A US security issued by the Government National Mortgage Association (GNMA, hence Ginnie Mae), an agency of the US Department of Housing and Urban Development. Ginnie Maes were the security base of the first interest-rate futures contract introduced on the Chicago Board of Trade in 1976, and are actively traded on all major US securities markets. (See also: Fannie Mae.)

Globex
An electronic 24-hour trading system developed by the Chicago Board of Trade, the Chicago Mercantile Exchange and the worldwide communications company Reuters.

Gold certificate — Singapore
Investors can buy gold certificates at selected Singapore banks. These certificates are equivalent to one kilobar of gold but are much more convenient to carry around and can be exchanged for physical gold or cash.

An investor can buy gold certificates of one kilobar up to a maximum of 30 kilobars of gold of 999.9 fineness. Banks that sell gold certificates include UOB, OCBC, OUB and DBS Bank. Some gold certificates do not have an expiry date and thus do not require annual renewal. The investor has to pay bank charges when buying certificates. Most banks charge $5 for the issue of each new certificate and charge an additional custodian fee.

Gold coins — Singapore

Gold coins are issued and sold by the Singapore Board of Commissioners of Currency. Examples are the Singapore Lion Gold Coin and the Singapore Bullion Coin. Gold coins originating from other countries are also available in the market. Common examples are the South African Kruggerands, the Canadian Maple Leaf, the British sovereigns, the American Double Eagle, the Dragon and Snake from Hong Kong, and the Australian Nugget. The Singapore Mint has issued some coin bars, which are in great demand. (See also: coin bars.)

Gold Exchange of Singapore (GES)

The Gold Exchange of Singapore (GES) started operations in 1978. Singapore Gold Clearing House Private Ltd (SGCH) was formed to provide the administrative support for the gold exchange. Its paid-up capital of S$1 million was equally subscribed by five shareholders, namely: DBS, OCBC, OUB and UOB and the Bank of Nova Scotia. The first four shareholders were the four largest local banks while the Bank of Nova Scotia had experience in the Winnipeg's gold futures market.

The SGCH would clear and guarantee all contracts entered into by members of the exchange with one another, that is, among the ten broker and dealer members. However, it did not clear or guarantee the contracts of overseas or local associate members. This meant that the associate members, like the public, had to channel their business through the full members.

In December 1983, when the Singapore International Monetary Exchange (SIMEX) was formed, it took over the functions of the GES. (See also: SIMEX.)

Gold savings account

These accounts are similar to savings accounts but instead of cash, the account holder withdraws and deposits gold. They are suitable for small investors as they can deal in grams rather than kilobars. An account holder is issued a savings passbook. If he decides to sell some of his gold deposits, he can exchange it for cash at prevailing market prices.

Gold trading account

These are bank accounts open for the purpose of trading in gold. The customer deposits a certain amount with the bank which then allows him the flexibility to trade up to ten times the deposit. To open a margin trading account, most banks require a minimum deposit of about $50,000.

Gold wafers

Some banks and jewellers offer gold wafers for sale over the counter. These gold wafers come in 1, 2, 5, 10, 20, and 50 gram sizes. They are produced by mints and are popularly kept as jewellery.

Golkar (Indonesia)

See Golongan Karya (functional groups)

Golongan Karya (Golkar) (Indonesia)

Golkar (functional groups) was set up by a group of military and civilian leaders to offset the influence of the Indonesian Communist Party, which was subsequently banned after being blamed for an abortive coup bid in 1965. The political upheavals that followed the abortive coup led to the ascent of General Soeharto as president. Golkar, which literally means functional groups, has been the dominant socio-political force during President Soeharto's 30-year administration. It claims a membership of 36 million out of the country's 200 million population.

Goods and Services Tax — Singapore

The Goods and Services Tax (GST) is a indirect tax on domestic cosumption. It came into effect in Singapore on 1 April 1994. The GST is collected by businesess which have registered with the Comptroller of Goods and Services Tax. Businesses with an annual turnover below $1 million are exempted from GST.

The objectives in implementing the GST are:

— to make the tax system fairer and broader-based;
— to lower corporate and personal income taxes so as to encourage enterprise promote growth and to be more competitive internationally;
— to encourage people to save and invest rather than to spend.

Government Housing Bank (Thailand)

The Government Housing Bank (GHB) was set up in 1953. It is a housing finance institution wholly owned by the Ministry of Finance. Its main activity is to finance persons of moderate income to buy their homes. However, it operates on a commercial basis without government subsidy. By providing the lowest mortgage rates, GHB has played an important role in providing loans to lower-income home-buyers.

Its sources of fund include deposits (interest-paying current account, savings and time deposits), long term domestic borrowings from the Government Savings Bank and the Bank of Thailand, and the issue of bonds guaranteed by the Ministry of Finance. The GHB has about 1,500 employees working in 20 branches in Bangkok, 20 branches and 80 sub-branches in regional cities.
(Website: www.ghb.co.th)

Government Investment Act 1983 (Malaysia)
The Act empowers the Minister to receive investments of moneys for a fixed period and to pay dividend thereon. The Act also appoints the Central Bank as the agent of the government and allows the issue of the investment by way of book-entry i.e. scripless.

Government Investment Certificate (GIC) (Malaysia)
These are non-interest bearing certificates issued in 1983 with the introduction of Islamic banking in Malaysia and the establishment of Bank Islam Malaysia Berhad. Maturities of these certificates range from 1 to 5 years.

Government Investment Corporation (GIC) — Singapore
The Government Investment Corporation (GIC) was formed in 1981 when the Monetary Authority of Singapore was reorganised. Funds previously managed by the MAS were transferred to GIC. Its board of directors was charied by the Prime Minister and included mostly ministers.

The role of the GIC is to manage the government's long term investments. Despite the size of the investments, it has maintained a low profile. It maintains overseas offices in London, New York and Tokyo to seek investment opportunities. Some of the investments have been made jointly with Temasek Holdings, the government-owned holding company.

Government Savings Bank (Thailand)
The Government Savings Bank in Thailand (GSB) was set up in 1947.

It is a non-profit organisation guaranteed by the government. Its main activity is to mobilise small savings and invest these funds in government securities. It encourages savings through the sale of popular savings certificates with a lottery feature.

Government securities market — Singapore

In the government securities market (GSM), the Singapore government issues various types of securities periodically to absorb the surplus funds of the Central Provident Fund. It also enables banks and finance companies to purchase government securities to meet their statutory liquidity requirements.

In 1987, the government securities market was revamped with the introduction of a computerised system and scripless trading procedures. Under the new system, several banks have been authorised as primary dealers or registered dealers.

The primary dealers underwrite the auctions of treasury bills, notes and bonds. All tenders are channelled through these dealers, who ensure liquidity in the market. As market-makers, the registered dealers buy and sell by giving 2-way quotes. But they do not bid in the auction of the new issues.

The dealer maintains two securities accounts, one for its customers' securities and another for its own holdings. It also maintains a cash settlement account with the MAS. Under the system, no physical transfer or scrip of bond certificate is necessary. A transfer of securities is shown by a book entry and daily settlement is done through the cash settlement account.

The revamp is part of the government's plan to further develop the capital market and to provide more instruments for fund management. It enables banks to mange their reserve and liquidity positions more efficiently by directly participating in government securities.

The objectives of a restructured government securities market are:

(a) to improve the liquidity and yield in the market so that investors have an effective additional avenue for investment;
(b) to develop a benchmark for pricing capital market instruments of other issuers;
(c) to develop skills in debt securities trading which can be applied towards offshore securities business, e.g. trading in US Treasury securities and Eurobonds.

Gross Problematic Assets (GPA)
GPA is an indicator used by international rating agency Standard & Poor's to measure stress in a financial system. Problematic assets include overdue loans, restructured assets (where the original terms have been altered), foreclosed assets, and non-performing assets sold to special purpose vehicles. GPA ranges are estimates of the potential level of problematic assets in the financial system in a reasonable worst-case economic recession, expressed as a percentage of domestic credit to the private sector and non-financial public enterprises.

Guidelines for bonus and rights Issues
See SES guidelines for bonus and rights issues

Hang Seng index
A Hong Kong Stock Exchange index compiled by the Hang Seng Bank in Hong Kong.

HKFE Clearing Corporation Limited (HKCC)
The HKFE Clearing Corporation (HKCC) is a clearing house wholly-owned by the HKFE. It clears and registers transactions effected on the Exchange's markets. Its board of directors ensures that operational procedures are consistent with the Exchange's market and risk management policies. The board comprises a minimum of six directors which include: the Chairman of the Exchange; the Chief Executive Officer of the Exchange; two members of the clearing house, or representatives of such members; and one independent director, unconnected with any exchange or Clearing House member.

The HKCC is obliged to meet counterparty liabilities when a member defaults on its settlement obligations. The maximum extent of the Clearing House's liabilities as counterparty is: the amount of margin collected by and on deposit with the clearing house pursuant to its rules; and the value of the Reserve Fund.

The HKCC has a Reserve Fund to meet its counterparty liabilities. The fund comprises the following components: members' cash deposits, insurance, bank guarantees, interest income, member's additional deposits; and resources appropriated by the clearing house from time to time out of its general revenue. (See also: Hong Kong Futures Exchange.)

Home Protection Insurance Scheme — Singapore
The Home Protection Insurance Scheme under Singapore's Central

Provident Fund was introduced in 1981. It enables CPF members to have their outstanding loans on their flats paid up by the CPF Board if they die or suffer permanent total incapacity. The scheme applies to members who have used their savings to buy Housing Development Board flats.

Under the scheme, the members pay a lump sum premium to be deducted from their CPF savings. The premium depends on their age at the time of cover, the amount of the outstanding loan, the repayment period, and the interest on the loan. Exemption from the scheme is granted to members who already have sufficient mortgage insurance cover for their flats.

Hongkong and Shanghai Banking Corporation (HSBC)
Hongkong and Shanghai Banking (Hong Kong Bank) has been associated with the economy of Hong Kong for more than a century. It is one of the three currency note issuing banks (the other two are Standard Chartered and Bank of China). In the past, the bank provided cheque clearing facilities on behalf of the Hong Kong Association of Banks and acted as lender of last resort.

In December 1990, a holding company HSBC Holdings plc was set up and registered as a non-resident company incorporated in the United Kingdom. The Hong Kong Bank is a wholly-owned subsidiary of HSBC Holdings and maintains its headquarters and management in Hong Kong.

Hong Kong Association of Banks (HKAB)
The Hong Kong Association of Banks replaced the Exchange Banks' Association in 1981. The statutory body has three permanent committee members: Hongkong and Shanghai Banking Corporation, Standard Chartered Bank and the Bank of China. Other members are the licensed banks in Hong Kong. The HKAB submits views and recommendations to the government on policies related to the banking sector.

In the past, the HKAB was authorised to fix the maximum interest rates for Hong Kong dollar deposits of less than HK$500,000 and with a maturity of less than 15 months. Since October 1994, retail deposit interest rates have been deregulated.

Hong Kong Bank
See Hongkong and Shanghai Banking Corporation

Hong Kong Banking Ordinance

The Banking Ordinance of Hong Kong provides the legal framework for banking supervision in Hong Kong. Under Section 7(1) of the Ordinance, the main function of the Hong Kong Monetary Authority (HKMA) is to promote stability and effective working of the banking system.

The regulatory framework is in line with international standards, especially those recommended by the Basle Committee on Banking Supervision. The objective is to preserve stability of the banking system and to provide flexibility for financial institutions to take commercial decisions.

The HKMA follows international practice as embodied in the principles of the revised Concordat issued by the Basle Committee. The Minimum Standards of the Basle Committee in July 1992 have also been incorporated into the authorisation criteria for overseas applicants for banking licences.

Institutions are required to maintain adequate liquidity and capital adequacy ratios, to submit periodic returns to the HKMA on the required financial information, to adhere to limits on loans to any one customer or to directors and employees, and to seek approval for the appointment of directors and senior management, and for changes in control. However, branches of foreign banks are not required to hold capital in Hong Kong and are not subject to capital ratio requirements or to capital-based limits on large exposures. (See also: Hong Kong Monetary Authority.)

Hong Kong Futures Exchange

The Hong Kong Futures Exchange (HKFE) was established in 1976. It is a leading derivatives market in the Asia Pacific. It provides for the trading of futures and options contracts by its more than 130 member organisations many of which are affiliated with international financial institutions.

Its broad range of products includes equity index, stock, interest rate and foreign exchange products. These products are traded either on the Exchange's trading floor via open outcry or electronically on its Automated Trading System (ATS).

The Exchange, with its subsidiary the HKFE Clearing Corporation, operates a rigorous risk management system, enabling members and their clients to meet their respective investment and hedging needs in a liquid and well-regulated marketplace. (See also: HKFE Clearing Corporation Ltd.)

Hong Kong Institute for Monetary Research

Hong Kong Institute for Monetary Research (HKIMR) was set up in August 1999. Its main objective is to conduct research in monetary policy, banking and finance areas that of strategic importance to Hong Kong and Asia. It is affiliated to the Hong Kong Monetary Authority and is funded by grants from the Exchange Fund.

Hong Kong International Airport

Hong Kong International Airport (HKIA) was opened in July 1998. The 1,250-hectare airport replaces the old Kai Tak Airport. The HKIA is built on reclaimed land on Chek Lap Kok island which is now linked to the city via train, bridges, tunnels and expressways.

In 1989, Sir David Wilson, then the governor of Hong Kong, announced the Airport Core Program (ACP) to construct a new airport at Chek Lap Kok as part of an ambitious development strategy. The ACP consisted of ten integrated infrastructure projects costing US$20 billion.

In 1991, the new Airport Projects Co-ordination Office (NAPCO) was formed to provide overall program management services in coordinating all ten projects. It worked closely with all government departments and private sector agencies involved in the projects. HKIA has a 500,000-square metre passenger terminal, one of the world's largest. It is about eight times larger than Kai Tak Airport. It is designed by renowned British architects Foster and Partners.

Hong Kong Monetary Authority (HKMA)

The Hong Kong Monetary Authority (HKMA) was set up in 1993 with the merger of the Office of the Exchange Fund and the Office of the Commissioner of Banking. The objective was to ensure that the central banking functions could be performed with professionalism and continuity, in the lead up to 1997 and beyond, in a manner that would command the confidence of the people of Hong Kong and the international financial community.

The HKMA maintains exchange rate stability within the linked exchange rate system through management of the Exchange Fund, monetary operations and other means. The linked exchange rate system adopted since 17 October 1983 is a currency board arrangement. Its core feature is the full backing of domestic currency notes by a foreign currency at a fixed exchange rate of US$1 to HK$7.80. In the foreign exchange market, the Hong Kong dollar exchange rate is determined by supply and demand.

The exchange rate of the Hong Kong dollar has remained remarkably stable since 1983 because of strong official reserves. These reserves form part of the Exchange Fund which is managed by the HKMA. The HKMA adopts a prudent investment strategy to ensure that the investment management process of the Fund keeps pace with international best practices. (See also: Hong Kong Banking Ordinance.)

Hong Kong Note Printing Limited

In 1996, the Hong Kong government bought the banknote printing plant of De La Rue and renamed it Hong Kong Note Printing Limited (HKNPL). The chairman of the company is the Chief Executive of the Hong Kong Monetary Authority (HKMA). Hong Kong dollar currency notes are issued by three banks: Hongkong and Shanghai Banking Corporation, Standard Chartered Bank and the Bank of China.

In 1997, the HKMA sold 15% of the shareholding to China Bank Note Printing and Minting Corporation. While retaining the controlling interest, it plans to sell some shares to the three note issuing banks.

Hong Kong Securities Institute

The Hong Kong Securities Institute (HKSI) is a professional body for practitioners in the securities, fund management and investment business. It was launched in December 1997. It is sponsored by the Hong Kong Securities and Futures Commission, and has the support of the Stock Exchange of Hong Kong, the Hong Kong Futures Exchange and the industry.

Its mission is to set professional standards for practitioners in Hong Kong's financial services industry. In cooperation with other professional associations, it will develop relevant training and qualification opportunities. The objective is to have a comprehensive development structure for securities and investment professionals. It will ensure that the industry will benefit from the maintenance of high professional standards of competence, integrity and ethics. (See also: Hong Kong Futures Exchange, Hong Kong Securities and Futures Commission, and Stock Exchange of Hong Kong.)

Hong Kong Stock Exchange

See Stock Exchange of Hong Kong

Housing Welfare Loan Scheme for Government Officials (Thailand)

This scheme began in 1993 as a government measure to prevent a brain drain from the public sector to the private sector. Low interest mortgage loan are offered through the Government Housing Bank which is wholly-owned by the Ministry of Finance. (See also: Government Housing Bank.)

IMF — Singapore Regional Training Institute
See Singapore Regional Training Institute (STI)

Incombank
See Industrial and Commercial Bank of Vietnam

Indonesian Association of Development Financing Institutions
(Asosiasi Lembaga Pembiayaan Pembangunan Indonesia, ALPPIA)
The Indonesian Association of Development Financing Institutions provides training and hold seminars on long term development finance.

Indonesian Bank Restructuring Authority (IBRA)
The Indonesian Bank Restructuring Authority (IBRA) (or Badan Penyehatan Perbankan Nasional, BPPN) was established in 1998 by Presidential Decree No. 27 of 1998. It is an independent body reporting to the Ministry of Finance. Its main mission is to improve the banking sector to an internationally accepted standard. It has set up the Asset Management Company to focus on debt recovery for banks which have failed.

Indonesian Clearing and Settlement Corporation (KPEI)
KPEI is a company which provides clearing service and guarantees securities settlement at the Jakarta Stock Exchange. Its shareholders are: Jakarta Stock Exchange Ltd (90%) and Surabaya Stock Exchange (10%).

Indonesian companies
Indonesian companies may be divided into three basic types: state-owned enterprises (Badan Usaha Malik Negara), public companies and private companies. (See also: Indonesian state-owned enterprises.)

Indonesian School of Mortgage Banking
The Indonesian School of Mortgage Banking was set up in 1997 by economist Professor Soemitro Djojohadikusumo through Yayasan

Dharma Tirta in cooperation with Bank Papan, Mortgage Banker Association of America, and Financial Analysis Development Institute of Indonesia (IPAF).

Indonesian state-owned enterprise
An Indonesian state-owned enterprise is basically a company owned by the government but has the flexibility of a private enterprise. During the transition from the "Old Order" administration of President Sukarno to the "New Order" administration of President Suharto, many state-owned enterprises were transformed from state corporations (Perusahaan Negara, PN) into one of the three new categories: government agency (Perusahaan Jawatan, or Perjan), public corporation (Perusahaan Umum, or Perum), or limited liability company (Perseroan Terbatas, or PT).

Indovina Bank (IVB)
IVB was licensed in 1990 as the first joint venture bank in Vietnam. Its partners are the Industrial and Commercial Bank of Vietnam (Incombank) and PT Bank Dagang Nasional Indonesia. It has offices in Hanoi, Ho Chi Minh City and Hai Phong City.

Industrial Adjustment Fund
This fund was set up by the Malaysian government in 1991 to restructure selected industries, such as the machinery and engineering, wood-based and textile industries.

Industrial and Commercial Bank of Vietnam (Incombank)
Incombank is one of the three state-owned commercial in Vietnam. Its clients are mainly from the industrial and commercial sectors. It has a joint venture bank with Bank Dagang Nasional from Indonesia.

Industrial Estate Authority of Thailand
The IEAT is a state enterprise attached to the Ministry of Industry. It implements the government's industrial development policy. It is also responsible for industrial estates in Thailand to ensure orderly industrialisation.

Industrial Finance Corporation of Thailand (IFTC)
The IFTC was set up in 1959 to provide medium and long term loans for the expansion and modernisation of industrial enterprises in the

private sector. The IFTC has been operating as a development finance company. With effect from 1992, the IFTC has been authorised to carry out activities related to the development of the capital market in Thailand.

Industrial Linkage Program (ILP) (Malaysia)
Malaysia's Industrial Linkage Program is a cluster-based industrial development program under the Second Industrial Master Plan (Second IMP) (1996–2005). The objective is to nurture local SMIs into reliable suppliers of critical components to larger companies. The priority areas include: electrical and electronic industry, transport equipment industry and machinery groups.
(Website: www.jaring.my/smidec/ilp.htm)

Industry-wide Automation Development Program (IADP)
Under this program, Singapore's Economic Development Board (EDB) encourages the development of automation systems which can be used by several companies. It covers direct costs of product development and acquisition of knowhow, including: cost of prototype, consultancy fees, salaries, cost of additional design and development equipment, airfare and overseas allowances. It grants up to 70% of approved costs subject to a maximum of S$1 million.

Infrastructure Development Fund (Malaysia)
The RM5 billion Infrastructure Development Fund was set up in June 1998. The fund was raised through domestic and foreign bond issues. It helps to revive deferred infrastructure projects to boost the Malaysian economy. The projects include monorail, sewerage and highway projects.

Initial Public Offer (IPO)
This refers to a new issue of share when a company offers its shares for the public to subscribe.

Initial Public Offer in Two Tranches — Singapore
The Stock Exchange of Singapore (SES) has introduced a two-tranch method for floating new issues. The method allows companies to opt for a combined fixed price and a Dutch-style tender system. The objective is to curb unnecessary speculation in new issues, especially during a bull market because pricing of the shares under the tender system will reflect prevailing market forces.

The idea was first discussed after the huge over-subscription rates chalked up by some of the IPOs in the 1990s. For example, the Kim Eng issue was over-subscribed by a record 783 times. This caused the overnight Singapore dollar inter-bank rate to soar to 28% because of the staggering S$23 billion in subscription monies involved.

Under this method, the IPO is issued in two tranches: one under a fixed price tranche and the other under a tender system. To ensure that small investors do not lose out, a specified proportion of the issue will be available for subscriptions under the fixed price portion. This may range between 20 and 40 per cent of the total share issue. Under the fixed price portion investors can apply for only 1,000 shares each, and multiple applications are not allowed.

An investor who wants to have a larger number of new shares can tender at a higher price. For the tender portion, an investor can submit more than one application provided that the tender price in each is different.

The new system also provides for shares under-subcribed in either category to be offered for allotment in the other, while if both tranches are under-subscribed the underwriters have to take up the shares. In case of over-subscription, the fixed price portion will be balloted.

The main features are:

— under the fixed price portion,investors can apply for only 1,000 shares each and no multiple applications are allowed
— in the event of over-subscription, successful applicants will be determined by ballot
— to ensure a reasonable spread of shareholding particularly among small investors, between 20 and 40% of each issue will be under the fixed price portion
— Under the tender portion, applications will be for 1,000 shares or in multiples
— applicants will be allowed to submit more than one application but only at different tender prices
— an applicant and "related parties" may apply for not more than 5% of the issue. (Related parties include the applicant's spouse and dependent children; a corporation in which the applicant, his spouse and dependent children have more than 50% interest; and if the applicant is a corporation, its holding company and subsidiary)
— the tender price will not be lower than the minimum application price fixed by the issuer (the subscription price of the fixed price portion).

— applications to the tender portion will be satisfied in full, starting from the highest price and progressing downwards until all available shares are allocated.

Institute of Banking and Finance — Singapore (IBF)
Singapore's Institute of Banking and Finance (IBF) conducts courses on the practical aspects of banking and finance for its member institutions. It has program for the Banking Certificate, Diploma in Banking and Finance, and Diploma in Investment.

IBF offers an undergraduate and two post-graduate program with degrees awarded by foreign universities. The Monash University's BBA degree program in banking and finance had its first intake of students in 1994. The Macquarie University's Masters of Applied Finance began in 1992. The Executive MBA in Finance offered by the Manchester Business School and University of Wales started in 1994.

The IBF administers 3 local examinations and 4 foreign examinations. They include the Dealers' Representatives' Examination (SES), the Futures Examination (SIMEX), the Chartered Financial Analysts Examination (USA) and the Chartered Institute of Bankers (London).

Insurance Act 1996 (Malaysia)
The Act deals with the licensing of insurers, brokers, adjusters and reinsurers. It also deals with setting up of subsidiary and offices, establishment of insurance fund, direction and control of defaulting insurers, the control on management of licensee, accounts of licensee, examination and investigation powers of the Central Bank, winding-up, transfer of business of licensee. The Act also deals in matters relating to policies, insurance guarantee scheme fund, enforcement powers of the Central Bank, offences and other general provisions.

Insurance Act 1993 Amendment — Singapore
The Insurance Act (Singapore) was amended in 1993. With effect from 31 December 1993, the distribution of surplus to policyholders and shareholders for life business was changed from the 80/20 to 90/10. This was phased over a period of five years commencing 1993. With effect from 1 January 1994, all direct life insurers are required to appoint a person as its actuary. The MAS is empowered to approve the appointment of the actuary and to prescribe the duties of the "appointed actuary".

Insurance business in Vietnam
In 1993, Vietnam opened up its insurance sector to foreign insurance companies, breaking the monopoly enjoyed by the state-owned insurance company Bao Viet. Government Decree 100-CP allows private enterprises and foreign insureres to apply for insurance business licence. There are four types of insurance business: insurance, reinsurance, insurance brokering and insurance agents. There are four types of insurance companies: mutual insurance companies, joint venture insurance companies, branches of foreign insurance companies and wholly-owned foreign insurance companies.

Insurance Trust Fund (Singapore)
The Insurance Trust Fund was set up in 1974, and was managed by a Board of Trustees nominated by the Insurance Commissioner, the General Insurance Association, Life Insurance Association and Singapore Insurance Brokers Association. Its main objectives were to promote education and research in insurance and to finance the Singapore Insurance Training Centre. In 1983, its role was taken over by the Association for Insurance Advancement.

Interbank Funds Transfer System (IFTS) (Malaysia)
IFTS is an automatic interbank fund transfer system launched in 1989 by Bank Negara Malaysia (Central Bank) to transfer and settle interbank funds.

International Advisory Panel (IAP) (Singapore)
IAP is a panel of international bankers which has been formed to advise the Monetary Authority of Singapore. Members are leading American, European and Japanese bankers. They provide the MAS with global perspectives on financial sector developments.

International Bank of Brunei Berhad
This is one of the licensed banks in Brunei. It was formerly known as the Island Development Bank Berhad.

International Bank of Singapore (IBS)
The IBS was set up by the Big Four local banks (DBS, OCBC, OUB and UOB) in 1974. The original objective was for the Big Four to move into international banking jointly. However, as each began to expand overseas separately, the joint venture became redundant. The IBS is

now wholly owned by Overseas Union Bank which bought over the shares of the other partners.

International Bank for Reconstruction and Development (IBRD — World Bank)
The formation of the IBRD or World Bank was proposed at Bretton Woods in July 1944 and commenced operations in 1946. The main objective is to provide or guarantee loans to member nations for development projects. Examples of such projects are electric power, roads, ports, telecommunications, education, tourism and family planning. The IBRD has two affiliate institutions: the International Finance Corporation and the International Development Association. (See also: Bretton Woods Agreement.)

International Committee on the Reconstruction of Cambodia (ICORC)
The ICORC comprises representatives from donor countries. They met in Paris in 1993, in Tokyo in 1994 and again in Paris in 1995. These meetings resulted in US$1.6 billion in contribution from 40 donor countries and international aid organisations such as the Asian Development Bank, World Bank and International Monetary Fund.

International Commodities Clearing House
This London-based clearing house provides clearing services for futures exchanges around the world, including the Hong Kong Futures Exchange, London International Financial Futures Exchange and the New Zealand Futures and Options Exchange.

International Fairs Development Assistance Scheme (IFDAS)
This scheme aims to promote Singapore as an international trade fair centre in Southeast Asia. Local or joint venture exhibition companies can get up to 50%, or a maximum of S$20,000 to cover promotion costs of trade shows. The company must be registered in Singapore. At least 30% of the company must be owned by Singaporeans, and its exhibitions must promote Singapore products or services.

International Federation of Stock Exchanges (Federation Internationale des Bourses de Valueurs)
The IFSE is a trade organisation for regulated securities and derivative markets worldwide. It promotes the professional business development of financial markets, both at the national and

international levels. Its secretariat is located in Paris. (Website: www.fibv.com)

International Maritime Organisation (IMO)
The IMO is an organisation regulating international maritime safety and the prevention of marine pollution from ships.

International Monetary Fund (IMF)
After World War II there were chaos in the international monetary system. In 1994, at the Bretton Woods conference, the formation of the International Monetary Fund (IMF) was proposed. The IMF was formed in 1947 to restore orderly exchange practices. Its objective is to promote international monetary cooperation in maintaining exchange stability and to encourage international trade. Member nations may borrow from the IMF to solve their balance of payments deficit.

The main objectives of the IMF are:

(a) to promote international monetary cooperation by providing an institution for consultation and collaboration on international monetary problems;
(b) to encourage international trade high employment and real income, and to develop economic policy;
(c) to promote exchange stability, orderly exchange arrangements among members, and to avoid competitive exchange depreciation;
(d) to assist in the establishment of a multilateral system of payments in respect of current tranactions between members and in the elimination of foreign exchange restrictions which hamper the growth of world trade;
(e) to give confidence to members by making the Fund's resources available to them under adequate safeguards, thus providing them with opportunity to correct maladjustments in their balance of payments without resorting to measures destructive of national or international prosperity.

International Monetary Market (IMM)
The IMM was set up in 1972 as a division of the Chicago Mercantile Exchange. It deals in futures contracts in currencies, gold and financial instruments.

International Organisation of Securities Commissions (IOSCO)
Membership of the IOSCO is open to a securities commission or a similar government body. Members agree to cooperate to promote high standards of regulation in order to maintain just, efficient and sound markets; to exchange information on their respective experience; to unite their efforts to establish standards and effective surveillance of international securities transactions. IOSCO has four Regional Standing Committees, which meet to discuss specific regional problems of the members: Africa-Middle East, Asia-Pacific, European and Interamerican regional committees. The IOSCO secretariat is located in Montreal, Canada. Since 1974, IOSCO members have been meeting every year to discuss issues related to world securities markets. The 1998 annual conference was held in Nairobi (Kenya), 1999 in Lisboa (Portugal) and 2000 in Sydney (Australia). (Website: www.iosco.org)

Internationalising the Singapore Dollar
See: Singapore Dollar — Internationalisation

Investment Adviser Licence (IAL) (Singapore)
Under Singapore regulations, investment advisers are required to have an Investment Adviser Licence. The licence has been granted mainly to investment management firms. Small firms with fewer than 30 clients are exempt from the requirement. Banks selling investment product such as unit trusts are also exempted.

Investment Allowance Scheme (IAS) — Singapore
This is a tax incentive scheme to encourage local Singapore enterprises to upgrade their machinery and equipment. The allowance can be applied against the company's taxable income in which the capital expenditure is incurred or it can be carried forward against a subsequent year's income. Even with IAS, the company's normal or accelerated depreciation schedules still apply.

Investment Coordinating Agency
An Indonesian government agency in charge of supervising private investment, both domestic and foreign.

Investment Credit Scheme (Indonesia)
The Investment Credit Scheme (Kredit Investasi) is supported by Bank Indonesia (Central Bank) to provide funds for industrialisation. Under

the scheme, medium and long term credits are provided to entrepreneurs to expand and modern their operations.

Investment Guidelines for life insurance companies in Singapore
Under the Investment Guidelines announced in 1992, life insurance companies in Singapore are required to observe maximum limits for investments in equities, real estate, unsecured loans and foreign assets. The measures also restrict investments in related companies. The guidelines stipulate the proportion of funds that can be invested in each asset-class.

Investment Management Association of Singapore
Investment Management Association of Singapore (IMAS) was registered in 1997. It is an organisation for fund managers to discuss issues of common interest. It represents the industry to the government and other organisations. Issues include a code of best practice and standards for the industry and the development of education and training programs.

Affiliate members include individuals from the industry as well as members of the Singapore Society of Financial Analysts (SSFA) or those with a dealer's licence.

IPE Brent crude oil futures
In 1995, Singapore International Monetary Exchange (SIMEX) launched a mutual offset energy contract in Brent crude oil futures. The agreement was signed with London's International Petroleum Exchange (IPE).

Under the arrangement, each Brent crude oil futures contract, worth 1,000 barrels of crude oil, can be bought or sold on either exchange during the 18 hours of combined trading on the two exchanges.

Pioneered by IPE, Brent crude is a cash-settled contract based on North Sea oil. Brent crude is used as a price benchmark for about 65 per cent of the world's oil. In terms of trading volume, Brent crude futures is the world's second largest after light sweet crude futures traded on the New York Mercantile Exchange.

Islamic bank
It is a bank whose activities are based on Islamic principles. For example, the bank accepts savings and demand deposits based on the principles of *Wadiah* (safekeeping). It accepts term deposits in the form

of general investment deposits and special investment deposits under the principles of *Mudharabah* (profit-sharing). The bank grants financing facilities such as project financing under the principles of *Mudharabah* and *Musyarakah* (joint venture), and hire purchase financing under the principles of *Bai' Bithaman Ajil* (deferred payment sale).

Islamic Banking Act 1983 (Malaysia)
The Act licenses and regulates Islamic banking business. It stipulates the financial requirements and duties of an Islamic bank, ownership, control and management of Islamic banks, restrictions on its business, powers of supervision and control over Islamic bank.

Islamic Banking in Indonesia
In Indonesia, Islamic banks were set up after the Banking Act of 1992 came into effect. There is one Islamic commercial bank, Bank Mua'malat Indonesia (BMI). Under the rural banking system (Bank Perkreditan Rakyat or BPR), there are three rural Islamic banks located in West Java: PT BPR Dana Mardhatilla, PT BPR Berkah Amal Sejahtera and PT Amanah Rabbabiah.

Jabotabek
Greater Jakarta Area (an area covering Jakarta, Bogor, Tanerang and Bekasi). It has a population of about 20 million people.

Jakarta Automated Trading System (JATS)
In 1995, the manual trading system at the Jakarta Stock Exchange (JSX) was replaced by the Jakarta Automated Trading System (JATS) to increase efficiency. JATS handles 50,000 transactions daily as compared to only 3,800 under the manual system. It is also an integrated system that connects trading, clearing, settlement, depository and broker accounting systems.

Jakarta Electronic Clearing System
The Jakarta Electronic Clearing System (SKEJ) was introduced in 1998. Initially, there were eight clearing participating banks: Bank Rakyat Indonesia (BRI), Bank Dagang Negara (BDN), Bank Central Asia (BCA), Bank Internasional Indonesia (BII), Citibank, Standard Chartered, Deutsche Bank and Bank Indonesia. Eventually, all banks within the Jakarta clearing area will become members of the system.

The system is based on the Electronic Clearing Data (DKE) which is transmitted by the clearing participant bank from the Clearing Participant Terminal (TPK) through the data communication network to the Electronic Clearing System Center (SPKE) at Bank Indonesia and is accompanied by the clearing notes.

Jaminan Peneliharaan Kesehatan Masyarakat (Guaranteed Health Maintenance for the People)

This health scheme was introduced in 1992 by the Indonesian government for its own employees. In 1997, a law was passed to allow the private sector to apply for licences to manage insurance plans for their own employees. Employees protected by managed care policies can only seek covered medical treatment from clinics and hospitals under contract with the employing company. In 1998, six of largest Indonesian companies launched their own managed care schemes. They were Bakrie, Astra, Pertamina, Bank Niaga, Lippo and Astek.

Jamsostek

Jamsostek is Indonesia's social security insurance scheme introduced in 1993. It is governed by the Social Security Law of 1992 and supervised by the Ministry of Manpower. It provides wider benefits than the provious workers' compensation scheme. It includes death, disablement, retirement benefits and work-related accidents insurance and health insurance for workers and their families. It is funded by compulsory contributions ranging from 7% to 11% of wages.

Jollibee Foods Corporation

Jollibee Foods Corporation is the largest Philippine fastfood chain with 208 domestic outlets and 24 outlets overseas. It has opened new branches in Brunei, Dubai, Hong Kong, Kuwait, Papua New Guinea, Xiamen (China), Saipan, United States and Vietnam. It is developing the Donut Magic concept in Saudi Arabia, Bahrain and Vietnam.

It has been recognised as the Philippines' most innovative corporation responding to customer needs by the Far Eastern Economic Review in its 1996 Annual Review 2000. Jollibee was cited by Forbes magazine as one of the world's 200 best small companies.

JPKM

See Jaminan Peneliharaan Kesehatan Masyarakat

JSX LQ 45 Index

The Jakarta Stock Exchange LQ45 Index was introduced in 1997. It consists of 45 stocks that are of high market value and liquidity. The aggregate market value of these stocks accounts for more than 70% of the total market capitalisation on the JSX. It also accounts for about 72% of the total value of transaction in the market. The index thus reflects the changes in the market value of all stocks that are actively traded. The LQ45 complements the Composite Index.

KDEI
See Kliring Deposit Efek Indonesia

Kepres (Indonesia)
Presidential Instruction (e.g. In February 1996, the government announced the enactment of Kepres #42, Presidential Instruction #42, which later became the "National Car" policy).

Khazanah Bonds (Malaysia)
These are bonds issued by Khazanah Nasional Berhad, the wholly-owned subsidiary of the Malaysian Ministry of Finance primarily for benchmarking purposes.

Kip
Currency of Laos

KLSE Bernama Real-time Information Services Sdn Bhd (KULBER)
KULBER was incorporated in 1986. It is a joint venture between Securities Clearing Automated Network Services Sdn Bhd (SCANS) (55%) and the national news agency Pertubuhan Berita Nasional Malaysia (BERNAMA) (45%).

It provides information about the Kuala Lumpur Stock Exchange to local and foreign information vendors. Information includes buy and sell quotes, closing prices, volumes and indices. (See also: Securities Clearing Automated Network Services Sdn Bhd, SCANS.)

Kliring Deposit Efek Indonesia (KDEI)
Indonesian depository and clearing agency formed in 1993 formed under the sponsorship of the seven state banks and Jakarta and Surabaya stock exchanges. It provides central custodian service and settles securities transactions. Its shareholders are: Bank Rakyat Indonesia, Bank Exim, Bank Tabungan Negara, Bapindo, Bank BNI, Bank Bumi Daya, Bank Dagang Negara (13.3% each), Jarkata Stock Exchange Ltd (5%) and Surabaya Stock Exchange Ltd (1.7%).

Koperasi Unit Desa (KUD)
KUD is a village unit cooperative established by Indonesian farmers. It distributes farm inputs, provides credit to farmers and markets farm products.

Kredit Investasi Kechil (KIK)
Indonesian investment credit scheme designed to finance the medium and long term needs of small entrepreneurs.

Kredit Usaha Kecil (KUK) (Small scale credit program)
KUK is an Indonesian financing program under which banks are required to channel a specified percentage of their loans to small businesses.

Kredit Usaha Tani (KUT)
KUT is an Indonesian credit scheme to finance the needs of farmers especially for food crops.

Krung Thai Bank
Krung Thai Bank was set up in 1966 after the merger of the Agriculture Bank and the Provincial Bank. As the Ministry of Finance is its main shareholder, the "wayupak bird" which is the official seal of the Ministry has been adopted as the bank's logo. In 1987, the bank was entrusted by the government to administer the "4 April Project" in succession of the Bank of Thailand (Central Bank) to solve financial problems faced by some Thai financial institutions and took over the Sayam Bank.

In 1989, Krung Thai was listed on the Stock Exchange of Thailand. In 1994, it was registered as a public company limited. In 1995, it was granted the status of "Group 1 State Enterprise". Its major shareholders are: Ministry of Finance (31%) and the Financial Institutions Development Fund (29%). It remains the government's only commercial bank. The bank has 16,000 employees working in about 550 domestic and 12 foreign branches. (Website: www.ktb.co.th)

Kuala Lumpur Commodity Exchange (KLCE)
The Kuala Lumpur Commodity Exchange was set up in 1980. In 1985, under the Malaysian Commodities Trading Act, KLCE was restructured and an independent Commodities Trading Commission was formed to supervise and regulate commodity futures trading in Malaysia.

The KLCE trades in crude palm oil futures, RBD palm olein and crude palm kernel oil futures, cocoa futures, SMR20 rubber futures and tin futures.

In 1996, KLCE set up a wholly-owned subsidiary, the Malaysian Monetary Exchange (MME), a financial futures market which trades in the 3-month KLIBOR financial futures.

In 1998, KLCE changed its name to Commodity and Monetary Exchange of Malaysia (COMMEX Malaysia) and merged with its subsidiary MME. (Website: www.klce.com.my)

Kuala Lumpur Composite Index (KLCI)
KLCI refers to the share price performance of 100 component stocks on the KLSE's main board.

Kuala Lumpur Interbank Offer Rate (KLIBOR)
KLIBOR is a rate quoted by banks in the Kuala Lumpur interbank market where the participants are banks and other financial institutions.

The KLIBOR 3-month futures contract is traded as a financial instrument on the Commodity and Monetary Exchange of Malaysia. The 3-month KLIBOR futures is based on the underlying three-month KLIBOR quoted in the interbank market.

Kuala Lumpur Options and Financial Futures Exchange (KLOFFE)
KLOFFE is Malaysia's first financial futures market. It trades in the Kuala Lumpur Stock Exchange Composite Index (KLCI) stock index futures and stock index options.

In January 1999, the KLOFFE was acquired by the KLSE.

Kuala Lumpur Stock Exchange (KLSE)
The Kuala Lumpur Stock Exchange was set up in 1983 when the Stock Exchange of Malaysia and Singapore was split up into two exchanges, the other one being the Stock Exchange of Singapore.

The operations are governed by the Securities Industry Act which was implemented by Registrar of Companies until 1993 when such functions were taken over by the newly formed Securities Commission. Similarly, the Capital Issues Committee (CIC) used to supervise the issue of shares and other securities by companies applying for a listing on the exchange. Its functions have also been taken over by the Securities Commission.

During the past decade, major events have taken place at the KLSE:

— 1983: computerise share script clearing system
— 1986: adopt the KLSE composite index
— 1987: set the Advanced Warning and Surveillance Unit (AWAS)
— 1988: introduce the second board
— 1989: introduce the semi-automated trading system SCORE (System on Computerised Order Routing and Execution).
— 1992: implement Central Depository System
— 1993: set up Securities Commission which replaced the Capital Issues Committee, the Panel on Takeovers and Mergers, and related functions of the Registrar of Companies.
— 1999: acquired the KLOFFE

Labuan as International Offshore Financial Centre
In 1990, Malaysia set up the Federal Territory of Labuan as an International Offshore Financial Centre (IOFC). Labuan focuses on four major offshore banking operations: trust and fund management, offshore insurance, offshore investment holding companies. Several measures have been introduced to stimulate the development of Labuan. They include:

— Extending the deadline for offshore banks and insurance companies which operate currently from Kuala Lumpur to move to Labuan.
— Allowing offshore banks and insurance companies in Labuan to have marketing offices in Kuala Lumpur.
— Permitting offshore banks to receive fees and commissions in ringgit arising from ringgit denominated transactions.
— Making premium ceded to Labuan offshore insurance companies fully tax deductible, compared to 95% currently.
— Allowing offshore life insurers to sell policies denominated in foreign currency to high net worth Malaysian individuals.

Land Bank of the Philippines (LBP)
The Land Bank of the Philippines provides financial support for agragrian reform in the Philippines. Its charter is contained in the Code of Agragrain Reforms. Its main activities include collecting deposits and granting loans to farmers' associations for the production, marketing of crops and commodities.

L3 Regulation
See Legal lending limit regulations

Lao PDR
Lao People's Democratic Republic

Law on Credit Institutions (Vietnam)
In 1997, Vietnam's National Assembly adopted the Law on Credit Institutions which took effect in 1998. Important provisions include the following areas: banking licences, board of management, internal control, loan security, credit risk, mandatory liquidity, capital adequacy ratio and bankruptcy.

Law on the Promotion and Management of Foreign Investment (Laos)
This law was passed in 1994 to replace the Foreign Investment Law of 1988. For a joint venture with local partners, the foreign investor must contribute at least 30% equity capital. Property and investments are fully protected by law.

There is no requisition, confiscation or nationalisation, except for "public purpose", in which case they will get prompt, adequate and effective compensation.

Major provisions include the following:

— Foreign investors may repatriate earnings and capital.
— There are no tax holidays.
— The corporate tax is 20% of profit (to be negotiated for investors exploiting natural resources).
— There is free transfer of funds subject to normal withholding tax: dividends (10%), interest (20%).
— There is an import duty of 1% on plant and equipment.
— There is exemption from export duty.
— Investors can lease and build on leased property and transfer rights to use both.

Lazard Vietnam Fund
This is a closed-end investment fund listed on the Dublin Stock Exchange.

Legal lending limit (L3) regulation
L3 is an Indonesian banking regulation. It is the maximum amount of credit allowed to be provided to a bank's owners or its business subsidiaries. According to new regulations which took effect from April 1997, a bank is only allowed to provide credit to its own group at a maximum of 10% of its equity.

LIBID (London Inter Bank Bid Rate)
LIBID is the rate of interest bid by the banks in London on the deposits they take.

Licensed deposit-taking company
See Restricted licence bank — Hong Kong

LIMEAN
LIMEAN is the average (mean) of LIBID and LIBOR

Lion Gold Coin
Singapore Lion Gold Coins are issued by the Board of Commissioners of Currency and are of 999 fineness. Although these coins are legal tender, they are often stored and seldom used as cash.

Liquid Asset Requirement (Malaysia)
Banks and other financial institutions are required by Bank Negara Malaysia (Central Bank) to maintain a sum equivalent to the Liquid Asset Ratio which is a specified percentage of their eligible liabilities.

Liquidity requirement — Malaysia
Commercial banks, finance companies and merchant banks in Malaysia are required to maintain a minimum percentage of their deposit liabilities in liquid assets. These are cash, balances with the Central Bank, money at call, treasury bills, government securities, Government Investment Certificates, Cagamas bonds, bills discounted or purchased, Bank Negara Bills, Bank Negara Malaysia certificates and state government securities.

Liquidity requirement — Singapore
Banks in Singapore are required to maintain a minimum percentage of their liabilities in cash balance with the Monetary Authority of Singapore (6%) and liquid assets (18%). Liquid assets are Singapore notes and coins, balance with the MAS, balances with banks in Singapore, net money at call in Singapore, Singapore government treasury bills maturiing within 3 months.

Listing on SESDAQ
The Stock Exchange of Singapore Dealing and Automated Quotation system (SESDAQ for short) was set up in 1987. This second board gives small and medium enterprises an opportunity to tap the equity market and to have their shares traded. Listing requirements are less stringent that those of the main board.

Loan Fund for Hawkers and Petty Traders
This fund was introduced by the Credit Guarantee Corporation of Malaysia to provide low-interest loans to hawkers and petty traders who are members of recognised trade associations. Loans vary from RM500 to 5,000 and may be used as working capital or for buying business assets. No security or guarantee is required for the loans.

Loan (Local) Ordinance, 1959 (Malaysia)
This ordinance authorises the raising of loans by the Malaysian government for the purposes of the Development Fund. The Act amongst other things appoints the Central Bank as the agent of the government and enables the raising of the loans by way of book-entry i.e. scripless.

Loan Stock
This is a loan raised by a listed company. It has a fixed repayment date and guaranteed interest. If it is a convertible loan stock, the holder can exercise the option to convert the loan stock into shares of that company.

Local
Persons who trade on the futures exchange on their own personal account, not as brokers.

Local Enterprise Accounting Program (LEAP) Singapore
This program is designed by the Enterprise Promotion Centre (EPC) to help local enterprises to improve their accounting system. EPC consultants assist the firm to computerise accounting and management control systems. Partial financial support comes from the Local Enterprise Technical Assistance Scheme.

Local Enterprise Computerisation Program (LECP) — Singapore
LECP is administered by Singapore's National Computer Board to help local enterprises to computerise their operations. It provides technical assistance (feasibility study, requirements specification, system implementation and training) and a grant to cover part of consultant's fee for feasibility study and for implementing the system.

Local Enterprise Finance Scheme — Singapore
Singapore's Local Enterprise Finance Scheme (LEFS) is administered by the Economic Development Board and participating financial

institutions. The objective is to assist local enterprises to upgrade their operations. It provides low-interest loans for these purposes: establish a viable new business; automate plant and machinery; expand manufacturing capacity; diversify product lines and augment working capital. A company should have at least 30% local equity and have fixed productive assets of not more than S$12 million. Service enterprises should employ no more than 100 workers.

Local Enterprise Finance Scheme (Overseas) (LEFS Overseas)
This is an extension of Singapore's Local Enterprise Finance Scheme to encourage companies to venture overseas. It provides low cost loans to buy equipment and industrial facilities needed for overseas operations. The overseas operations must complement the activities in Singapore and result in economic spin-offs to Singapore. It is administered by the Economic Development Board and participating financial institutions. (See also: Local Enterprise Finance Scheme.)

Local Enterprise Technical Assistance Scheme (LETAS)
LETAS was formally known as Small Industry Technical Assistance Scheme (SITAS). It is administered by the Economic Development Board to assist local enterprises to get external expertise to upgrade their operations. The EDB pays up to 70% of the cost of engaging external experts on short term assignment. Experts may be local or foreign. The amount depends on the scope, depth and effectiveness of the assignment and its relevance to Singapore's economic development objectives. Grants are based on 30%, 50% or 70% of costs (the expert's fees, airfare and accommodation in Singapore).

Local Industry Upgrading Program (LIUP)
The Local Industry Upgrading Program (LIUP) was started in 1986 by the Economic Development Board to foster closer business development between local companies and MNCs in Singapore. The objective is to upgrade local suppliers to meet the stringent requirements of MNCs. The MNCs contribute to the transfer of technology and management skills to their local suppliers to help them upgrade their business. In return, local suppliers provide good quality parts and services at competitive prices.

Loco
This term is used in commodity markets, meaning 'at' (from Latin word locus or place). A trader talks of gold traded "loco London" meaning deliverable in London.

London Inter Bank Offer Rate (LIBOR)
It is the interest rate charged by London banks on the deposits they place.

London International Financial Futures Exchange (LIFFE)
Established in 1982, LIFFE offers traders an extensive list of financial futures contracts and financial options. In 1992, the exchange merged with the London Traded Options Market to form the London International Financial Futures and Options Exchange.

LQ45 Index (Indonesia)
LQ45 is a stock index used in the Jakarta Stock Exchange. It consists of 45 stocks of high market value and good liquidity listed on the exchange.

L-Star 1 and L-Star 2 (Laos)
These are two multimedia satellites owned by Laostar, a joint venture by the Laotian government (20%) and Asian Broadcasting and Communication Network (80%). Each satellite is equipped with 32 KU band transponders to provide multimedia telecommunications including direct TV broadcast which will service South East Asia. The launch service was provided by Arianespace.

Mahkamah Agung (Indonesia)
Supreme Court of Indonesia. It is the judicial branch of the State.

Majelis Permusyswaratan Rakyat (MPR)
People's Consultative Assembly in Indonesia consists of 1000 members drawn from a broad cross-section of the community, including all members of the Parliament. The President is elected for five years by the Assembly. The MPR approves the guidelines of the state policy and can amend the Constitution.

Majlis Tindakan Ekonomi Negara (Malaysia)
See National Economic Action Council (Malaysia)

Makati Stock Exchange (MkSE)
The Makati Stock Exchange (MkSE) was organised in 1963 by five businessmen: Hermenegildo Reyes, Bernard Gaberman, Eduardo Ortigas, Aristeo Lat and Miguel Campos. Due to several difficulties encountered from those who opposed its creation, MkSE's operations

started only in 1965. It was located in Makati, the financial district of Metropolitan Manila.

It operated side by side with the Manila Stock Exchange, trading in the same securities. In 1992, the two exchanges unified to form the Philippine Stock Exchange. Trading on the new exchange began in March 1994. (See also: Manila Stock Exchange, Philippine Stock Exchange.)

Malaysian Accounting Board
See Financial Reporting Act 1997 (Malaysia)

Malaysian Central Depository (MCD)
MCD is a subsidiary of Kuala Lumpur Stock Exchange set up in 1990 to provide central clearing and settlement of securities. The Securities Industry (Central Depository) Act 1991 authorised the setting up of a Central Depository and provided the legal framework and safeguards for users in the Central Depository System (CDS).

MCD operates the CDS for shares, bonds, debentures and other securities. Investors use CDS for safekeeping of shares. Stockbroking companies are appointed Authorised Depository Agents (ADAs) to provide CDS services to investors. All individual and corporate investors must open CDS accounts with ADAs to trade in securities.

Financial institutions (banks, finance companies, insurance companies, unit trusts) and other institutional investors participate in CDS as Authorised Direct Members.

Malaysian External Trade Development Corporation (MATRADE)
MATRADE was set up in 1993 as the external trade promotion arm of Malaysia's Ministry of International Trade and Industry (MITI). It promotes the export of Malaysian goods and services.
(Website: www.matrade.gov.my)

Malaysian Derivatives Clearing House Berhad (MDCH)
MDCH was a clearing house for trade transacted at the Malaysian Monetary Exchange. In 1998, the Futures Industry (Amendment & Consolidation) Act 1997 came into force and repealed the Commodities Trading Act 1985. It rationalises the regulation of the futures market in Malaysia and authorises the merger of the Commodities Trading Commission (CTC) with the Securities Commission. The MDCH merged with the Malaysian Futures Clearing Corporation (MFCC). (See also: Malaysian Monetary Exchange.)

Malaysian Futures and Options Registered Representative (MFORR) Course
The MFORR course is for persons who are interested to register as futures broker's representatives, futures fund manager's representatives, futures trading advisers and their representatives in Malaysia. In addition to knowledge on futures and options, it covers rules, regulations, trading procedures and operations of the Kuala Lumpur Options and Financial Futures Exchange (KLOFFE), Commodity and Monetary Exchange of Malaysia.

Malaysian Futures Clearing Corporation (MFCC)
In 1998, the Futures Industry (Amendment & Consolidation) Act 1997 came into force and repealed the Commodities Trading Act 1985. It rationalises the regulation of the futures market in Malaysia and authorises the merger of the Commodities Trading Commission (CTC) with the Securities Commission. The Malaysian Derivatives Clearing House (MDCH) also merged with the Malaysian Futures Clearing Corporation (MFCC).

Malaysian Institute of Economic Research (MIER)
MIER is a government-backed economic think-tank. One of its activities is to make forecast of economic growth.

Malaysian Monetary Exchange (MME)
Malaysian Monetary Exchange (MME, formerly known as the Kuala Lumpur Futures Market) was incorporated in 1992 as a wholly owned subsidiary of the Kuala Lumpur Commodity Exchange (KLCE). In 1998, MME merged with KLCE to become the Commodity and Monetary Exchange of Malaysia (COMMEX Malaysia). (See also: Kuala Lumpur Options and Financial Futures Exchange; Malaysian Derivatives Clearing House.)

Malaysian National Focal Point (MNFP)
The Malaysian National Focal Point (MNFP) was set up in 1992 as a unit in the Ministry of International Trade and Industry. It compiles and disseminates online information about government policies, programs, incentives and facilities for investment, trade, technology and industry in Malaysia. Its database contains information on the country profile of Malaysia and a directory listing of important business contacts in Malaysia.

Malaysian National Insurance Sdn Bhd
Malaysia's largest local insurance company.

Malaysian Palm Oil Promotion Council (MPOPC)
The MPOPC was incorporated in 1990 to take over the activities of the Palm Oil Promotion Fund Committee. Its objective is to promote Malaysian palm oil in the world. (Website: www.mpopc.org.my)

Malaysian Rating Corporation Bhd
This is Malaysia's second rating agency launched in 1996. (See also: Rating Agency Malaysia Berhad.)

Malaysian Share Registration Services Sdn Bhd (MSRS)
MSRS was incorporated on 7 March 1996 to provide the services of a share registrar. Formerly known as SCANS Registration Services Sdn Bhd, it changed to the present name on 12 March 1998.

MSRS uses a share registry system called SCANS Electronic Registration and Transfer Services or SERTS. The system is linked to the Central Depository System (CDS), which is operated by the Malaysian Central Depository Sdn Bhd (MCD).

MSRS is owned by SCANS (51%) and MIDFCCS (49%) and has a share capital of RM10 million. (See also: SCAN Electronic Registration and Transfer Services.)

Malaysian Shipping Finance Fund
This fund was set up in 1993 by the Malaysian government to provide long term finance to shipping companies. Part of the fund is used to create a RM300 million Ship Financing Facility to be administered by Bank Industri Malaysia Berhad (BIMB) to finance shipping companies. Another RM500 million is used to set up a Shipping Venture Facility (SVF) to encourage new investment in the shipping industry. The SVF is set up as a venture company whose shareholders are BIMB, commercial banks, insurance companies and other corporations.

Manila International Futures Exchange (MIFE)
The MIFE was incorporated in 1984. It trades in financial and commodity futures contracts. In 1990, MIFE launched an interest rate contract based on the Central Bank 91-day treasury bill. In 1991, currency contracts were introduced.

Manila Reference Rate

Manila Reference Rate (MRR) is the weighted average interest rate announced by the Bangko Sentral ng Pilipinas (Central Bank). It is based on the combined promissory note and time deposit transactions of commercial banks. It is used by financial institutions as a reference to price their floating rate loans. The Old Manila Reference Rate was based only on promissory note transactions.

Manila Stock Exchange (MSE)

Manila Stock Exchange (MSE) was set up in 1927 by five American businessmen: Eric Little, Gordon Mackay, John Russell, Frank Wakefield and W.P.G. Elliot. Originally located in downtown Manila, it transferred to Pasig in 1992. When the Makati Stock Exchange started in 1965, the two exchanges operated side by side, trading in the same securities. In 1992, the two exchanges unified to form the Philippine Stock Exchange. Trading on the new exchange began in March 1994. (See also: Makati Stock Exchange, Philippine Stock Exchange.)

Manpower Development Assistance Scheme (MDAS)

This scheme is administered by Singapore's National Science and Technology Board (NSTB) to provide financial assistance to strengthen a company's R&D team. Activities may range from academic to on-the-job training. They are jointly funded by the NSTB and the company. Successful candidates completing the programs must be deployed in R&D work or in the management of technology and R&D. Examples are the Joint-Industry Masters Program, the Part-time Masters Program, the Management of Technology Program, the Research Exchange Local Program, the Research Exchange Overseas Program.

Margin account

A trader operating a margin account uses funds borrowed from a broker or bank.

Margin call

A margin call requires a client to deposit more money to bring a margin account up to the initial margin or the minimum maintenance level.

Market and Investment Development Assistance Scheme (MIDAS)
This scheme is administered by the Trade Development Board (TDB) to provide financial assistance to Singapore companies which under take market and investment development activities. Types of assistance under the scheme are: (a) individual marketing and preliminary investment development trips, participation in overseas trade fairs and missions; (b) setting up of overseas marketing offices for business development; (c) tendering for overseas projects under the International Bidding Assistance Scheme (IBAS); (d) product and packaging design under the Design Venture Programme; (e) developing global franchise network under the Franchise Development Assistance Scheme (FRANDAS); (f) certification for exports under the Certification Assistance Scheme (CERTAS); (g) licensing for market development under the Licensing Development Assistance Scheme (LIDAS).

Market capitalisation
The stock market's assessment of a company's value, calculated by multiplying the number of shares on issue by the individual share price.

MAS Electronic Payment System (MEPS)
The MEPS was launched by the Monetary Authority of Singapore in 1998. It is a real-time gross settlement (RTGS) system for Singapore-dollar high-value interbank fund transfers and for settling scripless Singapore government securities. The system allows payment instructions between banks to be processed and settled individually and continually throughout the day. The transfer of funds is instant, final and irrevocable as long as the paying bank has sufficient funds in its RTGS account with the MAS. The MEPS has replaced the previous payment system SHIFT (System for Handling Interbank Transfer).

Maybank-RAM Property Index (MRPI)
MRPI is an index developed by Malayan Banking Berhad (Maybank) and Rating Agency Malaysia Berhad to track performance in the property market. The index is based on the actual transacted values of terrace and semi-detached houses from 24 housing estates in Kuala Lumpur, Petaling Jaya and Shah Alam.

Medisave account (Singapore)
Medisave is Singapore's national health care savings scheme whereby Central Provident Fund (CPF) members set aside part of their savings in the Medisave Account to meet their personal or immediate family's hospitalisation expenses.

Since July 1991, the total CPF contribution rate has been 40%. Of the 40%, 30% were allocated to the Ordinary Account, 6% to Medisave and 4% to the Special Account.

From 1 July 1992, members above 35 years are required to contribute 7% to Medisave. From 1 July 1993, those above 45 years are required to contribute 8% to Medisave. For these two groups of members, their contributions into the Ordinary Account are reduced correspondingly by 1% to 29% and 28% respectively.

Medisave for self-employed (Singapore)
With effect from 1 July 1992, Medisave scheme in Singapore was extended to self-employed persons so that they or their family members could also enjoy its benefits. The contribution rate was 3% of their yearly net trade income. This rate was increased progressively over the years. (See table)

Self-employed: Medisave contribution rates, 1992–98

Date	Rate to be paid (%)		
	Age < 35	35–44	45 and >
1.7.92	3	3	3
1.1.94	4	4	4
1.1.95	5	5	5
1.1.96	6	6	6
1.1.97	6	7	7
1.1.98	6	7	8

Source: Central Provident Fund.

Medishield scheme (Singapore)
Medishield scheme in Singapore was introduced in 1990. It is a low-cost medical insurance scheme for Central Provident Fund (CPF) members and their dependants. It helps to meet the cost of prolonged hospitalisation and medical expenses. It is different from Medisave which is a savings plan. Under the Scheme, an insured member can

claim up to a yearly limit of $20,000, and a lifetime limit of $70,000. Annual premiums, ranging from $12 to $132, depending on the insured's age. They are payable from the Medisave Account. Coverage is up to 70 years of age.

One reason why Medishield has been introduced is that Medisave may only be adequate for basic hospitalisation needs and insufficient for expensive and long-term treatment of illnesses.

Memorandum of Association

To be registered as a limited liability company in Singapore, every business enterprise must have a Memorandum of Association and Articles of Association.

The Memorandum of Association states the company's name, registered office, share capital, objectives and main business activities. The Articles of Association specify the company's internal regulations, administration and management.

In Singapore, the memorandum and the articles of association have to be submitted when a company is registered at the Registry of Companies and Businesses (RCB). By paying a fee at the RCB, any person may inspect the Memorandum and Articles of Association of any registered company.

Mendaki Growth Fund

This is a unit trust launched by Singapore's DBS Bank in 1991 for the Muslim community. The trust is sponsored by Yayasan Mendaki, the foundation for the development of the Muslim community in Singapore.

Merchant bank

It is a financial institution which serves mainly corporate clients. Its activities include offshore banking, corporate finance, underwriting securities, merger and acquisition, portfolio management and investment advice. In some countries, it may be called an investment bank.

Metro Pacific Corporation (Philippines)

Listed on the Philippine Stock Exchange, it is the investment holding company of the Hong Kong-based First Pacific Company Limited. [See also: PDCP Development Bank Inc (Philippines).]

Metropolitan Bank and Trust Company (Philippines)

Metropolitan Bank and Trust Company is a universal bank listed on the Philippines Stock Exchange. It has about 340 branches in the Philippine and has numerous overseas branches and representative offices. The bank's overseas branch network has enabled it to process remittances from Filipino overseas contract workers.

Its major banking-related subsidiaries include: First Metro Investment Corp, First Metro Leasing & Finance Corp, Unibancard Corp, Metropolitan Bank (Bahamas) Ltd, First Metro International Investment Co. Ltd, Asia Money Link Corporation, MB Remittance Center (HongKong) and MBTC International Finance Ltd.
(Website: www.sequel.net/metrobank)

Metropolitan Insurance Company Inc
Metropolitan Insurance Company Inc is listed on the Philippine Stock Exchange. It provides non-life insurance coverage for fire, marine, motor car, casualty and bonds.

Minimum cash balance
Banks are required by the central bank to maintain a minimum cash balance or cash reserve ratio. The central bank may vary this ratio as to regulate liquidity in the money market.

Minimum Sum Scheme (CPF)
Singapore's Central Provident Fund (CPF) Minimum Sum Scheme came into effect in 1987. The objective is to ensure that CPF members will have a minimum sum to live on after age 60. It is protected by law from seizure by creditors.

In 1986, the minimum sum was set at $30,000 to ensure that the basic needs of a CPF member would be met. The amount set aside at age 55, plus interest earned, was calculated to provide him with a regular income of about $230 per month from age 60. The income would be available for about 20 years depending on the interest rate.

A CPF member may set aside the minimum amount in any of these three ways:

(a) deposit it in an approved bank account which will pay the member $230 per month from age 60 until the sum, plus tax-free interest, is exhausted. If he dies before the entire amount is exhausted, the balance will be paid to his nominee or his estate;
(b) use it to buy an approved annuity policy from an insurance company which will pay him monthly from age 60. Depending on the annunity plan, his dependants may also receive some money if he dies before a specified age;

(c) keep it with the CPF Board in his Retirement Account. The Board will act like the approved bank as in (a) above.

Members with balances of $10,000 or less need not set aside any amount under the scheme as they may need to live on their low CPF balances after age 55. Those with balances between $10,000 and $20,000 can withdraw $10,000 at age 55 and set aside the rest after age 60. For those with balances of $20,000 or more, the sum to be set aside will be half the CPF balance subject to a maximum of $30,000.

Not all CPF members need to set aside the minimum sum. These include the following:

(a) those who were above 55 on 1 January 1987 when the scheme started;
(b) those who own property with a market value of at least $30,000 at age 55;
(c) those who are already assured of a retirement income of not less than $230 per month;
(d) those who have only $10,000 or less in their CPF account at age 55;
(e) non-citizens and non-permanent residents (unless they continue to work or live in Singapore after age 55).

Subsequent Increase of Minimum Sum

Since its introduction, the minimum sum has been increased gradually to ensure that the CPF members have sufficient monthly income during their retirement years. The Minimum Sum will go up by $5,000 each year until it reaches $80,000 on 1 July 2003. With $80,000, a retiree can expeet a regular monthly income for about 20 years from age 60.

The cash portion of the Minimum Sum is to ensure CPF members have a monthly income during retirement without having to sell their homes. Members can use the Minimum Sum to buy a life annuity from an approved insurance company, keep it with a bank, or leave it with CPF.

CPF minimum sum, 1995–2003

55th birthday on or after	Minimum sum	Amount in Cash	Amount in Property
1.7.1995	$40,000	$ 4,000	$36,000
1.7.1996	$45,000	$ 8,000	$37,000
1.7.1997	$50,000	$12,000	$38,000
1.7.1998	$55,000	$16,000	$39,000
1.7.1999	$60,000	$20,000	$40,000
1.7.2000	$65,000	$25,000	$40,000
1.7.2001	$70,000	$30,000	$40,000
1.7.2002	$75,000	$35,000	$40,000
1.7.2003	$80,000	$40,000	$40,000

Source: Central Provident Fund.

Ministry of Planning and Investment (MPI) (Vietnam)
MPI was formed in 1995 as a result of merging several development agencies including the State Committee for Cooperation and Investment (SCCI) and the State Planning Committee (SPC). Since its formation, the MPI has been liberalising the economy to attract foreign investment.

MPI has five departments dealing with foreign investments: Foreign Investment Department (FID), Project Monitor Department, Monitoring Department for Industrial Parks and Export Processing Zones, Foreign Investment Legislation Department, and Office of Project Evaluation (OPE).

Monetary Authorities (Philippines)
The monetary authorities in the Philippines consist of the Bangko Sentral ng Pilipinas (BSP, or Central Bank of the Philippines) and the Bureau of the Treasury (BTr). The BSP is responsible for the policy directions in money, banking and credit, and the supervision of financial institutions. The BTr manages the cash operations of the government.

Monetary Authority of Singapore (MAS)
The MAS was set up in 1971. It performs all the functions of a central bank except that of issuing currency which is done by the Board of Commissioners of Currency.

Its Board of Directors is chaired by the Minister for Finance. As the central bank of Singapore, the MAS promotes stable growth of the economy in general, and of the financial services sector in particular. Its main objectives are:

— to conduct monetary and exchange rate policies appropriate for steady and non-inflationary economic growth;
— to maintain conditions conducive to a sound financial services sector;
— to act as banker to, and financial agent of the Government;
— to develop a competitive and progressive financial services sector;
— to foster sound working relationships with other central banks, international financial institutions, and public and private institutions in Singapore.

The MAS formulates and implements Singapore's monetary policy. It works closely with the Ministry of Finance to ensure that monetary policy forms an integral part of the overall economic policy for the nation. The MAS frames its monetay policy to influence monetary aggregates as well as money market conditions.

It regulates the monetary base through the use of monetary instruments such as the statutory minimum cash balance requirement imposed on the banks and finance companies, variation in rediscount rates, special deposit requirement, credit ceilings, and money market operations.

The MAS also intervenes in the the foreign exchange market to smoothen exchange rate fluctuations in order to maintain an appropriate exchange rate for the Singapore dollar.

MAS Rediscounting Scheme (Singapore)
The MAS Rediscounting Scheme provides pre-export and export financing. It was introduced in 1975 by the Monetary Authority of Singapore (MAS). Under this scheme, exporters obtain finance through their own commercial bank which acts as the intermediary between the exporter and the MAS. The commercial bank provides the funds to the exporter at the stipulated interest rate, and in turn receives re-financing from the MAS. The bank receives a commission for discounting the bill. Each bank is allowed a fixed total amount of export bills it may rediscount with the MAS. If that amount has been exhausted by this bank, the exporter will have to go to another bank for the facility.

Monetary Board
See Central Bank of the Philippines

Money brokers in Singapore
Money broking business in Singapore existed as far back as the early 1900s when such services were provided by firms such as Ong Bock Yew, Hung Chue, Tan Swee Hee and Degani & Company.

In the 1970s, the Monetary Authority of Singapore encouraged international money brokers to set up offices in Singapore. They were Marshalls, Murray-Jones (now Astley and Pearce) and Charles Fulton. Many of the locals joined hands with foreign firms to benefit from their expertise and contacts. Herbert Ong (formerly Ong Bock Yew) partnered with Harlow Meyer Savage. Hung Chue joined Peddar Martin. Degani linked with Tullett and Riley. Tan Swee Hee partnered Guy Butler.

In the early 1980s, new broking firms joined the fold. Keppel Shipyard went into joint venture with Tokyo Forex to form K-T Forex. Stockbroker Ong and Company joined Tradition Service of Switzerland to form Ong Tradition. Herbert Ong sold his shareholding to a local stockbroking firm, J. M. Sassoon. In 1983, Degani, Tullett and Riley merged with K-T Forex to form KTD Forex which became the largest broking firm. In 1984, Keppel Shipyard backed out from the partnership.

MSCI-Hong Kong Index
MSCI-Hong Kong Index futures contract was first traded in Singapore on SIMEX in March 1993. The MSCI-HK index is widely used to measure the performance of the Hong Kong stock market. It is a broad-based representation of 36 stocks, as compared to Hang Seng's 33 stocks. Like the Hang Seng Index, it is market capitalisation weighted. It is adjusted regularly to maintain its representativeness of the Hong Kong bourse.

MSCI Singapore stock index futures contract (SIMSCI)
In September 1998, SIMEX launched the MSCI Singapore stock index futures contract, or the SIMSCI, based on the Morgan Stanley Capital International (MSCI) Singapore index. It is the first electronically traded stock index futures contract on SIMEX. It is the third stock index futures contract to be traded on SIMEX, after the MSCI Taiwan stock index and the Japanese Nikkei 225.

Multimedia Development Corporation (MDC) Malaysia
MDC is a Malaysian government-owned company which promotes the Multimedia Super Corridor (MSC). Its main objectives are to attract world-class companies and to facilitate knowledge transfer and wealth creation. It provides information on the MSC, assists in seeking licence approvals and introduce companies to local partners and financiers.

Multimedia Super Corridor Research and Development Grant Scheme (MGS)
The objective of the scheme is encourage R&D in multimedia products and services to be used in the Multimedia Super Corridor (MSC). It helps local companies or joint ventures to develop relevant multimedia technologies and applications which would contribute to the overall development of the MSC. The applicant must be at least 51% Malaysian-owned.

Mutual offset system
Mutual offset is a system of substitution between two participating exchanges whereby a trade executed on one exchange may be used to offset a position on the other exchange. For example, Singapore's SIMEX has a mutual offset arrangement with Chicago Mercantile Exchange's (CME) International Monetary Market (IMM) for several of its financial futures contracts. SIMEX also has a mutual offset agreement with London's International Petroleum Exchange (IPE) for Brent crude oil futures contract.

Myanmar Agricultural and Rural Development Bank (MARDB)
The MARDB was set up under the Myanmar Agricultural and Rural Bank Law. It took over the functions of the Myanmar Agricultural Bank which was established under the 1975 Banking Law. The MARDB supports the development of agricultural livestock and rural socio-economic enterprises. In 1993, it introduced the Rural Savings Scheme to encourage savings among the farmers and to develop a rural banking system.

Myanmar Economic Bank
Myanmar Economic Bank is the largest state-owned commercial bank for domestic banking in Myanmar. It has a nation-wide network of more than 300 branches. Its total deposit is about seven times of all the other 15 domestic banks. It acts as an agent of the Central Bank

in treasury matters. It handles state fund accounts and replenish local cash requirement throughout the country.

Myanmar Electric Power Enterprise
Myanmar Electric Power Enterprise (MEPE) is a state-owned enterprise under the Ministry of Energy. It plans, designs, constructs, maintains and operates electric supply facilities and sells electricity throughout Myanmar.

Myanmar Five Star Line
Myanmar Five Star Line (MFSL) is a state-owned shipping line. It operates coastal and overseas transport services with a fleet of about twenty vessels. It has no direct service to US and Canada. It has a transhipment agreement with Japan's Nippon Yusen Kaisha Line (NYK). MFSL serves the Myanmar-Japan sector while NYK serves Japan and US-Canada sector.

Myanmar — Foreign Banks
As of 1995, there were 28 foreign banks with representative offices in Myanmar. They were from Thailand (6), Singapore (5), France (4), Malaysia (3). Others were from Indonesia, Bangladesh, Hong Kong, Japan, United Kingdom, the Netherlands and Canada.

Myanmar Foreign Trade Bank
It was established in 1976 in Yangon. It has a network of about 130 foreign banks in 60 countries. It focuses mainly on foreign trade and foreign currency transactions.

Myanmar Investment and Commercial Bank (MICB)
MICB was set up in 1989 to specialise in commercial lending and investment banking. It serves mainly foreign and local private corporations and individuals. It has a worldwide network of more than 120 correspondent banks.

Myanmar Mines Authorities (MMA)
The MMA organises annual gem emporiums where state-owned Myanmar Gems Enterprise and local merchants market their gems, jade and jewelry. The events attract gems merchants from other countries. The emporiums have been held every year since 1962.

Myanmar Oil and Gas Enterprise (MOGE)
The MOGE is jointly developing Yadana oilfield with America's

Unocal, France's Total, and Thailand Petroleum Authority. A 350-kilometre pipeline is being constructed from Myanmar's offshore Yadana oilfield to Thailand where the gas will be sold.

Myanmar Insurance Corporation
The Myanmar Insurance Corporation is the sole state-owned insurance company in Myanmar. It provides a wide range of insurance coverage. It also has a reinsurance program with international reinsurers. The Myanmar Insurance Law was enacted in 1993 to encourage insurance business.

Myanmar — Private Banks
There are 15 domestic private banks which have been granted banking licences by the Central Bank. Examples are Myanmar Citizens Bank Ltd, Cooperative Bank Ltd, Myawaddy Bank Ltd, and Yangon City Bank Ltd.

Myanmar Securities Exchange Centre
The Myanmar Securities Exchange Centre is a joint venture between the Myanma Economic Bank and the Daiwa Research Institute of Japan. Its main objective is to set up a stock exchange. In 1997, it issued the shares of Union of Myanmar Forest Products Joint Venture for subscription by Myanmar citizens.

Myanmar Small Loans Enterprise
A state-owned finance company in Myanmar dealing in small loans.

Nakornthon Bank (Thailand)
Nakornthon Bank was known as Wang Lee Bank Ltd until 1985. Founded in 1933, it is the second oldest commercial bank in Thailand. In 1973, it expanded into worldwide banking, and entered into a joint venture with Citibank which helped to improve its management system. In 1983, the Bank was listed on the Stock Exchange of Thailand (SET). It has 44 branches in Bangkok and 22 in the provinces. It was the first bank to issue the multi-function global ATM / debit card in Thailand.

NASD-SES Link
The Stock Exchange of Singapore (SES) is linked up with the US-based NASDAQ through an arrangement called NASD-SES link whereby NASDAQ counters can be traded in Singapore. However, this market is not active.

National Bank of Brunei
The National Bank of Brunei was the largest bank in Brunei Darussalam. It was closed down in 1984 due to mismanagement.

National Bank of Cambodia (NBC)
Formerly known as the Bank of the People of Cambodia, the National Bank of Cambodia (NBC) is the central bank of Cambodia. It is supervised by the Council of Ministers and has the status of a ministry. It has the power to approve, supervise and regulate all financial institutions in Cambodia. It fixes foreign exchange rates and interest rates for the purpose of the purchase and discounting of commercial papers. It has the power to intervene in the financial markets to stabilise the national currency.

National Development Policy (NDP)
Malaysia's National Development Policy plans to enable Malaysia to become a developed country by the year 2020. The NDP will continue the basic strategies of the New Economic Policy (NEP) of eradicating poverty and restructuring the economy to correct social and economic imbalances. It will add new emphasis on the following: focusing on hardcore and relative poverty, rapid development of a Bumiputera commercial and industrial community, private sector involvement in the restructuring process, and relying on human resource development to achieve growth and distribution. (See also: New Economic Policy.)

National Economic Action Council (NEAC) (Malaysia)
(Website: www.topspot.com/neac)
The NEAC was set up in January 1998 by the Malaysian government as a consultative body to the cabinet in its efforts to deal with economic problems. The NEAC is chaired by the Prime Minister. Its members include economic ministers, representatives from various fields in the private sector and selected organisations. Its main objectives are to:

— ensure that the country does not enter into an ecoomic recession as a result of the decline in the value of the ringgit and the fall in the share market,
— restore public confidence, particularly that of foreign investors with regard to the economy which is still fundamentally strong,
— revive the national economy and make it competitive globally,
— strengthen the economic base of the country so as to achieve a

developed nation status through rapid and sustainable economic growth.

National Economic Recovery Plan (NERP)
Malaysia's National Economic Plan was formulated as a response to the 1998 financial crisis. It has six major objectives:

1. stabilise the ringgit
2. restore market confidence
3. maintain financial market stability
4. strengthen economic fundamentals
5. continue the equity and socio-economic agenda
6. restore adversely affected sectors.

National Electronic Commerce Committee (NECC) (Malaysia)
The NECC was established in February 1998 with the Multimedia Development Corporation as the secretariat. Its main role is to establish a framework of E-commerce and a National Strategic Plan which includes the charter for e-commerce development.

National Housing Authority (NHA) (Thailand)
The NHA was set up in 1972 by the Thai Government to embark on a large scale public housing program. It works closely with the Government Housing Bank (owned by the Ministry of Finance) which provides low interest mortgage loans to low income households. (See also: Government Housing Bank.)

National Private Bank Association (Indonesia)
Perhimpunan Bank-Bank Umum Nasional Swasta (PERBANAS). It was formed in 1952 and has about 165 members.

National Savings Bank (NSB) — Malaysia
The National Savings Bank of Malaysia was set up in 1974 after a reorganisation of the former Post Office Savings Bank. Its main objective is to mobilise private savings, especially of small savers, and to finance national economic development. It has an extensive network of branches and also operates through post offices and mobile postal vans. All deposits are guaranteed by the government.

Negative Investment List (Indonesia)
The Negative Investment List (DNI) is a list of industries in which foreigners may not invest.

Network for Electronic Transfers (NETS) (Singapore)
NETS (Network for Electronic Transfer Pte Ltd) is a joint venture company formed in 1985 by the POSBank and the Big Four local banks (DBS, OCBC, OUB and UOB) to operate the electronic fund transfer at point-of-sale (EFTPOS) system. NETS provides a cashless payment service which allows ATM cardholders to pay for purchases at retail outlets.

New Airport Projects Co-ordination Office (NAPCO)
See Hong Kong International Airport

New Economic Mechanism (NEM) (Laos)
The New Economic Meachanism (NEM) in Laos was launched in 1986 to transform the economy from a centrally-planned economy to a market economy.

New Economic Policy (NEP)
Malaysia's New Economic Policy (NEP) was formulated after the 1969 racial disturbance. It had two basic objectives: to eradicate poverty and to restructure society so as to eliminate the identification of race with economic function. The NEP expired in 1990 and was succeeded by the National Development Policy or NDP. (See also: National Development Policy.)

New Entrepreneurs Fund (Malaysia) (Tabung Usahawan Baru)
The RM 1.25 billion fund was set up in 1989 to stimulate the growth of small and medium bumiputera enterprises and to encourage the development of bumiputera entrepreneurs. Participating financial institutions include commercial banks, Bank Pembangunan Malaysia Berhad, Bank Industri Malaysia Berhad and Malaysian Industrial Development Finance Berhad.

New Zealand Futures and Options Exchange
The New Zealand Futures and Options Exchange was set up in 1985. Its futures contracts include NZ$, US$, NZ$, 5-year government stock, 10-year government stock, 90-day bank-accepted bill, New Zealand wool and the NZSE40 capital share price index. Options include 5-year government stock, 10-year government stock, 90-day bank-accepted bill and the Forty index options.

New Zealand Stock Exchange
New Zealand Stock Exchange was formed in 1983. Its forerunners

were the Auckland Stock Exchange formed in 1897 and the Stock Exchange Association of New Zealand. In 1991, the exchange replaced its open outcry trading method with a computerised stock exchange automated trading system (SEATS).

Nikkei 225 Futures Options

The Nikkei 225 Futures Options was first traded on Singapore's SIMEX in 1992. This was SIMEX's first futures options contract to be based on a stock index. The underlying commodity of the Nikkei futures options contract is the SIMEX Nikkei 225 futures contracts.

Nikkei 225 Stock Average Index Futures

The Nikkei 225 Stock Average Index Futures was first traded on Singapore's SIMEX in 1986. The Chicago Mercantile Exchange (CME) had secured the rights to trade the Nikkei Index in the US and Asia outside Japan from Nihon Keizai Shimbun and had sub-licensed it to SIMEX.

The Nikkei Stock Average is the best known index covering the Japanese stock market. Published since 1949, the index is calculated and managed by Nihon Keizai Shimbun Inc., a newspaper information and communication group. The average is based on 225 stocks and accounts for 21% of the First Section of the Tokyo Stock Exchange. It represents about 50% of the market value and 60% of the turnover. (See also: Nikkei 300 Index.)

Nikkei 300 Index

In 1994, Singapore's SIMEX became the first non-Japanese exchange to get licensing rights from the Nihon Keizai Shimbun to trade futures and options contracts based on the newly created Japanese stock index, the Nikkei 300.

The Nikkei 300 is a market capitalisation-weighted index consisting of 300 representative stocks listed on the Tokyo Stock Exchange. In contrast, the Nikkei 225 is a price-weighted index comprising 225 representative stocks. The Nikkei 300 is traded alongside SIMEX's existing Nikkei 225 and offers investors a wider choice of instruments for managing their portfolios.

Nikkei index

This is the Japanese equivalent of US's Dow Jones index. It tracks the value of 225 representative stocks. The index was devised by the

Nihon **Kei**zai Shimbun (Japanese Economic News), Japan's leading daily financial newspaper.

Offshore banking unit (OBU)
OBU is a financial institution borrowing, lending and trading with non-residents.

Offshore Banking Unit (Philippines)
The Philippine offshore banking system was established by a Presidential Decree in 1976. An offshore banking unit (OBU) may be a branch, subsidiary or affiliate of a bank which is authorised by the Central Bank as a separate accounting unit to transact offshore banking business in the Philippines. An OBU may transact in any currency other than the Philippine peso.

Old Manila Reference Rate
See Manila Reference Rate

Open outcry system
A trading method where dealers shout their bids and offers on the trading floor of the exchange.

Organisation of Petroleum Exporting Countries
OPEC includes Saudia Arabia, Venezuela, Kuwait, Libya, United Arab Emirates, Iran, Algeria, Nigeria, Qatar and Indonesia. Non-OPEC countries include Norway, Oman, Egypt, Russia, Brunei.

OTC Fixed Income Service
Over-the-counter bond trading system at the Surabaya Stock Exchange in Indonesia.

Over-the-Counter Market — Singapore
Shares traded on Singapore's over-the-counter market or CLOB International were mostly Malaysian counters. Trading of Malaysian shares ceased with effect from September 1998.

Trading on several Asian and Australian companies listed on CLOB International continue but the volume is small.

Overseas Enterprise Incentive (OEI) (Singapore)
This is one of the tax incentives announced in the 1993 Singapore Budget Statement. The purpose is to support local enterprises to invest overseas to access new markets, resources and technology. Tax

exemption is granted on qualifying income from approved overseas investments for up to 10 years. The company will be issued an Approved Overseas Enterprise certificate which specifies the projects covered by the incentive.

Overseas Investment Tax Incentive (OII) (Singapore)
The objective of this tax incentive is to encourage local enterprises to venture overseas to access new markets and technology. OII allows capital losses from overseas investment to be deducted against the investor's other income. The loss may be carried forward if there is insufficient income in the year of claim. The deduction allowed is up to 100% of the approved equity invested. The overseas investments should create significant spin-offs for the Singapore economy by providing access to new technology and overseas marketing channels.

Pacific Economic Cooperation Council (PECC)
The PECC was set up in 1980 as an international organisation consisting primarily of members drawn from the public, academic, and private sectors with the objective of bringing into fruition the Pacific Basin Cooperation Concept advocated by the late Japanese Prime Minister Masayoshi Ohira. PECC holds a general meeting every 18 months. By 1997, PECC had 22 member economies from the Asia Pacific region. PECC enjoys the status of official observer at the APEC ministerial meetings.

Pakfeb
See Paket Februari (February reform package)

Pakdes
See Paket Desember 1988 (December reform package)

Paket Februari or Pakfeb
Pakfeb is a banking reform package introduced by Bank Indonesia in February 1991. It is designed to improve bank supervision. Its provisions include decrees on ownership and management of new banks. It also required all banks to maintain the internationally adopted standard of 8% capital adequacy ratio (CAR) as recommended by the Bank for International Settlements.

Paket Disember 1988
The December 1988 Package was one of the reform packages introduced in Indonesia to liberalise the financial system. It provided

incentives for the entry of joint ventures in leasing, factoring, venture capital and securities trading. Further reform packages were introduced in 1991 and 1993. For example, the package in 1991 included measures to improve bank supervision and capital adequacy for the banks. These reforms resulted in the introduction of a new banking act in 1992 which replaced the act of 1967. (See also: Paket Februari, Paket Oktober.)

Paket Mei or Pakmei
Pakmei is a banking reform package introduced by Bank Indonesia in May 1993. It covers capital adequacy, lending limits and provision of loan losses. One of the important aspects is the revision of the legal lending limits which restrict lending to individuals and groups. The previous restriction of group lending to 50% was reduced to 20%, with implementation to be completed within 4 years up to 31 March 1997.

Paket Oktober 1988
The October 1988 Package was one of the reform packages introduced in Indonesia to liberalise the restrictive regulatory financial framework. (See also: Paket Februari; Paket Mei, Paket Disember.)

Pakmei
See Paket Mei (May reform package)

Pakto 1988
See Paket Oktober 1988 (October reform package)

PAKSI (Malaysia)
In Malaysia, PAKSI or Financial Package for SMIs (small and medium industries) provides SMIs with a soft loan scheme for project financing and working capital financing.

Palm Oil Registration and Licensing Authority (PORLA)
PORLA's mission is to enhance the position of the Malaysian palm oil industry as the leading supplier to the world oils and fats market by providing services and assistance to the industry.
(Website: www.porla.gov.my)

Palm Oil Research Institute of Malaysia (PORIM)
PORIM was set up in 1979 to conduct research on oil palm and its products. Its objectives are: to promote the use of palm oil products,

to find new uses and to improve quality of the products. (Website: www.porim.gov.my)

Pan Electric crisis — Singapore

In November 1985, the financial collapse of the Pan Electric Industries Group triggered a crisis on the Stock Exchange of Singapore. The solvency of several stockbroking firms was threatened as a result of over-trading and over extending loans to their clients. Some banks were affected as they had lent to these stockbrokers. Trading of the SES was suspended from 2 December 1985 for three days so that remedial arrangements could be made to restore confidence in the market.

The Big Four local banks (DBS, OCBC, OUB and UOB) set up a special S$180 million "lifeboat" fund for stockbrokers. Other banks agreed on a 3-month moratorium on loans they had granted to stockbrokers. Meanwhile, the brokers graudally repaid their loans to the banks and reduced the amount of forward contracts. In spite of these rescue measures, a few stockbroking firms ceased operations because of financial difficulties.

Panin Group

Panin Group is an Indonesian financial conglomerate with diversified activities. Its affiliates include PT Panin Bank, PT Panin Life and PT Panin Insurance.

Patent Application Fund (Singapore)

This fund is administered by the National Science and Technology Board (NSTB) to encourage local organisations and individuals to register their invention in order to gain intellectual property rights. The fund defrays the cost of patent application. The research work that leads to the patent must be conducted in Singapore, and the patent must belong to a Singapore organisation or individual.

PCI Leasing and Finance Inc (Philippines)

PCI Leasing and Finance Inc is listed on the Philippine Stock Exchange. It is a wholly-owned subsidiary of listed Philippine Commercial International Bank (PCI Bank) and focuses on leasing and financing. Its leasing products include direct leases, sale and leaseback arrangements, and dollar-denominated leases. Its financing products include commercial and consumer loans, installment paper purchases, receivables discounting and factoring. (See also: Philippine Commercial International Bank.)

PDCP Development Bank Inc (Philippines)
PDCP Bank, formerly called Private Development Corporation of the Philippines (PDCP), is a development bank established in 1963 as a development finance institution cum investment house. It was set up with the assistance of the World Bank and the USAID and the sponsorship of the Philippine government. It was converted into a thrift bank in 1992 while in 1996, it acquired the First Philippine International Bank (FirstBank). In 1998, it received approval to operate as a commercial bank. It has a network of 77 branches nationwide. Its subsidiaries include PDCP Insurance Brokers Inc.

Among its shareholders is Metro Pacific Corporation — also a listed company, which is the investment holding company in the Philippines of the HongKong-based First Pacific Company Limited.

PDI bonds
Past Due Interest bonds

Pelita V
Fifth Five-year Development Program (Indonesia)

Pemberitahuan Ekspor Barang Tertentu (PEBT) (Indonesia)
Certificate of export for special products

Penanaman Modal Asing (PMA)
Foreign joint venture company in Indonesia.

Pension institutions (Indonesia)
As of 1996, there were 262 pension institutions comprising 239 employer pension funds (DPPK) and 22 financial institution pension funds (DPLK). About 80% of their assets came mainly from their members' and employers' regular instalments. Investments by pension funds are mainly on fixed-income instruments such as bonds and deposits.

People's Bank of the Union of Burma
The People's Bank of the Union of Burma was set up as a result of merging all the nationalised banks. It acted as the central bank of Burma. In 1975, its name was changed to Union Bank of Burma. (See also: Central Bank of Myanmar.)

Perbadanan Kemajuan Negeri Selangor (PKNS) (Malaysia)
Selangor State Development Corporation

Perhimpunan Bank-Bank Umum Nasional Swasta (Perbanas)
See National Private Bank Association.

Peringkat Efek Indonesia (PEFINDO)
PEFINDO is Indonesia's first securities credit rating agency set up in 1994. Its main function is to rate bonds and other debt instruments. It provides investors with information about the ability of companies to pay their loans and interest.

Permodalan Nasional Berhad (PNB)
This is wholly-owned subsidiary of the *Bumiputera Investment Foundation* in Malaysia. Its function is to evaluate, select, purchase and hold a portfolio of shares of companies that intend to issue shares to the Bumiputera community in compliance with the New Economic Policy. The shares are then transferred to the national unit trust company, *Amanah Saham Nasional Berhad.*

In 1988, an International Fund Management Unit was set up to undertake foreign portfolio investments. In 1990, PNB set up a wholly-owned subsidiary company PNB Equity Resource Corporation to participate in joint venture projects and venture capital investments with local and multinational corporations. (See also: Amanah Saham Nasional Berhad, Bumiputera Investment Foundation.)

Persahaan Dagang (PD)
Trading enterprise in Indonesia

Persahaan Persaorangan (PP)
Sole proprietorship in Indonesia

Persehoan Terbatas (PT)
Limited liability company in Indonesia

PERTAMINA
Perusahaan Pertambangan Minyak dan Gas Bumi Negera (state-owned Indonesian petroleum and natural gas company).

Perum PKK
See Perusahaan Umum Pengembangan Keuangan Koperasi

Perusahaan Umum
Public corporation in Indonesia. (See also: Indonesian state-owned enterprises.)

Perumka
Indonesian state railway company. After undergoing management restructuring in the early 1990s, Perumka turned losses into profits. In 1991, it lost Rp 92.2 billion. Its profits totalled RP 6.41 billion in 1994, Rp 11.87 billion in 1995, and Rp 17.89 billion in 1996. Much of its profits have come from new commercial trains which have better facilities and cater to executive class. These include: Argo Bromo (Jakarta-Surabaya) Argo Gede (Jakarta-Bandung), Bima (Jakarta-Surabaya), Mutiara (Jakarta-Surabaya) and Parahiyangan (Jakarta-Bandung). It has also expanded its cargo trains called Antaboga from Jakarta and Surabaya.

Perusahaan Dagang (PD)
Trading enterprise in Indonesia

Perusahaan Inti Rakyat (PIR)
PIR is a scheme in Indonesia for developing smallholders by assigning more agricultural estates as a nucleus to provide guidance in cultivating, managing, processing and marketing products. The scheme is carried out in plantations, poultry farms and fisheries.

Perusahaan Jawatan (Perjan)
Government agency in Indonesia. (See also: Indonesian state-owned enterprise.)

Perusahaan Listrik Negara (PLN)
Indonesia's state-owned electric company. In 1995, it set up a subsidiary PT Pembangkit Listrik Jawa Bali (PJB) which now operates the Surabaya coal-fired plant and the Saguling hydro-power plant in West Java, the Tambak Lorok steam power plant in Central Java, and steam and gas power plants in Bali. In 1996, PJB made profits totalling Rp 350 billion and was the largest contributor to PLN's earnings.

Perusahaan Negara (PN)
State corporation in Indonesia (See also: Indonesian state-owned enterprise.)

Perusahaan Perseorangan (PP)
Sole proprietorship in Indonesia

Perusahaan Pertambangan Minyak dan Gas Bumi Negera (PERTAMINA)
State-owned Indonesian petroleum and natural gas company

Perusahaan Umum (Perum)
Public corporation in Indonesia. (See also: Indonesian state-owned enterprise.)

Perusahaan Umum Pengembangan Keuangan Koperasi (Perum PKK)
Perum PKK is an Indonesian state-owned corporation which covers risk on credit extended by banks to cooperatives.

Petrolium Nasional (Petronas) (Malaysia)
Petronas is Malaysia's national oil company. It has 25 fully-owned and 13 partly-owned subsidiaries, e.g. Petronas Gas Berhad (publicly listed in 1995), Petronas Penapisan (Terengganu) Sdn Bhd, Petronas Penapisan (Melaka) Sdn Bhd.

Petronas Gas Berhad (Malaysia)
Petronas Gas is a subsidiary of Petronas whcih has a monopoly over gas processing and distribution in Malaysia. When Petronas Gas shares were floated on the Kuala Lumpur Stock Exchange in 1995, the 117 million shares at RM5.80 each attracted more than 645,000 applications for about 990 million shares worth RM5.25 billion, with an over-subscription rate of about 8 times.

PetroVietnam Insurance Company
An insurance company that specialises in the oil and gas industry.

Philguarantee
See Philippine Export & Foreign Loan Guarantee Corporation

Philippine Association of Securities Brokers and Dealers, Inc.
The Philippine Association of Securities Brokers and Dealers, Inc. is an organization of all licensed stockbrokers and independent securities brokers and dealers, as well as investment houses in the Philippines. It serves as the voice of the securities industry *vis-à-vis* the public and the government in all matters affecting the members.

The PASBDI is tasked to undertake projects for the development of the securities industry and to protect its members whenever their interests are affected by certain factors, i.e., proposed government measures, which may have an adverse effect on the securities industry. [Address: 9/F SEC Building, EDSA, Mandaluyong City, Philippines. Tel: (632) 724-0355]

Philippine Bank of Communications
Philippine Bank of Communications is listed on the Philippine Stock Exchange. It provides a wide range of financial services and credit facilities. Its major subsidiaries include PBCom Venture Capital Corp.

Philippine Banking Corporation
Philippine Banking Corporation is listed on the Philippine Stock Exchange. It started in 1935 as a mutual savings bank and loan association in Tanauan, Batangas. A few years later, it was converted into a commercial bank. It now provides a wide range of banking services. Its subsidiaries include Philbancor Venture Capital Corporation and the PBC Capital Investment Corporation.

Philippine Central Depository Inc (PCD)
The PCD is a private institution that implements the scripless book-entry system in the Philippine Stock Exchange. The securities include stocks listed on the Philippine Stock Exchange and debt securities such as treasury bills and treasury bonds. [Address: Makati Stock Exchange Building, Ayala Triangle, Ayala Avenue, Makati City, Philippines. Tel: (632) 893-5636 Fax: (632) 893-5591]

Philippine Commercial International Bank
PCI Bank is listed on the Philippine Stock Exchange. It provides a broad range of banking services in the Philippines through its extensive branch network. Its banking-related major subsidiaries include: PCI Capital Corporation, PCIB Savings Bank Inc, PCI Leasing & Finance Inc, PCIB CIGNA Life Insurance Corporation. (See also: Bankard Inc Philippines; PCI Leasing and Finance Inc.)
(Website: www.pcib.com)

Philippine Deposit Insurance Corporation
PDIC is the official insurance corporation in the Philippine banking system. It requires banks to insure their deposits up to 100,000 pesos per depositor.

Philippine Export & Foreign Loan Guarantee Corporation (Philguarantee)
Philguarantee is a government agency that provides guarantee cover to Filipino exporters on their loans obtained from domestic and foreign sources. It enhances the credit-worthiness of these exporters and enables them to obtain funds.

Philippine National Bank (PNB)
The Philippine National Bank, formerly controlled by the government was privatised in 1995 with the private sector owning 51% of the bank. It is the largest Philippine bank in terms of assets. It provides a full range of financial services through a network of 320 branches. PNB also provides banking services to the Philippine Government, and government corporations. Its major banking-related subsidiaries include: Century Bank, PNB Credit Card Corp, PNB General Insurers Co.Inc, PNB International Finance Ltd, PNB Remittance Centers Inc, PNB Securities Inc. PNB Venture Capital Corp, RPB Venture Capital Corp, PNB Corp Guam and PNB Italy S.p.A.
(Website: www.philnabank.com)

Philippine Savings Bank
The Philippine Savings Bank is listed on the Philippine Stock Exchange. Its main thrust of operation is the retail sector and the small and medium clientele. For example, its "Negosyo Na" working capital loan is a credit facility for small and medium scale enterprises.

Philippine Stock Exchange (PSE)
The Philippine Stock Exchange (PSE) was incorporated on 14 July 1992 as a result of unifying the Manila Stock Exchange (MSE) and Makati Stock Exchange (MkSE).

The MSE was set up in 1927 while the MkSE started operations in 1965. Although the two exchanges operated as separate entities, they were basically trading the same listed issues. With persuasion from President Fidel Ramos administration, the PSE was set up to unify the two exchanges in order to develop a more efficient capital market. The Securities and Exchange Commission granted the PSE its licence to operate as a securities exchange on 4 March 1994. It simultaneously canceled the licences of the MSE and MkSE. On 25 March 1994, the one price-one market exchange was achieved through the successful link-up of the two existing trading floors. From then on, the PSE has been the sole exchange in the Philippines. (See also: Manila Stock Exchange, Makati Stock Exchange.)
(Website: www.pse.com.ph)

Philippine Trust Company
The Philippine Trust Company is listed on the Philippine Stock Exchange. It offers a full range of banking services through branches located at key business centers in the Philippines. Philtrust Finance Limited is its subsidiary in Hongkong.

Pilgrims Management and Fund Board
This is a specialised savings institution in Malaysia set up in 1969 to promote and coordinate activities connected with Muslims going on pilgrimage. It manages a fund derived from the accumulated savings of Muslims and organises the pilgrimage. The fund is invested in securities based on Islamic principles.

Planters Development Bank (Philippines)
Planters Development Bank is listed on the Philippine Stock Exchange. It is a privately-owned development bank which is also involved in commercial banking. It has had about 40 years of experience in financing rural small and medium enterprises. It is active in the lending programs funded by the Government and multilateral institutions channeled through the Development Bank of the Philippines and the Land Bank of the Philippines. Its subsidiaries and affiliates include: Filrice Incorporated, PDB Leasing Corporation, and PDB Insurance Agency Inc.

Port Development Board (PDB)
In 1998, Hong Kong's Port Development Board has been renamed Hongkong Port Maritime Board. Its functions have been increased to include all aspects of the port and to promote it as an international shipping centre.

Post Office Savings Bank (POSBank Singapore)
The Post Office Savings Bank (POSB) was opened in 1877 and is one of the oldest financial institutions in Singapore. It was so named because it was part of the Postal Services Department. The objective was to encourage people with small income to save. In 1972, the POSB became a statutory board and separated from the Postal Services Department. Over the decades, the number of depositors had increased. The POSB has many branches and ATMs conveniently located all over Singapore. In addition to its savings and current accounts, the POSB provides a wide of services which include: salary crediting scheme, giro payment service, Save-As-You-Earn (SAYE) scheme, POSBLine, and electronic share application facility. The POSB has a wholly-owned subsidiary Credit POSB Pte Ltd which provides housing loans at competitive interest rates. In 1990, the bank adopted a new corporate name "POSBank" for easy identification. In 1998, the Singapore government sold POSBank to DBS Bank, a government-linked commercial bank.

Presidency Bank of Bengal (Myanmar)
This was the first bank set up in Burma (now Myanmar) in 1865 under the British rule.

Prevailing quota premium (PQP) — Singapore
PQP is a moving average of the quota premium of the respective vehicle categories over the past 12 months. Existing vehicle owners can revalidate their vehicle entitlements by paying the PQP.

Pribumi
Ethnic Indonesian

Prime rate
Interest rate banks charge to their most creditworthy customers.

Principal Guarantee Scheme (Malaysia)
This scheme is provided by the Credit Guarantee Corporation of Malaysia to assist small enterprises with no or inadequate collateral to obtain financing from commercial banks. (See also: Credit Guarantee Corporation Malaysia Berhad.)

Private development banks (Philippines)
Private development banks in the Philippines accept savings and time deposits. They use the funds to provide medium and long term loans to finance industry and agriculture. They may act as correspondent and collection agents and rediscount papers with any bank.

Private Development Corporation of the Philippines (PDCP)
See PDCP Development Bank Inc (Philippines)

Privatisation Exchangeable Note (PEN)
PEN is a new bond introduced in Singapore in 1999 by government holding company Temasek Holdings through its subsidiary Finlayson Global Corporation. Guaranteed by the Singapore government, PENs were offered to privatise the DBS shares it received from the DBS Bank and POSBank merger. The US$765 million bond issue was available in US dollar and Euro. There was also a S$30 million Singapore dollar tranche for retail investors.

PENs are zero-coupon bonds that mature in five years on 19 February 2004. Holders will not get any interest during the 5-year period. Upon maturity, they receive $11,333 for their initial investment of $10,000.

PENs can be exchanged for DBS shares after the third year, from 19 February 2002. Each lot of $10,000 PEN may be exchanged for one of the following:

(a) 345 DBS foreign and 518 DBS local shares, or
(b) 345 DBS foreign and 518 warrants, or
(c) 345 DBS foreign and cash in lieu of DBS local shares.

Option (b) is not available if the investor has used Central Provident Fund money to buy the notes. The warrants allow foreigners to own DBS local shares without the voting rights and to just get the proceeds from the sale of local shares when they excercise them.

The PEN is a blend of 40% DBS foreign and 60% DBS local shares. The initial price was $11.58 each, which was the blended closing price of DBS shares of $9.65 on 8 February 1999 plus a 20% premium.

Product Development Assistance Scheme (PDAS) (Singapore)
The PDAS is administered by the Economic Development Board. It provides cash grants to encourage local companies to develop new products (including hardware and software), or substantially improve existing products or processes related to their manufacturing activities. The grant covers 50% of the approved costs.

Prudential Bank (Philippines)
Prudential Bank is listed on the Philippine Stock Exchange. It offers a wide range of banking services. It also has investments in Prudential Venture Capital Corp and AEA Development Corporation. In 1987, the Prudential Bank and Bank of Tokyo jointly acquired Pilipinas Bank. (Website: www.prudentialbank.com)

PSE Foundation, Inc. (PSEFI)
The PSE Foundation, Inc. (PSEFI) is a private non-stock, non-profit corporation engaged in social welfare, charity, culture, business, education, science and research projects.

PSEFI seeks to assist cultural, academic and charitable institutions. It supports projects that promote the well-being and development of society; improve social and economic conditions; heighten youth involvement in productive activities and encourage self-sufficiency and self-reliance. Among the Foundation's beneficiaries are the Interact Pamilya Foundation, the Missionaries of Charity, Tuloy sa

Don Bosco, UNICEF, Foundation for Adolescent Development and the Clean and Green Foundation. [Address: 4/F, PSE Centre, Exchange Road, Ortigas Centre, Pasig City, Philippines. Tel: (632) 636-0122 Fax: (632) 634-5113]

Public Bank Berhad (Malaysia)
Public Bank is Malaysia's third largest bank. It was set up in 1966. It has a network of more than 150 branches in Malaysia, Hong Kong, Sri Lanka and Laos. It also has offices in Cambodia, Vietnam, New Zealand, Australia, China and Myanmar.

Public Information Services Office (PISO) (Indonesia)
In 1993, BAPEPAM (Indonesia's Capital Market Supervisory Agency) set up PISO to make capital market information easily accessible to investors. Services include information on listed companies, stock exchanges, clearing settlement, depository institutions, investment funds, securities companies, custodians, securities administration agencies and trust agents.

Quezon City Development Bank (Philippines)
Old name of Asiatrust Development Bank Inc. (See also: Asiatrust Development Bank Inc.)

RAS Commodity Exchange — Singapore
In 1992, the RAS Commodity Exchange (RASCE) was formed to manage the rubber futures market in Singapore. In 1994, it was renamed the Singapore Commodity Exchange (SICOM) to reflect the extended role of the exchange which also deals in other commodities such as coffee. (See also: Singapore Commodity Exchange.)

Rating Agency Malaysia Berhad
Incorporated in 1990, RAM is one of the two rating agencies in Malaysia. The other agency is Malaysian Rating Corporation Bhd which was launched in 1996. The major shareholders of RAM are IBCA (UK) and the Asian Development Bank. Other shareholders include local banks, merchant banks and other financial institutions. Ratings undertaken by RAM include specific corporate ratings as well as rating of securities which are of interest to investors.

Real-time Analysis Stock Information Service (RASIS)
RASIS is a service launched by the Kuala Lumpur Stock Exchange in 1992 to provide investors with up-to-date information.

Real Time Electronic Transfer of Funds and Securities (RENTAS) (Malaysia)
RENTAS is a real time gross settlement system (RTGS) to transfer ringgit-denominated interbank funds and scripless securities transactions. It was introduced in July 1999 to replace the former SPEEDS system for interbank payment and scripless securities. (See also: Sistem Pemindahan Elektronik untuk Dana dan Sekuriti or SPEEDS.)

Red Herring
It is a draft prospectus used by an issuer of a share offer to attract investors.

Regional Investment Company (RIC) Fund (Singapore)
RIC is a venture capital fund set up in 1994 to support small and medium enterprises in Singapore. The S$82 million fund was jointly set up by Economic Development Board's (EDB) investment holding arm, EDB Investments Pte Ltd (EDBI) and local venture fund manager Transpac Capital Pte Ltd. The RIC fund is managed by RIC Management Pte Ltd. Investee companies are also eligible for loans from the Entrepreneur Development Fund at attractive rates.

Regional Venture Funds Incentive — Singapore
The objective of RVF Incentive is to encourage the setting up of venture funds for Singapore investments in the region. The fund should be involved in active investment, not portfolio investment in regional stock exchanges. The minimum fund size is S$20 million. The regional investments by the fund should have spin-offs to other local Singapore companies, including co-investment with Singapore investors, increased business for other Singapore companies or the use of Singapore as a regional hub. The fund management expertise should be developed in Singapore.

The RVF Incentive comes under Section 13(H) of the Income Tax Act. It provides for an exemption of tax up to 10 years for gains from foreign investments.

Regionalisation Training Scheme (RTS) for overseas employees
This scheme is administered by Singapore's Economic Development Board's International Manpower Division. The objective is to assist Singapore-based companies to provide training in Singapore for key employees from their overseas subsidiaries. RTS provides training

grants to offset the foreign worker's levy. Training may be in-house or in an approved institution. The number of trainees is limited to 100 or 10% of the company's workforce in Singapore, whichever is lower. Maximum duration is 6 months. Trainees must be of supervisory rank and above.

Reinsurance in Vietnam
See Vietnamese Reinsurance Company

Relocation Assistance Program (Singapore)
The Relocation Assistance Program was introduced in September 1998. It gives grant to SMEs relocated to new industrial estates under the Redevelopment Program and to upgrade at the same time. The Relocation Assistance Program is administered by the Productivity and Standards Board (PSB) while the Redevelopment Program is administered by the Housing Development Board. HDB tenants who take up the upgrading program receive help in planning factory layout and automating their operations. Grants will be given to pay up to 90% of the consultancy costs unde the Local Technical Assistance Scheme.

Remisiers
See Dealers and remisiers

Repo
Repurchase agreement

Requirement Assessment Service (RAS) (Singapore)
This low-cost service is provided by the National Computer Board to help local firms to assess their computerisation requirements. NCB consultant reviews the firm's operations and submit a report covering: (a) business functions to computerise; (b) hardware and software requirements; (c) costs and benefits of computerisation; (d) suggested approach for computerising. The firm may then seek further assistance under the Local Enterprise Computerisation Program (LECP).

Research & Development Assistance Scheme (RDAS) (Singapore)
The RDAS is administered by the National Science and Technology Board to promote private sector R&D activities in Singapore. It provides grants to companies conducting R&D of technological and commercial merit. RDAS is open to all projects arising from industry,

or those in collaboration with the public sector. Projects should involve R&D that are carried out in Singapore and the products or processes must have economic spin-offs for Singapore. RDAS funds up to 50% of the total direct project costs such as cost of manpower, new R&D equipment and consumables.

Research Exchange (REX) Local Program (Singapore)
The REX Local Program is administered by the National Science and Technology Board under its Manpower Development Assistance Scheme. It facilitates technology transfer and increases collaboration between industry and the local universities and research centres. Companies may send their R&D staff to local universities and research centres or to bring in researchers from these organisations to the company for a period to work on R&D projects. (See also: Manpower Development Assistance Scheme.)

Research Exchange (REX) Overseas Program (Singapore)
The REX Overseas Program is administered by the National Science and Technology Board under its Manpower Development Assistance Scheme to upgrade the research capability of companies in Singapore. Companies may send their local R&D staff overseas for training, or to bring in foreign experts to train local R&D staff. (See also: Manpower Development Assistance Scheme.)

Research Incentive Scheme for Companies (Singapore)
The Research Incentive Scheme for Companies (RISC) in Singapore is administered by the National Science and Technology Board to support companies to develop their R&D capabilities in Singapore. RISC supports activities in strategic technology, with the objective of increasing the company's competitiveness. Companies must develop specified R&D to increase their competitiveness. The RISC funds part of the research spending, up to a maximum of 50% for a maximum of 5 years. This covers manpower, training, materials and equipment.

Research Institute of Investment Analysts Malaysia (RIIAM)
RIIAM was incorporated in 1985. It is affiliated to the Kuala Lumpur Stock Exchange (KLSE). Its main objectives are to do research and organises courses on investment. It provides training for the KLSE group, investment professionals and the public. As of 1999, it had 1224 individual and 51 corporate members. RIIAM is a member of the

Asian Securities Analysts Federation which is part of the International Council of Investment Analysts.

The Kuala Lumpur Stock Exchange-Research Institute of Investment Analysts Malaysia Information System (KLSE-RIS) is a service available on the website: www.klse-ris.com.my

Restricted Licence Bank (Hong Kong)
Restricted licence banks in Hong Kong were known as licensed deposit-taking companies before 1990. They must have a minimum paid up capital of HK$100 million. They may collect deposits in amounts of not less than HK$500,000 from the public.

Restricted Licence Bank (Singapore)
The first restricted licence was granted by the Monetary Authority of Singapore to a foreign bank in 1971. A bank with a restricted licence may engage in the whole range of banking except that it is: (1) not permitted to accept time deposits of less than S$ 250,000; (2) not allowed to operate savings accounts; (3) not allowed to open new branches in Singapore. In all other aspects, it is free to carry on business in the same way as a full licence bank. It is authorised to deal in foreign exchange as well as in the Asian Dollar Market.

RHB Islamic Index
This stock index tracks Syariah-approved companies traded on the main board of the Kuala Lumpur Stock Exchange. These companies include Telekom Malaysia Bhd, Tenaga Nasional Bhd, Petronas Gas Bhd and others.

Rho
A measure of the amount an option price is expected to change in response to changes in interest rates. (See also: Delta, Gamma, Theta, Vega.)

Riel
Cambodian currency

Rizal Commercial Banking Corporation (Philippines)
Rizal Commercial Banking Corporation (RCBC) is listed on the Philippine Stock Exchange. It started in 1960 as a development bank. In 1963, it acquired a commercial bank licence, and in 1989 a universal banking licence. Through its 160 branches, it serves a diversified

market which includes corporate to retail banking. It has a strong Filipino-Chinese and Japanese market niche. Its major banking-related subsidiaries include: RCBC California International Inc, RCBC Capital Corporation, RCBC International Finance Ltd, and RCBC Savings Bank. (Website: www.rcbc.com)

Robusta Coffee Contract
This coffee futures contract was launched by Singapore Commodity Exchange in 1995 based on the Singapore Robusta Standard Grade. The contract price is denominated in US dollars and the size of each trading lot is 10 tonnes. The contract is Asia's only Robusta coffee futures.

Roundtripping
Under a directive from the Monetary Authority of Singapore, a bank in Singapore is not allowed to accept a Singapore dollar deposit placed with its overseas branch which then sends the sum back to Singapore as a "balance held for banks outside Singapore". When a bank carries this act of "round tripping", it circumvents the liquid asset requirements. The MAS expects banks to comply not only with the legal requirements on liquid assets, but also the spirit of these requirements.

In 1982, several banks, including local institutions, were fined for roundtripping. The Corrupt Practices Investigation Bureau was called in to investigate several bankers for allegedly receiving kickbacks involving the deposits. A few foreign bankers were asked to leave Singapore for condoning roundtripping. In February 1995, banks were once again reminded by the MAS not to be involved in roundtripping.

Royal Air Cambodge (RAC)
RAC is the national carrier of Cambodia. It is a joint venture between the Cambodian government and Malaysian Air Service.

Rural banks (Indonesia)
See Bank Perkreditan Rakyat

Rural banks (Philippines)
Rural banks in the Philippines provide credit to small farmers and merchants. They can only be owned by Filipino citizens. With the permission from the Central Bank, some are allowed to collect deposits, open current accounts, act as collection agents or act as

trustees for farmers' estates. They may also invest in the equities of companies engaged in related businesses.

Rural Savings Scheme (Myanmar)
The Rural Savings Scheme in Myanmar was introduced in 1993 to encourage savings by farmers.

Saham dwi warna (Indonesia)
A golden share in a public company which gives the shareholder (usually the government) a veto right in major decisions.

Samurai bond
Yen-denominated bonds issued in Japan by a foreign borrower.

San Miguel Corporation (Philippines)
San Miguel Corporation (SMC) is the largest Philippine beverage and food conglomerate listed on the Philippine Stock Exchange. It has expanded into other Asian Pacific countries through joint ventures, licensing and exports.

In 1998, it combined its soft drinks interests with those of Coca-Cola Amatil Ltd of Australia in a transaction valued at US$2.7 billion. It has entered into a licensing agreement with the American brewer Miller Brewing Co. to produce and distribute Miller Genuine Draft in the Philippines.

San Miguel has expanded its distribution network in China with sales offices in 16 cities. Through its subsidiary company San Miguel Foods International, it bought over 49% of the feeds and poultry business of PT Dharmala Agrifood (a subsidiary of the Dharmala Group, one of Indonesia's top ten companies). The Company has also diversified into property development through San Miguel Properties Philippines Inc (SMPPI). It has numerous subsidiaries including: San Miguel International Ltd, San Miguel Foods Inc, SMC Juice Inc. (Website: www.sanmiguel.com.ph)

Satuan Tugas Khusus (STK) (Indonesia)
See Bad debt work-out team

Savings and loan associations (Philippines)
Savings and loan associations in the Philippines accept saving deposits from members and grant small personal loans and long term loans for home building.

Savings and mortgage banks (Philippines)
Savings and mortgage banks in the Philippines collect savings from depositors and invest them in loans secured by bonds, real estate mortgages and long term loans for home building.

SCAN Electronic Registration and Transfer Services (SERTS)
SERTS is an integrated electronic share registry system used by the Malaysian Share Registration Services Sdn Bhd to serve its clients many of whom are companies listed on the Kuala Lumpur Stock Exchange (KLSE). The system is electronically linked to the Central Depository System (CDS) at the KLSE. The SERTS-CDS linkage improves the performance of company registrars and benefits company shareholders. (See also: Malaysian Share Registration Services Sdn Bhd or MSRS; Securities Clearing Automated Network Services Sdn Bhd, or SCANS.)

Scripless Securities Trading System (SSTS)
SSTS is a scripless trading system launched in Malaysia in 1990 as an on-line book entry system for Malaysian Government Securities, treasury bill, Cagamas papers and Bank Negara Certificates and Bills.

Second Board at KLSE
The Kuala Lumpur Stock Exchange (KLSE) set up a Second Board in 1988 to enable small companies with a minimum paid up capital of RM5 million to raise funds from the stock market. (See also: Kuala Lumpur Stock Exchange.)

Second Outline Perspective Plan (OPP2)
Malaysia's Second Outline Perspective Plan or OPP2 covers the period 1991–2000. It has been formulated based on the National Development Plan (NDP) to accelerate the eradication of poverty and to provide a broader framework for achieving socio-economic objectives. (See also: First Outline Perspective Plan OPP1, National Development Policy, New Economic Policy.)

Secondary Mortgage Corporation (SMC) (Thailand)
The Secondary Mortgage Corporation (SMC) was set up by the Thai government in July 1997 to securitise housing loans by issuing mortgage-backed securities of up 40 billion baht. Bank of Thailand has also accorded SMC bonds, the instrument to be used in the exchange of mortgage loans, the same status as state enterprise bonds. This

status makes them eligible for financial institutions to hold as reserve assets.

Securities Analysts Association (SAA) (Thailand)
The SAA is a professional organisation representing financial analysts in Thailand. Its main objective is to promote the standards of investment decision-making through the education of financial analysts. SAA's main program leads to the designation of Certified Investment and Securities Analyst (CISA) which is recognised by the Securities and Exchange Commission. (Website: www.saa-thai.org.th)

Securities and Exchange Commission (SEC) — Philippines
In the Philippines, the securities industry is regulated by the Securities and Exchange Commission. The SEC is a quasi-judicial government agency whose role is to protect investors in securities transactions. It derives its power from Presidential Decree, the Revised Securities Act, Corporation and Partnership Laws, Investment Company Act and Investment Houses Law.

It issues certificate of incorporation to financial institutions. It performs functions in connection with the licensing of finance companies and investment houses. It registers commercial papers of all financial institutions. [Address: SEC Building, EDSA, Mandaluyong City, Philippines. Tel: (632) 726-0931 Fax: (632) 726-8459]

Securities and Futures Commission of Hong Kong (SFCHK)
The SFCHK was formed in 1989 as an autonomous statutory body to regulate the securities and futures markets. It has replaced the Securities Commission, the Commodities Trading Commission and the Office for the Commissioner for Securities and Commodities Trading. It is a self-funded body outside the civil service but is accountable to the government and reports to the Financial Secretary.

The SFCHK oversees the operations of the Stock Exchange of Hong Kong, the Hong Kong Futures Exchange and their clearing houses to ensure the sound functioning of their systems. It also administers the two statutory Investor Compensation Funds.

It has five executive directors and five non-executive directors. There are four operating divisions: (a) The Supervision of Markets Division oversees the operations of the Stock Exchange of Hong Kong, the Hong Kong Futures Exchange and their clearing houses. (b) The

Corporate Finance Division regulates takeovers and mergers and share buy-backs of public companies as well as administers securities legislation relating to listed companies. (c) The Intermediaries and Investment Products Division grants licences and supervises securities dealers and regulates the marketing of unit trusts, mutual funds and other collective investment schemes. (d) The Enforcement Division enquires into alleged breaches of relevant Ordinances and Codes, including possible insider dealing and market manipulation offences. (Website: www.hksfc.org.hk) (See also: Stock Exchange of Hong Kong, the Hong Kong Futures Exchange.)

Securities Clearing Automated Network Services (SCANS)
SCANS is the clearing house, network and facilities manager for the Malaysian Exchange of Securities Dealing and Automated Quotation (MESDAQ).

Securities Clearing Corporation of the Philippines (SCCP)
The SCCP is a private institution which acts as the clearing and settlement agency for trades executed in the Philippine Stock Exchange. It also manages a Trade Guarantee Fund for these transactions. The Philippine Stock Exchange owns 51% of SCCP while the other 49% is owned by commercial banks. [Address: Philippine Stock Exchange, Exchange Plaza, Ayala Avenue, Makati City, Philippines. Tel: (632) 848-6609 Fax: (632) 848-6610]

Securities Commission (Malaysia)
Malaysia's Securities Commission was set up in 1993 under the Securities Commission Act. Its mission is to promote and maintain fair, efficient, secure and transparent securities and futures markets and to facilitate the development of an innovative and competitive capital market.

It has absorbed the functions of the Capital Issues Committee, the Panel on Takeovers and Mergers and some related functions of the Registrar of Companies. It is responsible for the regulation and development of the securities industry, financial futures and options markets, unit trust and property trust schemes, and the takeover and merger of companies. However, its functions do not include commodity futures contracts which remain under the purview of the Ministry of Primary Industries and governed under the Commodities Trading Act.

Securities Exchange Commission (Thailand)
The Securities Exchange Commission in Thailand was set up in 1992 to supervise all institutions related to the capital markets and securities.

Securities Exchange of Thailand (SET)
The Securities Exchange of Thailand was set up in 1975 for the listing and trading of securities in Thailand. The SET was reorganised in 1992. It is now known as the Stock Exchange of Thailand. (See also: Stock Exchange of Thailand.)

Securities Industry Act (Malaysia)
In 1998, new sections were added to the Securities Industry Act 1983. They allow the Securities Commission to require a person to disclose the names of persons on whose behalf any dealings in securities are carried, which impose a duty on chief executives and directors of a corporation to disclose their interest in securities to the Commission, which allow the Commission to apply to the court to disqualify a chief executive or director who has been adjudged bankrupt or who has contravened provisions of securities laws or who has been convicted by a court of law of a criminal offence, and which enable the Commission to require a listed corporation to submit its audited annual accounts and periodic financial reports to the Commission.

Securities Industry Act — Singapore
The Securities Industry Act is administered by the Monetary Authority of Singapore. Its main aim is to maintain a proper balance of prudential control and self-regulation. It ensures that the Stock Exchange of Singapore (SES) exercises proper regulation of the market. While the SES Committee is responsible for the operation of the exchange, the MAS is enpowered to review, overrule or vary the decisions of the Exchange.

The major sections of the Act cover the following:

(a) establishment and operation of stock markets;
(b) licensing of dealers, dealer's representatives, investment advisors and investment representatives;
(c) records to be kept by dealers, dealer's representatives, investment advisors, investment representatives and financial journalists;
(d) conduct of securities businessmen;

(e) accounts to be kept by dealers and investment advisors and the audits thereon;
(f) fidelity funds;
(g) trading in securities.

Securities Industry Council (Singapore)
The Securities Industry Council (SIC) was established under the Securities Industry Act. Its main functions are to advise the Minister for Finance on matters relating to the securities industry. It advises the Stock Exchange of Singapore Committee regarding listing requirements, suspension or delisting of companies, and on action to be taken or to prevent or expose unlawful or dishonest forms of trading. It also advises the Exchange on applications by companies wishing to raise money by a public issue in any form. It advises the Registrar of Companies on the activities of suspect companies. It enforces the Singapore Code on Takeovers and Mergers. The Council is represented by the Monetary Authority of Singapore, the business sector and the government.

Securities Industry Development Centre (Malaysia)
The Securities Industry Development Centre is a department within the Research and Development Division of the Securities Commission of Malaysia. Its main objective is to promote research within the industry as well as a better understanding of the capital markets. It undertakes and disseminates non-proprietary research relevant to the needs of industry.

Securities Investors Protection Fund Inc (Philippines)
The Securities Investors Protection Fund Inc (SIPFI) in the Philippines is a non-profit corporation which administers a fund to protect investors and members of the Fund. All licensed brokers and dealers are members of the SIPFI. The fund is collected as a levy imposed on brokers based on a percentage of turnover. It is managed by a board of trustees, including representatives of the Philippine Stock Exchange and the Securities and Exchange Commission. It is used to compensate investors if a broker goes into liquidation. [Address: 9/F SEC Building, EDSA, Mandaluyong City, Philippines. Tel: (632) 724-0355]

Securities Trading Automated Quotation System (STAQS) (China)
STAQS was set up in 1992 by the Stock Exchange Executive Council.

In 1993, the National Electronic Trading System (NETS) was launched by China Securities Trading System Corporation, which is owned by the Peoples Bank of China, four large banks, three securities companies and the Peoples Insurance Company.

Security Bank Corporation (Philippines)
Security Bank Corporation is listed on the Philippine Stock Exchange. It obtained its universal banking licence in 1994. It provides a full range of financial services. Its subsidiaries are engaged in credit card, leasing, forex brokerage, investment banking, fund management and non-life insurance services. They include: SB Capital Investment Corporation, SB Forex Inc, Security Diners International Corporation and Security Finance Inc.

Sendirian Berhad
Malay word for private limited denoting a private limited liability company in Malaysia

Sertifikat Bank Indonesia
See Bank Indonesia Certificate

SES Review Committee (Singapore)
This is one of the three committees within the Financial Sector Review Group which was set up by the Singapore government in 1997 to review the financial sector. It studied the conceptual framework that will make Singapore's capital market more international and competitive. It reviewed the rules and by-laws of the Stock Exchange of Singapore (SES) and the Securities Industry Act. It examined the roles played by the SES and the Monetary Authority of Singapore. It also recommended initiatives to develop the capital market. (See also: Banking Disclosure Panel, Corporate Finance Committee, Financial Sector Review Group.)

SESDAQ
SESDAQ (Stock Exchange of Singapore Dealing and Automated Quotation System) is the second board set up by the Stock Exchagne of Singapore (SES) to provide a market for small and medium enterprises which would not otherwise be eligible for admission to the main board of the SES. The admission criteria are less stringent than those of the main board.

Share Depository Centre (SDC) (Thailand)
The Share Depository Centre in Thailand was set up in 1988. Its main functions are to clear and settle securities traded at the Stock Exchange of Thailand (SET).

Share Ownership Top-Up Scheme (Singapore)
In 1993, the Singapore government introduced the CPF Share Ownership Top-up Scheme (SOTUS) to help Singaporeans own shares. A cash grant of $200 was given to Singaporeans who had contributed at least $500 in their CPF account during the qualifying period from 1 March 1993 to 31 August 1993. The cash grant and the CPF contributions could be used to buy Singapore Telecom shares which were floated in October 1993. As a result of the first SOTUS, 1.26 million Singaporeans received $242 million in government contribution and it led to some 1.48 CPF members to subscribe for Telecom shares.

In 1994, the government implemented the second SOTUS. It paid $300 into the CPF account of each Singaporean member aged 21 and above, provided he had contributed at least $750 into the account between 1 March 1994 and 31 August 1995. The second SOTUS is meant to help Singaporeans to build up enough CPF savings to subscribe for shares when the next statutory board is privatised.

Share price indices
Share prices fluctuate as a result of supply and demand in the market. Share price indices have been designed to measure the overall movement of all the share prices. These indicators are closely studied by analysts to forecast price movements. The Dow Jones Industrial Average, the Financial Times index, the Nikkei index are closely watched by investors in New York, London and Tokyo.

In Southeast Asia, the popular popular indices are: Straits Times Index (Singapore), Kuala Lumpur Composite Index (Malaysia).

Shari'ah Supervisory Board (SSB) (Indonesia)
The SSB oversees the operations of Indonesian Islamic banks.

SHIFT (System for Handling Interbank Fund Transfer)
See MAS Electronic Payment System

Ship Financing Facility
See Malaysian Shipping Finance Fund

Shipping Venture Facility
See Malaysian Shipping Finance Fund

Shogun bond
A bond issue made in Japan by a foreign borrower, denominated in a non-yen currency.

Singapore bullion coins
The Singapore bullion coins are gold coins issued by the Board of Commissioners of Currency and are of 999 fineness. Although these coins are legal tender, they are often stored and seldom used as cash. (See also: Gold coins.)

Singapore Code on Takeovers and Mergers
The Singapore Code on Takeovers and Mergers was introduced in 1974 and revised in 1979 to provide guidance on the principles of good business practice to be observed in takeover and merger transactions.

The code is administered and enforced by the Securities Industry Council and is modelled on the City Code on Takeovers and Mergers of the United Kingdom. Although the code is drafted with public companies in mind, it also applies to unquoted companies and private companies.

The Code extends to cover offeror companies which are incorporated outside Singapore. Thus, if an offeree company is incorporated in Singapore, the Code will apply if it is to be taken over by a company incorporated elsewhere. If both the offeror and offeree companies are incorporated elsewhere, the Code obviously does not apply even though there may be Singapore shareholders of these companies who may be disadvantaged by the transaction.

Singapore College of Insurance
The Singapore College of Insurance was set up in 1994 as a non-profit charitable and self-financing educational institution for the Singapore insurance industry. With the setting of the college, the role of the Singapore Insurance Institute has become that of a professional body. (See also: Singapore Insurance Institute.)

Singapore Commodity Exchange (SICOM)
In 1994, the RAS Commodity Exchange (RASCE) was renamed the Singapore Commodity Exchange (SICOM).

SICOM trades in the following futures contracts:

— 1RSS (ribbed smoked sheet grade 1)

— 3RSS (ribbed smoked sheet grade 3)
— TSR 20 (technically specified rubber grade 20)
— RCS index contract.

SICOM has two types of members: clearing and non-clearing members. Clearing members are owners of the exchange, and consist of brokers who are market makers, brokers who are not market makers, and dealers who trade for their own accounts. Though all clearing members can guarantee trades and share in the profits of the exchange, only market makers can register trades done. Non-clearing members may be trade members or associate members.

Clearing members must buy at least four exchange seats each. Their privileges include voting rights and authorising and registering trades. Non-clearing members must buy at least one seat and have voting rights but cannot solicit customer business.

Singapore Dollar — Internationalisation
For many years, the Monetary Authority of Singapore (MAS) has advised financial institutions against any attempt to internationalise the Singapore dollar.

As stated in the MAS Notice to Banks, dated 1 November 1983, banks are required to consult the MAS before considering S$ credit facilities exceeding S$5 million to non-residents, or to residents for use outside Singapore.

The MAS would consider favourably on credit facilities in S$ for financing trade with Singapore or for generating economic activity directly benefiting Singapore. Examples of such activities will be manufacturing, construction, transport and communication services. However, financial and portfolio investments do not fall within this classification.

The MAS discourages any attempt to facilitate external speculative activities in the local financial or property markets. Banks have been advised not to finance in S$, for whatever amounts activities which have no bearing on Singapore, for example third country trade or activities outside Singapore, without consulting the MAS.

Non-residents borrowing S$ for other uses in Singapore would be considered favourably by the MAS. Examples include payment for equipment or other expenses that accrue from their operations in Singapore; working capital of their Singapore operations; guarantees and performance bonds issued to the Comptroller of Income Tax, statutory boards, or other Singapore parties.

Singapore Dollar Negotiable Certificate of Deposit (S$NCD)
Singapore Dollar Negotiable Certificate of Deposit (S$NCD) is a certificate of deposit issued by a bank acknowledging the deposit of a specific sum in Singapore dollars for a fixed time period at a determined interest rate. The main feature of a NCD which distinguishes it from the ordinary fixed deposit is its negotiability. It can be bought or sold before the date of maturity through institutions in the secondary market. (See also: Negotiable certificate of deposit.)

Singapore Foreign Exchange Market Committee
The Singapore Foreign Exchange Market Committee was formed in 1986. Its purpose is to foster the growth of the Singapore market as a leading international centre for transactions in foreign exchange and financial instruments. Its specific objectives are:

(a) to monitor the development of the markets and to take appropriate measures for their continued growth;
(b) to discuss technical issues in the markets and to recommend standards;
(c) to maintain and enforce the Code of Conduct and Market Practices of the Singapore foreign exchange and money markets;
(d) to serve as a channel for information and dialogue between market participants and the MAS;
(e) to enhance the stature and maintain the reputation of the Singapore markets by promoting high standards of professional conduct;
(f) to arbitrate in disputes between market participants where the parties involved agree to such arbitration.

Singapore Gold Market
The Singapore gold market comprises the spot market and the futures market. In the spot market, settlement takes place two business days after the contract date. In Singapore, there are two spot markets operating side by side depending on the place of delivery. They are: (a) the Loco London market, (b) the Singapore Kilobar Market or Loco Singapore market. Gold futures are traded in SIMEX. (See also: SIMEX.)

Singapore Inc Website
The Singapore Inc website was launched in 1997 jointly by several government agencies (EDB, NSTB, JTC, PSB, TDB, NCB, STB, PSA

etc.) to provide information to investors. The website: www.singapore-inc.com

Singapore Insurance Group (SIG)
In 1997, all the 12 local general insurance companies in Singapore signed an agreement to form the Singapore Insurance Group in order to compete in the world market. The group will underwrite up to $500 million in general insurance in any one risk.

Singapore Insurance Institute (SII)
The mission of the Singapore Insurance Institute is to help Singapore develop into a insurance and reinsurance centre of international repute.

Singapore Interbank Offer Rate (SIBOR)
SIBOR is a rate quoted by banks in the Singapore money market where participants are banks and other financial institutions.

Singapore International Monetary Exchange (SIMEX)
The Singapore International Monetary Exchange (SIMEX) was formed in 1983. It replaced the Gold Exchange of Singapore (GES) and trading in financial futures began in 1984.

Contracts traded on SIMEX include the following:

Catergory	*Futures Contracts*	*Options Contracts*
Interest rate	Eurodollar	Eurodollar
	Euroyen	Euroyen
	Euromark	Euromark
Stock index	Nikkei 225 stock average	Nikkei 225 stock average
	Nikkei 300	Nikkei 300
	MSCI-HK index	
Currency	Japanese yen	
	Deutschemark	
	British pound	
	Deferred spot US$/DM	
	Deferred spot US$/JY	
Bond	10-year Japanese Govt	
Precious metal	gold	
Energy	high sulphur fuel oil	
	IPE Brent crude	

In SIMEX, there are three types of corporate membership and one type of individual membership. These are: corporate clearing members, corporate non-clearing members and commercial associate members.

Corporate clearing member
— own one share and three seats on SIMEX
— minimum paid up capital: S$5 million
— minimum adjusted net capital: S$5 million or 10% of customer funds whichever is higher
— security deposit of S$250,000 or 2.5% of its maintenance margin, whichever is higher
— full trading rights on the trading floor
— authority to accept customers' business
— authority to clear trades

Corporate non-clearing member
— own three seats on SIMEX
— minimum paid up capital: S$2 million
— minimum adjusted net capital: S$2 million or 10% of customer funds, whichever is higher
— full trading rights on the trading floor
— authority to accept customers' business
— no authority to clear trades

Commercial associate member
— own one seat
— minimum adjusted net capital: S$100,000
— standing letter of credit: S$1 million
— trade energy futures contracts only
— trade for own account or associated companies
— no authority to clear trades

Individual non-clearing member
— own or lease one seat, or hold a trading permit
— seat owner or lessee: trade on all contracts
— trade permit holder: only trade on specified contracts
— full trading rights on the trading floor
— trade only for own account

All transactions done in SIMEX must be cleared through the clearing members. They constitute the clearing house and the basis of the exchange financial integrity. A clearing member must be a Singapore company or the branch of a reputable foreign firm.

A corporate clearing member must become a shareholder of SIMEX which is constituted as a public limited company. It must own three seats on the exchange. Each seat enables the clearing member to have a trader to deal on the exchange floor. Among the clearing members are leading financial institutions from Singapore and other financial centres. They serve both institutional and retail investors from all over the world.

The corporate non-clearing members, like the clearing members can act as brokers for their clients or trade on their own account. They must own three seats. Though they can execute their own transactions on the trading floor, they have to clear the trades through the clearing members.

In 1984 and 1985, SIMEX issued 450 seats at $50,000 each. In 1987, another 100 seats were made available at $75,000 each. By May 1992, when 25 new seats were offered, each of them cost $180,000.

Individuals may join SIMEX by buying a seat or by leasing a seat from a corporate member. They may act as floor brokers or floor traders but are not permitted to act for retail customers. As floor brokers, the individuals may execute orders on behalf of corporate members. As floor traders, they may trade for their own account. By being willing to take positions, individual members provide liquidity in the market.

SIMEX also issues trading permits to individuals to trade in energy futures or other specified contracts for a monthly rental.

SIMEX-CME Mutual Offset System

SIMEX has a mutual offset arrangement with Chicago Mercantile Exchange (CME) whereby a trader can open a contract in one exchange and close it in the other.

There is a computer link-up in the clearing system between SIMEX and CME. The offset eliminates overnight risks, reduces transaction costs and bridges the 13-hour time gap between the two cities. The mutual offset trading is done for two types of financial futures contracts: Deutschemark and the Eurodollar deposit interest rate.

SIMEX-IPE Mutual Offset System

In 1995, SIMEX launched the world's first mutual offset energy contract with London's International Petroleum Exchange (IPE) to trade in Brent crude oil futures. Under the mutual offset agreement, Singapore and London traders can square off positions by opening a contract in one exchange and closing it off in the other. (See also: IPE Brent crude oil futures.)

SIMEX Trading System

Trading in SIMEX is done by the open outcry system. It is an auction conducted in designated pits on the exchange floor. In these pits, bids and offers are openly shouted by the traders who can be easily identified by the designated code names. The system enables orders to be transacted at the most competitive prices. Information about the transactions is quickly made available to the public.

Singapore kilobar market

In the Singapore physical kilobar market, or Loco Singapore market, delivery of the gold takes place in Singapore. The gold traded is of 999.9 fineness. Since the Singapore kilobar is of finer quality than the gold traded in Loco London, it has a premium over the London gold price. The prices of the Singapore gold are based on prices quoted in London plus a mark-up for the transport, insurance cost, and profit margin in addition to the premium for quality.

Kilobars are usually bought on full payment for immediate physical delivery. The buyer may lodge the gold bar with the selling bank for a fee. Instead of physical gold, a buyer may purchase kilobar gold certificate from any of the authorised banks such as DBS, OCBC, OUB, UOB and Bank of Nova Scotia.

The certificate is issued for a standard lot of 3 bars each weighing 1 kilogram of 999.9 fineness and an orignal validity period of 12 months. The OCBC also issues certifcates for one kilobar. The certificate may be endorsed to a third party during the validity period. However, the third party may not further endorse the certificate.

Singapore Merchant Bankers' Association

The Singapore Merchant Bankers' Association was formed on 24 July 1975 with the objectives of (1) promoting a sound merchant banking system and practice in Singapore with the cooperation of the MAS, and (2) promoting a forum for discussion and exchange of views and information among members.

Singapore Mint

Although not directly related to the Board of Commissioners of Currency, the Singapore Mint, a subsidiary of the Government-linked Chartered Industries of Singapore, mints all Singapore coins. It also mints coins for other countries. It has set up several coin centres to sell both Singapore Mint proof coins and those of other national mints.

Under the SMART (Singapore Mint Advance Reservation) scheme, a person may open an account with the Mint by paying a deposit. The account holder will be allocated all coins, medals, souvenirs issued by the Mint. He will also be given advance information of all issues.

Singapore Mint Advance Reservation Scheme (SMART)
See Singapore Mint

Singapore Regional Training Institute (STI)
The IMF-Singapore Regional Training Institute (STI) was opened in 1998. It is a joint initiative of the International Monetary Fund and the Singapore government. It offers courses on macroeconomic adjustment and reform policies, financial programming, monetary and exchange operations, public finance, banking supervision and statistics.

The STI is administered by the IMF Institute, the training arm of the IMF in collaboration with the Monetary Authority of Singapore. The STI will initially be located at the MAS Building pending the completion of its own premises.

Singapore Reinsurance Corporation
The first reinsurance company, Singapore Reinsurance Corporation, was established in 1973 to function as a professional reinsurance company and to serve as a clearing-house for all the registered insurance companies in the republic. The paid-up capital of S$ 35 million has been jointly subscribed by all the insurance companies. The shareholding of domestic companies is 75% and that of foreign companies is 25%.

The Singapore Reinsurance Corporation has been set up with these objectives:

(1) to reinsure business at the national and international level;
(2) to serve as an information centre for both local and foreign insurers;
(3) to establish and administer insurance pools covering specialised risks;
(4) to provide and coordinate training facilities and expertise.

Insurance companies registered in Singapore have agreed to cede to the corporation a quota share of 5% of their fire business on their

Singapore register and 2 1/2% of their marine cargo, hull, motor, and miscellaneous accident departments. The establishment of the corporation has also helped to decrease reinsurance premiums currently going abroad and to attract the placement of foreign reinsurance business in Singapore.

Singapore Securities Research Institute (SSRI)
The SSRI was formed in 1974. Its main function is to conduct research related to the securities industry. It is wholly owned by the SES which determines the policy of the Institute. The SSRI conducts courses related to securities and investment analysis.

Singapore Technical Analysts and Traders Society
The Singapore Technical Analysts and Traders Society (STATS) was formed in 1985. Its primary objective is to promote the use of technically oriented research in decision-making.

Singapore-United States Business Council (SUBC)
The SUBC was formed in 1996 to promote trade and investment between Singapore and the US as well as joint ventures in other countries. It comprises 6 US and 8 Singapore chief executives from both countries and is chaired by Deputy Prime Minister Tony Tan. The council meets every 18 months. In May 1998, it had its second meeting and the theme was the region's economic crisis. The council also visited Suzhou Industrial Park in China.

Single strike price method
This is one of the methods to tender in a public share offer in the Stock Exchange of Singapore. Under the single strike price method, successful applicants will pay the price submitted by the lowest successful bidder. (See also: Dutch method of tender.)

Sistem Pemindahan Elektronik untuk Dana dan Sekuriti (SPEEDS)
SPEEDS was a computerised scripless trading system introduced by the Central Bank of Malaysia for trading, registration and settlement of government securities. It has been replaced by the Real Time Electronic Transfer of Funds and Securities or RENTAS.

Sistem Transit Aliran Ringan (STAR)
STAR is a Light Rail Transit system in Kuala Lumpur, Malaysia.

Skim Khas Perumahan Kos Rendah dan Sederhana (Malaysia)
See Special Scheme for Low and Medium Cost Houses

Skim Perbankan Tanpa Faedah (Malaysia)
Interest Free Banking Scheme

Small & Medium Industries Development Corporation (SMIDEC)
Malaysia's SMIDEC was set up in 1996 to provide advisory services, guidance and assistance to small and medium industries in Malaysia.
(Website: www.jaring.my / smidec)

Small Industries Finance Office (Thailand)
The Small Industries Finance Office in Thailand provides low-interest loans and technical assistance to small industrial enterprises including cottage and handicraft industries.

Social Security Organisation (SOCSO) (Malaysia)
Malaysia's SOCSO was set up in 1971 as a government department to provide social security benefits to low-income workers in the industrial and public sectors through the Employment Injury Insurance Scheme and Invalidity Pension Scheme. In 1985, SOCSO became a tripartite statutory board with representatives from employers, employees and the government.

In 1992, the eligible monthly wage ceiling of an employee was doubled to RM2,000. The scheme is optional for employees earning more than RM2,000 subject to a mutual agreement between the employers and the employees. Contribution to the scheme is calculated on a sliding scale based on the employee's wage. The rate is 1% of the wage in for the Invalidity Pension Scheme and 1.25% for the Employment Injury Scheme.

Solid Bank (Philippines)
Solidbank is listed on the Philippine Stock Exchange. It was set up in 1963. Its major subsidiaries include Solid Insurance Brokers Inc and Solid Phil. Venture Capital Corp.
(Website: www.solidbank.com.ph)

Special Fund for Tourism (Malaysia)
This fund was set up in 1990 by the Bank Negara Malaysia (Central Bank) to finance tourism-related projects. The RM200 million fund

was used mainly for construction of new hotels and renovation of existing hotels and resorts.

Special Purpose Vehicle
A special mechanism or organisation set up as part of an economic rescue plan.

Special Scheme for Low and Medium Cost Houses (Malaysia) (Skim Khas Perumahan Kos Rendah dan Sederhana)
The special scheme is a RM2.0 billion revolving credit facility set up by Bank Negara Malaysia (Central Bank) in May 1998. The objective is to provide bridging finance to developers for building houses costing RM150,000 and below. Participating financial institutions include commercial banks, finance companies and Bank Islam Malaysia Berhad.

Special Standard for Application of Banking Accounting in Indonesia (Standar Khusus Akuntansi Perbankan Indonesia or SKAPI)
These are accounting guidelines developed by the Bank Indonesia and the Indonesian Accountants Association in order to meet international standards.

Specialised Government Banks (Philippines)
Specialised government banks in the Philippines are government banks set up by special laws to provide credit for specific projects to promote economic development. Examples are the Development Bank of the Philippines, the Land Bank of the Philippines and the Al-Amanah Islamic Investment Bank of the Philippines. (See also: Al-Amanah Islamic Investment Bank of the Philippines, Development Bank of the Philippines; Land Bank of the Philippines).

Standar Khusus Akuntansi Perbankan Indonesia
See Special Standard for Application of Banking Accounting in Indonesia.

State Committee for Cooperation and Investment (SCCI)
SCCI is now part of the Ministry of Planning and Investment (MPI). See Ministry of Planning and Investment (Vietnam).

State Economic Development Corporation (Malaysia)
In the late 1960s and early 1970s, the Malaysian Federal Government decentralised many of its economic activities by setting up State Economic Development Corporations to fulfill the objectives of the New Economic Policy (NEP). Many government-owned companies were incorporated to undertake massive public projects to create jobs and improve the standard of living of the people.

State Law and Order Restoration Council (SLORC)
See State Peace Development Council

State Peace Development Council (SPDC)
In 1988, the military in Myanmar declared martial law and set up the State Law and Order Restoration Council (SLORC) to restore stability in the country. In 1997, the SLORC was renamed the State Peace Development Council (SPDC).

State Securities Committee (SSC)
Vietnam's State Securities Committee (SSC) was set up in 1996. It is responsible for developing a stock market in Vietnam.

StatLink (Singapore)
StatLink is an interactive trade statistics service introduced in 1996 by Singapore's Trade Development Board through the world wide web at http://www.tdb.gov.sg/singbiz.html/ It contains data covering a period of 48 months and is updated every month.

Statutory reserve requirement (SRR) — Malaysia
Commercial banks, finance companies and merchant banks in Malaysia are required to maintain part of their deposit liabilities as statutory reserves with the Central Bank. On 1 June 1996, the SRR was raised from 12.5% to 13.5%.

Stock borrowing and lending (SBL) arrangements (Malaysia)
These are arrangements introduced by the Securities Commission (Malaysia) in 1997 to allow for regulated short-selling and hedging activities to develop the derivatives market. During the 1998 financial crisis, these arrangements were suspended.

Stock Exchange of Hong Kong
The Stock Exchange of Hong Kong (SEHK) is the eighth largest stock market in the world in terms of market capitalisation and the second largest in Asia, after Japan.

Historically, although trading of shares started in 1866, the first formal stock market, the Association of Stockbrokers in Hong Kong, was established in 1891. It was renamed the Hong Kong Stock Exchange in 1914. A second exchange was incorporated — the Hong Kong Stockbrokers' Association in 1921. The two exchanges merged to form the Hong Kong Stock Exchange in 1947. In the late 1960s and early 1970s, as a result of rapid economic growth, three more exchanges were set up: the Far East Exchange (1969), the Kam Ngan Stock Exchange (1971) and the Kowloon Stock Exchange (1972).

After the 1973 market crash, there was a need to strengthen market surveillance. In 1977, the Hong Kong government set up a working party in 1977 to consider the unification of the four stock exchanges. On 7 July 1980, the unified exchange — the Stock Exchange of Hong Kong (SEHK) was incorporated. The four exchanges ceased trading on 27 March 1986. A new era began with trading via a computerised system on the SEHK on 2 April 1986.

After the October Crash in 1987, the SEHK underwent a complete reform, including the establishment of a wider representative Council and a professional management team, to safeguard the interests of all participants and to operate and develop the market effectively.

Stock Exchange of Singapore

The Stock Exchange of Singapore Limited (SES) was set up on 24 May 1973 after the split of the joint Stock Exchange of Malaysia and Singapore. SES started full operation as a separate exchange on 4 June 1973. However, many of the 300-odd companies were co-listed on the Kuala Lumpur Stock Exchange (KLSE) and their prices moved in tendem due to arbitraging.

In 1987, SES introduced a second board known as SESDAQ (Stock Exchange of Singapore Dealing and Automated Quotation). It now enables smaller Singapore companies with growth prospects to raise funds in the capital market.

In 1989, the KLSE delisted about 180 Malaysian companies from the SES main board. As a result, the amount of capitalisation of the exchange was affected. In order to overcome the reduced depth and breadth of the exchange, SES introduced an over-the-counter market known as CLOB International to facilitate trading of Malaysian shares. Later, companies from Hong Kong and Philippines were also added to the list.

The objects of the SES are spelt out in the Memorandum and Articles of Association which include the following:

(1) to regulate and control the stockbroking business in Singapore
(2) to protect the interests of members of the Exchange;
(3) to record transactions between member firms;
(4) to furnish quotations of share prices transacted on the Exchange;
(5) to provide investors service and to promote interest in the securities market as a whole;
(6) to work in close cooperation with the Securities Industry Council and the MAS;
(7) to interpret and enforce the Rules and Bye-laws of the Exchange and to arbitrate between members of the Exchange;
(8) to prepare, publish, and circulate reports and records;
(9) to provide and enact listing requirements and to enunciate and enforce a code for mergers, take-overs, and acquisitions;
(10) to institute a policy of market surveillance and corporate disclosure.

Stock Exchange of Thailand
Formerly known as the Securities Exchange of Thailand, the SET was set up in 1974 and trading was computerised in 1991. The SET was reorganised in 1992 as a non-profit organisation to serve as a secondary market for transacting securities. It is self-regulated with powers to enforce standards and rules against unfair practices. It is supervised by the Securities and Exchange Commission.

Stock Price Index (Philippines)
In the Philippines, the Stock Price Index (SPI) measures the changes in the average prices of shares traded on the Philippine Stock Exchange. The classification follows the Philippine Standard Industrial Classification (PSIC) prepared by the National Economic and Development Authority (NEDC). The 1985-based index covers 76 stocks in the following sectors: mining and quarrying (31), manufacturing (18), construction (3), wholesale and retail (3), transport, storage and communication (2), finance, insurance, real estate and business services (16), community, social and personal services (3).

Strategic Response Quotient (SRQ)
SRQ is an indicator of how well a bank respond to fulfilling capital adequacy requirement, managing costs, credit risk and interest spread. SRQ is derived by dividing net interest income by net non-interest costs.

Surabaya Stock Exchange (SSX)
The Surabaya Stock Exchange was established on 16 June 1989. It commenced operations in 1994. It was the first private stock exchange in Indonesia. Its formation was one of the results of deregulating the Indonesian financial market under the October 1988 reform package (October Package, Paket Oktober or Pakto). In 1995, Bursa Paralel Indonesia merged with Surabaya Stock Exchange to form Surabaya Stock Exchange Limited Company.

Members of SSX are broker-dealers which have been granted a licence by BAPEPAM and are shareholders of the Surabaya Stock Exchange Limited Company. SSX uses the new Eldistra (Electronic Long Distance Trading) system.

Surat Berharga Pasar Uang (SBPU) (Indonesia)
These are short term Indonesian money market instruments comprising mainly promissory notes issued by Indonesian banks and non-bank financial institutions.

Sushi bond
Sushi bond is issued in the euromarkets by a Japanese company, aimed at Japanese investors, mostly insurance companies and trust banks who can claim they are not buying a foreign bond because the bond has been issued by a Japanese entity.

Syarikat Takaful Malaysia Sendirian Berhad
An Islamic insurance company in Malaysia set up in 1985. It provides insurance services in accordance with Islamic principles. (See also: Islamic bank.)

Sydney Futures Exchange
Sydney Futures Exchange began in 1960 as the Sydney Greasy Wool Exchange. In 1975, it introduced live cattle futures. In 1979, it became the first exchange outside the US to trade financial futures. It now trades in wool, cattle, 90-day bank bills, All-Ordinaries share price index, government bonds, semi-government bonds and ASX Fifty Leaders Index.

System for Handling Interbank Fund Transfer (SHIFT) (Singapore)
Before the launching of the System for Handling Interbank Funds Transfer (SHIFT) in 1985, interbank payments were done by bank messengers assembling at a central location and exchanging cheques.

With the introduction of SHIFT, banks in Singapore were linked by a computerised system. Local dollar interbank payments were effected within seconds. When a payment transaction had been approved by the sending bank, the information was transmitted to the SHIFT Central Computer at the Automated Clearing House managed by Banking Computer Services Pte Ltd. This central computer processed the transaction and transmitted an advice to the receiving bank's computer, thus effecting the fund transfer. In 1998, SHIFT was replaced by the new MAS Electronic Payment System. (See also: MAS Electronic Payment System.)

System on Computerised Order Routing and Execution (SCORE)
SCORE is an automated trading system used in the Kuala Lumpur Stock Exchange in Malaysia.

Tabung Angkatan Tentera
See Armed Forces Fund (Malaysia)

Tabung Haji
An Islamic institutional fund in Malaysia. It invests in Syariah-approved stocks on the Kuala Lumpur Stock Exchange.

Tabung Usahawan Baru
See New Entrepreneurs Fund (Malaysia)

Takaful Act 1984 (Malaysia)
The Act registers and regulates takaful business in Malaysia. "Takaful" means a scheme based on brotherhood, solidarity and mutual assistance which provides for mutual financial aid to the participants in case of need whereby the participants mutually agree to contribute for that purpose.

Taxes in Vietnam
The direct business taxes in Vietnam include the business income tax, turnover tax, profit remittance tax, personal income tax, contractor tax, royalties tax, land and housing taxes.

Telecom share floatation
Singapore Telecom was listed on 1 November 1993. It was the single largest share issue in the stock market history. Response from the Singapore public was overwhelming. The company received 2.4

million applications for 4.5 billion shares, and raised S$4.3 billion from the market.

Telecom and SOTUS

The overwhelming response to the Singapore Telecom share floatation was partly the result of wide publicity given to the issue and the encouragement from the government. In order to enable Singaporeans to own shares, the government had earlier introduced a Share Ownership Top-up Scheme (SOTUS) whereby the CPF account of each eligible Singaporean was topped up with S$200 by the government. As a result of SOTUS, 1.26 million Singaporeans received S$242 million in government contributions. The scheme encouraged some 1.48 million CPF members subscribing to Telecom shares. (See also: Share Ownership Top-up Scheme.)

Templeton Vietnam Opportunities Fund

This is a closed-end investment fund listed on the New Stock Stock Exchange.

Tenaga Nasional Berhad

Malaysia's privatised national power company which was listed in 1992.

Tender method (Singapore)

This is one of the methods of offering shares for subscription by the public in Singapore. In the tender method, applications are for 1000 shares or in multiple of 1000. Multiple applications are allowed but only at different tender prices. Each individual investor and his related parties are limited to 5% of the issue. The minimum tender price must be higher than the fixed price.

Applications by tender will be satisfied in full, starting with the highest bid price downwards until all shares are allocated. If the number of shares applied for at a particular price exceeds the number of available shares or if the total number of shares applied for are less than the available shares, the allocation will follow Stock Exchange of Singapore guidelines.

The tender method may either be a "Dutch method" or a "single strike price method". Under the Dutch method, successful applicants will pay the price they tendered for. Under the single strike price method, successful applicants will pay the price submitted by the lowest successful bidder.

The advantages of the tender method are: (a) it gives issuers some flexibility in raising capital; (b) it offers investors a better chance if they wish to subscribe for more shares; (c) it allows the forces of supply and demand to determine the price: (d) it is an attractive method when the issuer expects a great demand for the shares. (See also: Dutch method of tender; Single strike price method.)

Termination of Interchangeability of currencies

On 16 January 1969, the currency notes issued by the former Board of Commissioners of Currency, Malaya and British Borneo, ceased to be legal tender. However, under the interchangeability arrangements, the Malaysian, Singapore and the Brunei currencies continued to be exchanged at par.

On 5 May 1973, the Malaysian Government terminated the Interchangeability Agreement with Singapore. Since then, the exchange rate between the two currencies has been subject to foreign exchange fluctuation. However, the Brunei dollar is still accepted at par with the Singapore dollar.

Thai Rating and Information Services (TRIS)

TRIS is Thailand's first credit rating agency. It was set up in 1993 with the sponsorship from Thai financial institutions. Its mission is to provide credit rating service and to disseminate the rating results and other related information in the Thai bond market for the beneift of investors. TRIS is a founding member of AFCRA, ASEAN Forum of Credit Rating Agencies.

TRIS's shareholders comprise four major groups: commercial banks (22%), finance companies (22%), securities companies (22%) and other institutions (34%). Other institutions include life insurance companies, investment management companies, Ministry of Finance, Stock Exchange of Thailand, Asian Development Bank, Government Savings Bank, and Industrial Finance Corporation of Thailand. No single shareholder owns more than 5% of TRIS. This is to ensure that TRIS is free from any outside influence. (Website: www.tris.tnet.co.th)

Thailand Development Research Institute (TDRI)

The TDRI was set up in 1984 as a non-profit, non-governmental organisation to do policy research and to disseminate results to the public and private sectors. It provides technical and policy analysis that supports the formulation of policies with long-term implications for sustaining social and economic development in Thailand.

TDRI is funded by users of its research and various local and foreign donors. During the early years, its supporters included the National Economic and Social Development Board, the Department of Technical and Economic Cooperation, the Canadian International Development Agency, and the United States Agency for International Development.

TDRI's major research programs include: human resources and social development, international economic relations, macroeconomic policy, natural resources and environment, science and technology development, and sectoral economics.

Theta
A measure of the amount an option price is expected to change in response to the time of expiration. (See also: Delta, Gamma, Rho, Yega.)

Thrift Banks (Philippines)
Thrift banks in the Philippines include savings banks, private development banks, and stock savings and loan associations. They cater to the lower income groups by mobilising small savings and provide loans at longer and easier terms than commercial banks. Cottage industry entrepreneurs, farmers and small businesses depend on thrift banks to finance their activities.

Tier-1 Capital
This refers to paid-up capital, non-cumulative perpetual preference shares, share premium, statutory reserve fund, general reserve fund, retained profits, surplus/loss arising from sale of fixed and long-term investments as well as minority interest (consistent with the components of Tier-1 capital) and after deducting goodwill.

Tier-2 Capital
This refers to hybrid capital instruments, minority interest arising from preference shares, subordinated term debt, revaluation reserves and general provisions for bad and doubtful debts.

Tokyo International Financial Futures Exchange (TIFFE)
TIFFE was set up in 1989. Contracts traded include: 3-month euroyen, eurodollar interest rate futures and yen/US$ currency futures. It also trades in options on 3-month euroyen futures. TIFFE does not have a trading floor. Transactions are done through a Fully Automated Computer Trading System (FACTS).

Tokyo Stock Exchange
The present Tokyo Stock Exchange was set up in 1949 but its history dates back to 1878. It started to trade in bonds in 1956 and government bonds in 1966. It also trades in futures and options contracts based on Topix (Tokyo Stock Price Index) and government bonds.

Topix
Topix is Tokyo Stock Exchange stock price index. It is a composite index calculated from the aggregate market capitalisation of about 1,200 stocks. Topix is a share-weighted index whereas the Nikkei is price-weighted. (See also: Tokyo Stock Exchange.)

Total Business Planning Program (TBP) (Singapore)
The objective of this program is to encourage local enterprises to implement a total business plan including strategies for market development, technology transfer, business diversification, business collaboration, mergers and acquisitions. The scheme pays part of the consultancy costs incurred in formulating the plan.

TPKP
Indonesian acronym for corporate employee housing savings scheme.

Trade Affiliated Member
A Trade Affiliated Member (TAM) is a member of the Manila International Futures Exchange (MIFE). It is a corporation that is interested in one particular contract by virtue of its business. It has to trade through a full member as it is not a member of the Clearing House, and has no floor trading rights.

Trade Input Driven System (Singapore)
Trade Input Driven System (TIDY) is the trading system used in Singapore Commodity Exchange (SICOM). It is an automated order-driven system where a computer matches buying and selling orders, which are subsequently registered in the clearing house.

Trading of IPOs on a "When Issued" Basis
In May 1993, after reviewing the procedures for processing IPO applications, the Stock Exchange of Singapore (SES) introduced a new facility to enable investors to trade in IPO shares on a "when issued" basis before confirmation of allotment of shares to successful applicants.

Investors wishing to sell their holdings or anticipated holdings in an IPO issue may do so soon after the close of an IPO, instead of after 3 to 4 weeks. This reduces the market risk of investing in IPO shares, thus enhancing the market's capital-raising efficiency.

"When issued" trading commences on the market day after the conduct of balloting to determine successful applicants of an IPO. Such trading will continue till the third day after the dispatch of notifications of allotment to successful applicants. Normal trading on a "ready" basis commences thereafter. There is one single settlement date for trades done on a "when issued" basis and that date coincides with the settlement date for trades done on the first day of trading on a "ready" basis.

Trading Practices and Market Development Committee
A committee set up by the Central Bank of Malaysia as provided for in the Code of Conduct and Market Practices for Scripless Trading in the Malaysian securities market. It plays a consultative role and serves as an important link between the Central Bank and market participants.

Tranche method of issuing CDs
This is a method of issuing certificates of deposit (CD) in the primary market. By the tranche method, the issuing bank decides on the amount to be issued, the period, and the interest rate. A manager is then appointed to solicit the deposits. By this method, the issuing bank does not have direct contact with the purchasers of its CDs. The only communication between them is by means of a Placing Memorandum prepared by the manager. The Memorandum contains sufficient information to assist the purchaser to evaluate the issue. The manager charges a commission of about 2.5% which covers management fees, underwriting fees, and the selling commission.

Treasury Bills Act (Malaysia)
The Act provides for issue of Treasury Bills in Malaysia. The Act amongst other things appoints the Central Bank as the agent of the government and permits the issue by way of book-entry, i.e. scripless.

Union Bank of Burma
In 1967, the People's Bank of the Union of Burma was set up as a result of merging all the nationalised banks. It acted as the central bank of Burma. In 1975, its name was changed to Union Bank of Burma. (See also: Central Bank of Myanmar.)

Union Bank of the Philippines

The Union Bank of the Philippines is listed on the Philippine Stock Exchange. It was among the first government institutions that were privatised. It started as the Union Savings and Mortgage Bank through capital provided by Land Bank and Social Security System (SSS) and advances from the Central Bank of the Philippines. In 1982, it was granted a commercial bank licence.

The bank started its privatisation in 1988 when Land Bank sold its 39% ownership to Aboitiz Group of Companies. The second phase followed through the sale of SSS' shares amounting to 30% of the shares. The third phase took place in 1992 when the SSS sold another 13.3% through a secondary offering.

The bank now offers a wide range of products and services to both corporate and individual clients. Some services are provided through subsidiaries such as UBP Capital Corporation, Crosby UBP Securities Inc and UBP Insurance Brokerage Inc and Union Bank Currency Brokers Inc.

Unit trust

A financial institution managed by professional fund managers who pool the funds subscribed by small investors and invest them in stocks and shares and other securities. Prices of the various units are publicised in newspapers by the fund managers. Investors buy from and sell to the managers at these prices.

Unit Trust Companies in Singapore

In Singapore, a unit trust is constituted by a Trust Deed which sets out the rights, responsibilities, and duties of the fund manager, the trustee, and the unit-holders. The Trust Deed must be approved by the Registrar of Companies before the units in a fund can be advertised for sale to the public. Before a fund can be set up, the fund manager must issue a prospectus to be approved by the Registrar.

The duties of a trustee are:

(1) collecting and holding all income of the fund;
(2) distributing income to unit-holders;
(3) keeping custody of all investment and other assets that form the capital of the trust fund;
(4) countersigning all unit certificates before they are issued to the unit-holders;

(5) approving all advertising material;
(6) ensuring that the provisions of the Trust Deed are adhered to;
(7) removing fund mangers if it is in the interest of the unit-holders.

Urban Bank Inc (Philippines)
The Urban Bank Inc is listed on the Philippine Stock Exchange. It has evolved from a development bank in 1980 to a universal bank in 1994. It provides a wide range of services. In 1995, the bank obtained an approval from the Securities and Exchange Commission to form a Special Purpose Trust Fund on the registration and sale of Asset-Backed Securities, thus making it one of the three institutions and the first Philippine bank to be so authorised. In 1998, Urban Bank's Virtual Banking Development Laboratory was awarded an ISO 9001 Certification for the development and serving of office and banking software. It was the first Philippine bank to be ISO certified by Certification International, an ISO-accredited certifying body based in England. Among its major banking-related subsidiaries are: Urbancorp Finance Inc, Urbancorp Investments Inc, Urbancorp Insurance Brokers Inc and Urbancorp Securities Inc.
(Website: www.urbanvirtualbank.com)

US Treasury bond futures
The US Treasury bond futures was first traded in SIMEX on 8 October 1986. The US T-bond futures is a long-term contract to complement the short-term Eurodollar futures. It is similar to that traded on the Chicago Board of Trade (CBOT). However, SIMEX does not have a mutual offset arrangement with CBOT, similar to that with the Chicago Mercantile Exchange for some of the other contracts.

Vantage Equities Inc (Philippines)
Vantage Equities Inc is a financial service company listed on the Philippine Stock Exchange. It started as Palawan Oil & Gas Exploration Inc. In 1996, the company acquired 100% of Vantage Securities Corporation (formerly AGJ Securities Corporation) and 65% of PMI, a fund management company. In 1997, it increased its holdings in the International Exchange Bank to 20.89%. On 1 September 1997, the company's name was changed to Vantage Equities Inc.

Vega
A measure of the amount an option price is expected to change in response to a unit change in the price volatility of the underlying instrument (See also: Delta, Gamma, Rho, Theta.)

Vereenigde Oostindische Compagnie (VOC)
Dutch East India Company

VID Public Bank
VID Public Bank is a 50–50 joint venture bank between the Bank for Investment and Development of Vietnam and Public Bank Berhad of Malaysia. It has offices in Hanoi, Ho Chi Minh City, Danang and Haiphong.

Viet Kieu
Overseas Vietnamese

Vietcombank
See Bank for Foreign Trade Bank of Vietnam

Vietindebank
See Bank for Investment and Development of Vietnam

Vietnam Bank for Agriculture (Agribank)
It was set up in 1990. It is now known as the Vietnam Bank for Agriculture and Rural Development. (See also: Vietnam Bank for Agriculture and Rural Development.)

Vietnam Bank for Agriculture and Rural Development (VBARD or Agribank)
Vietnam Bank for Agriculture and Rural Development (VBARD or Agribank) was set up in 1996 to succeed the Vietnam Bank for Agriculture which was set up in 1990. It is one of the three state-owned commercial banks in Vietnam. It concentrates on the agricultural sector. It has the largest domestic network and undertakes agriculture related foreign trade transactions.

According to its 1996 Annual Report, Agribank's statutory capital was VDN 2,200 billion and had 21,000 employees working in 2,564 branches. The bank had business relationship with 7 million farmer households, 3,300 state enterprises, 8,000 production cooperatives and 1,000 limited companies with outstanding loans of VDN 17,574 billion.

Vietnam — Commercial Law
See Commercial Law of Vietnam

Vietnam — Credit Institutions
See Law on Credit Institutions

Vietnam — Economic Court
See Economic Court (Vietnam)

Vietnam Enterprise Investments
A closed-end investment fund listed on the Irish Stock Stock Exchange.

Vietnam Frontier Fund
A closed-end investment fund listed on the Irish Stock Stock Exchange.

Vietnam insurance business
See Insurance business in Vietnam

Vietnam International Arbitration Center (VIAC)
The VIAC settles disputes which arise from foriegn trade contracts.

Vietnam International Assurance Company (VIA)
VIA is a joint venture insurance company whose partners are Vietnam's state insurance company Bao Viet (51%), London's Commerical Union (24.5%), and Japan's Tokio Marine & Fire Insurance Co (24.5%). VIA offers general insurance, life insurance and reinsurance to domestic and foreign investors. (See also: Insurance business in Vietnam.)

Vietnam International Leasing Company (VILC)
VILC is the first company to be granted a leasing licence by the State Bank of Vietnam. It is a 5-party joint venture involving Korean Industrial Leasing Co. (32%), Vietnam Industrial and Commercial Bank (19%), Nippon Credit Bank (17%), Banque Francaise du Commerce Exterieur (17%) and International Finance Co. (15%).

Vietnam — Law, Ordinance, Decree and Regulation
In Vietnam, laws are passed by the National Assembly and are the highest form of legal documents. Ordinances are passed by the

Standing Committee of the National Assembly when the Assembly is not in session. Decrees are passed by the government and implement the laws and ordinances. Decrees are accompanied by regulations which provide the details.

Vietnam Singapore Industrial Park (VSIP)
VSIP is an industrial park located in Song Be Province, about 17 kilometres north of Ho Chi Minh City. The 500-hectare park is jointly developed by Vietnam's state-owned company Song Be Export Import Trading Company (Becamex) and a consortium of Singapore companies led by government-linked Sembawang Group. They include Sembawang Industrial, Sembawang Engineering, Jurong Town Corporation, Temasek Holdings, UOL Overseas Investments, KPM Group, LKN Construction and MC Development Asia. During the first phase, 500 hectares will be devleoped for infrastructure to support ready-built factories to attract investors. The park offers one-stop service to simplify the application process for investors to set up operations. Foreign companies from France, Japan, Malaysia, Singapore, Switzerland, United States and others are expected to employ about 10,000 workers producing electronic goods, food products and supporting services.

Vietnam Singapore Technical Training Centre (VSTTC)
Vietnam Singapore Technical Training Centre is located in the Vietnam Singapore Industrial Park. It trains Vietnamese workers in a wide range of technical skills.

Vietnam — Taxes
See Taxes in Vietnam

Vietnamese Reinsurance Company (VINARE)
First reinsurance company in Vietnam, started operations in 1995. In Vietnam, an insurance company is allowed to re-insure with another insurance company provided that it must re-insure part of the liability with VINARE.

"When Issued" trading
See Trading of IPOs on a "When Issued" Basis

World Bank
The World Bank, or International Bank for Reconstruction and

Development (IBRD) was set up in 1944. Its main objective is to provide credit to member countries for development purposes. It provides loans for projects related to economic growth. Examples are electric power, ports, telecommunication, water supply, tourism and family planning.

Yankee bonds

These are bonds denominated in US$, issued in the US by a foreign borrower.

Yield to maturity

Yield to maturity is a measure of the expected total return from bonds when held to maturity. The calculation takes into account the appreciation of par from the current market price when bought at a discount or depreciation when bought at a premium.

INDEX